MW01633846

Photography and Politics in America

Published in cooperation with
THE CENTER FOR AMERICAN PLACES
Sante Fe, New Mexico,
and Harrisonburg, Virginia

Photography and Politics in America

From the New Deal into the Cold War

Lili Corbus Bezner

The Johns Hopkins University Press Baltimore & London

 Published 1999
Printed in the United States of America on acid-free paper
1 3 5 7 9 8 6 4 2

The Johns Hopkins University Press
2715 North Charles Street
Baltimore, Maryland 21218-4363
www.press.jhu.edu

Library of Congress Cataloging-in-Publication Data will be found
at the end of this book.

A catalog record for this book is available from the British Library.

ISBN 0-8018-6187-X

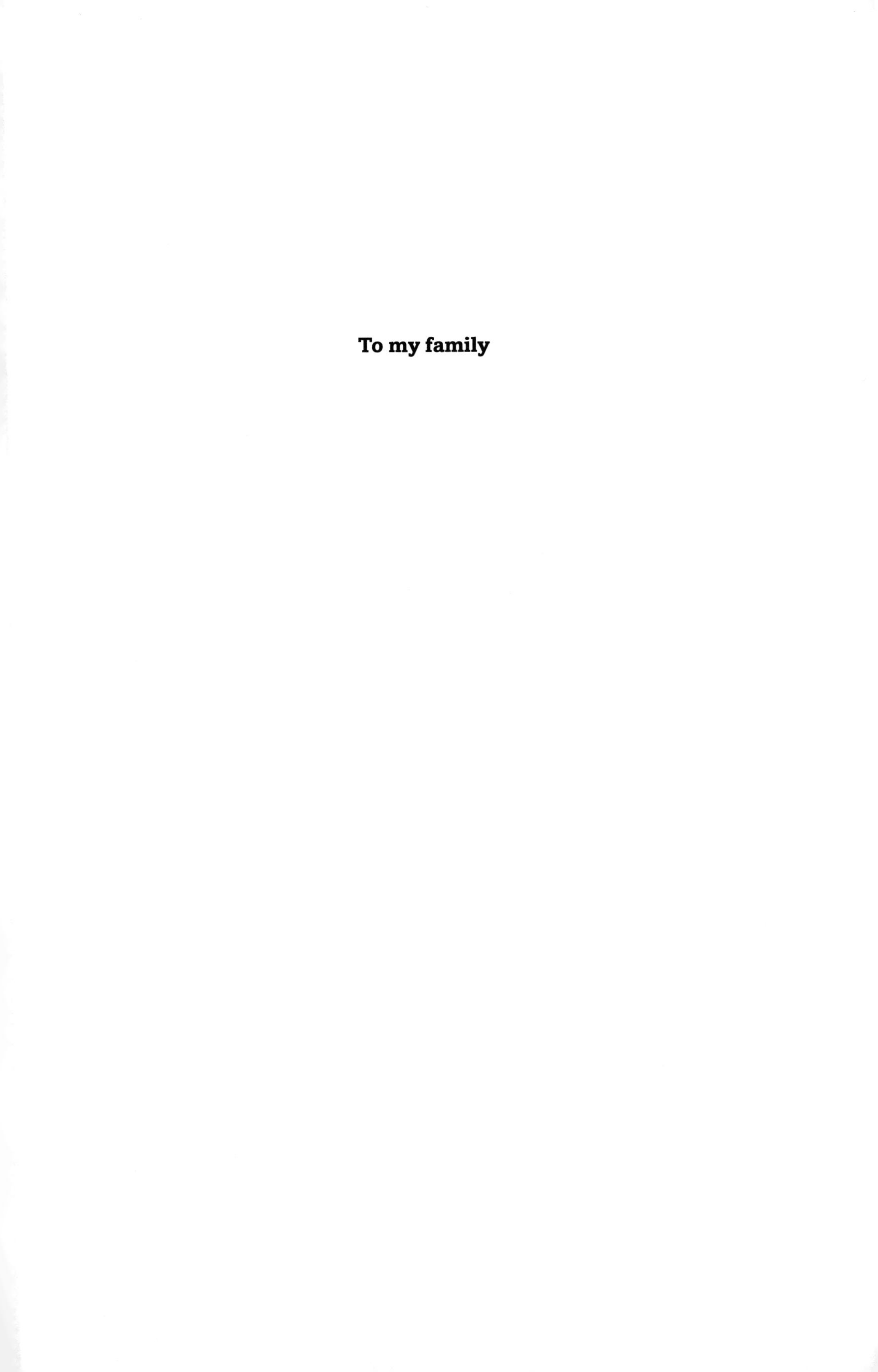

To my family

Contents

Illustrations

Preface

This book traces photography's history in the United States during the early cold war years. Although broad-based photographic histories seem rare today, my interest in this topic is not merely academic. At the time the book was researched and edited, various assaults continued on the arts and expression, even though the freedom enjoyed by artists today seems ideal in comparison to what those in the Photo League faced during the 1940s. But controversies in regard to "correct" content or financial support of the arts endure, as they always have, and as they always will. This book will, I hope, inspire readers to contemplate the lessons of the past in context to art of the present and of the future—to internalize the complexity of ideology's relationship to the image.

I believe such histories of repression and subsequent formations of canons are timely; for instance, as I relate the stories of the Photo League photographers to undergraduate students today I find the classroom silent, eyes alert, attention focused on what seems to them, today, unbelievable. Someone invariably says, "But we have a constitution, the government couldn't blacklist like that!" Such comments reinforce the fact that my research is charged with the most controversial partisan politics of the twentieth century. Interrogating this past, however, allows us to consider and question more profoundly the present.

Histories, of course, are frequently ambiguous and painful; they do not unfold in tidy linear scrolls but are found in tangled webs of narratives. The histories discussed in this book present a veritable thicket of voices and conflicting perspectives, not unlike Akira Kurosawa's *Rashomon*, complete with old animosities and even cruel treachery. It was painful to witness the tears of men and women in their seventies or eighties recalling the difficult disintegration of friendships and careers. The cold war bred hostilities and misunderstandings as citizens scrambled to protect themselves, their work, their families, and their friends. Conversely, it was rewarding to hear these stories of survival and courage in the face of such adversity.

Despite my commitment to represent a complex history in this book, I seek not to simplify the events but to invigorate readers' appreciation for the dulling effects of repression on creative expression as well as the skewed effects of hagiographic canon-formation. While I have tried to be fair and balanced to the various points of view and loyalties encountered in my research, I found passionate, committed figures such as Sid Grossman and Robert Frank both compelling and misunderstood; I wish not to mythologize such artists but to assess more realistically the impact of the surrounding social context on their work and subsequent criticism. Grossman suffered descent into absolute and even deliberate obscurity, while Frank rose to saintly mythological prominence on a pedestal few mortals could endure: neither treatment, I believe, is fair to either artist.

I regret any irritating sweeping generalizations about complex political issues during the three decades discussed and urge all readers to continue studying this crucial period in additional contexts. But I celebrate retelling the stories of many photographers who have been neglected over the years—whose stories, I have found, can create a disturbing silence in audiences who are unaccustomed to history's thorny discourse and who desire neat packages and happy tales of financial success and deserved reputations. The cold war years, instead, offer a paradoxical model to all of us today; its study challenges readers' ideal notions of what it means to be a "good American" or the promotion of "positive" values in art. Hardly the neatly contained *Zeitgeist* many take it to be, the cold war and its histories offer the opportunity to debate key issues in democratic theory. In the end, then, I hope this book promotes a continuing and deepening dialogue on the relationships between society and art as a testament to the lives of the photographers discussed.

Finally, in a world awash in images, I hope, too, that this book encourages renewed contemplation of context, intent, and purpose in the media. The ability of photographic images to contort, enhance, or alter reality is certainly realized by many contemporary viewers of the digital universe. My original, ironic (but ultimately romantic and ambiguous) title of the text, "We Believed in Truth," signified the extraordinary commitment to "real" social criticism that many past documentary photographers maintained from the 1930s through the 1950s. In interviews today, many long-forgotten photographers seem confused by a contemporary world in which "meaning" is contested or derided. While in our own times such nostalgic ideals are often (and sometimes very deservedly) suspect, this book is ultimately a tribute to those documentary photographers who longed to engage more broadly, whatever the price, with the most complex challenges of their contemporary world.

Acknowledgments

After working on the research for this book for almost ten years, the number of people to thank runs in the hundreds. Most importantly, this book provided me with the rewarding experience of meeting and interviewing a number of sources who generously shared their time and memories during the course of my research. The artists and writers, some of whom have since passed away, were invaluable sources for my research and, at times, submitted to prolonged hours of often distressing conversation as they shared their insight, reflection, or encouragement. Many Photo League sources were especially kind and eagerly shared their stories with a stranger. I would like to thank all those I was able to interview both formally and informally: Walter Rosenblum, Helen Gee, George Gilbert, Aaron Siskind, Rosalie Gwathmey, Morris Engel, Miriam Cohen, Erika Stone, Grace Mayer, Rebecca Lepkoff, Arthur Goldsmith, Sol Libsohn, Joe Schwartz, Rae Russel, Vivian Cherry, Ruth Bernhard, Ida Wyman, John Cage, Burt Glinn, John Grillo, Fred McDarrah, Arnold Gassan, John Haines, Miles Forst, Louis Faurer, Bob Adelman, Saul Leiter, Ed Roth, and David Vestal. Without such dedicated, generous, and sincere sources, I could never have come close to appreciating the cold war experiences of artists in New York City during the 1940s, 1950s, and early 1960s.

A number of archives and research institutions whose helpful staff were indispensable to my work deserve my gratitude. First, thanks to Howard Greenberg and his staff at the Howard Greenberg Gallery, New York, who generously shared crucial unpublished Photo League archival material and allowed me full access to its bountiful collection of photographs. Thanks, especially, to Anne Tucker, who graciously allowed me to ransack her copious personal files in Houston. Other essential sites include: the Humanities Research Center, University of Texas, Austin; the Museum of Modern Art, New York; the Museum of Fine Arts, Houston; the Metropolitan Museum, New York; the Witkin Gallery, New York; the New York University Bobst Library; Julia van Haaftan and the staff at the New York Public Library; Miles Barth and the International Center of Photography; Barbara Millstein at the Brooklyn Museum; Leslie Noland and the Museum of the City of New York;

Dianne Nilsen and the Center for Creative Photography, Tucson; Janice Madhu, at the George Eastman House; the Scheinbaum and Russek Gallery, Sante Fe, New Mexico; and Emily Goldstein at Glenn Horowitz Booksellers.

Enduring colleagues and friends I met at the University of Texas, Austin, include Anne McCauley, John Clarke, Joe Thomas, Susan Webster, Janis Bergman-Carton, and Bill Stott. Their patience with my exuberant and sometimes irritating focus over the years inspires my own aspiration to listen and encourage others. This gratitude also extends to other colleagues and friends whose advice, editorial comment, support, and general encouragement was greatly appreciated: James Enyeart, Mike Weaver, Naomi Rosenblum, Adam Cohen, Peter Bunnell, Pam Veerhusen, Cindy McAllister, and Charlotte Simpson. Helen Gee deserves thanks, again, for her invaluable insight on all matters.

For their help in guiding my search for reproductions and sources, I thank Jim Hughes, Eric Sandeen, Mary Engel, Patricia Hills, Nancy Neel, Charles Traub of the Siskind Foundation, Robert Frank and the staff of PaceWildensteinMacGill Galleries, New York, Misty Moye at the Museum of Fine Arts, Houston, the staff at the National Gallery of Art, Washington, D.C., the George Eastman House, and the Robert Miller Gallery.

The University of North Carolina at Charlotte provided needed financial support through a Faculty Research Grant to study women in the Photo League and a Faculty Research Support Grant to help offset costs of copyrights for this book. My thanks, too, to the many friends, colleagues, and students at the University of North Carolina, Charlotte, who supported me during the final stages of this book, especially Martha Strawn, whose encouragement never wavered.

My deepest appreciation extends to my editor, George F. Thompson, president of the Center for American Places, his assistant Randy Jones, and the always helpful professional staff at the Johns Hopkins University Press, especially my incomparable manuscript editor, Celestia Ward.

And finally, I thank my family, to whom this book is dedicated. I am grateful for my grandmother, Jackie Koonce Guynup Gibbons, whose own history out of poverty inspires and humbles me every day; my parents, Burton and Patricia Corbus, who encouraged my work through their emotional support, often sharing their own memories of these decades in long, patient discussions; Kevin Bezner, whose uncompromising ability to analyze and encourage is invaluable; and our son Nate Bezner, whose expertise in film, photography, and computers deepens my awareness of traditions and innovations today.

Photography and Politics in America

Introduction

What Is Documentary Photography?

> Documentary? That's a very sophisticated and misleading word. And not really clear. You have to have a sophisticated ear to receive that word.
>
> WALKER EVANS, 1971

Ever since photography's invention in the early nineteenth century, the concept "documentary" has been burdened with fascinating complexity. Even the most sophisticated minds falter in attempts to define its style and attitude. The term *documentary* often serves to define a photographer's relationship to content and form, text, and publication. It presumes to explore larger societal issues beyond the individual photographer's personal concerns and typically delves into more overt "political" realms of class and economics. In reality, documentary photography frequently intrudes into contradictory categorizations; it exists uneasily, therefore, within the supposedly distinct domains of journalistic, artistic, landscape, fashion, and advertising photography.[1] Even though such categories are problematic and ambiguous, documentary photography has been a useful trope that distinguishes a humanistic perspective many image makers embraced and explored in twentieth-century photography, as exemplified in the work of the Farm Security Administration (FSA) photographers of the Depression. As Edward Steichen stated in 1938, "one of the favored words . . . today is *documentary*."[2] But the positivist ascendancy of documentary style and attitude did not survive subsequent decades. Why then, in later years, did documentary photography's influence and prestige wane?

This book traces the rise of abstract and personal photography by the late 1950s and early 1960s, a rise that coincided with the slow decline of documentary photography after the Depression years and led to abstract and personal photography's eventual domination of the field. Until that time, organizations such as the Photo League carried on the documentary vision of earlier work, especially that of Lewis Hine and the FSA photographers, expressing its members' views of American society in the 1930s and 1940s. Like Hine and the FSA workers, most league photographers sought human subjects who illustrated the class distinctions and inequities of their time. The photographic career of Sid Grossman, a key figure in the Photo League, serves as an example of one member's difficulties in maintaining a political and documentary artistic stance in the post–World War II years. Steichen's 1955 exhibit, *The Family of Man*, represents a late populist but critically flawed moment in the history of documentary photography as it was subsumed, and diluted, within the safer (or less extreme) realm of photojournalism. Finally, the rising celebration of artists such as Robert Frank and Minor White heralded the movement toward more ironic or personal visualizations of the American scene. By the 1960s, the increasingly self-conscious "artistic" image that communicated cultural fragmentation and personal alienation, not populist social reform, prevailed as the primary signifier of talent and the true aesthetic ambition in photographic histories and criticism. Documentary photography, in turn, increasingly became categorized as professional photojournalism as its ideological presumptions and hegemonic hold were questioned more and more by critics of the medium.

Although art history categories are traditionally constructed and seldom exist as clearly delineated patterns, most historians of photography depict the movement toward self-conscious formalism as a natural and positive progression up the evolutionary art ladder (just as the "triumph" of American abstract expressionism was hailed as an improvement over social realism). The decline of documentary photography during these decades is much more complex than this summary.[3] Documentary photography's decline and dissolution into the category of quasijournalism, apart from the category of art, coincided with the disruptive social upheavals and politically repressive years of the cold war. New cultural and ideological conditions in the cold war years forced traditional presumptions concerning social documentary to become inexorably altered, regarded as suspect and even dangerous. This parallel between the decline of documentary photography and the rise of political repression is no mere coincidence—a redbaiting, blacklisting climate forced many artists to retreat into safer, more private realms.

Photographic categories such as "documentary" or "photojournalism" are not necessarily or immediately obvious to viewers; often we must be told which is which, a function of textbooks, museums, gallery owners, critics and historians. A single image can belong to more than one category, or its characteristics may change through time (for instance, a nineteenth-century image, such as a daguerreotype portrait, may become increasingly artistic, a transformation usually related to its age and its increased market value). In reality, any photograph—or any visual image—conveys multiple fields of meaning that alter and shift through time. Because it is rooted in mechanical reproduction, the photograph seems, to most viewers from Baudelaire's time to our own, to project a sense of objective reality in its rendering of concrete objects in space. At this most basic level, every photograph could be judged to *document* a person, place, or event. But each photograph also contains a symbolic order with cultural determinants, a message both sent and received.[4] The documentary photographer is primarily concerned with sending messages of social realities beyond his or her own personal inner world (or "other-centeredness").

It was during the lean years of the Depression that documentary work enjoyed a more consensual and dominant aesthetic among the majority of known photographers (such as Dorothea Lange, Russell Lee, Jack Delano, Arthur Rothstein, Ben Shahn, and other FSA workers). More formally engaged photographers, following Alfred Stieglitz's modernist tradition, were less recognized publicly and had fewer publication and exhibition venues as compared with those available to FSA photographers. That such photographers coexisted alongside documentarians during the 1920s and 1930s is clear by the work of the more formally engaged f/64 group on the West Coast as well as that of other photographers such as the surrealists and Bauhaus artists, among others in the European scene. As evidenced in disparaging comments by writers in the Photo League's publication *Photo Notes* and from other sources, however, documentarians in the 1930s often found their modernist contemporaries disengaged from crucial societal issues. In contrast, FSA work is rarely called "art" in photographic histories of the time—instead readers find an emphasis on the documentary artists' social attitudes and their work's humanistic content rather than its aesthetic concerns.[5]

A full history and critical exploration of the federal patronage of photography during the 1930s (much less the century-old history of documentary photography) is not possible within this context, but the general background of the FSA program illustrates the healthy activism of documentary during the Depression. In 1935, Franklin Delano Roosevelt formed the Resettlement Administration (RA) as part of his New Deal for America, which established assistance programs and agencies during the Depression years. The initial impetus of the RA's formation was the need to provide rural relief and land-use administration; its projects included rehabilitation loans and grants to farmers, debt adjustment, flood and erosion control, cooperative rural settlements, suburban resettlement, and migrant camps. The RA was absorbed into the Department of Agriculture and became the Farm Security Administration (FSA) in 1937. Franklin D. Roosevelt appointed Assistant Secretary of Agriculture Rexford Tugwell (previously a professor of economics at Columbia University) to head the FSA. The coordination and reorganization of these programs was, according to Tugwell, the "rehabilitation of poor people and poor land together in one federal agency." Tugwell decided to hire photographers to create a pictorial survey of rural areas in the United States (to "show Americans America") and appointed his former student Roy Stryker head of the Historical Section.[6]

The FSA was headquartered in Washington D.C., where the printing, filing, and distribution of images took place. It employed a staff of thirteen photographers, including Walker Evans, Arthur Rothstein, Carl Mydans (hired in 1935), Ben Shahn, Dorothea Lange, Russell Lee (replacing Mydans in 1936), Jack Delano, John Vachon, Marion Post Wolcott, and John Collier. Stryker was not always easy for these photographers to work with, and there are numerous stories of the battles that developed. Beaumont Newhall's recollections of Stryker illuminate the director's ideology of documentary with an emphasis on content, not aesthetics. When Newhall was curator of photography at MoMA, he showed Stryker "a superb set of prints" by Ansel Adams of a few of Dorothea Lange's negatives: "They were beautifully mounted on museum board, with each carefully signed by both artists. To my surprise, Stryker burst into a rage of vociferous deprecation. The print quality was to him elitist, unfair to his printer. He wanted to give the museum a pile of eleven-by-fourteen glossy prints for visitors to look at. 'And when those become dog earned and worn out,' he said, 'I'll send you another batch.'"[7]

Earlier, during his study of sociology, Stryker had frequently used photographs to aid his research. Finding such visual data useful, the FSA asked its photographers to record America's problems and show what the agency was doing to improve conditions across the nation. Their images typically focused on the poor, disenfranchised, and unempowered, who were struggling to cope under adverse (and potentially reversible) conditions—classic subjects essential to documentary photography's humanistic spirit. But despite all its good intentions, the FSA was always in danger of being shut down, threatened by budget cuts and lack of support by Congress. The agency limped on until the more prosperous pre–World War II years (when many of the unemployed were able to find work in the army and war factories), and in 1943 the FSA was replaced by the Office of War Information. The legacy of the FSA is impressive—in its brief six-year existence, the staff of thirteen photographers, hired to document "long-standing rural distress," produced some 270,000 prints and negatives.[8]

As William Stott demonstrated in his *Documentary Expression and Thirties America*, documentary photography during the Depression years was a distinct genre that implied rhetorical conceits such as "truth" and "honesty." Lange stated, in concert with many other documentary photographers, "We were after the truth . . . not just making effective pictures."[9] The clear black-and-white "straight" images they produced, without any *seeming* manipulation or alteration, helped create compelling presumptions of authenticity and realism in FSA work. In a classic sense, this "honest" documentary style is defined as the presentation of objective facts, but in reality such objectivity is complex and unfixed, as it is put into question by each individual photographer's own biased, ideological background. The prevailing beliefs held by FSA photographers, however, included a faith in the common people as subjects and a concern that content should evoke viewers' emotions. In what Stott more specifically defines as "social documentary," photographers typically focused on human subjects and created images that could, theoretically, encourage social improvement or, according to Walter Lippmann, "public education."[10] Stott adds: "Documentary deals with people 'a damn sight realer' than the celebrities that crowd the media. These people, far from being the society's rulers, are often its most deprived and powerless subjects. . . . [Documentary] makes vivid the unimagined existence of a group of people by picturing in detail the activities of one or a few of its number . . . [and] makes them visible, gives the inarticulate a voice." Documentary photography, then, characteristically focuses on the underclasses in a society, the disenfranchised, the poor, or "common man." Few documentary essays exist on the rich or powerful members of a society, as documentary photographers' partisan agenda dictates seeking those who need empowerment economically.[11]

Documentary photography's central concern has always been legible content (not form, style, or presentation, although such issues were not neglected) and the image's capacity to arouse viewers' sympathetic emotions. To argue that content took precedence over form is not to say that the two were mutually exclusive or in a simplistic war against each other. In reality, for FSA photographers (or any artists), form is always an extension of content, and vice versa.[12] But historically, documentary photographers emphasized the subject, particularly the human subject, while each individual artist stressed formal issues to varying degrees.

Given the complex dynamics of reading images, a documentary image's potential ability to excite viewer response is problematic. No visual information is neutral; it is always received and manipulated through the viewer's own bias. Few documentary photographers believe that viewers respond in a simple cause-and-effect manner of communication. Beaumont Newhall's recollection of a story concerning Lange indicates photographers' awareness of the critical pitfalls in the category of documentary work. Lange sent two images of a pueblo to Newhall, his wife, Nancy, and Peter Bunnell in 1969, asking "Which one is documentary?" After spending an entire evening trying to answer this question, they decided on "the plain one," although neither, they felt, without caption or text, could be truly considered documentary.[13] Like Lange, many photographers realize that social documentary images raise complex questions by implying sociopolitical situations demanding thought, action, or even answers.

That the FSA stressed social content is evidenced, too, by Walker Evans's more troubled career in the organization. Stryker accused Evans of making "insufficiently 'political'" images with "ivory tower" aesthetics.[14] This dialectic between form and content is not so much an either-or situation as a matter of emphasis somewhere between the extremes. The FSA photographers were told to record, primarily, agrarian scenes of human distress, and they responded to these demands. Despite aesthetic differences, a clearly humanitarian focus linked the photographers of the FSA with other social documentarians.

While the FSA photographers faced complex issues such as the function of images, federal patronage, the problem of audience reception, the photograph's communicative ability, and individual control of images, most of the photographers were interested, to varying degrees, in the photograph's ability to incite change. In subsequent historiographies of the period, Lange's success at altering conditions of California pea-pickers through the use of her pictures has taken on mythic proportions as an instance of photography improving the conditions of real people's lives.[15] Mass circulation of such images assured many photographs the possibility of viewer response. The FSA images, organized from bureaucratic headquarters in Washington, D.C., were also well circulated in the growing arsenal of picture magazines during the 1930s. The bourgeois viewers in Washington or the privileged elite elsewhere were not the only audience for these documentary images; they were used in Department of Agriculture brochures and, more generally, in press magazines and newspapers. By 1940 the FSA's Historical Section claimed a picture distribution of approximately 1,406 images per month in magazines such as *Time*, *Fortune*, *Today*, *Nation's Business*, *Life*, and *Look*, among many other periodicals.[16]

Within the context of early twentieth-century photography, the specific term *documentary* was coined by John Grierson, a British film producer and sociologist who came to the United States in 1924 to study mass media. His

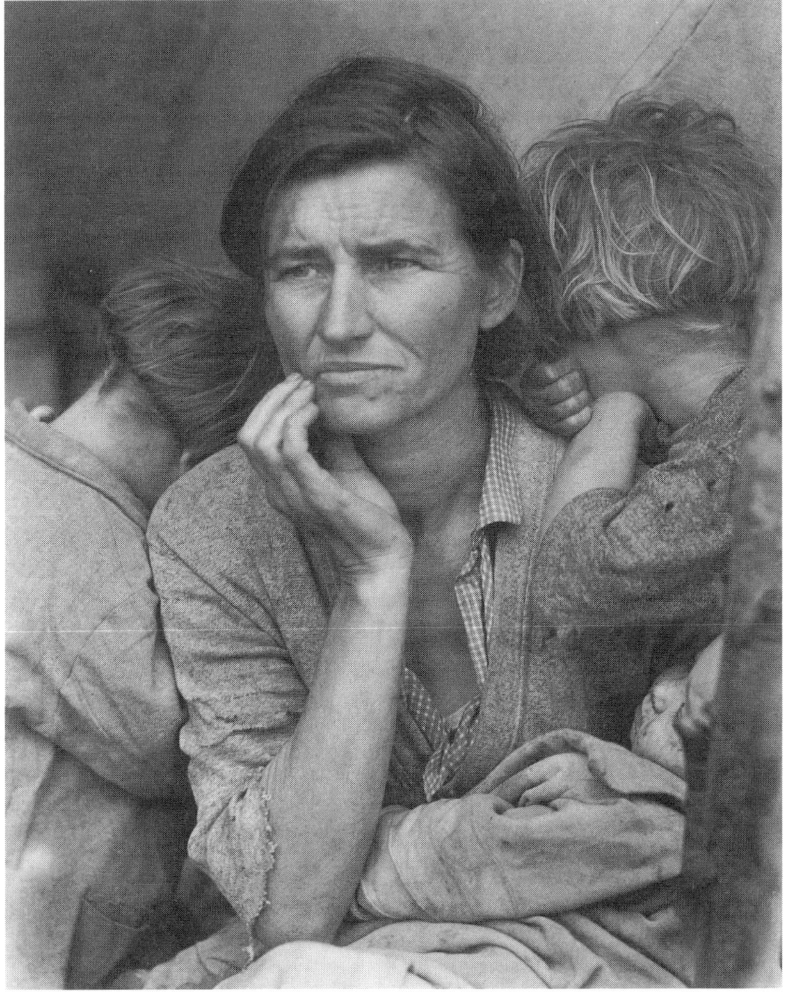

I.1. Dorothea Lange, *Migrant Mother,* 1936

Lange's iconic *Migrant Mother*, a peapicker in Nipomo, California, symbolized for many (such as FSA director Roy Stryker) the concern of the federal government for economically distressed farmers and their families during the Depression years. U.S. Farm Security Administration, Prints and Photographs Division, Library of Congress.

films mixed historical and sociological fact with fiction, creating images that could inform, educate, and dramatically evoke feeling, typically toward working-class subjects. One of Grierson's early films was *Drifters*, a 1929 work about the British herring industry. As a trained sociologist, Grierson sought to create not just informational worker-education films or sensationalized Hollywood movies but informed films that excited emotional response: "I look to register what actually moves: what hits the spectator at the midriff: what yanks him up by the hair of the head or the plain bootstraps to the plane of decent seeing." Such ideals, again, emphasized content, not form: as Grierson said, "documentary was from the beginning an anti-aesthetic movement."[17]

William Stott points out the different philosophies between modes of documentary work, maintaining that some documentarians worked to inform the intellect through the presentation of visual evidence while others, such as the FSA photographers and Grierson, sought to inform both the intellect and the emotions with a political motivation in mind (for instance, economic improvement for a disenfranchised minority, as in John Steinbeck's *The Grapes of Wrath*). Such implicit, although abstract, political ideals frequently led to charges of propagandistic potential. As Grierson said, "there is hardly any avoiding [the] accusation of propaganda," for documentary work clearly dealt with social conditions that could be changed by human choice and action.[18] Propagandistic art, to most Americans, then and now, was often associated with totalitarian regimes such as the Soviet Union and Nazi Germany; it deceptively manipulated subject matter in order to present false, corrupt political histories and ideologies in a positive light. Unlike documentary work, then, propaganda was not an attempt to be either true or honest. Given America's fears of escalating fascist and Communist states during the 1930s and 1940s, the perception of creating propaganda was to be avoided at all costs. But the distinctions become tenuous between propaganda and documentary at times; certainly persuasive, partisan image-making, in general, risked accusations of deceptive purpose.

Even so, the period of the FSA's photography was far more politically active than other times in the history of American photography. While all eras could be broadly labeled "political," artists during the Depression years enjoyed more government patronage and proactive union agitation than those in any other period of American art. Many artists during these hard economic years believed that "art is a weapon," a principle also held by radical socialists and Communists. Certainly propaganda, deceptive images with overt political functions, can mislead viewers, but, as Stott claims, during the Depression more "honest" forms of propoganda existed as well, which sought to influence public opinion in positive ways. He writes: "At the very least we now admit that some propagandas are less reprehensible than others. We understand that propaganda has a 'double face'" with shades of grey between each extreme.[19] The more committed Communist or socialist artists believed in agitational propaganda (or "agit-prop"), work that substantiated, in every form and expression, the (usually revolutionary) ideals of economic equality. Less didactic radical artists involved in the production of documentary work generally wished to deal with facts of life that could be altered, hoping to move the audience to outrage, sadness, or an emotional state conducive to changing the conditions. At the very least, documentary photographs made visible the subjects FDR called the "forgotten"; they professed to empower those with no voice, oftentimes in book-length essays (such as Walker Evans's and James Agee's *Let Us Now Praise Famous Men* and Margaret Bourke-White's and Erskine Caldwell's *You Have Seen Their Faces*).[20]

This desire to correct social wrongs and promote social activism has many precedents within the history of photography, but to the FSA photographers (and later to the Photo League) Lewis Hine and Jacob Riis were illustrative and inspirational examples to follow. Both photographers were engaged in social activism and reform at the turn of the century, Riis as a police reporter and Hine as a sociologist. The two men turned to photography as a way to affect further social reform, believing that images are more convincing than words. As Hine said, "If I could tell the story in words, I wouldn't need to lug a camera."[21]

FSA photographers, following the philosophy of Hine, Riis, and other documentarians, looked to socioeconomic research during the Depression, as scripted by director Roy Stryker, in order to find subjects who needed economic empowerment. After the FSA program was discontinued, Stryker wrote his own definition of the type of photographer he wanted to hire at New Jersey's Standard Oil for a company-sponsored documentary photographic foray he later headed: "Their education should never stop, but should go ahead, step by step, day by day. They should know something about economics, history, political science, philosophy, and sociology. They have to be able to conduct research, gather and correlate factual information, and think things through. Then they can go out and take pictures that mean something."[22] In the 1930s, Stryker's FSA photographers assumed that content, researched factually and meaningfully, could actually approximate "truth." The FSA style of presentation, with clear and precise prints rendering every detail, made their content seem unquestionably valid and factual. As John Tagg has pointed out, documentary realism assumes and encourages photography's "privileged status as a guaranteed witness of the actuality of the events it represents."[23] Empirical, visual evidence of poverty, unemployment, or racial discrimination made the existence and effects of these problems undeniably real and alive, especially when combined with crucial textual information or captions. As Stryker said, "Truth is the objective of the documentary attitude." But, he also added, "A good documentary should tell not only what a place or a thing or a person *looks* like, but it must also tell the audience what it would *feel* like to be an actual witness to the scene."[24] In this manner, the viewer participates visually in multiple dimensions of fact and feeling, so that the images can evoke feeling and inform in concert.

In recent studies, many scholars have emphasized FSA photographers' own biased manipulations of content and subject in order to influence and heighten emotional response (for instance, choosing images of sharecroppers who are scowling instead of those smiling). Through such images, documentary photographers sought to incite viewers' efforts toward implementing social relief reforms. For some viewers, the images succeeded. One woman came to Stryker's office to get a copy of Walker Evans's shot of an urban landscape in Pittsburgh picturing a cemetery and steel mills. Stryker recalled her reason for wanting the photograph: "I want to give it to my brother who's a steel executive. I want to write on it, '*Your* cemeteries, *your* streets, *your* buildings, *your* steel mills. But *our* souls. God damn you.'"[25] The focus, it was hoped, on industry, itinerant workers, labor strikes, poverty, and the unemployed could make viewers, such as the woman Stryker quoted, feel compassion for those with pitiable lives and long for such conditions to change. The hard task was to depict the poor as *able* to rehabilitate; to make them appear overly victimized or too downtrodden risked failure, as viewers might not believe conditions could improve.

Most documentarians, then, believed in the primacy of evoking *feeling* in order to move the audience to action. FDR felt that social change was difficult if not impossible "in our civilization unless you have sentiment."[26] Many images from the FSA files, especially those that have been subsequently reproduced, have the dramatic capacity to make viewers feel sadness, pity, or despair over someone else's plight. The photographer's manipulation of poignancy and sentiment is often a powerful and necessary tool for documenting victims of society. Thus, the human subject and human difficulties are the centerpieces of most FSA images. As Stryker wrote, "However they might have differed in skill and insight, our photographers had one thing in common, and that was a deep respect for human beings."[27] For Roosevelt, too, the suffering individuals who made up the masses were the key to his own New Deal political agenda. And during this time of social injustice and mass deprivation, many artists felt that to turn to the imagery of personal imagination, in the modernist tradition, was not only escapist but irresponsible. This sentiment was evident in literature as well; many writers of the 1930s felt that individually focused fiction was "frivolous" in an era of social upheaval.[28] Even Walker Evans, Stryker's most "difficult" photographer, perhaps put it more simply: "Don't talk about it, go out and do it."[29]

While documentary photography during the 1930s was never universally agreed upon in terms of visual execution or definition, its ideals became even more blurred after World War II. During the early 1950s, especially, more and more photographers and critics began to question many of the assumptions held by documentarians. The social ideals of documentary photography were also frequently grouped with journalistic philosophy, whether or not such images were published in or patronized by mass circulated magazines. Edward Steichen, in the foreword to *Memorable Life Photographs* (1951), discussed photojournalism in terms that also could be applied to documentary work: "Photographic journalism is generally accepted as an authoritative source of visual information about our times. It now regularly reaches audiences all over the world on a scale unheard of a decade or two ago. It is becoming a new force in the molding of public opinion, and explaining man to man. . . . On occasion [it] create[s] images that reach into the nebulous and controversial realm of the fine arts."[30] With the rising acceptance and patronage of more personally directed images in the modernist tradition of Stieglitz, many photographers like Steichen still clung to the realist function of photography, which clearly communicated to a more democratic, populist array of potential viewers. Andreas Feininger, a commercial photographer who published many books on technique and process, wrote in 1954 that the "first requisite for a good photograph is that it have some meaning," that it "get ideas across" that are "apparent" and legible. "A picture that does not 'say' anything is pointless."[31] But for many photographers, meaning and purpose were more nebulous; might one's own personal, inner vision have equal, if not superior, truth and meaning?

The rise in acceptance of "art for art's sake" philosophies was seen again and again in periodicals such as *Aperture* and general history books of the 1950s. In *Photography at Mid-Century* (1959), Beaumont Newhall defines just four stylistic trends in contemporary photography: The first is the "straight approach" which never loses "contact with reality" (such as work by Paul Strand, Edward Weston, and Ansel Adams). The second is "experimental," as seen in the more abstract, manipulated work of Lázló Moholy-Nagy and Man Ray. A third category is the "equivalent," wherein photographs are treated as symbols, "even, at times, a trigger to a stream of consciousness" (such as Alfred Stieglitz's or Minor White's work). And Newhall calls the final type "photojournalistic" (illustrated by the work of Henri Cartier-Bresson), in which images clearly "desire to communicate." Documentary work, one presumes, if it still existed at all for Newhall, would be contained within this last category—as, he continued, photojournalism "essentially [has] a desire to communicate, to tell about people, to record without intrusion the moment."[32]

By the 1950s, any amount of the consensus that had previously existed concerning the dominance of documentary photography was negligible. In a later edition of *The History of Photography* (originally published in 1937), Newhall writes:

> "Documentary," in the sense in which we have described it, has been accepted as the definition of a style. Since World War II the movement has lost impetus in the organizational sense. Its tenets have been absorbed and have become essential to the fabric of photojournalism and, especially, to the style of factual reporting developed by television. Substitutes have been suggested for the word "documentary": "historical," "factual," "realistic." While each of these qualities is contained within "documentary," none conveys the deep respect for fact coupled with the desire to create the basically subjective interpretation of the world in which we live that marks documentary photography at its best.[33]

During the repressive cold war decades after World War II, documentary ideals became suspect, like the individuals investigated by the CIA and FBI, of overt (or naive) political purpose and function.[34] In concert with growing suspicions of documentary photography's clarity, this style was also aestheticized into museum collections, its political possibilities diluted by a concern for formalism.[35]

In all levels of the photographic press during the 1950s, one finds articles on how to "read" photographs, as critics and artists endeavored to educate the public about the complex, multiple levels of photographic signification. Even *Popular Photography*, in a March 1958 article by Ralph Hattersley, discussed "How to 'Read' a Photograph." *Aperture*'s articles of the 1950s included Ansel Adams on "Defining 'Documentary'" (a type of image-making "'costumed' with ideological intention") and a special issue in 1953 by Minor White, on "reading" photographs, in order to "help the spectator get more out of it."[36] Whereas in previous years, many viewers presumed the legibility of documentary images, by later decades critics such as White questioned all conceits of professed photographic clarity. Increasing numbers of American photographers in periodicals of the 1940s and 1950s questioned the ability of documentary photography to convey any objective "truth;" as Newhall noted in an *Aperture* article of 1956, visual communication is biased: "The photographic image implies authenticity. How often have we heard the cliché: 'The camera does not lie.' We know that it does, outrageously so, yet we refuse to believe our common sense."[37]

In other *Aperture* articles, White similarly disparaged the documentarian and photojournalist's "outward drive . . . where anything less than a crisis gets scant attention." The "inward-going drift" of the photographer-artist, however, "leads towards a world of contemplation, where violence violates an active life." White's consistent underscoring of the categories' differences increasingly marginalized documentary photography. The two become distinct: "The mirror-to-life photo reporter does not have the same purpose that the beauty-evoking photographer-artist has, and to cross or mix their purposes is to cloud the truth of each."[38]

Many historians and critics of photography, even today, in the tradition of White and Newhall, keep the camps distinct, organized into discrete, functional categories, as if such categories exist naturally and are not defined by the market, galleries, critics, and museums of the world. And the differences between documentary photography (or photojournalism) and art photography are now more fixed than ever. Newhall's *The History of Photography* includes separate chapters on "photojournalism," "art photography," and "documentary photography." The more recent *International Center of Photography Encyclopedia of Photography* has numerous entries defining such terms, indicating the entrenched, popular notions of categorization. "Documentary and Social Documentary photography" is defined as work in which events are minimally altered with little influence on the part of the photographer and that attempts to document or influence social conditions (the encyclopedia lists examples of documentary groups, including the FSA, the Photo League, and photojournalists such as W. Eugene Smith and Robert Capa). Cornell Capa, the ICP's founder, calls such photojournalists "concerned photographers," following Hine's example, who try "to show things that had to be corrected, and the things that had to be appreciated." Other entries in the encyclopedia include "art photography" and "photojournalism," which, as a broad category, includes documentary work but more specifically involves the assignment of a particular story and narrative with the inclusion of text.[39]

This book does not seek to entrench these categories even further but instead, by exploring the complex relationship between documentary work and artistic photography, attempts to re-create the contemporary tensions that existed between the two extremes during these years. Art and documentary are not simply two mutually exclusive realms—together they create a conceptual photographic field rich in creative options and aesthetic avenues. Yet, by the late 1950s, more and more photographers aspiring to "high art" (in the newly expanding academic art photography programs growing across the nation) traveled the road toward the more elite, sophisticated, formal school espoused by White and others in *Aperture*. Meanwhile, traditional documentarians entered careers working in the more populist but less prestigious (in terms of photographic histories and critical categories) field of commercial photography and journalism, even as the popularity of illustrated magazines waned after World War II.

That such ingrained categorical notions become accepted photographic lore by the 1960s and 1970s is witnessed in John Szarkowski's influential *Mirrors and Windows* (1978), in which he publicly stated the growing interest in "art" over more documentary photojournalism: "The failure of photojournalism stemmed perhaps from the sin of hubris. Like President Johnson, it thought it could deal with anything. This opinion was eventually proved fallacious in public. Good photographers had long since known—whether or not they admitted it to their editors—that most issues of importance cannot be photographed. . . . As the influence of the professional diminished, the content of American photography became increasingly personal, and often progressively private."[40] Szarkowski, in later decades, certainly played a role in devaluing photojournalism in favor of aestheticized, private, and personal artistic photography. The growing popularity of television, displacing the mass media picture magazines, radio, and newspapers, also contributed to this developing hierarchy in photographic expression. The influx of European Modernists, fleeing the war and destructive political regimes, would also infuse the American art scene with new energies devoted to more abstract directions.

The Austrian writer Ernst Fischer, in his Marxist art criticism of the late 1950s, was not surprised by the formation of such hierarchies: "In the late bourgeois world of today," he wrote, intensified by class struggles, "art tends to be divorced from social ideas," driving the individual "further into his desperate alienation, to encourage an impotent egoism, and to turn reality into a false myth surrounded by the magic rites of a bogus cult."[41] Hierarchical categories, Fischer believed, encourage the mystification of art into arenas of personal angst, indefinable alienation, and fragmentation, rather than collectively sought activism. Shahn similarly wrote, also in the late 1950s: "As during the thirties art had been swept by mass ideas, so during the forties there took place a mass movement toward abstraction. Not only was the social dream rejected, but any dream at all."[42] By the 1950s, Shahn's perceptions surely intensified as he defended his politics and art in court trials mandated by the House Un-American Activities Committee.

In short, photographic distinctions and categorical definitions were determined by cultural events and wider sociological-historical conditions pressuring artistic communities to expand, question, or retreat from previously held notions of meaning since each society historically, in the words of Michel Foucault, "has its [own] regime of truth."[43] What was accepted and even glorified as documentary realism in the Depression underwent sometimes violent and occasionally subtle transformations during the 1940s and 1950s, when America entered one of its most repressive political climates of the century. There is no mere irony in this story; the parallels between the decline of documentary work and the rise of more formally engaged photography relate to clear, real, historical events in time.

1

"Where Do We Go from Here?" The Demise of the Photo League, 1947–1951

> The artist stands alone. He has lost his shadow. As his art can find no direction from society, it must invent its own destiny.
>
> SUZI GABLIK, *Has Modernism Failed?*

The late 1940s in the United States were a difficult and confusing time for many documentary photographers. Artists born of liberal New Deal politics, as were many of the photographers in New York City at that time, found themselves in a more prosperous but more repressive climate in America. Roosevelt's era ended with his death, in 1945, after four terms in the presidency. Harry Truman continued FDR's vision with "the Fair Deal" during his tenure in office, from 1945 to 1952, and faced the escalating cold war challenges of Communist aggression, both domestically and internationally.

No single event initiated the chill of the cold war in the United States; the period must be seen as a complex accumulation of events and attitudes at every level of American social behavior throughout the late 1930s, 1940s, and 1950s. Historian Robert Goldstein more specifically dates the initiation of America's cold war to the period from 1947 to 1950. Factors contributing to his conclusion include campaigns to ferret Communists out of American political and social life, legislation passed with strong anti-Communist overtones, and the initiation of government loyalty programs.[1]

Concerns over containing the domino effect of Communism in the late 1940s led to expensive policies such as the Truman Doctrine. American-led covert activities aimed at combating the spread of Communism spanned the globe, active in such places as Iran, Guatemala, and Indochina, among other "hot spots" in danger of potential Communist takeover. As an integral aspect of Communist containment, politicians also supported increased efforts in the development of A-bomb and H-bomb technology, and the United States gathered a growing arsenal of international scientists to pursue this goal.

America's confidence in its nuclear superiority dissolved in 1949, however, when Russians exploded their own experimental A-bomb ("Joe-One," named after the Soviet Communist dictator, Joseph Stalin). The subsequent "space race" of the 1950s escalated experiments in ballistic weaponry as well as Soviet-American tensions for world dominance. The fear of Soviet aggression increased with the trials of Klaus Fuchs (1949) and the Rosenbergs (1951), all of whom were convicted of supplying the Soviets with secret documents relating to nuclear weaponry.

The climate offered one obscure Republican Wisconsin Senator, Joseph McCarthy, a perfect setting for his "redbaiting" smear tactics of the 1950s, as he hounded out suspected Communist sympathizers who, he believed, threatened the democratic future of the United States. As McCarthy's prestige and popularity grew (until his censure in 1954), the House Un-American Activities Committee (HUAC) courts were the busiest they had ever been. They had been created in 1938 and monitored the loyalties of federal workers by forcing testimonies from "witnesses" concerning defendants' past associations with Communism. J. Edgar Hoover and the covert operations of the FBI and the CIA waged a relentless war against internal subversion, compiling ever-growing secret files on "suspect" individuals which provided damning materials to support HUAC investigations. Further legislation underscores the strain of the times: In 1947 Truman supported the creation of a Loyalty Review Board to check federal employees and their families and dismiss any with suspicious connections to dangerous left-wing, subversive, or Communist organizations. After millions of dollars had been spent on such investigations, no evidence of actual espionage was found—although careers were often left in ruin. Workers were often forced to sign loyalty oaths forbidding "seditious" behavior and membership in "subversive" organizations. Suspect individuals called into HUAC courts included not only those known to have belonged to Communist organizations but also those more abstractly identified as "fellow travelers." The U.S. government was not required, because of "security risks," to provide the specific evidence behind such accusations, and some workers found themselves dismissed on the basis of innuendo, family associations, or past affiliations—tenuous evidence, in short, of subversive activity. It is no wonder this period has been called an "age of anxiety."

The fears of Communist infiltration in American politics escalated in 1948, when Whittaker Chambers named Alger Hiss as a former Communist Party member working for the federal government. The next year, eleven Communist Party leaders in the United States were prosecuted and convicted for advocating the overthrow of the American government. By 1950, the McCarran Act, or Internal Security Act (passed over Truman's veto), prohibitively monitored the activities (and civil liberties) of those suspected of involvement with Communist and Communist front organizations. In 1952, the election of Republican Dwight Eisenhower ended two decades of Democratic presidents. Not surprisingly, his successful campaign had emphasized the threat of Communism, the conflicts in Korea with North Korean Communists, and the containment of Chinese and Russian aggression. Such events set the tone of the times as America's cold war intensified.

In short, the late 1940s and 1950s were not a supportive climate for political liberalism, the very attitude that had earlier drawn so many image-makers to documentary ideals. By the end of the 1940s, in fact, one documentary-oriented photographic organization, the Photo League (1936–51), had been blacklisted by the U.S. Attorney General and was dissolving because of political pressure. Meanwhile, league members were also witnessing the rise of abstraction and formalism over their own social documentary tradition. The years the Photo League experienced the strongest hostility from the U.S. government were years tense with fear of Communist aggression. Suspicion and paranoia affected many Americans' lives, not just those of artists in the Photo League. Goldstein points out that in 1947, the American Civil Liberties Union reported increased challenges to civil liberties cases, "a sharply unfavorable change." Put together, these social conditions created a climate, as Oliver Larkin describes in his book *Art and Life in America* (1949), that "was not one in which the artist could feel at home, as he had in the 1930s."[2]

In the minds of right-wing politicians of the time, art, too, became a key element in their scenario of a Communist takeover, even the little-known art of the New York–based Photo League. While the art world was hardly embraced by right-wing politicians of the 1930s, by the 1940s the climate had changed more drastically and led to repressive legislation that made the art scene during the Depression years seem ideal in comparison. William Hauptman dates the beginning of this cold war in art at 1946, when conservatives halted the State Department–sponsored "Advancing American Art" show after Republican representative George A. Dondero (Michigan) pointed out modern art's "sympathies" to Communism. As a leader of the crusade against what he and others like him considered subversive art, representative Dondero repeatedly attacked modern art in 1949 as Communistic. Dondero's conception of just what constituted subversive art was never fully defined (he found the work of social-realist Ben Shahn particularly loathsome), but nonetheless he viewed some artists as a threat to the moral fiber of American liberty and cried "Throw the Marxists out." Perhaps the most succinct illustration of the government's antagonism toward modern art comes from President Truman's reference to the cancellation of a State Department art exhibition in 1947: "If that's art, I'm a Hottentot." The cold war in the art world had begun.[3] Photographers soon learned that painters such as Shahn and Philip Evergood were not the government's only concern.

In December 1947, the Photo League was listed as a subversive organization by U.S. Attorney General Tom Clark. Two years later the league was mentioned again during testimony against Communist leaders. Members of the organization reacted with angry surprise. In retrospect, the government's suspicion, given the political climate, was predictable. For decades the Photo League had flirted with left-wing ideals and partisan policies, which, in the cold war years, generated the explosive potential of an ideological H-Bomb.

To fully comprehend the reasons behind the government's blacklisting the league in 1947, one must first appreciate the radical nature of the organization's history in the 1930s and early 1940s. The Photo League was founded in 1936 and was strongly rooted in the Depression and the radical politics of that era. Throughout its existence, the league offered lectures, classes, use of darkrooms, and a mimeographed newsletter, *Photo Notes*, for a small fee to members, both amateur and professional. The organization was loosely organized by volunteer officers who kept track of the finances and operated the classrooms and newsletter, among other activities. Presently, there is no unified league archive, some issues of *Photo Notes* are missing from collections of the journal that do exist, and there are no known membership lists. Even though the league enjoyed illustrious membership and exerted tremendous influence on American photography during its time, it has been historically neglected, if not ignored. The complex and controversial politics of the league's history have discouraged some historians from investigating the organization. Even so, the material evidence—articles, reviews, and letters in *Photo Notes*, as well as member photographs—combined with oral interviews with former Photo League members prove the humanist, documentary emphasis of the organization while also indicating its potential to be classified as subversive in the climate of the cold war.

The league's beginnings reach back to 1930, when the Film and Photo League was founded as a branch of Workers' International Relief (WIR). Headquartered in Berlin, this organization assisted striking workers.[4] The WIR organized branches called Workers' Camera Leagues throughout Europe and the United States; the New York City branch produced documentary films concerning the struggles of workers and contributed photographs to leftist publications such as the *New Masses* and the Communist Party paper, the *Daily Worker*. In 1934 a splinter organization, Nykino, was formed by filmmakers who were inspired largely by Russian filmmaking and sought to explore expressive form as well as social content.[5] The photographers and filmmakers eventually broke into distinct groups, and in 1936 the still photographers organized the Photo League. As Trager points out, "the important distinction between the new organizations and their parent group was their commitment to documentary photography as an art form, not just as a tool for mass communication."[6] The central philosophy of the Photo League, throughout its existence, was its focus on the creation of documentary photographs imbued with overtly partisan social commentary.

The Photo League's lineage in the documentary tradition also extends far beyond the boundaries of New York, with branches reaching into the history of the German and international worker photography movement. German magazines such as the *Arbeiter Illustrierte Zeitung*, founded in 1925, had distinct Communist leanings and served as a counterbalance to the popular bourgeois press while providing, by 1926, centers for amateur workers or photographers. Such publications and artistic movements inform American photographic history in that they display an ideological as well as aesthetic model by which to document the world. *Arbeiter Illustrierte Zeitung* and other German magazines invigorated photographic layout design while extolling documentary vision. As Ute Eskildsen points out, "by the mid-twenties, German photography was changing its relationship to reality."[7] The Photo League, by the 1930s, similarly confronted new forms of *Sachlichkeit*, or objectivity, in New York by reviling pictorialist photographic conventions such as soft focus, which mimicked painterly strokes, while discussing the vital role of social commitment in art.

The league's lineage was also linked to the history and styles of the FSA photographers. Various FSA photographers (John Vachon, Arthur Rothstein, Dorothea Lange) are consistently mentioned within the pages of *Photo Notes* as members, teachers, and speakers. But most of the league's initial inspiration came from Lewis Hine, whose photographs the league received in a memorial collection.[8] Hine was mentioned reverently in *Photo Notes* as the spiritual leader of documentary photography. Just after the turn of the century, Hine was enlisted by the National Child Labor Committee to provide photographic evidence of labor abuses and led a photographic crusade against child labor. Between 1908 and 1921 he made more than five thousand photographs for the committee, powerful images proving the need for labor reforms. Yet by the late 1930s, "nobody was paying attention to him and we felt we could be of assistance," league member Walter Rosenblum

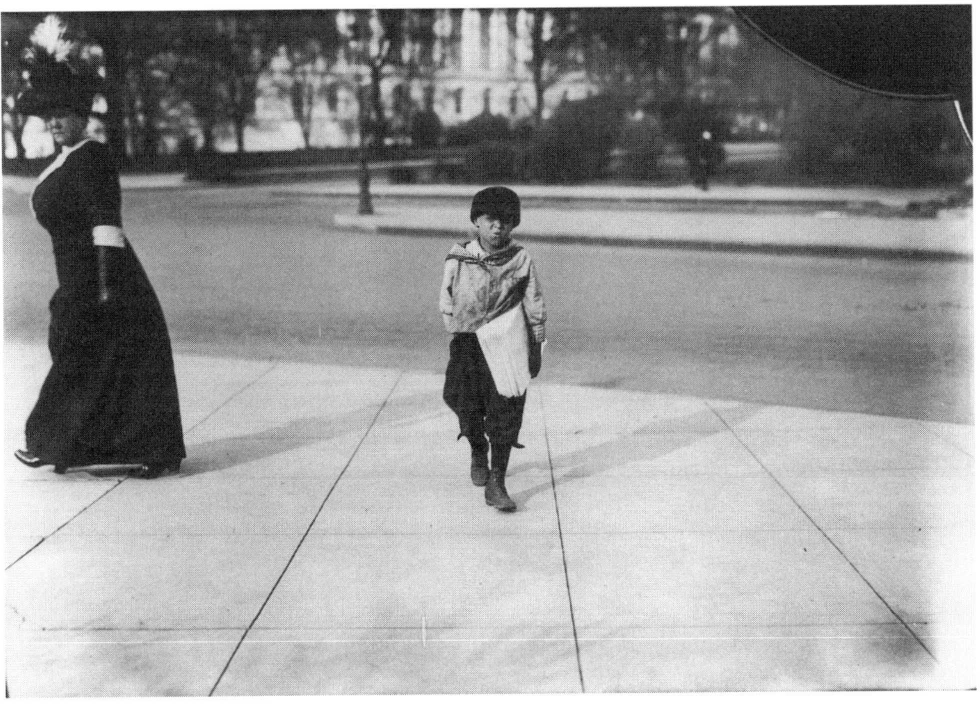

1.1. Lewis Hine, *Newsboy, Washington, DC,* 1912

Newsboy demonstrates Hine's concern for child laborers; he stands small and isolated in urban concrete as a woman walks away. Hine reported: "I found them wandering about until 1:00 and 2:00 A.M."; they were also subject to aggressive assaults by rival newspapers' gangs. Courtesy George Eastman House.

recalls. Hine was poverty stricken in the 1930s, and his prints were selling for $5. "We loved him," Rosenblum said, "he was always threatened by people who would kill him [for exposing such abject cultural conditions]."[9] To young Photo League members such as Rosenblum, this heroic "journeyman" photographer represented the dedicated documentarian for whom photography was not only an art form but also a social mission.

Hine's interest in the conditions of American class and working conditions is clearly presented in *Newsboy, Washington, DC,* 1912. Hine photographed the small, isolated figure of a boy selling newspapers, an occupation that kept children awake during the late night and early morning hours and exposed them to dangerous thugs working for rival news publications who tried to pull the boys from the streets. Hine's focal point, the child, is, in formal terms, centered in the composition, surrounded by the concrete city which accentuates his small form, his vulnerability, his loneliness. A woman walks out of the picture frame, ignoring the newsboy's plight. For many league viewers, images such as these demonstrated the photograph's potential ability to instruct, initiate reform by alluding to social ills, and raise viewers' consciousness.

When reading league discourses on Hine, one has to assume that if a photographer's intentions are pure and noble, an empirical social "truth" can, and should, be achieved in order to educate viewers about injustice. The concept of "truth" seems rarely questioned (by today's standards), although some Photo League members, such as W. Eugene Smith and Lisette Model, balked at the concept of a concrete, objective photographic reality.[10] More often, however, Hine's admirers embraced his heroic struggles as inspiration for their own photography, although none seem to have worked consistently for any specific reform organizations, as Hine had.

Despite its admiration of Hine, the league as a whole had no single, hard-line political agenda, especially by the mid-1940s. Member photographers were investigating various areas of image-making. Rosenblum says that there was a small clique within the league of photographers who "felt that all photography should have an agit-prop basis for being," while others, inspired by league instructor Paul Strand, had a broader vision of photography beyond didactic political uses. As Mike Weaver points out, however, Strand's work "must be seen in the context of his socialist vision if it is to be fully understood."[11] Strand's photography had begun under the influence of Hine at the Ethical Culture School in New York. After a pictorialist phase, Strand produced sharply focused work—a new realism called straight photography. Such images blended Strand's concern for aesthetics with his commitment to social awareness, as seen in *Blind Woman*, 1917.

While Strand and Hine provided inspiration, the active participation in the 1940s of photographers such as Strand (on the advisory board) and members Walter Rosenblum, Ansel Adams, Edward Weston, W. Eugene Smith, Lisette Model, and Dan Weiner illustrates the aesthetic range within which the men and women of the Photo League worked. But hints of member dissent, controversy, and the questioning of "correct" purposes of art were constantly voiced in *Photo Notes* (and later by former members in other forums). The humanist, left-wing, documentary photographers combing the streets and slums of New York City consistently overshadowed the artists more engaged with formalist or modernist issues within the pages of the Photo League's publications.

Political overtones abound in the monthly *Photo Notes* issues. Common terms charged with meaning include *masses*, *progressive*, and, especially,

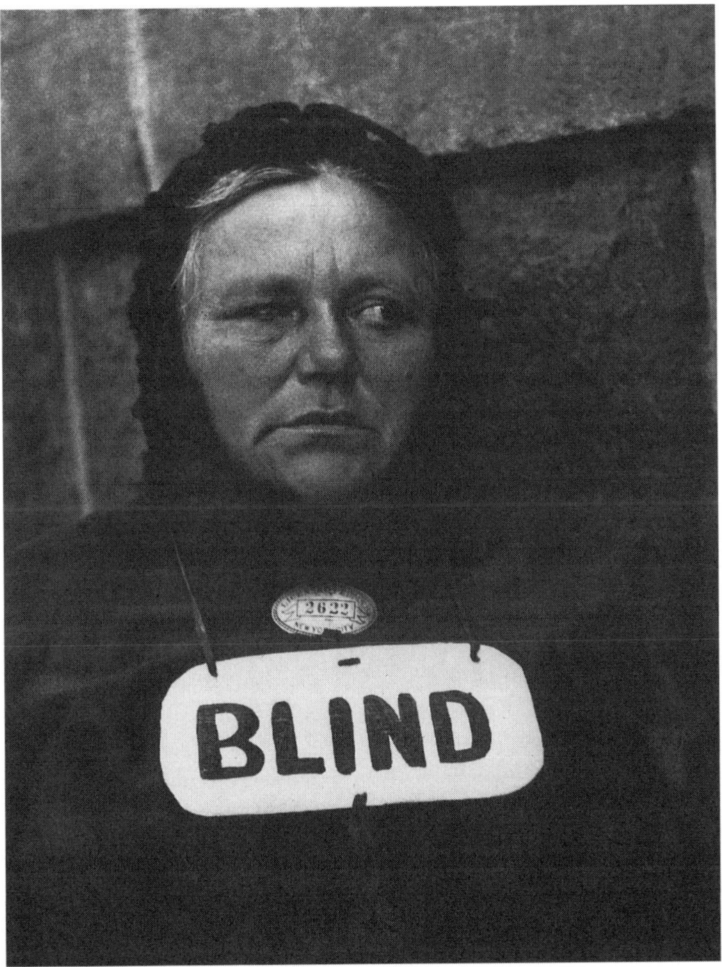

1.2. Paul Strand, *Blind Woman,* 1917.

A leading figure in American photography, Strand studied with Lewis Hine in 1908. Alfred Stieglitz's galleries, circle of friends, and publications (Strand was featured in the last two issues of *Camerawork*) inspired Strand to explore photographic aesthetics and modernism based on the objective nature of reality. Photograuve print from *Camerawork* 49/50: 13. Courtesy George Eastman House.

worker. Within the league, in fact, members were consistently referred to as *workers* rather than photographers or artists, especially in the 1930s and early 1940s. Edward Hunt, for example, in "The Photo Magazine Craze," an article published in the August 1938 issue, claimed that "photographic pictorials [are] . . . supported by the masses of people, workers and middle classes" and so "should be progressive in character." He also discussed two "really progressive photo magazines," *Photo History* and *Focus*; the latter he praised for "daring to tell the truth about the disgusting disease-ridden conditions under which the workers live and work."[12] Years later, in June 1949, the Photo League organized an exhibition called "New Workers." While terms such as *worker* may seem antiquated to modern readers, an anachronistically harmless label, at the time these were the code words many Americans associated, at a superficial level, with Marxism and Communism. The Photo League members were encouraging art with social purpose, photography that could improve living conditions and better civil liberties, and they were doing this, at times, in a language popularized by radical Depression-era politics and born from the Marxism of the Russian revolution.

No one aspect of the Photo League better demonstrates the organization's commitment to the social documentary tradition than the "feature groups," organized collectives of members who would document particular areas in New York City in need of reform and attention. These photographic forays, which began in the 1930s and tapered off in the 1940s, allowed members to explore fully the documentary photo essay. There was no federal funding or organization of league feature group production, however, as there had been for FSA photo essays; league photographers were largely motivated by the desire to document the more negative aspects of the Depression or poverty in general. And while there were few opportunities before the rise of the large picture magazines to sell Photo League work, members' photographs sporadically circulated in newspapers, magazines, and to labor groups and other organizations interested in social reform.

One of the better known of the Photo League feature groups in the Depression years was the *Harlem Document*, organized by Aaron Siskind. An active socialist in his early years, Siskind had joined the league in the early 1930s, while the Film and Photo League was still associated with WIR, and was already producing images of men huddled around fires in New York City streets and May Day parade scenes. With Siskind as their leader, a group of Photo League photographers set out to chronicle aspects of everyday life in Harlem. Siskind also consulted with Michael Carter, an African American social worker and writer in Harlem who provided the group with contacts to the community. Siskind, in an effort to portray a comprehensive visual and textual statement of Harlem, even discussed the project with New York University professor of economics Sol Prom. The project culminated in a forty-print exhibition that was shown at the New York City YMCA, the Harlem Branch Library, and the New School.[13]

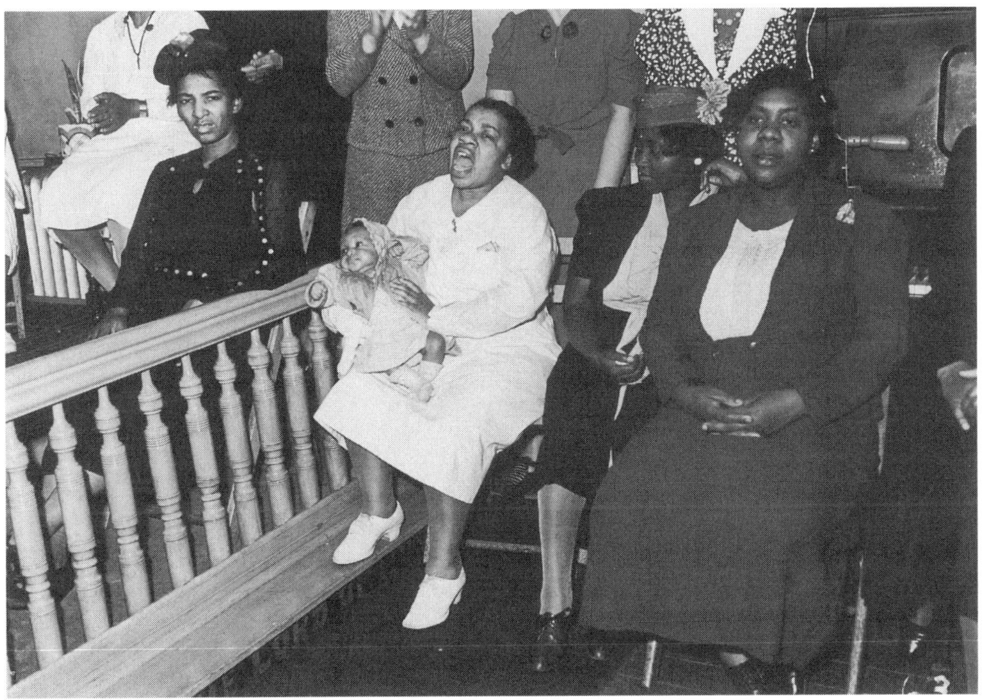

1.3. Aaron Siskind, *Interior of Church* from the *Harlem Document, ca. 1937–38.*

The *Harlem Document* was compiled in 1937 and 1938 by a Photo League feature group led by Aaron Siskind. Working with social workers and economists, the photographers aimed to depict multiple and complex social relationships in the community. © The Aaron Siskind Foundation/courtesy Robert Mann Gallery.

The *Harlem Document* aimed to depict many facets of social relationships within the community, combining aesthetic photographic issues with social reform. One image from the series included *Storefront Church*, ca. 1937–39, in which several women sit within a confined space, the back row a series of headless forms. A central figure with an open mouth (visually signifying singing or an emotive response) sits in the audience with a baby on her lap. Another woman, separated by a divider, looks penetratingly at the camera. The image, like many of the others in the collection, does not didactically disclose any particular social or economic phenomenon but glimpses more generally into the cultural life of Harlem, displaying women in dignified clothing within a rather spartan place of worship. Siskind and the others on the project sought out various scenes to depict the dynamism of Harlem: a woman in her well-equipped kitchen, outdoor markets, little boys on the street, a stripper, jazz musicians, and nightclubs. Siskind (revealing in part the white photographers' projections of Harlem) recalled in 1989: "I think we were angled toward revealing conditions in terms of how poor they were. Our study was definitely distorted. We didn't give a complete picture of Harlem. There were a lot of wonderful things going on in Harlem. And we never showed most of those. So [the photographs] were politically motivated in that sense. We offered, in the book, no solutions."[14] Looking back, Siskind was critical of the overt political agenda of many Photo League members and felt that the images fell short of their lofty ideals to reveal poverty, arouse sympathy, and incite change.

Even by the late 1930s Siskind was suspicious of some league members' dedication to social reform in photography. As Carl Chiarenza writes, "Political dogma and the reformer's simplistic solutions to symptomatic injustice had worn thin." Earlier, while working on a league exhibition, "America Today," Siskind had been outraged by the supposed blackballing and expulsion of another member, Isador (Izzie) Lerner, whose accounts of his trip to Russia were interpreted by other league members as critical of the Soviet Union.[15] By the late 1930s many previously pro-Soviet Americans were disillusioned with Russian revolutionary ideals, especially upon learning of the Hitler-Stalin pact in 1939. Siskind's skepticism of Soviet policies was not unusual within intellectual circles of the time, although his accounts indicate he was within a minority at the league.

Despite his complaints about the overt politics and inflexible ideology lurking in many league images, Siskind still helped organize the *Harlem Document*, one of many group efforts at documentary photography in the Photo League. Examples of other league production groups and exhibitions included: *Portrait of a Tenement* (1936): *May Day* (1937, 1938); *Rural America*, FSA work by Russell Lee, Dorothea Lange, Arthur Rothstein, and Ben Shahn (1939); *The Catholic Worker Movement* (1939–1940); *16th Street Lost Generation* (1939–40); *Men-at-Work*, a title also used earlier by Hine (1940); and *War Comes to the American People* (1941). Such titles indicate the degree to which league photographers dedicated themselves to documenting collectively the American scene, even the distressing elements of social injustice and discomfort. During the war years, when many league members were overseas or busy in civilian positions in the United States, the feature groups' activities tapered off significantly. After the war, these projects all but disappeared, especially when compared to the group activities of the prewar years.

Articles in *Photo Notes* also chart the gradual dilution of prewar collective social ideals within the Photo League. Articles by Elizabeth McCausland (between 1939 and 1940) stridently called for a photography of social change that valued a humanist, if not leftist, orientation. McCausland was an art critic and historian who wrote monographs on George Inness, Alfred Maurer, and other American painters, while publishing articles in *Art in America*, *American Contemporary Art* (the American Contemporary Art Gallery publication), *Arts Digest*, *American Magazine of Art*, and *Parnassus*, among others. She was the art critic for the *Springfield (Massachusetts) Sunday Union and Republican*, and her diverse interests led her to write articles on many topics, including the artists I. Rice Periera, Arthur Dove, Philip Evergood, and Kathe Kollwitz, as well as thematic articles such as "Labor and Art." In 1943–44 she was honored by a Guggenheim Fellowship, an indication of her serious dedication to writing and research on the arts. She was also an active member of the Photo League as well as its best, and most serious, critical writer. McCausland's commitment to "social photography" was reflected in her publications, her organization of a 1939 Hine exhibit, and her lectures to league members on the history of photography and "the documentary ideal." McCausland served on a 1939 symposium discussing the "Functions of Photography," moderated a debate on documentary "versus" pictorial photography in 1940, and lectured on the relationship between words and pictures (1942) and "Photography and Myth" (1947). Her close relationship with documentary photographer Berenice Abbott, another league member, surely fostered and intensified McCausland's interest in this field of study; as early as 1935 she wrote an in-depth article on Abbott, discussing the documentary aesthetics in her work.

In another article, "Documentary Photography" (1939), McCausland described her concept of documentary work. The "greatest objective of such work," she wrote, "is to widen the world we live in, to acquaint us with the range and variety of human existence, to inform us (as it were forcibly) of unnecessary social horrors such as war, to make us aware of the civilization in which we live and hope to function as creative workers. This is a useful work, and as such beyond claims of mere personality or clique."[16] Her definition stressed a concentration on human activity, and she especially called for exposing negative political behavior that created "unnecessary social horrors." McCausland found "hard-working" FSA photographers the most inspiring of documentary artists and wrote that "the somewhat remote and abstruse manner of the spiritual heirs of the Photo-Secession may seem too refined." An FSA image of a woman's knarled hands, she added, "is a human and social document of great moment and moving quality. . . . This is the vanguard of photography today." Photography with purpose, "useful work" in the tradition of Hine, could, she believed, better social conditions. McCausland also disdained any cults of personality or art cliques that placed individual needs over societal concerns. In her brief summary of photographic history, she bemoaned modernist styles such as the abstract photogram by Man Ray and Moholy-Nagy: "Before the documentary, the technical 'capricci' of Moholy-Nagy and Man Ray; before the 'photogram' and the 'rayograph,' the Photo-Secession; before that, the pictorialists. What came of these? . . . Against this pattern of sterility, of ideas which could not reproduce themselves, we have the new function . . . of documentary photography, an application of photography direct and realistic, dedicated to the profound and sober chronicling of the external world." McCausland likened modernist traditions to sterile humans, who cannot propagate, unlike the fecund documentary tradition, which, according to laws of natural selection, spawns new hopes and truths for humankind: "We want the truth, not rationalization, not idealizations, not romanticizations." She described modernist, abstracted images, supposedly less legible, with fewer levels of social signification for viewers, as dangerous during "the arduous struggle that is existence in eras of crisis."[17]

Photo League cofounder Sol Libsohn's photograph, *Loneliness of Longshoremen*, from the *Chelsea Document*, illustrates many of McCausland's ideals. Libsohn, like most of the league members, had been born in New York City and was a self-taught photographer. An instructor at the league through the 1930s, he also worked for the WPA. His commitment to the documentary realist tradition of exposing the underclass can be clearly seen in photographs made during his years in the league. As Libsohn said, "unless you feel an involvement with people, with the human condition, you should not photograph them at all."[18] Libsohn often photographed working-class figures of diverse ages and "types" populating the streets of the Lower East Side. Although Libsohn's photograph displays obvious interest in the drama of light and line, to Libsohn it is also an image of the "shape-up," a practice before the days of legal union protection for longshoremen. Every day workers lined the streets early in the morning, hoping to be chosen for work by virtue of their youth, size, or any other criteria. While no didactic text outlines specific social conditions, the image's documentary politics are more abstractly communicated. It is both "direct and realistic"; it has not turned the central concern, the longshoremen, into abstract, modernist tools of composition, but it combines evocative formal values with the humanism of social realism. Such an image broadens viewers' exposure to human variety and informs them, perhaps quietly, of "the human condition." One makes acquaintance with souls one might otherwise ignore.

Libsohn, like many league workers, often sacrificed high-focused clarity

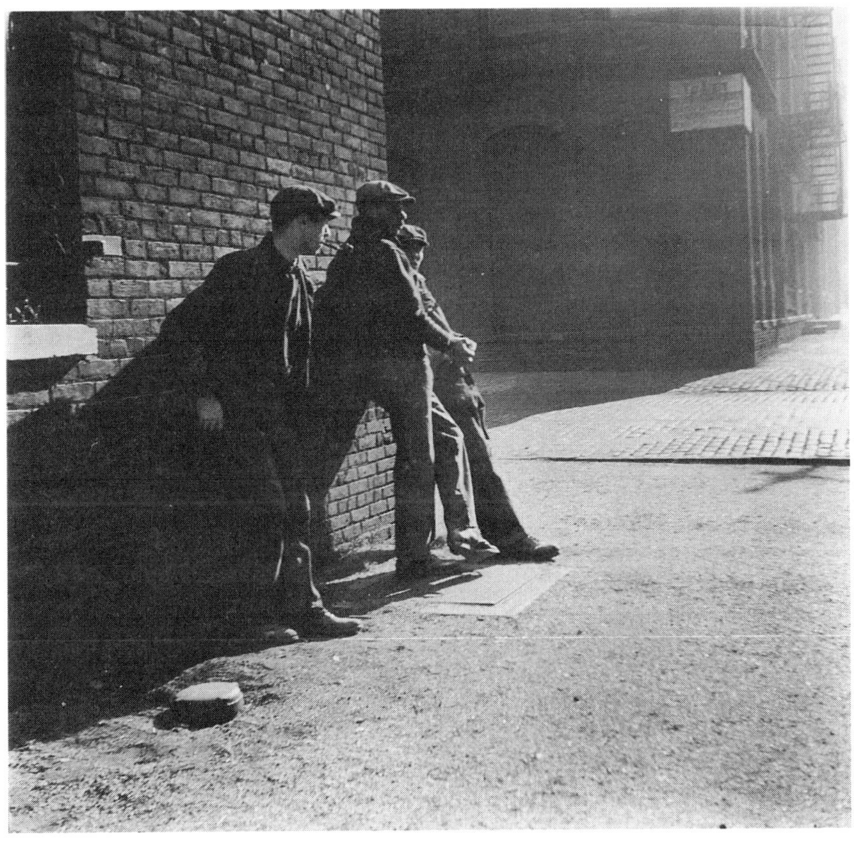

1.4. Sol Libsohn,
Loneliness of Longshoremen,* from the *Chelsea Document, ca. 1938–39.

Sol Libsohn (one of the Photo League's founders) photographed longshoremen, he said, during a "shape-up" before legal union protection. Libsohn's dedication to exposing the human condition demonstrates his strong social documentary ideals. Courtesy Sol Libsohn.

(while also avoiding the dated cliché of fuzzied pictorialism) for the grain and blur of a "street photography" or "shot from the hip" aesthetic. The graininess born of 35mm technology and faster film speeds became a formal device for many in the league—for some, who had poor equipment or were faced with difficult lighting situations, this was by necessity. Others found this technique could impart a formal equivalent of the desperation of the poor. In any case, to the serious documentary photographer of the New York scene, technical issues dear to the likes of Ansel Adams or Edward Weston (such as the use of small apertures, large format clarity, and zone systems) were outré; they had missed the point and failed to place content alongside or even over form. Such documentary photographers never dismissed formal issues from their art; they simply experimented with the expression of photographic "truth," seeking a strong, satisfying blend of form and content.

In her photographic reviews, McCausland continued to champion humanist ideals, not modernist "capricci." In 1940 she published another article in *Photo Notes* concerning the *Chelsea Document*, a project led by Sid Grossman and Sol Libsohn to photograph the neighborhoods in this New York City neighborhood. Her review again positively emphasized the social realist philosophy characteristic of league photography. She praised the document, which she said stood as "witness against the chaos and brutality of housing in New York City today." Chelsea, an "urban hell" as she called it, contained some of the city's worst slums and had alarmingly high tuberculosis and infant mortality rates. To McCausland, picturing the dignified, surviving citizens of economic depression amounted to a visual crusade for their lives. A document such as this, she wrote, vanquished "esthetic snobbery . . . and art speaks not only to the people but for the people."[19]

To jaded, postmodern sensibilities, reviews such as this might read like a Frank Capra script: overly sentimental in their belief in truth and justice. Yet most liberals in prewar America, who were children (or adults) of the Depression, believed in the necessity of federal programs to enhance the quality of life for the underprivileged, such as Chelsea residents, in the tradition of Roosevelt's New Deal policies. For many Americans, those federal programs had kept their own families alive and employed, or at least offered the hope of assistance during the Depression years. Federal funding and a supportive climate benefited scores of Americans during the 1930s—in their demands for government aid, painters, musicians, and theatrical groups agitated and organized to a degree never before witnessed in the history of American art. Although few of these demands ever became realized, the ideals and energies directed toward the creation of federally supported arts programs (for example, the Artists' Congress and the Artists' Union) were actively sought throughout the 1930s.[20] Such activity in the arts, however, would decrease considerably during the 1940s.

Nevertheless, the voices in *Photo Notes* maintained this tone of artistic social consciousness throughout the early 1940s. One of the magazine's writers who most consistently called for social awareness in photography was Walter Rosenblum. Having grown up in the same neighborhoods he photographed, Rosenblum was an active league member from 1937 to 1951 and served as its president for several terms. In December 1941 he reviewed a photography exhibition at the Museum of Modern Art, *The Image of Free-*

dom. While he proudly noted that 13 percent of the work had been done by Photo League members, he was very disappointed that the "photographs were not sufficiently representative of America." The overall image portrayed was "too beautiful" for his documentary taste—where are the farmers, he asked, the workers in mills? "Isn't [America] the people who organized Ford at the cost of their lives, the American boys who went to Spain to stop the fascist invader. . . . Let us photograph the people who are making America a finer place for us all. . . . These are the things which we must affirm."[21] Rosenblum, in all his contributions published in *Photo Notes*, demonstrated the partisan documentarian's concern with class and economy, the belief that photography concerned with human values could speak for disenfranchised Americans. Within the repressive context of the later 1940s, when federal agencies ferreted out so-called subversive organizations, such ideals became ideologically charged, potentially suspect, and dangerous.

Rosenblum's photograph *Pitt Street*, 1939, from the *Pitt Street Document*, done for a workshop conducted by Sid Grossman, forcefully illustrates Rosenblum's focus on the underprivileged and impoverished New Yorkers often found on the street corners of the Lower East Side. Rosenblum said of the boy photographed, "I wanted to express the strength of character in his face, the toughness his spirit had developed, growing up among those tenements in the background."[22] The image is less pointedly political than some viewers who have read Rosenblum's clearly leftist prose in *Photo Notes* may expect. But most league photographers sought to combine personal, artistic vision with attention to social conditions. Many recall being called the "Ashcan" school of photography, a superficial comparison to the early-twentieth-century American realist artists such as Robert Henri, who painted scenes of poor economic environments, people in everyday, unidealized dress, more often in moments of happiness than sorrow.

In this particular image by Rosenblum, a boy dominates the scene and towers over the camera, his face conveying a determined, tough expression that seems far older than his years. Hands hidden in pockets, he stares at the viewer while the tenements loom behind him. As in many league photographs of this time, nature—the sky, clouds, grass, or trees—is practically nonexistent in the sea of buildings, as if it were a privilege not accorded to the lower classes.

Rosenblum's own background reinforced the league's documentary ideals; for him New York City was not simply a place to photograph but also, as for most league members, home. Born in the City, Rosenblum came from a Russian orthodox Jewish family. During the 1930s, his father worked for the WPA while Rosenblum joined the National Youth Administration, which

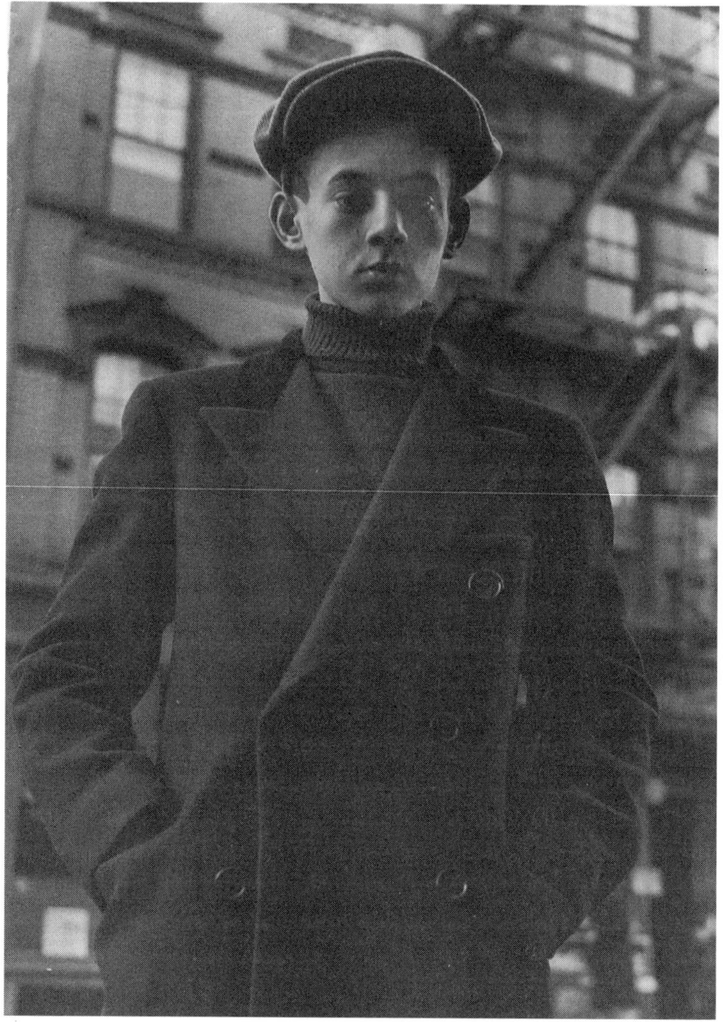

1.5. Walter Rosenblum, *Boy in Black Coat,* from the *Pitt Street Document, 1939*.

The *Pitt Street Document* was created by Rosenblum while he was taking a workshop with Photo League instructor Sid Grossman; its images often focused on the "have-nots" populating the Lower East Side. Courtesy Walter Rosenblum.

paid, he recalls, $5 a week. Through the WPA he took a photography class in one of the community centers run by unemployed artists. By word of mouth he discovered the Photo League and met Grossman, who asked him to be secretary of the league (the only paid position). An unknown source told the WPA that Rosenblum had a second job, which was not allowed, and he was fired from the Youth Administration. The league therefore became his sole source of income. One day he took over Berenice Abbott's photo workshop class at the league when she was ill and found he also enjoyed teaching.

The Photo League was more than a photographic school for Rosenblum; it was "a training ground for young photographers," an environment that gradually defined his photographic outlook through workshops and friendships with photographers and critics such as Strand, Newhall, and Grossman. The league was particularly useful to a poor, aspiring photographer in New York City: "It was a marvelous, strange time, when nobody had money. . . . You'd have meetings where different people would come in to speak. You'd have print critiques. . . . In the Photo League you had a home." Like Libsohn, Rosenblum had grown up in a less affluent section of New York City. He, like many others, photographed where he had lived. It was at the league that Rosenblum's social consciousness deepened, thanks to the community of like-minded artists he found there: "We thought it was wrong for one-third of a nation to be ill-housed, ill-clothed, and ill-fed, certainly we did, because we were the one-third."[23]

There is no doubt Rosenblum was among that one-third. His background is typical of many of the children of immigrants during that time. In many ways, his is the story that Jane Addams, Riis, and Hine had documented. Rosenblum's recollections of his life create haunting verbal equivalents of many Photo League images: "I was born on the Lower East Side; three floor walkup. Toilet in the hall, cold water flat. Bathroom in the kitchen. My mother did the laundry for seven people and carried it up to the roof to dry. We never lit the coal stove in the winter until 2:00 in the afternoon because we had no money for coal. You didn't eat properly; my breakfast was a roll soaked in coffee. All my teeth were rotten when I was little. Life was not easy."[24] Rosenblum's family, like countless others, suffered extreme economic poverty. "My mother, she died in her fifties from overwork. My father, I think, was driven nuts by the environment that he was part of. They lost their first two children from diseases that were so curable, my mother had a nervous breakdown." With such conditions commonplace, the reasonable response for many disenfranchised New Yorkers of the lower classes, Rosenblum believes, was to question the capitalist ideal that seemed to limit upward mobility for many Americans. This belief was shared by others in the league and translated, for some, into a sense of mission which was not only documentary in terms of its photographic vision but also political in its activism: "That we had members of the Communist

Party, absolutely, but they were not people who would overthrow the government. They just thought communism made more sense than capitalism. . . . They thought the Russian Revolution was a great idea. But that's because you were poor, you were exploited, you had no job, you had no work and you were looking around for another, better way to live."[25] Many league members came from similarly impoverished roots; this aspect of personal experience, combined with the then thriving tradition of documentary photography, certainly affected the league's communal outlook at a profound ideological level.

Social change, however, alters convictions. During World War II, fewer issues of *Photo Notes* were published and many members were sent to war posts throughout the world. Women active in the league, such as Rosalie Gwathmey, maintained the organization's visibility and production. During these years *Photo Notes* issues included pleas to "Buy More Bonds" and "Donate Blood" for the war effort. In the August 1945 issue a "Welcome Home" was extended to many of those who had served overseas (such as Sergeant Walter Rosenblum and Corporal Sid Grossman). Although in earlier league essays some members had criticized America's seeming eagerness to enter into war, strong displays of patriotism and antifascist fervor appeared in *Photo Notes* during World War II.

In the May 1942 issue, one article praised the controversial film *Native Land* by Paul Strand and Leo Hurwitz. Hurwitz was Strand's associate in Frontier Films as well as in the Photo League. Both organizations were allied in their commitment to documentary ideals. One of Frontier Films' major projects, *Native Land* became a source of contention within the organization. The film concerned the disintegration of American democratic ideals and premiered on May 11, 1942, just five months after the bombing of Pearl Harbor. Hurwitz, who was later blacklisted for his film work, recalled: "The ACLU was reluctant to sponsor [the film]: they feared it was too left, too labor conscious." Other members split from Frontier Films because *Native Land* was "too dangerous, too left, too scary." But the anonymous reviewer in *Photo Notes* praised the film, especially its narration by the "great" Paul Robeson—"well known and beloved by millions for his life-long struggle in the cause of Democracy."[26]

This comment sounds innocent, yet Robeson was becoming one of the most controversial figures in cold war America. In the eyes of many government officials, Robeson, a singer and actor, was tainted with ties to Communism. According to Victor Navasky's research, suspicions of Robeson's disloyalty culminated in 1949 when Jackie Robinson, the first black player to break color barriers in major league baseball, was called as a HUAC witness to express his views on "Robeson's statement in Paris to the effect that American Negroes would refuse to fight in any war against Russia because [they] love Russia so much." That same year, participants at two of Robeson's interracial concerts in Peekskill, New York, were attacked by white mobs. Navasky, who researched blacklisting in *Naming Names* (1980), notes that African Americans brought before HUAC "were not automatically required or expected to name names. Instead, they had a number of options, among which the most effective was to denounce Paul Robeson." Robeson had an enviable and award-winning background (having been a football player at Rutgers and a member of Phi Beta Kappa, graduating with a law degree from Columbia University, and later playing the lead in *Othello* on Broadway), but he had sung for the antifascist troops in Spain, was very popular in the Soviet Union, and had taken the Communist Party line or strongly left-wing stances on some issues. In the 1930s, for instance, Robeson donated his proceeds from the play *All God's Chillun Got Wings* to Jewish refugees escaping Nazi Germany, and he actively supported antifascist forces in the Spanish Civil War.[27]

In the 1940s Robeson continued to fight racism, support organized labor, and protest the deteriorating U.S.–Soviet relations. Later in the decade HUAC committee members accused Robeson of being a Communist. Because of Robeson's "suspect" activities, the American government revoked his passport in 1950. His career plummeted as concerts were cancelled, and it would be many years before whites in the government or the media would praise his life's work.

Photo League member Joe Schwartz, like others in the organization, admired Robeson's efforts to improve America's labor and race relations. The child of eastern European immigrants, like so many others in the league, Schwartz joined the Photo League in the late 1930s. Schwartz says his honeymoon, in 1938, consisted of hitchhiking to the South and photographing images of racism. Working as an offset printer, he also served as president of the tenants' union of the Brooklyn housing project in which he lived. Schwartz, committed to social documentary photographs of what he calls the "have-nots," photographed Robeson campaigning for the 1948 Progressive Party presidential candidate Henry Wallace in Brooklyn. His photograph of the famous man or short quotations on Robeson in *Photo Notes* may seem rather insignificant, but during the cold war years such affiliations, associations, and praise, in enough quantity, signified to already paranoid forces a certain political position—left-wing or, even worse, Communist.[28]

By 1947 several articles in *Photo Notes* indicated the increasing presence of an intolerable, distrustful, and conservative (if not, in some opinions, fas-

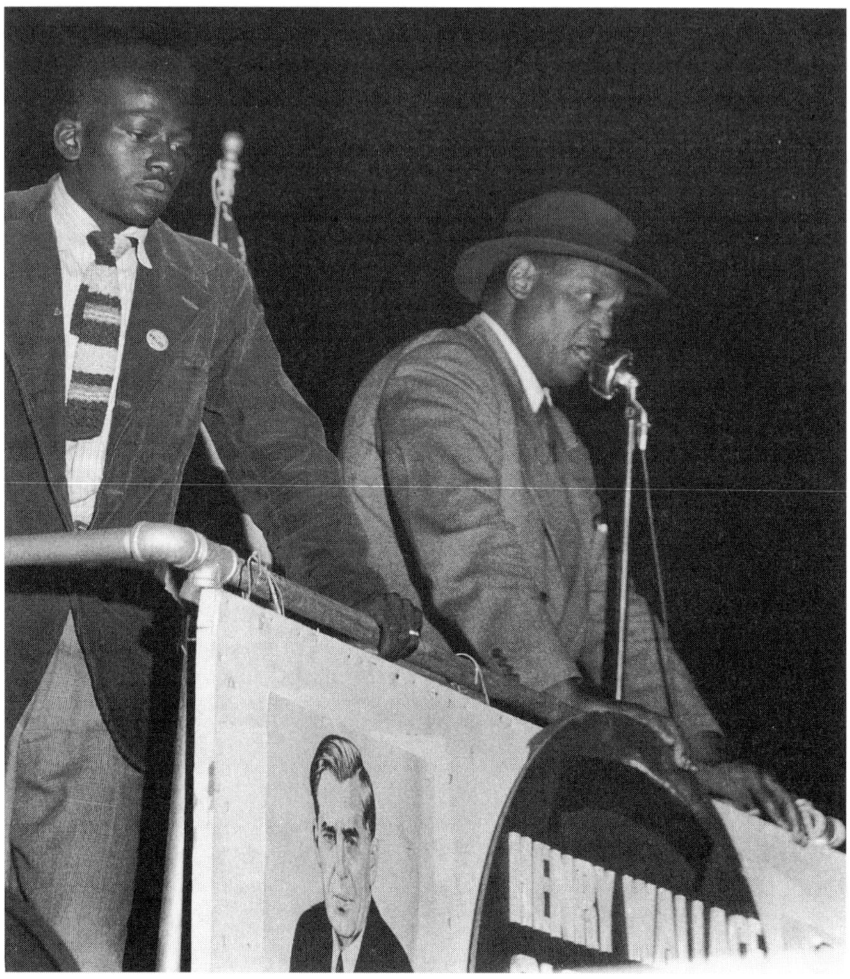

1.6. Joe Schwartz, *Paul Robeson at Fulton Street Rally in Brooklyn,* 1948.

Photo League member Joe Schwartz photographed activist artist Paul Robeson as he campaigned for the Progressive Party presidential candidate Henry Wallace in Brooklyn. Courtesy Joe Schwartz.

cist) orientation in American society. In the May-June issue, painter Irene Rice Pereira wrote an essay on the vital importance of Artists' Equity, which Strand and others had founded. She declared that photographers should be eligible for membership and argued that artists must *organize* (a word usually associated with unions) for protection even in "nonpolitical" realms such as rental issues and copyrights.[29] In line with league ideals, taking pictures was not enough; political beliefs were also made manifest through personal engagement and activity.

Positive energy and enthusiasm in the league increased with growing membership; new members listed in 1947 issues of *Photo Notes* included Ansel Adams, Barbara Morgan, Beaumont and Nancy Newhall, W. Eugene Smith, Paul Strand, and Edward Weston, among others. Tucker notes that after the war there was a gradual shift away from a social to personal vision in the Photo League's aesthetic philosophy.[30] While artists who were more concerned with "personal" issues joined in growing numbers after the war, an adamant core of members still emphasized the social utility of documentary images. Others joining in 1947 included Clemens Kalischer, David Vestal, and FSA photographers Jack Delano, Edwin and Louise Rosskam, and John Vachon.

Further emphasizing the social documentary tradition in photography, McCausland railed again against the potent, dehumanizing potential of modernism in her article "Camera and Brush in Service of Humanity." In this piece she discussed the concept of realism in the history of art and thankfully noted a return "to realism as a language intelligible to people at large." Citing photography as "by nature an instrument par excellence for realism," McCausland asked, "shall we face confusion and spiritual retreat? . . . Will art find ways to voice the song of free humanity?" Separating art from life, distinguishing between craft and medium, leads us, she argues, to a nihilistic "no" to the last question, with all its "despair and futility."[31]

While McCausland discussed a renaissance of realism in photography, other voices of the times indicate a gradual move toward modernist modes of personal exploration in art (as was witnessed in painting circles with the "triumph" of abstract expressionism). More recently, Serge Guilbaut has also noted that this retreat from social to more personal values in the New York visual art scene occurred, not surprisingly, within a specific context—the cold war years.[32] A parallel shift in aesthetics gradually occurred in the Photo League, especially after it was blacklisted by the U.S. government in late 1947. And, compared to earlier years, by the mid- to late-1940s fewer and fewer voices in *Photo Notes* argued openly against the repressive motions accelerating in civil court cases and the right-wing political machinations of the federal government overseas. The repressive political climate, combined with the growing numbers and influence of European modernists in the United States after the war, created an increasingly hostile climate for politically engaged artists.

In the November 1947 issue of *Photo Notes*, Nancy Newhall (whose husband, Beaumont, was also an occasional writer in *Photo Notes* and a recent league member) wrote an article on Ben Shahn, an artist who would endure strong accusations from HUAC courts in the 1950s. She concluded that in his recent exhibition Shahn was a better painter than photographer and explained why she felt he so appealed to photographers: "First of all, I think, because he deals with the same problems, themes, and concepts as we do. He has not evaded actuality but penetrated it." Newhall embraced Shahn as "one of us," implying her own solid standing with the league.[33] While the Newhalls were champions of many photographers during their careers, there are several instances that imply their (especially Nancy's) belief in documentary photography within the classic FSA tradition. The Photo League, as Nancy Newhall wrote again and again, fulfilled this role in its education of photographers.

Yet, in his own historical survey of American photography, *The History of Photography* (originally written in 1937, revised in 1982), Beaumont Newhall ignored the Photo League and its impact on midcentury American photography in subsequent editions of the book. Although he was a league member, he contributed less frequently to *Photo Notes*. Unlike his wife, Nancy, Beaumont enjoyed longer stretches of employment at mainstream institutions, such as the Museum of Modern Art (as librarian, 1935–42, and as curator of photography, 1940–45) and, later, the George Eastman House. However, the very politics he seemed, on occasion, to endorse, might have become anathema to him later.[34]

The cold war battles the league endured certainly played a role in the Newhalls' perception of the organization. Their presence in the league was quite strong until the redbaiting tactics of the government intensified from 1947 to 1949. Eventually they left, as Rosenblum recalls, "with that same stupid excuse" that Ansel Adams and Barbara Morgan had used: that there may have been Communist activity that they were unaware of in the group. As evidenced in letters between Morgan and Nancy Newhall, they all felt somewhat betrayed by the league, wanting the organization to fight the accusations with assertions of their lack of Communist activity. When no such statements appeared, Morgan, especially, began to feel that perhaps they had been duped or misled. She even telephoned Adams to warn him that Communists had taken over the board of directors and advised him to resign with her after Grossman had been named (which Adams ultimately did, sending a copy of his letter of resignation to the FBI).[35]

Tense times create many types of victims, and the fears engendered by the repressive legislation of the decade must not be taken lightly. Photo League membership and association could adversely affect one's career by the late 1940s. For instance, Robert Capa was one of many photographers facing discrimination during this era. His passport was revoked in 1948 based on evidence from an extensive FBI–State Department dossier compiled against him. The dossier includes "evidence" that he had either been a member or honorary member of the "radical, anti-fascist" Photo League. Lou Stettner remembers a call from the local FBI while in Paris asking for the names of Communists in the league, which he adamantly declined to answer. The same day, he was fired from his job at a Marshall Plan project. By the late 1940s, mere innuendo became evidence of potential subversive activity; suspicions mounted as repercussions increased, and members dropped out.[36]

Others held their faith in the league, whether or not it had Communist members, and continued to support its documentary ideals, as fraught with partisan politics as they were. In the November 1947 issue of *Photo Notes*, a small blurb entitled "Thought Control in Photography" appeared, criticizing the censorship of photographs in the *Utah Centennial*. An FSA photograph of children with unbrushed hair had offended a "gentleman from Utah. . . . School children in Utah must not have unbrushed hair. So all modern photographs were withdrawn." The defiant anonymous writer used a liberal dose of brazen sarcasm as the verbal weapon at hand, as if there were no real reason, yet, for Photo League members to be afraid of repressive action or repercussions. In the same issue, Rosenblum's "Some Thoughts about the Photo League" discussed the "creative worker" and stated that photographers must organize in their struggles as they are thrown into the "fires of economic insecurity." He also added that membership in the organization had tripled, with dues at $7 per year (up from $5), and that $15,000 was needed for new, bigger headquarters. Indeed, in November 1947 membership was clearly up (with 200 members, its greatest number ever), and activities, exhibitions, and the school program were expanding and growing.[37]

One month later, on December 5, 1947, the Photo League was taken by surprise: Attorney General Tom Clark included it in a published list of "totalitarian, fascist, communist or subversive" organizations. The headline on page one of the *New York Times* read: "90 Groups, Schools Named on US List as Being Disloyal." One subtitle alluded to the league: "These Are Among 11 Classed as Adjuncts of Soviet–Klan and Film Body Accused." The article, by Lewis Wood, noted that many associations were "named for the first time," including the Ku Klux Klan, Hollywood Writers' Mobilization for Defense, Veterans of the Abraham Lincoln Brigade, and the National Council of American-Soviet Friendship. The list, according to the Attorney General, resulted from FBI investigations and the recommendations of Department of Justice officials after President Truman's executive order creating a "loyalty board" just weeks before. One year earlier, Truman's diary reflected more generally the fear of Communist organization: "The Reds, phonies, and 'parlor pinks' seem to be banded together and are becoming a national danger. I am afraid they are a sabotage front for Uncle Joe Stalin."[38]

Repressive measures against suspect organizations, such as the Attorney General's listing, were effective in escalating public fear of Communism and kept the American sociopolitical (and economic) climate in a state of cold war fear. Suspect groups, as indicated in the *New York Times* article, were made public: all "Groups Called Disloyal" were published on page 18, and included the National Negro Congress, the Protestant War Veterans of the USA, the American Youth Congress, and the U.S. Communist Party, among many others. The Photo League was found under "Names on the New Listing," which included the Civil Rights Congress, Veterans Against Discrimination, Communist Party affiliates (such as the Southern Negro Youth Congress, the United May Day Committee, and the American Polish Labor Council), the Nature Friends of America, the National Committee to Win the Peace, and the KKK, among others. On the same page, another article, "Accused Groups Deny Disloyalty," quoted irate members in various named organizations. This article also reported that "Officials of the Photo League said they could not comment until they had studied the matter more closely."[39]

Rosenblum remembers finding out about the listing while in Dan Weiner's studio, when a journalist from the *New York Times* called asking for his reaction. The Attorney General's office was not required to provide any reason for the listing, and it did not. As Rosenblum pointed out, answering a question from one member, "Clark says we are subversive but has neglected to say why, when, where, or how." Furthermore, as a press release Rosenblum drafted on December 5, 1947, stated: "The Photo League repudiates this irresponsible and reckless smearing of its purposes and its membership. It regards itself as one more victim in the campaign, spearheaded by the Un-American Activities Committee, to stifle progressive thought in every walk of life, and to intimidate by threat cultural workers in every field."[40] These were bold words, but, as the league would soon discover, there were severe consequences to the listing; one was being required by law to print on their stationary that they were a "subversive organization."

The Photo League members called for a meeting on December 16 to discuss a plan of action and protest. The special January 1948 issue of *Photo Notes* included statements from Rosenblum, a copy of a speech given by an outraged Paul Strand, encouraging letters and telegrams received (from Dorothea Lange, Ben Shahn, Jack Levine, Philip Evergood, Edward Weston, and Ansel Adams), a transcript of the floor discussion among league members, and Rosenblum's conclusion, "Where Do We Go from Here?" In this essay, Rosenblum tried to make sense of the league's situation while lifting the spirits of members by saying that they all "rejected the smear technique." Discussing the reasons for the listing, he said that perhaps the old Film and Photo League (ca. 1929–34) may have been a factor, since it had been so concerned with the social scene of its day. He elaborated further: "We have developed a tradition based on social realism because our members concern themselves deeply with the world they live in. At one time the Pictorialists labeled documentary photography as the Ashcan School. It is true that many of our members did not concern themselves of [sic] the natural scene." However, this orientation was to be expected, he felt, because most of the members themselves grew up in tenements; Harlem and the Lower East Side contained, he said, their "own flesh and blood." Thus, "How can one be censured for being interested in one's fellowman?"[41]

Rosenblum continued to search for reasons the league was blacklisted. Certainly it had supported controversial government policies of the day. He recalled the members passing a resolution and sending a telegram to Congress urging them not to pass the Taft-Hartley Bill (1947), as the Photo League felt it "to be a menace not only to labor but to the entire American people." Furthermore, the league "membership felt that the State Department was destroying an important cultural program when it repudiated its own collection of American paintings and recalled them from Czechoslovakia and South America. We informed the State Department how we felt. Inflation, the lack of adequate housing, and the threat of another war affect all people regardless of craft. We are and always will be citizens as well as photographers." He concluded that the government must understand artists' power: "Scare the artist now and you might shut him up when 1948 rolls around. But we will not be frightened by this flagrant attempt at thought control." Still hopeful of resolution and vindication, Rosenblum ended by stating that all races, creeds, and colors were accepted within the league, as was "every shade of political opinion." The league was not a political organization at all, according to Rosenblum's essay; it was a photographic organization, and the best revenge was to turn it into "a real center of American photography." Barbara Morgan suggested assembling an exhibition of league work in which "the type of photography being attacked—documentary photography" could be presented to a large audience so that the public could "see it and understand its important function in ameliorating evils." With Beaumont Newhall appointed as chairman of this project, it would later culminate in a show entitled *This Is the Photo League*, 1948.[42]

Rosenblum, president of the league at the time of the listing, recalls that the Photo League was "never even socialist orientated" and that "the ironical thing is that at the time of the listing we were less political than we had been when we started." He remembers a concerted effort among members to *not* become a political organization. There may have been Communists in the league, he went on to say, but "there was no organization" of them: "Nobody asked anybody; if you had $7 you were a member." He also recalls the fear generated by the listing: "It's hard to understand the terror that existed at that time [of the listing]. . . . It said from now on you must print on your stationary 'The Photo League is a subversive organization.' But there were no penalties if you didn't do it. Nobody threatened you. . . . We fought back. . . . We organized. . . . People came and there was no problem. But the pressure got worse and worse and worse and people began to feel it more and more and people began to drop out." Rosenblum does not deny Communist Party ties within the Photo League; he identifies himself as a socialist at the time: "Sure, I was a socialist, but I wasn't going to throw bombs at anybody or overthrow the government by force and violence." While the leftist orientation of many league photographers was undeniable, a uniform, organized, anti-American platform did not exist within its membership. However, enough of a threat existed in the minds of cold war officials for the league to be marked as suspect.[43]

But Aaron Siskind remembers the earlier years of the league differently, in a distinctly minority opinion: "The whole organization, especially in the thirties, was very much a Communist front organization. And they had their operators in, their party people and all that. . . . The Communists were the only ones who had any program for solving our conditions, and everybody went over to help them. They didn't join the Party, they came to the meetings, they worked with them. . . . Everybody was for them, was with them. It was unbelievable." During Siskind's years at the league, Communist ties had been stronger than they were in later years. There were certainly enough ties in the 1930s to raise the FBI's suspicions of Communist activity within the Photo League. During the cold war, the FBI monitored any organization suspected of affiliations, since their attitude was that anyone associated with the Communist Party of America was "contaminated with the disease of communism," which could then spread, like a domino effect, throughout an organization.[44]

Most members' accounts, however, maintain that the Attorney General's office grossly overestimated the extent of Communism in the league by the 1940s; while a number of members acknowledged CPA membership, most were more generally "left-wing" in orientation. To the FBI, the distinctions between left-wing and Communist were specious—they investigated the league from 1942 to 1952, reporting that "The League has been used for recruiting Communist members and follows the Party Line. Mass organization activity credit is given by the Party to the leaders of the League. Emphasis on social and industrial documentary photography products and the members' photographic efforts are available as the Communist propaganda organs." League images, in short, were found to support the CPA ideals of class struggle. The FBI garnered much of its data, as Fiona Dejardin's research ably proves, from primary left-wing, socialist, and Communist periodicals of the time, which published articles and photographs associated with league workers. She also finds it unsurprising that league members were monitored by the FBI, adding that the evidence "does not mean that the Photo League was a 'subversive' organization; membership in the CPA was not a crime."[45]

Members in subsequent years seldom wanted to make specific allegations of Communist activity, even today. Others "named names," years later, but the usefulness of such activity is questionable. The bottom line is that some league members were members of the CPA, others were not, and in the later years of the league, fewer and fewer members had Communist ties. Whether or not the league had been a front organization in the 1930s, by the late 1940s there was no one party line in its eclectic membership. What alerted suspicion in the General Attorney's office, beyond some members' affiliations with the CPA and other suspect organizations, was the leftist philosophy that underlay the documentary photographic tradition, the belief that images could effect social change in people's lives. Conservative officials, superficial as their reasons for listing an organization often were, perhaps understood that many league members were not just out to make "pretty pictures" of an idealized, healthy, growing post–World War II America—they were engaged in describing visually the lives of those *not* participating in the American capitalist dream. In addition, many of the photographs made by the league obviously sacrificed popular glossy technique for the integrity of strong social content; the members wrote their government officials on numerous occasions concerning issues they disagreed with; and a few truly were or had been Communists. In retrospect, with the understanding of just how far the United States government went during the cold war with superficial suspicions, the Photo League's listing is no longer a great surprise.

The December 1947 listing inspired many photographers to rally to the aid of the Photo League. The articles and editorials within *Photo Notes* also track the course of the repressive measures taken by government officials. The January 1948 issue vehemently attacked the listing, especially in the reprinted "Address by Paul Strand." In this public speech, given to attending members of the league, Strand stated: "We are the co-victims of something happening in the country today that is widespread and which threatens every American. In reality, we have the honor, along with a lot of other people of being in the front line, defending American democracy." In the address, Strand compared the repression of the league and "the summary dismissal of federal employees under the President's loyalty purge," to the events at Nuremberg after World War II (stating that Nazi war criminals were accorded more civil rights than hounded American citizens), the blacklisting of Hollywood writers, and even Hitler, who had used redbaiting because it so effectively "divides and confuses." Strand recalled, as did other writers, the earlier cancellation by the State Department of an exhibition of American paintings which had included works by artists of "various shades of New Deal Communism," including Ben Shahn, who was present at Strand's address to Photo League members. "That is why we here tonight have to stand up to this thing. No use in trying to run away and be afraid and say, 'Please, I am a good boy.' It won't do any good. . . . The artist himself, if he is really an artist, has to tell the truth as he sees it. He can't help himself . . . and that is why they want to silence us. . . . We are, in a sense, honored by being placed in the front ranks of the fight for the Bill of Rights. It is our job to defend it, not only for ourselves, but for all the American people today."[46]

Strand, associated with the league off and on since 1936, was, in Rudy Burckhardt's words, "a kind of patron saint" to some Photo League members. As politically aware as he was, however, Strand continually stressed form and technique as well as content in photography. Rosenblum, in his "Personal Memoir" of Strand, praised Strand's awareness of aesthetics, saying he showed students that there was "more to life" than the Lower East Side.[47] Most importantly, although some critics and historians categorize Strand within the elite, fine art tradition of photography, he defended and fought for the Photo League throughout these difficult years.

Rosenblum's memories of Strand as an influential teaching force at the league demonstrate his importance within the organization. He remembers Strand as "always a member," showing "unusual" photographs to league students. "We were dealing with life in New York. If someone shows you a cobweb in the rain you have no idea what it's about. . . . but the advantage of that is that if you didn't understand what was going on, you could follow it up" by seeing Strand and talking to him about the photograph. Rosenblum described how his own growth was fostered by exposure to Strand's aesthetic:

> I said [to Strand] "I want a photograph." He gave me a picture. Barn windows, just windows. I said, "Holy God, what did he give me this picture [for]? I don't like this photograph. Why doesn't he give me something that I can appreciate?" I came back three weeks later and said, "Paul, I want to buy another photograph." He said, "okay" . . . I said, "Holy God, he did it again." Of course they are my two favorite photographs. I didn't understand that at the time . . . he was no fool, and he was educating me by what he gave me.

For Strand, the league's documentary ideals were not completely incompatible with his own. Yet, as a teacher he obviously sought to counterbalance some students' views of documentary photography with a broader vision, beyond that of the Lower East Side. Rosenblum also compared Strand to Hine, another key influence on league students. While Hine would allow any amount of print manipulation in order to publish his work, "if you took a 16th of an inch off [Strand's] photographs you were dead."[48] While Hine's work emphasized the "journeyman" potential of documentary photography, Strand's stood for the fine art tradition, following his friend Stieglitz's lead.

Throughout his life, Strand remained committed to leftist political ideals, although such ideology was not always clearly seen in his still photographs. His own personal politics strongly allied him with many at the league, as evidenced by his periodic writings and contributions to the newsletter. In one issue of *Photo Notes* Strand authored a plank aimed at "helping the artist" through federal aid and proposing the creation of a Federal Bureau of Fine Arts.[49] Rosenblum recalls another level of leftist political commitment in Strand's life: "Sure, Strand signed the Communist Party nominating petition for [Ben] Davis, he did that, [but] it was never like it was an arm of the Communist Party."[50] By the late 1940s, such details and historical distinctions did not matter to suspicious government forces. Strand's move to France, in the summer of 1949, can be seen as his having given up on contemporary American society, not just the specific trials and tribulations of the Photo League.[51] More simply, as Rosenblum recalls, "He was in trouble with the government. [They] wanted to take his passport away, and they did for a while." Not only was Strand associated with the blacklisted league, he and Shahn were also presidents of another "suspicious" group, the National Council of the Arts, Sciences, and Professions, so "the FBI had a big list about what he was [doing]." Rosenblum summarizes: "He got fed up with the United States."[52]

During the early months after the listing, much league energy was spent countering accusations of questionable loyalty and suspicious activity. In January 1948, one month after the listing, the revolutionary spirit of league members soared in the pages of *Photo Notes*. At the same time, there were realistic fears of reprisal. The January issue, in a transcript entitled "Discussion from the Floor," reported that "The Petition submitted by the Executive Committee was read and discussed. One proposal that the phrase 'cultural workers' be deleted was vetoed on the ground that it is this group we shall approach for signatures." Numerous reprints of letters and telegrams received in response to the listing communicate the angry tone of this 1948 issue. Notes on discussion topics at this special meeting also voiced the outrage most members felt. Paul Strand and Nancy Newhall drafted a unanimously approved telegram to be sent to Attorney General Clark, New York Congressmen, and local newspapers: "We one hundred and three members of the Photo League assembled tonight at the Hotel Diplomat categorically deny the charges of disloyalty you have made against us. We consider your action made without specific charges, fair trial and opportunity to defend ourselves in the American way a grave violation of constitutional rights. We call upon you to retract the charge against us and restore these rights not only to us but to all Americans." As Barbara Morgan noted at this meeting, the type of art often attacked by right-wing politicians was documentary photography, or art, as Shahn put it, that was "interested in the people."[53]

The league's taste for social documentary nevertheless continued to dominate. Antimodernist references still appeared in *Photo Notes*, recalling McCausland's earlier denunciation of the dreaded photogram. Art historian Milton Brown contributed his negative review of the MoMA show, "In and Out of Focus," curated by Steichen, in the June 1948 issue. The review reiterated Brown's preference for social realist (or social documentary) art. His fury over the MoMA show was due to the "tastelessly commercial" and "socially infantile" photographs displayed in this "circus." Brown found the photography of 1948, as represented in this show, "torn between the news and the fashion magazine . . . without a shred of ethics or esthetics" and, most crucially, lacking the social purpose of the past. Instead, he viewed the work as the "dry skin of pointless and dull recording of accidental and fragmentary facts of human activity," evidenced in the "mediocre" (i.e. insufficiently "documentary" in narrative and overly formalistic) works by Walker Evans, Henri Cartier-Bresson, and Robert Capa.

Photographers Brown did admire included Photo Leaguers Morris Engel, Sid Grossman, and Rosalie Gwathmey. Brown judged the MoMA work from a narrow ideologically critical position that required the photographer to have a more narrative point of view. He wrote: "What [photography] needs today is the same kind of social and artistic purpose, the same fervor, the same insistence upon integrity, the same faith in photography as an art form which motivated the earlier generation of American photographers" (presumably the FSA).[54] As an art historian, Brown championed social realism and the Ashcan painters; the same ideals applied in his criticism of photography that, he felt, too often catered to capitalist exploitation or mere individual exploration. Given the rising number of dissenting voices in *Photo Notes* as the 1940s ended, the increasingly unpopular, strident, social realist philosophy was still very much alive even after the listing.

In the same June 1948 issue of *Photo Notes*, active league member Elizabeth Timberman negatively reviewed league expatriate Siskind's photographs at the Charles Egan Gallery. Siskind's work revealed a competing taste in contemporary photography at the time—one that balked romantic social realism. Siskind, as shown in his *New York*, 1947, had moved toward more abstract directions in the wake of modernism. His experiments irritated Timberman: "Here was a whole roomful of photographs—some thirty or more—and not a single specimen of the human race in any picture, not even so much as a footprint. No people. No trees, birds or flowers either. Photograms, perhaps? I was relieved to find they were not." She complained that his works were "just abstractions" full of "brooding emotion," "richly eloquent but [which] seldom sparkle." Rosenblum also questioned Siskind's abstractions and closeups of graffitied walls as being "limited" in their comprehension of experience: "With the whole world to look at he began to look at little pieces of peeling paint on the wall. . . . Strand once said to me about him, 'the trouble with Aaron is he is up against a brick wall.'"[55]

Siskind would later bemoan the league's strict and parochial attitudes toward subject matter and intent in photography, feeling the sting of disapproval over his newfound, more abstract imagery that seemed, to some, to focus on middle-class or elite values. Siskind remembers: "That was one of the reasons why I finally gave up on the Photo League." Ironically, Ruth Bernhard remembers a young Siskind, alongside other members, angrily accusing her of making overly formal photographs during her visit to the league in the late 1930s. League member Bill Witt had a similar memory from the late 1940s: "I had become interested in nature and abstract photography. I had some pictures of that type in the [Photo League] show and they raised eyebrows."[56] Gradually, more and more new voices entered league discussions on photography's purpose and function, loudly heralding

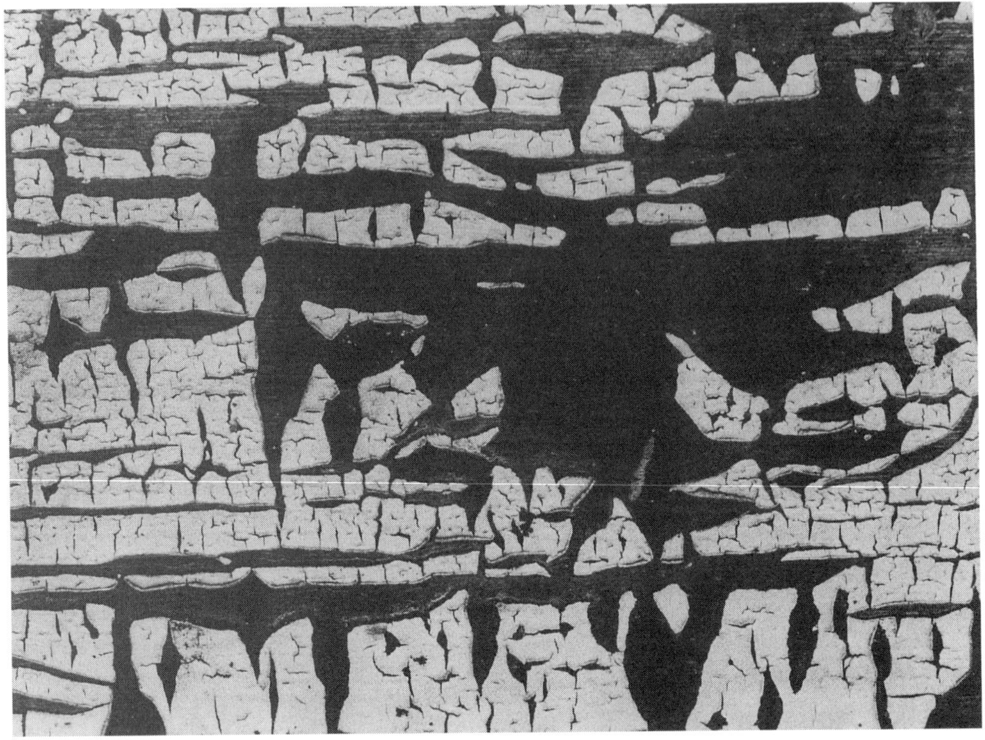

1.7. Aaron Siskind, *New York*, 1947.

Siskind's move toward modernism and abstraction in the 1940s was unpopular with many in the Photo League. This change, questioning the power of photography to influence ideology, was provoked during a trip to Cape Cod, where he concentrated on mood and formal elements. By 1947 (and through the 1950s), his associations with abstract expressionist painters in New York and Black Mountain College had reinforced these experiments. © The Aaron Siskind Foundation/courtesy Robert Mann Gallery.

the transcendence of, and tolerance of, formally engaged explorations. Those who once had felt like outcasts from the league, like Siskind, would become part of the celebrated mainstream in later years.

Documentary dominance, with its assumption of social purpose, was declining gradually not just in the league but more generally as well. During 1948, one *Photo Notes* writer mentioned another battle between Congress and an American documentary organization, the FSA. In the fall issue, an article entitled "FSA Attacked" outlined Congressional fear of perhaps potentially "political" photography. As described in *Photo Notes*, a debate in the House on May 13, 1948, centered on the use of taxpayers' funds for photography (specifically the 1935–43 FSA photographs, housed in the Library of Congress). Mr. Johnson of Indiana, the article reported, decried giving precious federal funds to photographers such as Marjorie Collins, whose work was of questionable "value." Citing more "ridiculous" illustrations, Mr. Johnson asked that the House "scrutinize them closely to see that things of this character are not carried on any longer. This sort of thing should be stopped immediately."[57]

The ideological and aesthetic connections linking the league with the FSA would require a book-length treatment of their own. Rosenblum said the league "felt a close connection with FSA," and he went on to describe a league-sponsored FSA show, naming some FSA members and mentioning Roy Stryker's lecture at the league. Stryker (director of the Historical Section, Division of Information, of the FSA), Rosenblum recalled, based the FSA "on what Lewis Hine had done earlier." This sense of lineage, from Hine to the FSA to the league, reinforced social documentary ideals.[58]

Ironically, with this same issue, *Photo Notes* began to use a more professional-looking, two-page spread format including illustrations and occasional advertisements (with contributing editors such as Ansel Adams, Beaumont Newhall, and Paul Strand, among others, at the helm). The cover photograph was by Atget. The articles published displayed a sense of diversity within the league: a synopsis of the Photo League school by Barney Cole; "Two Schools" by Beaumont Newhall; "A Visit to Brassai" by Stettner; Ferdinand Reyer on "Atget"; and Strand's "A Platform for Artists." The editors, led by Rosalie Gwathmey, announced plans to widely circulate the magazine and define the organization's expanded editorial vision by listing the best photographers in history (including not only Hine and Strand but Octavius Hill and, a name not typically praised in *Photo Notes*, Alfred Stieglitz). But while the introduction to the "new" *Photo Notes* proclaimed the editors' interest in "broadening the scope of our material" in this medium "capable of creative expression," many league photographers continued to explore traditional social documentary.

One image by a Photo League member, dated 1947, the year of the listing, illustrates the league's continued partisan espousal of documentary humanism. In *Rebecca of Harlem*, by Morris Engel, the viewer confronts an intimate window scene of a woman and three children placed in front of a gauzy curtain and formally integrated within the framing borders of the window itself. As was quite common in Photo League images, the content focuses on African Americans, and in this case their worn clothing signifies their social class and rank. Yet, a spirit of survival, love, and togetherness links the figures both metaphorically and physically. The image does not outrage

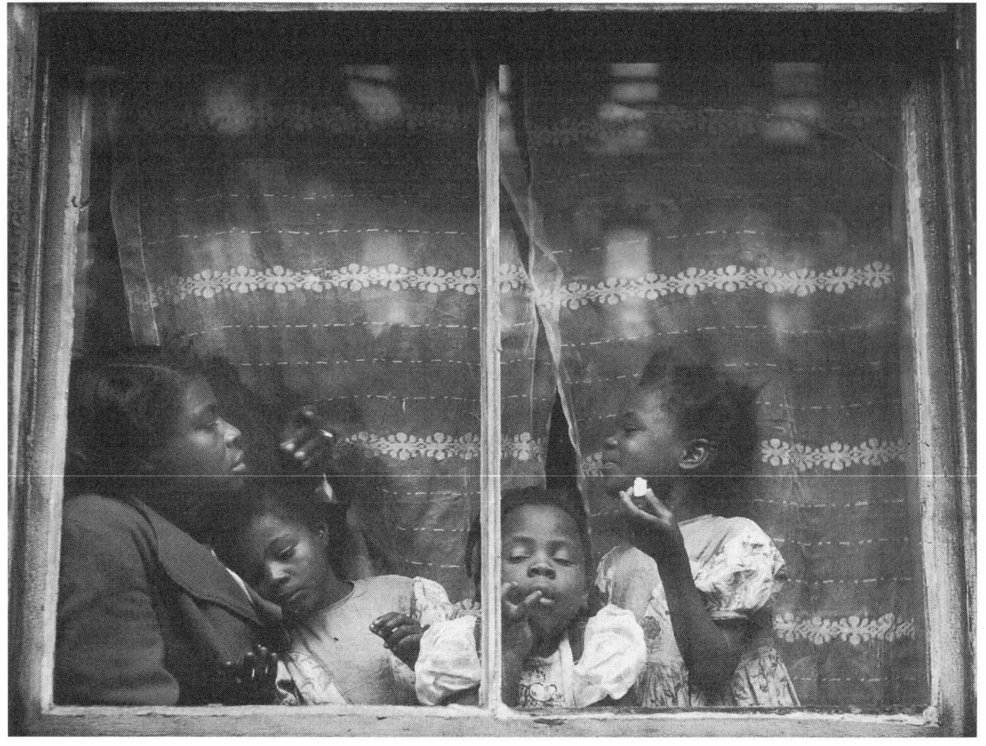

1.8. Morris Engel, *Rebecca of Harlem*, 1947.

Morris Engel's forceful image of a family group in Harlem illustrates social documentary ideals in the Photo League of the 1940s. The intertwining figures are physically linked yet isolated within the window's frame. © Morris Engel.

viewers with a horrific scene of deprivation (as Hine might have envisioned) but, rather, symbolically suggests cultural loneliness and isolation as the boxed figures cling to one another. The Communist Party might have a difficult time using an image such as this to argue the evils of capitalism on minority groups in America, yet conservative forces might also balk at such a "sympathetic" view of African American life.

Engel's image is not unusual. That league photographers frequently turned to African American subjects, especially urban children, is a significant aspect of their documentary approach and interest in developing an art that both visually excites and educates the viewer. The history of blacks' representation in American art is, of course, far too complex for a complete analysis here. But it can be said that historically African Americans have been generalized, idealized, and superficially reduced to sociological "types" as subjects of a contorted, white, and often male gaze. League photographers' images of African Americans, however, cannot be easily fit into any one type, as each individual brings unique backgrounds and sympathies to his or her image. Generally, when looking at the mass of images produced by league photographers, one is surprised by how many portray African American subjects with a unique, sustaining, or sympathetic point of view. Some images offer distinct contrasts to clichéd, picturesque views of the impoverished, sentimentalized, or ennobled scenes of African American life.

African Americans endured social and economic discrimination few whites could imagine. Documenting their lives within multiple contexts provided a platform for change; such images, league members hoped, could help humanize and individualize a largely ignored social group. Similar league photographs exist in other ethnic worlds, including that of Italians, Jews, and Latinos, among others, but a majority of league photographs frame African American subjects. Interviews with surviving league members indicate there were few if any black members, although some African Americans did participate in league activities (race was never mentioned in member rosters so it is impossible to accurately judge all league members' ethnicity). Despite the league's sympathy toward discrimination faced by blacks in society, then, it still remains that most of these images were made by white artists from working-class, immigrant backgrounds. Nevertheless, they indicate many members' own identification with others outside the American mainstream. Over the spectrum of the thousands of photographs of black subjects, it is clear that artists in the league pictured African Americans in different fashions, depending upon the photographer's individual background and political orientation. Images fall within a broad array of "types," each endeavoring to document others' lives with a sympathetic nod to the sociopolitical discrimination the subjects faced.

Contemplation of the history of African American lives in the 1940s forces an appreciation for cultural despair but also for hope. African Americans would not attain the incremental privileges, such as desegregation, won during the Civil Rights movement until the 1950s and 1960s, following the organized protests encouraged by leaders such as Rosa Parks and Martin Luther King (struggles that Photo Leaguer Dan Weiner often chronicled). In New York City, as many league photographers observed during their own lives, African Americans were consistently and routinely discriminated against in housing, employment, and education. But during the cold war even a mere interest in the improvement of African American lives could be construed as a decidedly left-wing, if not Communist, orientation.

A brief assessment of the government's attitude toward African Americans during the escalating cold war years demonstrates the fear and suspicion many whites felt toward the black population. Morris L. Ernst and David Loth's *Report on the American Communist* (1952), detailed the statistics concerning ethnicity and Communist Party membership:

> The minorities usually feared [by anti-Communists] are the Negroes, the Jews, and the foreign-born. The fear seems to be based much more on the uncomfortable feeling that these groups are unfairly treated than on any success the Communist party has had in recruiting members among them. . . . But the ones that the Communists are supposed to be able to attract in substantial numbers are those minorities which have good reason to be dissatisfied with their standing in their communities. Of all of them, of course, the Negro has the most reason for complaint.[59]

The report argued that, statistically, a smaller percentage of African Americans existed in the Communist Party than did in the American population at large (411 out of a total of 5,395 CPA members in 1948) and that such fears were overstated. However, the report also noted that African Americans did have a "very high percentage" of leadership positions within the party. A typical highly charged question during the federal loyalty hearings was "*Have you ever had Negroes in your home?*" This indicates that even social interaction with African Americans could signify leftist sympathies.[60] Since such an association was often considered suspect during the cold war years, photographing blacks (indicating, to some, a sociopolitical as well as an artistic interest in their lives) could similarly be viewed as potentially damaging to one's status as a "loyal" American.

African American writer Richard Wright's personal experiences in the 1940s illustrate the difficulty faced by many Americans, like some in the league, who longed to initiate social change yet avoid the extremism of Communism. In "I Tried to Be a Communist" (1944), Wright said he had been a party member for twelve years but ultimately repudiated the organization and withdrew (a not uncommon scenario for many left-wing workers and intellectuals of the time). His biographer, Margaret Walker, claims he joined the party "because he believed in world revolution, particularly as the correct solution for the American black man," but left upon realizing that black liberation was not a primary agenda of the Communist Party. She adds that his greatest difference with the party was ideological (Wright valued Russian revolutionaries Trotsky and Lenin but not Stalin).[61] Indeed, the Communist Party frequently tried to enlist African Americans within their ranks, as Ernst and Loth discussed; "peak Negro membership was claimed in

1939," with 5,005 black members, but by 1940 only 250 of those remained.[62] Wright's dissatisfaction with the party was due to its exploitation of the American race problem and the racism within the ranks of the party.[63]

In a fundamental sense, the statistical actualities of black membership in the party had little bearing on the paranoid rumors and innuendos of the cold war years. Other ethnic minorities, which league photographers often belonged to and recorded repeatedly, were also suspect throughout this era. Many Photo League images certainly belied the traditional, popular, and typically white conceptions of American society after the war. Today these pictures may seem routine in their views of poverty, showing the faces of African Americans, workers, and other lower-class members of society. Seen collectively and repeatedly, such images provide a forceful indication of the political leanings of many league members, who felt artists must engage themselves with the disenfranchised classes in need of empowerment.

The Attorney General most likely did not care about the specific images the league produced or their content but instead decided to blacklist the league based on some members' past activities within suspect left-wing and Communist movements. It is unlikely government officials saw specific league photographs such as Engel's; if they did, no records or accounts are yet known. The government's primary concern was that the league could be a possible front for Communist activity. However, given that Congressmen cited specific FSA works in their denunciations of that organization, it may be that some league photographs were similarly scrutinized. We cannot know the definitive answers to such questions, as much of the material in the government files has been blacked out.[64]

The government's suspicions certainly would have grown if officials had undertaken a close examination of league photographs. Plenty of the members' photographs sought to visually empower the various ethnic and working classes in the United States that the government most worried might become Communist. George Gilbert, a young student of Sid Grossman's and an energetic league member, visualized concern for the lower classes of New York City neighborhoods in *American Faces, New York City* (ca. 1940). Here an almost toothless man, smiling broadly, holds a sign reading "All Out with FDR for Victory in '42." Beside him, a better dressed man claps and a woman smiles, while in the background figures stand in various poses, their features hardly those of the upper crust of America's elite. It was to these New York inhabitants that most Photo League cameras turned—the poor or working class, who coped and persevered. A specter of authority clouds the sign in the form of a police officer's shadow. This juxtaposition resonates; by the cold war years, the mere symbol of FDR, a heroic champion of federal assistance

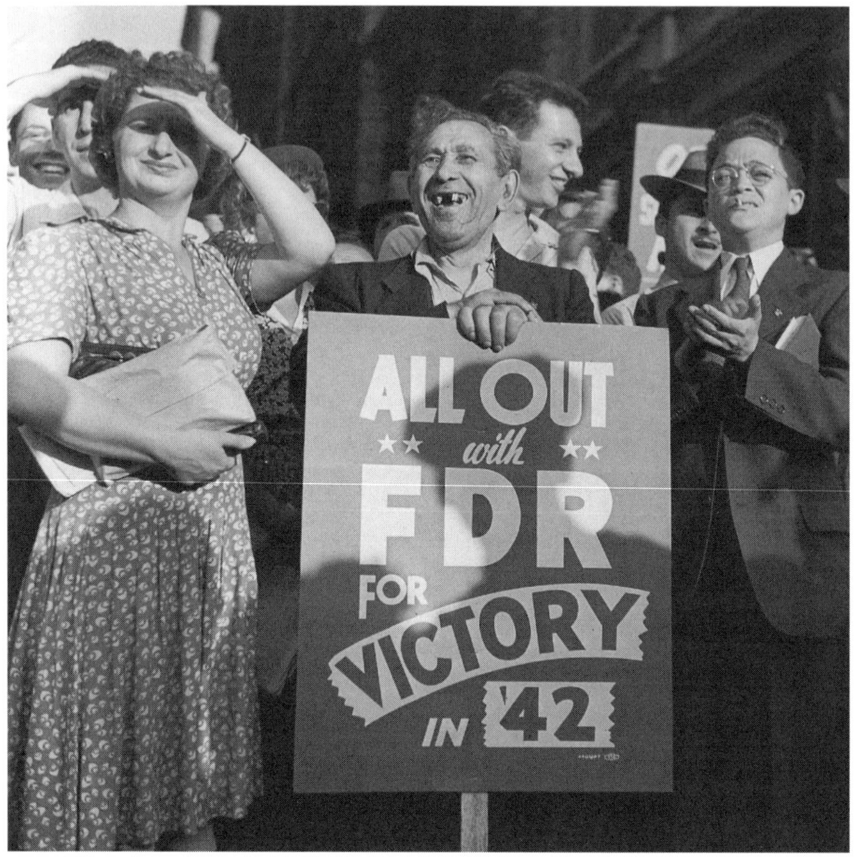

1.9. George Gilbert, *American Faces, New York City,* 1940.

George Gilbert, a student with Photo League instructor Sid Grossman, combed the streets of New York City documenting events and citizens' unidealized lives. At a rally for FDR, the shadow of a policeman is cast on the poster. © George Gilbert, 1940.

for such citizens, might be enough to incite overzealous HUAC suspicions. As Strand said in his January 1948 address to the league, muralist Anton Refregier was forbidden to represent a large portrait of FDR in a San Francisco Post Office, even though "fifteen other prominent Americans had been approved. . . . It is symbolic that the forces now in control do not want us to remember Roosevelt or his policies."[65]

To combat the listing, members decided to mount a massive exhibition—"the best photography show ever seen anywhere"—so that the public could see members' works and "understand" the Photo League's "important function in ameliorating evils."[66] With Beaumont Newhall as chairman of the project, the show, *This Is the Photo League*, opened one year later, in December 1948, featuring the works of ninety-six photographers and a catalog with an essay by Nancy Newhall. Photographs by older leaguers as well as more recent members (some of whom had joined in sympathetic reaction to the listing) were included: Berenice Abbott, Ansel Adams, Richard Avedon, Sid Grossman, Consuelo Kanaga, Dorothea Lange, Lisette Model, Nancy Newhall, Aaron Siskind, W. Eugene Smith, Paul Strand, John Vachon, Dan Weiner and Minor White, among others. But it is in Nancy Newhall's prose that one discovers the political impetus for *This Is the Photo League*.

Newhall praised the "driving force of the League"—its "hunger and thirst after photography." The league students, she wrote, were curious and engaged; they "wheedled everybody whom they thought had something to say to come talk to them and listened avidly, no matter how divergent the speaker's viewpoint from their own. . . . Growing up in the bitter years of the Depression, they found the tragic vision of the early Documentary movement—Lange, Evans, Shahn, and others in the FSA—natural and logical as their guide. . . . Their studios, by necessity and conviction, were the streets."[67] After surveying the league's history, which by 1947 included growing membership and interest, Newhall finally gets to the main point—the defense of the league in the face of blacklisting: "Plans for building . . . a center were maturing when the Attorney General's listing of the League as one of some thirty 'Un-American and subversive' organizations cut like a lash across all activities. Un-American? Subversive?" Newhall then discussed the cultural diversity of the membership in respect to birth, age, race, political affiliation, and gender. The listing, she wrote, spurred members to define the focus, action, and meaning of the league. She asked why the league never reached the status of the Photo Secession or Group f/64, even though they had "more photographers of outstanding vision and power. . . . Yet they remain peripheral. . . . Again, why?" Newhall could not, given the situation, connect such marginalization to contemporary repressive sociopolitical legislation, although the league's peripheral status today seems a natural result of the paranoic mood.

Many of the images in the exhibition catalog are by no means politically inflammatory, didactic, or obvious (such as Weston's *Church Door*, Adams's *Aspens*, or Strand's *Mullen in Sun*). Others carry the ideological baggage associated with documentary photography—for instance, Grossman's wildly cropped tangle of *Coney Island* revelers, Engel's truncated black man's head peering ominously from the clutter of a store window, from the *Harlem Document*, or Model's unidealized faces on the street in *Wartime Block Party*.[68]

More surprising are the photographs that seem safe choices given the oeuvre of the artist: Marian Palfi's image of a *Jehovah's Witness* (the catalog featured no KKK members or abused children, subjects she had documented throughout the 1940s); Jerome Liebling's Brooklyn cityscape; and David Vestal's still life of a bowl of eggs.

Such images point to the gradual decline in classic, partisan documentary ideals from this point on in the league, as documentary's supposed legibility, viability, and very foundations were increasingly questioned by photographers and critics throughout the repressive postwar years. Furthermore, it was in the Photo League's best interest to include diverse images in this show, not just those of poor New Yorkers. Aesthetic diversity, from documentary to formalized still lifes, undercut the accusation of social realist didactics and, league organizers hoped, could fight the perception of the league as a Communist front.

One of the nineteen halftone reproductions published in the exhibition catalog, Rosalie Gwathmey's *Charlotte, N.C.* (1948), is a riveting visual reminder of Photo League documentary convictions. Gwathmey, then editor of *Photo Notes*, was dedicated to documentary's partisan ideals and active in radical politics. She frequently photographed her birthplace, Charlotte, North Carolina, focusing almost exclusively on the lives of poor African Americans in the segregated South of the late 1940s. After studying painting at the Pennsylvania Academy of Fine Arts, where she met her future husband, the social realist painter Robert Gwathmey, she attended the Art Students' League in New York. In 1942 she joined the Photo League and started to study with Strand and Grossman. The league's influence profoundly affected her photographic purpose: "I am particularly interested in photographing the Negro in my native South because of the problems that face him—housing, jobs, discrimination. These things I would like to see bettered."[69]

Such professed beliefs provoked the FBI to monitor the Gwathmeys. Her husband was followed and approached by government officials for information because of his political views and involvement with the National Council of the Arts, Sciences, and Professions, which was viewed at the time as a Communist front organization. The couple was scared. As she recalls, they "threw scads of books out . . . we just . . . threw them in the garbage can at the corner. We were afraid somebody would come in and look through our bookshelves and accuse us of being Reds." Discouraged after the Photo League disbanded, Gwathmey quit photographing, having only sold one photograph—to Stanley Praeger, a blacklisted actor, for $15. She gave all of her equipment away (to the league) and threw out her negatives, convinced

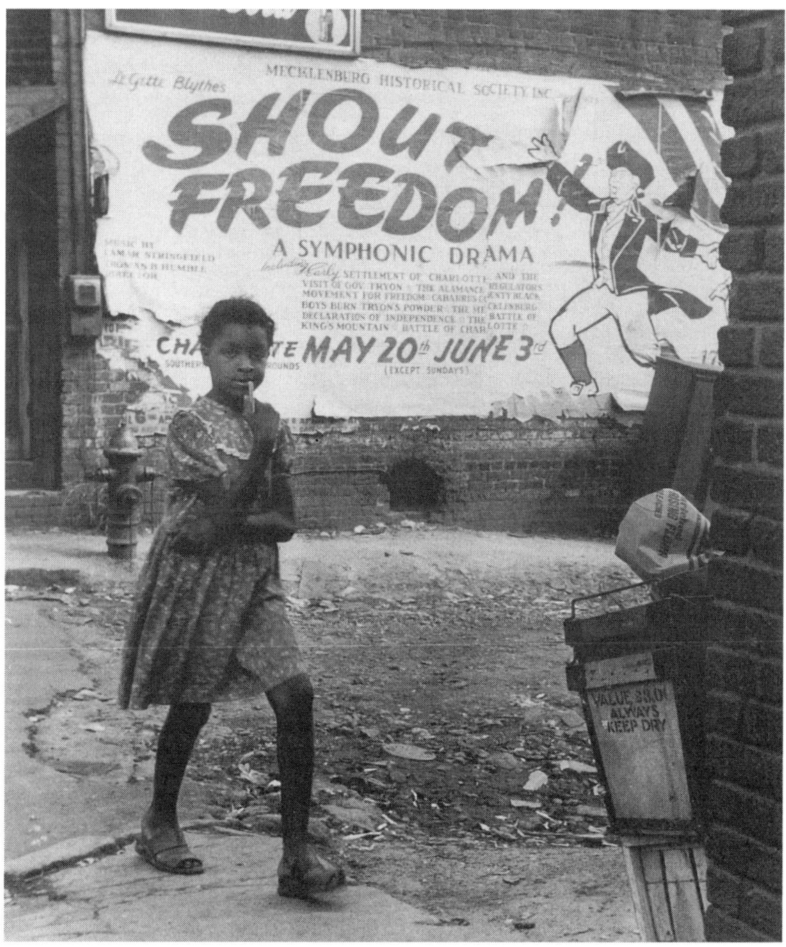

1.10. Rosalie Gwathmey, *Shout Freedom, Charlotte, North Carolina*. ca. 1948.

Rosalie Gwathmey's photographs of African Americans in her hometown, Charlotte, N.C., demonstrate the documentary lessons fostered at the Photo League. © Rosalie Gwathmey. Courtesy Howard Greenberg Gallery.

she had no future in photography.[70] The Gwathmeys were representative of many in the league whose careers, interests, and lives would be inexorably altered by the tensions of the cold war era.

The image by Gwathmey that was included in *This Is the Photo League* exhibition realizes her ideals. An African American girl walks on a sidewalk, a painted wall behind her proclaiming "SHOUT FREEDOM." The brick wall in the background is crumbling; included within the composition is a fire hydrant, an empty lot with no greenery, and a scarred, uneven sidewalk. The girl herself is boxed and isolated within the borders of the framed edges and by a brick wall, which she walks toward. The visual irony of the girl contained within such an environment hawking "freedom" is strong, especially in light of the cultural context of the burgeoning Civil Rights movement of later years. Gwathmey's potent image displays the most evocative political possibilities afforded by the documentary photographic tradition within the Photo League. Few saw the shot (it was not reproduced in any picture magazines), but it projects key documentary ideals in its style, composition, and subject matter. Such beliefs, then, were still strong in the minds of some members even after the league had been listed.

Reviews of the exhibition were included in the spring 1949 issue of *Photo Notes*. "This Is the Photo League," by Leo Hurwitz, noted that "despite the tolling of Mr. Clark's bell," the Photo League was very alive, the photographs revealing "a rawness that seldom faces you on the pages of our magazines." The artists Hurwitz singled out for praise were numerous: "Rosenblum's life-heavy faces watching an event off screen . . . Witt's shrouded, faceless woman pouring water from a jar . . . Model's acid comments on slum-destroyed people . . . Joseph's sad-eyed little girl who has often wanted and seldom received." His text betrays a respect for the documentary agenda when he lists the qualities uniting these images, such as "a fascination with the fractions of life, . . . a keen sympathy for the struggles of everyday people, and a warm interest in the textures of their lives."

After this praise, however, Hurwitz articulated a concern for improved technique among league photographers. He condemned the "common disregard of the potentialities of photography: to yield a wide scale of values, truth of texture and tone." Furthermore, "The photographer is too early satisfied with the arresting discovery, the socko fact, and too little concerned with the other expressive materials available to him. Such satisfaction prevents the completion of the picture and restricts its effect." In contrast, Hurwitz continued, superior works by Strand, Weston, and Adams illustrate "organic integration of form and content," creating "a new living object, the picture whose overall meaning and mood is more than the sum of its visual facts."[71] In this respect, Hurwitz's review illustrated a growing taste and appreciation for expressive photographic form and print quality over stale content—a taste coinciding with an increasingly repressive political climate.

The press notices reprinted in this issue of *Photo Notes* included both positive and negative reviews from contemporary newspapers and popular publishers, an indication of the league's encouragement of various, even opposed, opinions.[72] "J. T.," in *U.S. Camera*, criticized the overemphasis of documentary content over technique: "The League's show tends to push the message rather than the work: to show the reporter, not the craftsman. . . . The Photo League's quarters look, to this writer, not so much like a photographic gallery as the offices of a crusading newspaper." This critique points to a more bourgeois taste for even-handed presentations of the human condition, including more scenes of joy and positive images of life. Similarly, the *American Society of Magazine Photographers Newsletter* (January 1949) condemned the negative thrust of league content: "too many of the pictures seem to show the gloomy, the dreary, and, often, the insignificant. Even in Harlem, and the lower East Side, there are scenes full of humor and vitality, which, photographed by men of strength and maturity, can be beautiful and tender." Such comments indicate that traditional documentary aesthetics still dominated at the league (or were perceived as dominant), even while popular taste for such images questioned their "truthfulness" in the increasingly prosperous postwar years.

Jacob Deschin, *New York Times* critic and active league supporter, detected a new direction among some league photographers toward a more individual point of view with less social crusading: "Although the league has been much criticized for its constant preoccupation with the seamy side of life, no patterns exist in the League today; only new, intimately personal sincere ways of seeing." Judging by this last review, the league had succeeded in convincing some critics of the expressive variety encouraged within the organization and offset accusations of didactic political extremism.

One of the reviews of *This Is the Photo League* reprinted in *Photo Notes* was from the Communist Party paper, the *Daily Worker* (January 14, 1949, by Charles Corwin). Corwin praised league photographers as "most progressive," and he did not resist the opportunity to state what would seem a logical fact concerning the blacklisting of the Photo League: "Perhaps for this reason [their progressiveness] the League . . . has been honored with the label 'subversive' by Attorney General Clark. Such witch-hunting has been answered by rank and file cameramen who continue to join in increasing numbers the only artists' organization which today continues the great tradition of social meaning of the period of WPA and the FSA." The interest of the *Daily Worker* in the league's exhibition was not unusual; the Communist Party paper reviewed many shows, plays, and books for its readers, especially those works concerned with lives of the underprivileged masses. A review in the *Daily Worker* was not an absolute indicator of Communist activity, but it could, in some minds, signal a possible sympathy for or affiliation with the party.

The mere mention of one's name in this publication was often noted in government files, as Herbert Mitgang points out in *Dangerous Dossiers*: German author Thomas Mann's record was tarnished by a mention in the *Daily Worker* (1939); Lillian Hellman's files note that her play *Watch on the Rhine* was favorably reviewed by a critic for the *Daily Worker*; Tennessee Williams's file cited a *Daily Worker* mention of his public condemnation of the jailing of the "Hollywood Ten" (1950). Ben Shahn, a periodic member and participant in league activities, had an extensive FBI file concerning his Communist Party ties. His dossier included this comment from an unknown FBI "art critic": "Ben Shahn's work in the modernistic art field has shown a tendency to play up the lower class and he has had occasion to do work which in former years appeared in the *Daily Worker*."[73] Apparently the FBI read every issue of the paper and monitored any person or organization it mentioned favorably. The Photo League collectively balked at such thought control by reprinting the *Daily Worker* critique within its own magazine. However, taken together the reprinted reviews also illustrate that critics were divided over the dominance of documentary content versus form and technique in photography.

A new surprise in 1949 would make such aesthetic distinctions, for a time, seem trivial. On April 26, a conspiracy trial of twelve Communist Party leaders at Foley Square (*Dennis et. al. v. the United States*) produced, as its star witness, Angela Calomiris. In her testimony, she named Grossman as the person who had introduced her to the Communist Party and named the Photo League as a Communist front organization.[74]

Calomiris's brief moment of fame in the glare of government investigations was sufficient enough for J. B. Lippincott to publish her memoirs, *Red Masquerade: Undercover for the FBI*, in 1950. In the book, Calomiris chattily discloses her rise and splendid fall from Communism by outlining her association with Grossman, who she says consistently, like "a typical Communist," blamed everything on the "system." At first, she writes, league Communists, with their petitions and literature, seemed a "harmless bore." Throughout this time, she claims, she was ideologically courted by Communists as well as the FBI. In short, Calomiris infiltrated the league for the FBI and served as the league's executive secretary in 1942 while participating in spy activities—for instance, she would take "scores of shots" of May Day Parades so she "could turn over prints to the FBI" (who used them to identify Communists in the crowds). [75]

When the league was listed in 1947, Calomiris proudly remembers, "I couldn't help feeling that my reports had been the main evidence. They had been conclusive enough, heaven knows. For once, I rather enjoyed the indignant outcries of my fellow photographers on the executive board." Furthermore, she describes Strand's eloquent address following the listing: "At a mass meeting sponsored by the League to 'clarify' the issue, a well-known photographer attacked the concept of art for art's sake as decadent. An artist—and we considered ourselves such—needs political interests as much as he needs food. Before he got through, he managed to drag in the evils of the Marshall Plan, the warmongers, and the universal military training bill, ending nicely with an appeal to keep the artists of America free."[76] Her summary of Strand's speech is misleading and superficial, although Strand had forcefully decried the eroding civil liberties of an America that was looking more and more uncomfortably fascist in orientation. Calomiris's glib, paranoid interpretation of Strand's speech strains her credibility while clearly placing her within the fearful, conservative mood of the times.

Another simple indicator of this conservatism was found in the April 30, 1949, issue of the *New York Times*, which included an additional article on Calomiris, "a quick-witted young woman with a confident, determined air." Headlines surrounding this text declared: "Witness Parries Red Trial Thrusts"; "State Communist Party Has Raised Its Quota in Fund Drive—About $100 for Every Red"; "U. of Chicago Reply Hits 'Red' Charges"; and "Ex-Communist Is Set for Anti-Party Tour." By the June 25, 1949, issue, even the movie page advertised *The Red Menace*, "daring . . . shocking *ENTERTAINMENT!*" "The most talked about *drama* of our time," as the hyperbole read, included treachery ("Party agents use friendly girls to lure the innocent!"); violence ("Brass knuckles slash the wanderer from the Party line!"); hate ("Red Fascism is spawned in twisted minds!"); and conflict ("The purge is on! You can't escape from the Party!").[77] From serious reports of HUAC trials to advertising of popular culture, the *New York Times* was filled with indicators of cold war fear. Calomiris's testimony against the Photo League was but one of many reports on the dangerous possibility of Communist activity in the United States.

Again, the members reacted with angry surprise. An anonymous press release was written on Photo League letterhead on April 28, 1949.[78] In it the writer expressed the league's collective shock over Calomiris's testimony and "its subsequent indiscriminate use in newspapers," perpetuating "the unfounded slanders that the Photo League is a Communist front organization." The release explained that Calomiris had been an inactive member since 1942 and that her scant activity as secretary had taken place during the War, when many members were overseas. In short, the member explained, "We regard this testimony and the subversive listing of the Attorney General as part of a tactic of intimidation and threat used against cultural workers and a violation of the fundamental American freedoms." While the authors of this draft are unnamed, the use of the word *worker* evokes the early, more overtly political days of the league. The statement itself seemed to be a semantic tongue-wagging to conservative detractors.

The minutes of a meeting held by the Photo League on July 14, 1949, supply more information concerning the Calomiris affair.[79] "Chairman Rosenblum" opened the meeting by remarking upon Calomiris and admitting that no decision had yet been reached as to what to do and that more facts were needed. The report of the executive committee was read and then followed by a letter in support from Grossman's students. A new member, Bill Golden, told of Calomiris's membership in a "fraternal lodge" to which he belonged and how she apparently took pictures of "important" members for the police. This, Golden concluded, "was conduct unbecoming a photographer," and he asked for her expulsion from the league. Indeed, her dues had not been paid for the last year and a half, and the vote was unanimous to expel Calomiris.

Another league document excerpted Calomiris's testimony of "skillful innuendo" and claimed no direct links were made between her involvement with the league and Communism. "Shameful witchhunts" such as these, the document continued, were yet another attack on civil liberties. It went on to discuss other recent repressive measures taken by the U.S. government while criticizing Calomiris's "treachery and disgrace": "She has no place among honest people, among people of trust, people that desire progress in our lifetime. . . . Her name should be forever removed from our books, not alone that our books should once more become clean, but as a warning to those debased elements who so misjudge the anger of American people, that they expect them to remain silent and apprehensive in the face of these attacks on their freedom."[80]

Calomiris's testimony was all the more shocking to league members because so few could remember her as an active member. In a 1976 interview, W. Eugene Smith could not remember ever having met Calomiris;[81] Rosenblum remembers her only as one of many who gathered at informal parties at Grossman's house. She did attend functions: George Gilbert photographed her at the league with *New York Times* photography critic Jacob Deschin. The government provided no documented evidence as to Calomiris's motive in naming Grossman and the league, but Rosenblum speculates, "My feeling was that the police had something on her and at that time there was an effort to get those leaders of the Communist Party into jail and to make that time as difficult as possible for any progressive. They wanted to scare everyone to death."[82]

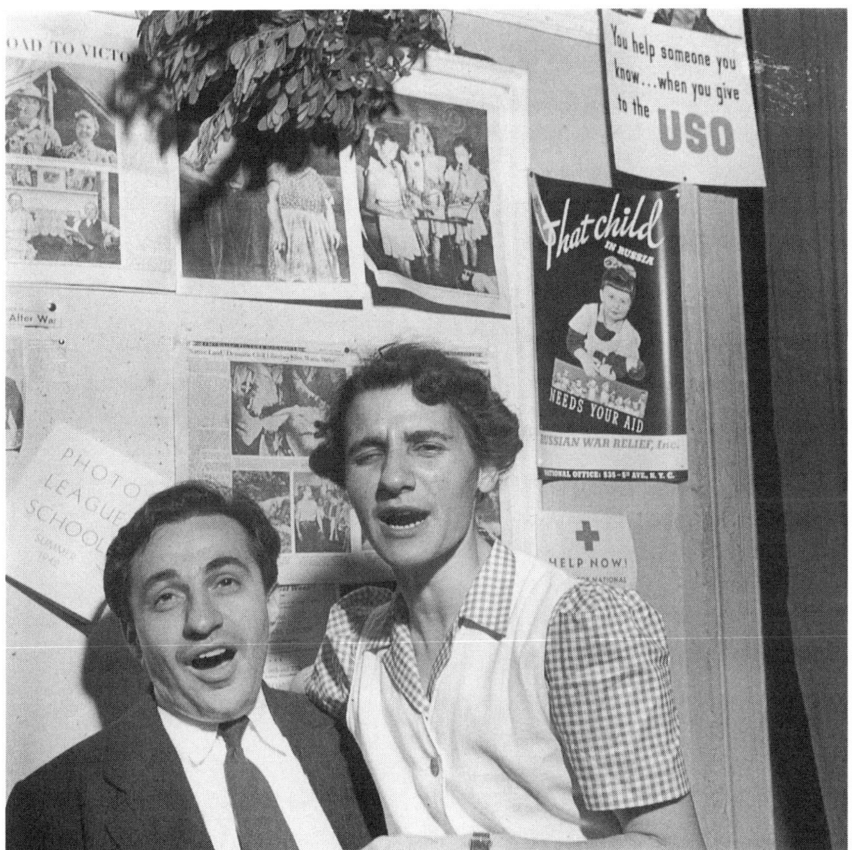

1.11. George Gilbert, *Jacob Deschin and Angela Calomiris at Photo League,* 1946.

Gilbert photographed Photo League activities during the 1940s, capturing this glimpse of Jacob Deschin, photography critic for the *New York Times*, and Angela Calomiris, who, it was later learned, had been spying on the league for the federal government. © George Gilbert, 1946.

Still the documentary tradition of social reform persevered in some artists' work, despite an increasingly hostile cultural climate discouraging such activism (if only at a visual level). Two images in particular demonstrate the humanist documentary vision emblematic of the urban working class and unglorified scenes of street life, as emphasized by many league photographers: *Sandstorm* (or *Summer Afternoon in the Slums*), 1949, by Ruth Orkin, and *Lower East Side*, 1949, by Dan Weiner.

Ruth Orkin (1921–1985) grew up in Hollywood, the daughter of a silent film actress. After moving to New York City in 1943, she earned an interna-

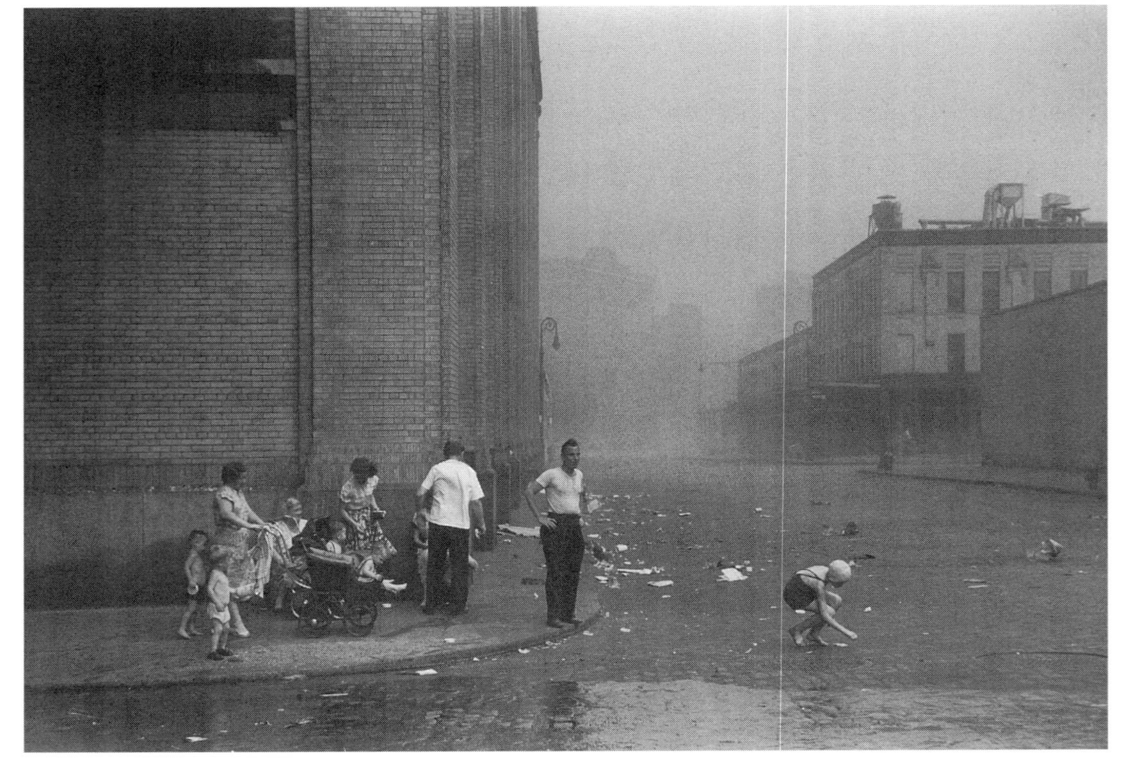

1.12. Ruth Orkin, *Sandstrom* (or *Summer Afternoon in the Slums*), *1949*.

Ruth Orkin was a successful commercial photographer and photojournalist who also belonged to the Photo League. This Greenwich Village neighborhood, she recalled, "was always alive with people, even in the midst of the dirt and decay." © 1981 Ruth Orkin.

tional reputation as a freelance photojournalist, publishing work in *Life*, *Look*, *Collier's*, and other magazines. She attended Photo League activities beginning in 1945 and married active member Morris Engel in 1952. She became an "actual" league member, she recalled, "as an act of principle, two weeks after the Attorney General's list came out." She shared with league members, according to Engel, "a people-oriented humanism." As Orkin stated, "To me, documentary photography is what's real. And reality is what moves people in the long run." It is this problematic philosophy that informs the image, *Summer Afternoon in the Slums*, which pictures a littered Greenwich Village neighborhood with a warehouse "clattering with noise all the time" and a wholesale meat market in the background. Orkin said: "I took the picture just as a gust of wind came up and blew grit swirling around the people who were sunning themselves on the corner. They were Polish and Irish, very poor, who lived there. It was a neighborhood that was always alive with people, even in the midst of the dirt and decay."[83]

Orkin composed disparate objects within a clustered mass of figures, including barefoot, barely dressed children and surrounding women. Two windblown men punctuate the misty darker tones with white shirt and undershirt. All are gathered at the corner of a sidewalk while debris flies through the empty, desolate stretch of background. One lone figure—a barefoot, crouching girl in the street bending to pick something up—breaks away from the others. These are not idealized post–World War II Americans (or "affluent society" as John Kenneth Galbraith would call them later in 1958) enjoying the prosperity of the times. Instead we see figures bleakly positioned within a desolate environment. Even so, they are photographed as a group, together against the elements of the Village with a man standing vigilant, protective and in a resolute hands-on-hips stance, gazing out into the street on the edge of the sidewalk. Orkin's image metaphorically speaks of the tenuous, delicate structure of human groups in the face of danger, symbolized by the wind in the streets, and evokes a potential narrative in regard to the precarious economic stability of the lower classes in American society.

Meanwhile Dan Weiner, a native New Yorker and successful photojournalist, grew up on 104th Street with his immigrant parents. He was greatly influenced by Hine's images of immigrants, Riis's portrayal of slum life, and the work of the FSA photographers.[84] A student of Grossman's and a league supporter, Weiner was also executive secretary (as noted in the spring 1949 issue of *Photo Notes*, published after Calomiris's naming). Not surprisingly, given Weiner's documentary ideals, his *Lower East Side* depicts a desolate urban environment littered with debris. A man, surrounded by trash, searches for meager treasures in a discarded box. This man, too, stands at the periphery of a turning sidewalk, carefully framed within the geometry of the landscape. He ekes out an existence yet is alone, surrounded by unpeopled buildings, brick, and cement.

Like most league members, Weiner was primarily interested in photographing people. The playwright Arthur Miller, upon viewing an impressive Manhattan skyline, recalled telling Weiner, "There's a picture for you to take," but Weiner "laughed and politely but firmly corrected" Miller, responding: "There's no people there. I'm not interested in scenery. . . . Those kind of pictures don't need me . . . I want to get people in some kind of relationship to meaning."[85] Other league members, such as Sol Libsohn (quoted earlier), corroborated Weiner's documentary focus on humanity: "unless you feel an involvement with people, with the human condition, you should not photograph them at all." Max Yavno claimed that "middle class people," in contrast to the poor, were just not as interesting photographically. And Rosenblum, concerning his Pitt Street project, recalled, "I learned that people, as bright as you are . . . understand what you're doing. . . . So, I always gave out pictures to the people I photographed."[86] The lower-class subjects of photographic forays by the artists quoted above were treated reverently, with dignity and respect for their conditions.

More and more Photo League members nevertheless began to question these documentary presumptions by the late 1940s. For instance, Ansel Adams's views in *Photo Notes* generated controversy over the increasing content-form debate. As early as 1940 he had cautioned photographers to pay more attention to technical quality and even equated good technique with one's manhood: "I am not arguing for merely empty precision. . . . you and I know thousands of swell pictures have been weakened—emasculated—by careless attention to the final vehicle, the print."[87] Again, in 1948, just months after the listing, Adams defensively argued against those who might accuse his work of being humanistically disengaged: "We have been accused out West . . . of doing too many mountains, rocks, and junipers. I for one have done most of my work in the natural scene. The choice of subject matter is somewhat determined by environment. Harlem does not exist in Yosemite Valley."[88]

Of course, the poor and disenfranchised existed in California as well as New York City and could have been the content of choice, just as the ignored Hudson River landscape existed right outside the league's back door. Adams did make some forays into traditional documentary subject matter, as evidenced by his images of interned Japanese Americans during the war. But Adams's work, overall, was tempered by his own West Coast background in the finely crafted tradition of photography by the f/64 group and the Western wilderness issues, which altered, or expanded, his own perception of "correct" subject matter. His ties to the Photo League, in retrospect, seem tenuous, even though league photographers, like the West Coast photographers, also produced "straight," clear, and representational images. The league entertained Adams's views, however; just as he supported the league, as evidenced by his letter to the league after the listing (reprinted in the January 1948 issue of Photo Notes): "I am no 'communist' or 'fellow-traveller.' I don't like the domination of any creed, theory, party or fashion. . . . Many of the League members think differently than I do about photography and other matters. This is what keeps the League alive. . . . *Protest* is not enough. This accusation demands . . . *action*. . . . Dust off your lenses and get going! Photograph the truth of America—the majesty of the Natural Scene, and the majesty of our people and their accomplishments."

His words testify to the league's tolerance for intelligent, alternate points of view. A "lively photographers' free-for-all" was provoked by Adams at the league on November 28, 1948 (as recorded by Lester Talkington). The ensuing discussion involved "new classifications of photography": the documentary approach (and Adams' suspicions of it), and "technique vs. message." Within this forum, Adams articulated his doubts about politically inspired art as "too closely identified with some political expedient." Documentary, he continued, was restricting ("to a certain aspect of society") and "two-dimensional." Too seldom, he complained, were viewers presented with answers to social problems, though such "positive photography" could have "great emotional value."[89]

Later in the transcription of this round-table discussion, Adams joined forces with many of the league members by saying that "Abstract or non-objective photography is escapism. . . . It is the disintegration of the relationship of the individual to the world. I don't like it any more than I like the idea of a photographer working along a particular ideological or propaganda line." Adams believed that more "guts and integrity" were needed in photography and admitted, "I am guilty of an awful lot of compromise. Sometimes I wake up in the night and think about it." Rosenblum concluded the symposium with a decidedly documentary point of view: "The important meaning of a work of art is its function—its effect on others. To make prints just for ourselves would be failure." To Rosenblum, the function of art involved an interactive audience of viewers who understood and appreciated meaning. The isolated modernist, alone in his or her studio and unengaged with the wider world, risked failure if emotive effect was not communicated. With role models like Hine and Strand, an ideal blend of both poles was sought by many league members.

Adams consistently, with good nature, tried to reconcile his own landscape photography with that of the more figural league work. Rosenblum maintains that Adams was one of the few members, however, who finally quit the league to avoid the political implications of belonging to a listed organization, resigning after Calomiris' testimony. While supportive of the lively photographic organization, he quit under the pressures of its final days. Until that time he was an admired member, voicing alternative aesthetics in photography.[90]

The spirited dialogue over the dominance of form or function in photography continued to grow throughout the remaining years of the league. This dialectic survives in many texts of the period. For instance, Oliver Larkin's 1949 book, *Art and Life in America*, quoted Shahn telling the young abstract expressionists, "You guys are just afraid of being emotionally involved in anything bigger than yourselves." Larkin added that "any reconciliation between the two [social realists and abstract expressionists] seemed as remote as the 'united and cooperating' world of Roosevelt's dream."[91] The older generation of artists, born of New Deal policies during the Depression (like the documentary photographers within the league), are positioned in this text as contradictory to the more modernist artists, who were exploring interior realms and formalist issues. American artistic circles were moving toward an increased taste for and acceptance of abstraction, not social realism. Concurrently, as Dejardin notes, documentary patronage in left-wing photo magazines decreased during the cold war, leaving fewer venues for publication of documentary work.

In October 1950, another special Photo League meeting was called; the allegations and difficulties arising from the listing and Calomiris's naming still haunted the league. Several handwritten and typed notes demonstrate the editing and composition of prose to best articulate the angry concerns of its anonymous writers (including Rosenblum). The drafts link the league's naming with other events in recent years, listing the rampant assaults on civil liberties: the McCarran-Wood Bill, monitoring Communist activities; General Clark's list of subversive organizations; the Mundt-Nixon Bill (or Subversive Activities Control Act), forcing possible subversive organizations to register as "Communist fronts" and authorizing the use of internment camps to detain possible subversives; the conviction of ten Hollywood workers accused of Communist activity; the imprisonment of Joint Anti-Fascist Committee leaders; "the sinister umbrella of the Korean War"; city ordinances removing the right of free speech; and (crossed out in one draft) the Taft-Hartley Law, regulating union activity.[92]

These rough drafts of Photo League notes clearly convey the anger some league members felt toward contemporary American politics. Specific acts of legislature that had affected the Photo League were also criticized. For instance, the McCarran-Wood Bill's repressive purpose was summarized as harassment of "all progressive organizations to the point of demoralization so that they will fold up and be unable to answer the attack." The writer of the draft then asked sarcastically, "what's a little thing like the Constitution?" The draft went on to defend the venerable history of the league, also arguing that they needed no defense but the truth. "Truth," the ideal sought in documentary, became more illusory as the cold war heated up. These drafts also mentioned that it now seemed obvious that the listing stemmed directly from Calomiris's activities for the FBI during her three-month period of active membership in 1942.

The present repressive climate was likened to a fearsome enemy: "the scepter of leadership in the 'Anti-Comintern Axis' has been disinterred in Berlin and is being loudly and profanely held aloft in Washington." This technique, the writer continued, induced a "creeping paralysis. And the whole thing can be made to look legal." One draft speculated that fighting the measures could take as long as two years and outlined the specific damages incurred by the McCarran-Wood Bill. While the final copy presented to league members is not included in these files, it is clear from the tone of the drafts that league leaders were not only angry about their specific troubles but also irritated with the wider political spectrum of eroding civil liberties in the United States.

As mentioned previously, Serge Guilbaut has argued that abstract art in the late 1940s was an escapist form of modernism which more safely kept suspicions of disloyalty at bay than did the social realism of the 1930s. A similar argument could be made for the changing philosophies in New York photography circles. While many league photographers continued their humanistic, vaguely leftist orientations, others began, in the 1950s, to produce "safer" images featuring their own children (not poor black ones) and abstractions taken from a closely regarded natural scene.[93] Others, in a transition that might be called "pre-postmodernist," questioned the capacity of documentary photographs to convey clear, sociological meaning to viewers and thus effect cultural change. More and more photographers left the Lower East Side streets to focus on private, more formally engaged scenes of nature or portraits. Or, at least, these are the images most often published within periodicals of the 1950s. Given the repressive restrictions placed on the league during the late 1940s, it is no surprise that *Photo Notes* articles reflect a shift in their acceptance of formalism.

By 1950, more and more articles in *Photo Notes* heralded a tolerance for and retreat into formalism. The newsletter also reflected other difficulties that faced the league. Because of financial problems, the spring 1950 issue of *Photo Notes* was delayed. It included an article by a new voice—Minor White. His article, "What is Photography?," articulated the more aesthetic and less documentary artistic direction taken by many artists during the cold war years.

White became involved in the league in its later years through his photographic career out West. As Rosenblum recalls, "in an effort to broaden its perspective the Photo League was in touch with the Minor White School on the West Coast at the time. We exchanged shows, we had shows here of his photography."[94] White emphasized, in the *Photo Notes* article of 1950, the personal, subjective, and formal potentials of art photography: "In brief, it's what any artist makes of it." White further elaborated upon the merits of artistic vision: "It serves the poetic artist with reality, which, if he can intensify—much as Alice through the Looking Glass—yields him the poetic. But photography will not serve him if he seeks to avoid the literal; its arms are only long enough to reach through, not around reality. It serves the mystic artist with a naive window giving on the world. With a burning glass as wondrous as a child before his fact and magic have come apart."[95]

This text manifests a completely different and new tone within the pages of *Photo Notes*—the modernist visionary. Certainly more formally engaged photographers already existed within the league (such as Strand, Adams, and Weston), but never before had the pages of the newsletter so strongly endorsed this aesthetic. The concepts of truth and justice, politically alive in the ideological potential of social realism, are poignantly questioned if not absent for White in this *Photo Notes* essay: "Nor can we say that documentary truth is the sole gift of the hand camera, or poetic truth the property of the view—such truths are in the person first, the world second, and in cameras not at all." The documentary photographer begins to sound more and more naively partisan in the face of such criticism.

Alongside the White article was a review entitled "A Photo League Symposium," which quoted Homer Page as saying "American documentary photography is in the doldrums today. The vital forces it inherited from the FSA group of the 1930's have been dispersed and lost." League members, in this symposium of 1950, tried to understand and explain the declining documentary tradition, citing "the present confusion of facts and values." "We are not sure of war or peace, prosperity or recession: not sure to strike between our freedom and our security." These issues were "clouded" and "in transition," which made "any attempt to record conditions extremely difficult."[96] The "real casualties" of the cold war and McCarthyism, Navasky has noted, were "the walking wounded of the liberal left," the "impaired momentum of the New Deal," and, it might be added, social documentary photography.[97]

More recently, John Tagg has explored the concept of "realism" that is so critical to most photographers' understanding of "documentary" work. His research exposes the cultural factors that determine "truth" and "realism" within a documentary context, proving that such terms are not universal nor ahistorical but instead are formed within specific social, theoretical, and ideological conditions: "We must see that here [with Berenice Abbott's understanding of "realism"], as generally, realism is defined *at the level of signification*, as the outcome of an elaborate constitutive process. . . . It is, rather the product of a complex process involving the motivated and selective employment of determinate *means of representation.*"[98]

The privileged status of the photograph, as guaranteed witness of actual events, encourages what Tagg calls "a regime of truth." This illusion of authority becomes a critical condition of social documentary, with its presumptions of visualizing *truthful* ideological constructs such as class, struggle, and economic forces. This connection between authority and documentary is neither "accidental or arbitrary." Documentary photography, flourishing under the ideological conditions set during the Depression, however, was beset with new cultural and historical challenges during the cold war years that inexorably altered its ideals and assumptions in representation. We may mourn or celebrate this growing awareness of subjectivity as a loss of innocence, but we cannot afford to neglect its history. If, as Tagg maintains, "a dream is a fulfillment of a wish," then by the 1950s the documentary dreams of the 1930s were redirected irrevocably toward interior, personal realms.

While reading the final issues of *Photo Notes*, one can hear the death knell of traditional documentary photography as its grip on artists gradually loosened. Through the final years, financial support for the league diminished as the repercussions of the Attorney General's listing forced many members to quit. Modernism was on the rise; documentary work, in gradual decline. The listing and Calomiris's naming of Grossman had effectively, with no objective evidence, scared most members away. Despite all efforts by remaining members, in June 1951 the Photo League disbanded permanently.

League members often express a sad, bitter surprise at the organization's decline and disappearance in a democratic society wherein ideals born of the Depression years could no longer hold. As the August 1951 statement on the final closing of the league, from its Executive Committee, noted, the cold war was on and the "people have been the victims. . . . The Photo League is but one of the casualties. . . . [but] the fight . . . is far from over."[99] And many former members, still working, carry the league's ideals with them to this day, an indication of their commitment to an politicized form of social documentary. They are often bewildered that the league's story has been submerged over time, like so many of the lives damaged during the cold war years. How, the curious and concerned ask, can histories disappear? They cannot; they leave ghostly tracks—as the career of one league member, Sid Grossman, shows.

2

Coming in from the Cold: Sid Grossman's Life in the League

> There ain' no usa draggin' no Communism in this thing, Mistah. Ah respecks yo' feelin's powerfully, suh; but whut yuh's astin jus' stirs up mo' hate. Whut this po' boy needs is understandin'.
>
> Richard Wright, *Native Son*

Sid Grossman (1914–55), a quintessential Photo League photographer, believed that art must have a moral imperative. His early work, especially, used art as a "weapon," visualizing a world of the poor and disenfranchised. It was, in part, this ideology that brought him to the attention of FBI hunters fearful of Communists who might subvert or overthrow the government of the United States. This unwanted and unwarranted government attention not only led to the demise of the Photo League but also destroyed Grossman's professional life. Grossman was a key personality within the league: he was a founding member (1936), the director of the league's school, and the only league member mentioned by name in Calomiris's 1949 testimony. Grossman's career in the league is an ideal example of the difficulties encountered by politically engaged documentary photographers of the cold war years.

Like other league workers, Grossman photographed the lives of more "ordinary" New Yorkers, in most cases haunting the less fashionable streets of the City in which he was born. Grossman's own childhood was hard. His working-class parents were Jewish immigrants from Austria, who, speaking a new language and trying to establish themselves, faced a difficult enough situation. Making matters worse, Grossman's father deserted the family, leaving his mother, a cook at Catskill vacation resorts, as the primary provider for her four children. After attending high school in the Bronx and taking classes at the City College of New York, he joined the Film and Photo League in 1934 or 1935; the following year he helped found the new splinter group, the Photo League. Largely self-taught in photography, Grossman

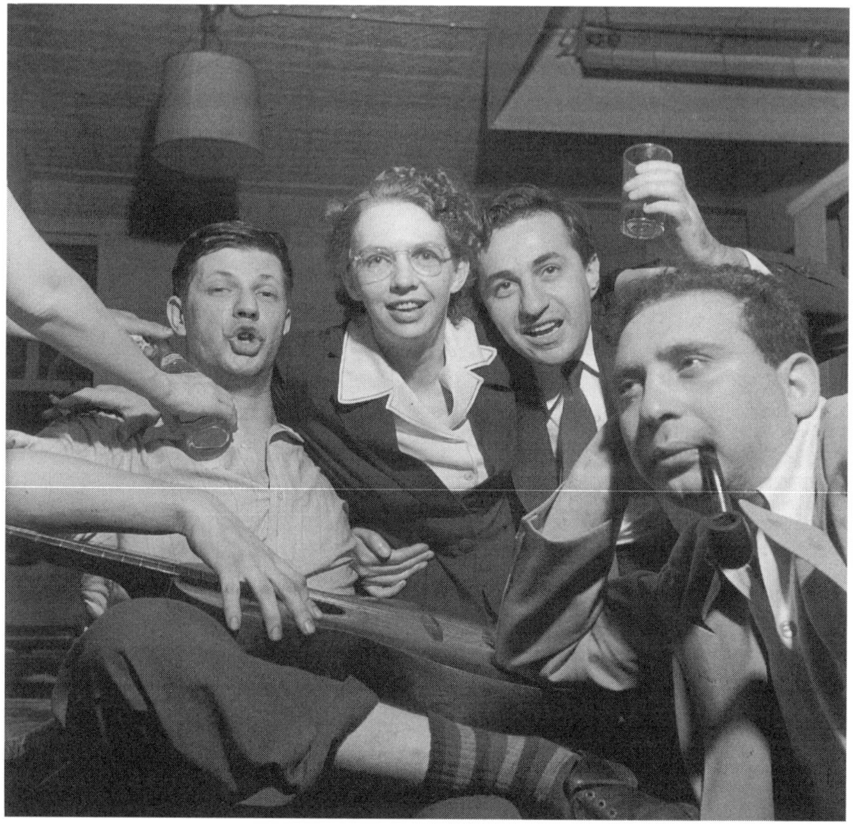

2.1. George Gilbert, *Photo Hunt Party,* 1947.

Gilbert snapped informal photographs of Photo League activities; here he caught the lively camaraderie between (left to right) instructor Sid Grossman, publicity chairman and *Modern Photography* editor Jacqueline Judge, *New York Times* critic Jacob Deschin, and photographer Arnold Eagle. © George Gilbert, 1947.

in the 1930s concentrated on freelance documentary work and also found WPA employment in the street repair crew as a pick-and-shovel man (1936).[1]

Grossman's first photographic project for the league began in 1938, the same year he began teaching, when he collaborated with Sol Libsohn on the *Chelsea Document.* Typical of members working on league projects, the photographers not only visually chronicled this area of New York City, they also worked with the tenants in an effort to understand the neighborhood's problems. Libsohn and Grossman worked with the Chelsea Tenants' League through 1939 to identify the character of the area as well as its problems; the images were exhibited in 1940 at the Photo League, the Chelsea Tenants League, and the Hudson Guild. Grossman also worked on other photographic documents, not always with league members, such as *Negroes in New York* (1939), a WPA assignment. Despite his busy career, Grossman earned little money from his photography and, though he hated doing so, often had to hustle for meager jobs doing portraits or weddings. Walter Rosenblum remembers him living on a salary of thirteen dollars a week during his early Photo League days.[2]

Most of Grossman's personal and professional time went to the league's school, which he designed, directed, and taught at from 1938 to 1949. This significant contribution earned him no salary, but his dedication to the school's success was inspiring. Grossman's influence on league photography is reflected consistently in this role, since the syllabus and readings list he compiled with Libsohn would influence many students coming to the league for guidance, including Rosenblum and Dan Weiner.[3] Grossman's instruction of young photographers extended beyond the bounds of league classrooms; he also conducted classes from various centers such as the Henry Street Settlement, the Harlem Art Center, and, later, at his own Chelsea apartment and the Provincetown School of Photography. His influence on most league students was profound, if controversial. Even those who dislike Grossman's opinionated techniques and critiques admit his devotion to his students. More typically, however, his students testify that he positively changed their lives and made them serious photographers. His first course, and one of his most famous, was, not surprisingly, "Documentary Photography."

As an important pedagogical force in the league, Grossman appeared frequently in *Photo Notes*. The spring 1949 issue announced, as it had many times before, that he would lead the next workshop class. The writer extolled Grossman, who had "been teaching this course over a long period" and noted "it is from this class that so many of the fine photographers that the league has developed have received most of their inspiration." The announcement outlined what it was like to take a course with Grossman or to study in the league—"This is a practical working course with a minimum of lecturing"—and stated the class was executed in more of a round-table basis. As one former student, Hal Greenwald, noted on the league school in the January 1948 *Photo Notes* issue: "It is unique in that it uses a progressive educational method: the student learns by doing. . . . To Sid Grossman, our school director, must go the majority credit for evolving this enriching method of teaching photography."[4]

The league's classes would enrich and educate hundreds of photographers in New York, who were hungry for experience with the various, often illustrious, (and unpaid) teachers, including not just Grossman but Paul Strand, Walter Rosenblum, Morris Engel, and others. Throughout the 1930s and 1940s, the league was the only organization offering New Yorkers such comprehensive photographic instruction. A shared aesthetic toward documentary photography dominated in upper-level course work; in the fall 1948 issue of *Photo Notes*, Barney Cole outlined the documentary direction of the school as directed by Grossman. "Basic Technique" introduced students to photographic techniques and important artistic ideas; "Advance Technique" encouraged students to "learn to 'see' in a new way" through specific assignments. Finally, in the description of the upper-level workshops, readers learned of the league's specific appreciation for the documentary tradition: "The student is taught to see himself in relation to photography, photography in relation to society."

A typical league student should become independent, the text emphasized, and eventually achieve "a personal style of photography—his own, and not the instructor's." However, a general ideological consensus is evidenced when league courses were compared to other photography classes (of which there were few), in which "instructors hold conflicting viewpoints," leaving students in confusion over incompatible dogmas and concepts.[5] Best of all, the league school, as directed by Grossman, was inexpensive ($30 a year for all three classes during the postwar years), courses were small and personal (often at night to accommodate working students), and darkroom equipment was available for a small fee.

Many of Grossman's students, recalling the league's classes and lectures in later interviews, still praise him. Louis Stettner, for instance, calls Grossman the "Ghandi" of photography, a great authority. Rosenblum reports he was "a marvelous teacher" and "the organizational genius at the league."[6] An impressive number of female students benefited from his teaching as well, including Lisette Model, Vivian Cherry, Erika Klopfer (Stone), and Helen Gee, among others. Arthur Leipzig said, "Sid was a truly wonderful teacher who knew how to motivate his students and how to help them tap into their feelings. . . . [He] introduced me to the world of art." As Leipzig recalls, Grossman sent introductory students to the Museum of Modern Art to encourage artistic questioning and increased sophistication. Ida Wyman notes, like so many others who were in the league, that classes at the Photo League demanded "honesty" and capturing "what exists" in synch with deeper questions of style and content. Others felt emotionally assaulted by his volatility and passion.[7]

Helen Gee took private classes with Grossman and other students in his Chelsea apartment after he left the league; her memories of his harsh teaching tactics still linger. By the time she knew him "he was still considered a pariah," "deserted, even by close friends" because of their fears of "guilt by association." She was warned about him: "Grossman's a tyrant. He'll either inspire you or crush you." Clashing with him from the start, she "swallowed hard and tried to ignore the pains" in her stomach from his "tyrannical behavior." But in the end she found that his "passion and commitment were lessons in themselves" and noted Grossman's frequent exhortation": "Live for photography![8]

Lisette Model's stormy relationship with Grossman endured through these difficult years. While she found Grossman's teaching methodology destructive at times, she attended his classes through 1950. As Grossman's widow, Miriam Cohen, relates, both were assertive, opinionated, and passionate artists who sparred but respected each other. Grossman helped Model learn the technical photographic skills necessary to get a teaching position at the New School; she supported him by attending his classes although she was already a mature artist.[9]

As school director, Grossman was a gruff taskmaster who pushed students to learn and grow, often uncomfortably and through confrontation. Les Barry wrote that Grossman's "manner of teaching was to create challenge and conflict for his students, define their goals, and inspire them to strive in those directions. He was merciless in his criticism of work that appeared pedestrian or showed a lack of creative effort." In the April 1943 issue of *Photo Notes*, he was gently and facetiously called "Simon Legree Grossman . . . stalking about to see that nobody wastes company time."[10]

Grossman did not consider himself a traditional instructor. He was not merely interested in teaching technical issues like print development and presentation; he also encouraged students' self-examination and independence: "I won't bear the responsibility for making something out of you. You must take that on yourself. You have to be searching, you have to be finding the courage to speak."[11] Rosenblum's recollections of his first class with Grossman reveal the emphasis placed on self-discovery. Grossman asked the students in the class to choose a project for the semester and report the following week on the topic, to which Rosenblum replied that he would like to photograph New York: "He said okay. He knew that was a stupid project for a young kid, to go photograph New York. But Sid was the kind of fellow who realized you had to learn it on your own; you learn by thinking a thing through rather than having someone say, 'No, you stupid kid, you can't do that.'"[12] Rosenblum soon realized on his own the project was too large and decided instead on the Lower East Side. But that choice also proved too much for Rosenblum to handle, and he ended up concentrating on one single block, Pitt Street.

Grossman shared with many league members and imparted to students a serious concern for the humanistic, documentary tradition. According to his friend and colleague, David Vestal, Grossman's earliest influences were the FSA photographers, as well as Hine and Strand, both of whom he knew personally. Vestal explained that "like other members of the Photo League, they believed photography should serve a social purpose. Grossman's street pictures from the 1930s typically show spirited or defeated people enduring hard times."[13]

His photograph *Shoeshine Boys*, 1939, illustrates his focus on images with the potential moral imperative of social consciousness. The photograph depicts two boys on a sidewalk; one, wearing battered sneakers, sits in a simple wooden chair with his feet propped on a shoeshine box. With a wrinkled brow and an open mouth, he appears worried, distressed. Another, smaller boy leans against a window, legs crossed and hand in mouth. The composition stresses the human figures—the lines of the background building and sidewalk lead our eyes to the boys, while a crack in the pavement contains them within the center space. They are not pictured in an act of labor, with a client, but in a liminal moment without business. The evocation of child labor in the tradition of the league's hallowed spiritual leader, Lewis Hine, is clear. Also poignant is the visual conflict with cultural ideals—children, according to most Americans' values, should play, attend school, but not hang out on street corners.

Concerning Grossman's humanistic vision, Rosenblum (in a review of the photographs in MoMA's *The Image of Freedom* show, 1941) specifically addressed this image: "Sid Grossman's three pictures deserve special mention. Look at his picture of the Arkansas farmer, of the farmer in the Tenant's Union in Oklahoma, of the two bootblacks on the sidewalks of New York. The power, the emotional intensity comes through with a great emotional impact to the observer."[14] Rosenblum praised Grossman's documentary desire to excite viewers' emotions. While the factual information of a photographic scene may be important to a viewer's appreciation of the image, as William Stott has written, "the essence of documentary is not information. . . . [It] is the . . . power to move."[15] Most photographers working from this ideological premise could then hope that social documents would encourage social improvements, an aspiration born of Depression-era and New Deal sentiments.

Another image done the following year, a portrait of union organizer and farmer *Henry Modgilin*, 1940, further exemplifies these typical documentary

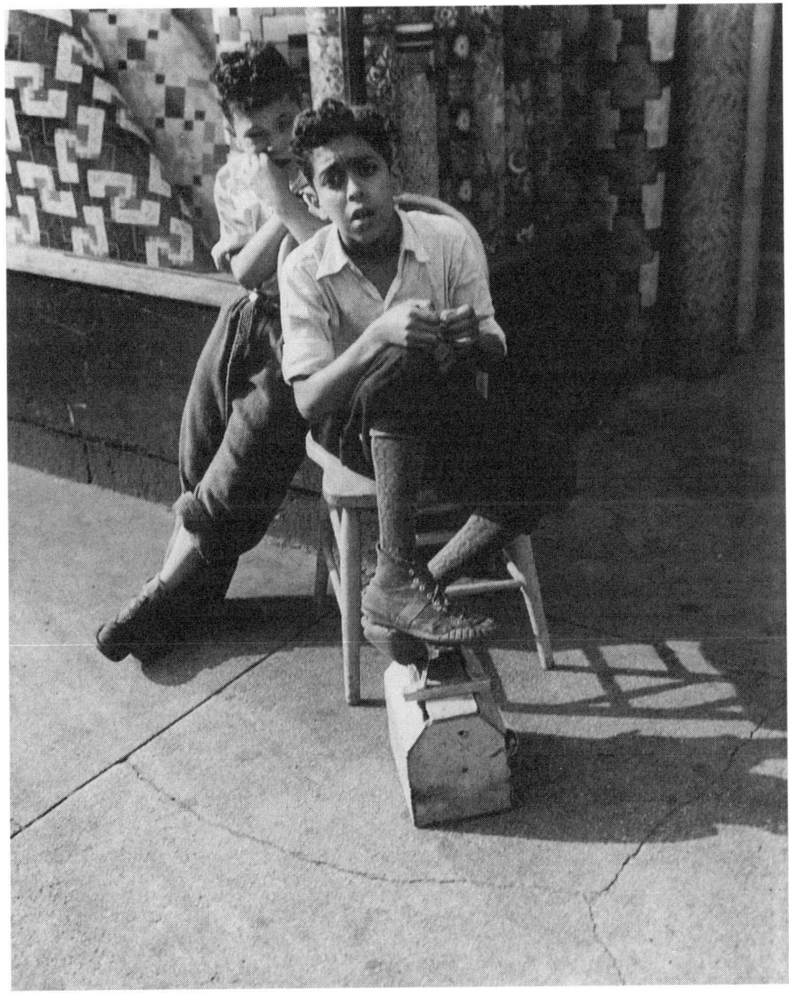

2.2. Sid Grossman, *Shoeshine Boys,* 1939.

Sid Grossman's street photograph of shoeshine boys dates from the period that Grossman photographed a feature project, the *Chelsea Document*, with Sol Libsohn (1938–39); the two worked with the Chelsea Tenants' League, identifying the neighborhood's character and problems. © Miriam Cohen. Courtesy Howard Greenberg Gallery.

concerns. The image was one of many photographs Grossman took when he traveled to Oklahoma, Arkansas, and Missouri on a self-assigned journey to photograph farmers and union activities with Marion Hille (whom he married around 1941). In Oklahoma, Grossman photographed oil well workers,

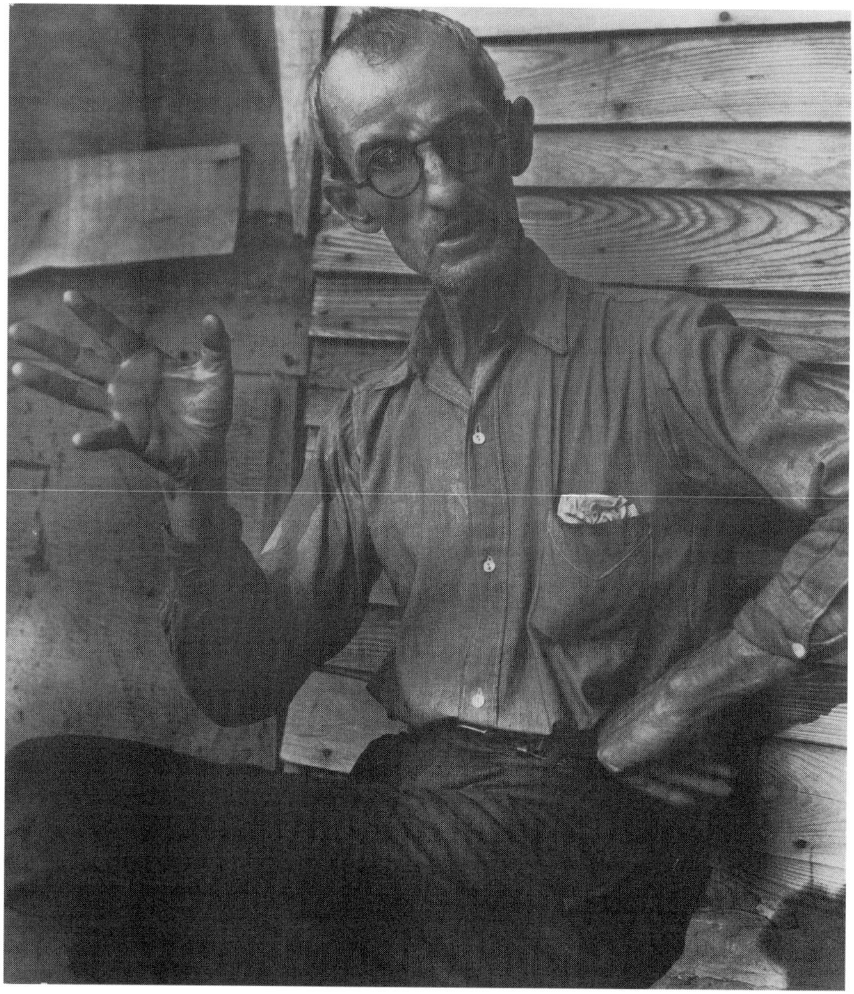

2.3. Sid Grossman, *Henry Modgilin, Oklahoma*, 1940.

This midwestern farmer was photographed by Sid Grossman in 1940 while Grossman was traveling to Oklahoma, Arkansas, and Missouri to document workers and union activities. Federal documents indicate that the FBI initiated surveillance of Grossman's activities during this trip. © Miriam Cohen. Courtesy National Gallery of Canada, Ottawa.

industry, and town scenes; in Arkansas he met and photographed people in the Southern Tenant Farmers' Union and the Farmers' Union Local 576 (documenting, for instance, their rural lives, families, and homes, as well as their union activities.)[16]

Grossman's aesthetic when photographing the farmers and union workers he met on the trip was clear, unaffected, and "straight," yet, like most documentary photographers, he worked his prints to create the desired response. As colleague David Vestal noted, "Almost every tone in the negative was changed drastically in printing; partly to clarify space, but mostly to dramatize this gaunt man's eloquent face, body and gesturing hand. Each finger, individually, is separated from the wall behind it by local manipulation in printing—fanatical and typical. No trouble was too great for a picture he cared about."[17] The same image was published posthumously in a book of Grossman's photographs, *Journey to the Cape*, accompanied with a text by his friend Millard Lampell: "Sure would like it to rain. Don't mind for myself, hell, I've seen it rain. But I'd like my kids to see it. I mean, this used to be good country. But now it's so dry a man's got to prime himself to spit. . . . You hungry? Come on in and set. We got plenty. We got a thousand things to eat . . . every one of 'em's peas."

Human survival and endurance in the face of social hardship and deprivation are emphasized in both the text and photograph. Grossman's portrait of the farmer reinforces and strengthened the humanistic, personalizing text as well. The title indicates the real man, by name, not symbolically (Grossman did not call the photograph, for instance *Poor*, *Destitute Farmer* or *Getting Along* or whatever). Modgilin's erect, angular body fills most of the picture plane, while his lively, gesticulating hand, with those fingers Grossman labored to accentuate, animate the frail form. His aged, stubbled, and bespeckled face is cocked, his mouth open as if in the middle of a spirited dialogue. Modgilin's clothes are simple but respectable—all buttons are intact, a handkerchief is placed in his pocket. In the background, the simple, unpainted pine structure does not distract viewers from the dominating figure. This older man's bearing is proud, ennobled, even quietly heroic; one can certainly imagine this man discussing the struggles involved in union organization of the 1930s. Grossman's camera sought such examples of "ordinary" people surviving difficult financial situations, not complacent, contented figures of the upper classes. But such attraction to the working class also earned him the attention of the FBI. Anne Tucker maintains that it was during this photographic trip that the FBI initiated surveillance of the league, because of Grossman's associations with known Communists during his travels.[18]

The following year, in the December 1941 issue of *Photo Notes*, Grossman reviewed *12,000,000 Black Voices: A Folk History of the Negro in the US*, a book published earlier that year by African American writer Richard Wright, illustrating three centuries of black experience and accompanied by FSA photographs chosen by league member Edwin Rosskam. Grossman's respect for this text emphasizes his dedicated interest in the troubled aspects of the human condition and, perhaps, implies an allegiance with Communism. Grossman quoted large sections of the book, finding it "one of the best photography books. . . . written with a profound, personal emotion, and a clear understanding of the needs and desires of the Negro people." He then extensively quoted passages by Wright ("we are not what we seem . . . for *we* are *you*") and praised Rosskam's use of photographs, derived from his years of experience with the FSA, in relation to the text, which resulted in a "splendid integration." Finally, in a world on the brink of war and social insecurity, Grossman argued: "when it is so necessary for us to find unity of all our nation, and the will to defend our essential right, is particularly the time to understand, and to bring into the fight with us, this one tenth of our people."[19] Today these words seem simple, maybe even self-evident, written as they were during a time of burgeoning world war. But within the historical context and in light of Wright's own controversial career, such praise could also be perceived as suspect by government forces. Wright's text had already drawn the attention of the FBI (Mitgang cites Wright among the many writers investigated by the FBI for activity in the Communist Party); Grossman's positive review linked Wright's "party-line" ideology to the Photo League and certainly added to Grossman's FBI dossier.[20]

Wright had been a party member during the first half of the 1930s and endured the testimony of informants through the 1940s as the government tried to establish his danger to American society. One bureau informer recalled Wright's conversation over dinner, during which he had discussed "the eventuality of a Communist takeover of the government."[21] Even though he was not a Communist after 1936, Wright was perceived as a "fellow traveler," sympathetic to revolutionary ideals. In 1948, bureau director Hoover declared that "the philosophical Communist might just as well be working as an agent of a foreign power because he is aiding its cause."[22] Such comments would bear on Grossman's life as well; as his second wife, Miriam, has voiced, even after he had tried to break with the party, suspicions followed him.

Wright's novel *Native Son* had been published in 1940, one year before his *12,000,000 Black Faces*, the book Grossman happily reviewed. This dramatic novel focused on Bigger Thomas, a black man from the Chicago slums tried and executed for the murders of his white employer's daughter, Peggy, and his black girlfriend, Bessie (this murder, although deliberate and far more brutal, does not figure as prominently in the trial). As Alan Wald points out, Bigger "is a product of society, but a close reading of the text shows that Wright, a Communist Party member of the time, intentionally avoided the temptation to make Bigger into a mere victim of circumstance." Wright, in fact, was critical of how members of the Communist Party viewed African Americans—as little more than symbols of capitalist abuse.[23]

Grossman was daring to participate in this discussion of African American life in the United States. As one chairman of Washington state's Un-American Activities Committee declared, "if someone insists there is discrimination against Negroes in this country, or that there is inequality of wealth, there is every reason to believe that person is a communist."[24]

Wright addressed such racist fears in *Native Son*. The text weaves together related associations involving unions, Communists, and workers for social reform. Bigger knows he should be afraid of such activities: "he had heard about unions; in his mind unions and Communists were linked." Despite the fact that he is not a Communist, police investigators consistently try to tie Bigger to the Communist Party by asking him whether he read the *Daily* [*Worker*], ever went to Russia, or even gesticulates "like he's been around a lot of Jews." Jan Erlone, a Communist friend of the murdered Peggy, is also asked a series of "damaging" questions concerning his interest in blacks by the coroner in Bigger's trial in order to discredit him. The passage reads like transcripts from a HUAC court:

> "Do you believe in social equality for Negroes?"
> The room stirred.
> "I believe all races are equal . . . " Jan began.
> "Answer *yes* or *no*, Mr. Erlone! You're not on a soapbox. *Do* you believe in social equality for Negroes?"
> "Yes."
> "Are you a member of the Communist Party?"
> "Yes." . . .
> "Did you *shake hands* with that Negro?"
> "Yes."
> "Did you *offer* to shake hands with him?"
> "Yes. It is what any decent person . . . "
> "Confine yourself to answering the questions, please, Mr. Erlone. We want none of your Communist explanations here. Tell me, did you *eat* with that Negro?"
> "Why, yes."
> "You *invited* him to eat?"
> "Yes." . . .
> "How many times have you *eaten* with Negroes before?"
> "I don't know. Many times."
> "You *like* Negroes?"

"I make no distinctions . . ."

"Do you *like* Negroes, Mr. Erlone?"

"I object!" Max shouted. "How on earth is that related to this case!"[25]

Wright's fictional Communists point to his distrust of the party; he does not heroicize or idealize Communist characters. His text serves to illuminate the times in which Wright and Grossman lived as left-wing, if not Communist, radicals. But as the novel's protagonist, Bigger, contemplates a Communist life, he considers popular culture stereotypes: "What made people Communists? He remembered seeing many cartoons of Communists in newspapers and always they had flaming torches in their hands and wore beards and were trying to commit murder or set things on fire. People who acted that way were crazy. All he could recall having heard about Communists was associated in his mind with darkness, old houses, people speaking in whispers, and trade unions on strike."[26] Margaret Walker points out that Wright was an ambivalent Communist who wrote for the *Daily Worker* with increasing disaffection. Nevertheless, because of Wright's known affiliations, the FBI examined his later book (so positively reviewed by Grossman in *Photo Notes*) looking for seditious statements in order to secure reasons for Wright's arrest as "a dangerous Communist," but in the end they were unable to establish charges of sedition. As his essay "I Choose Exile" recounts, Wright left America in 1947 for Paris (like Strand), where, he felt, "there was more freedom in one square block" than in all of the United States.[27] In short, Wright, during the early 1940s, was not a name to praise publicly if one valued an untarnished image.

Yet Grossman valued artists such as Wright, who, in agreement with the aesthetics nurtured within the Photo League, gave voice to the underprivileged workers in America. In fact, there was a strong anti-authoritarian tradition within the league that reached almost cliché proportions in league images of the police. The numerous negative representations of police collectively demonstrate the dominant ideology among many league photographers working in the documentary tradition (most of whom passed through Grossman's workshops or influence). Seen individually, the images might provoke some mild interest in light of the increasingly repressive legislation enacted in midcentury America; seen together, they forcefully demonstrate why, during this era, the league (and, especially, Grossman himself) was perceived as "progressive," or even threatening to mainstream American values. Police figures are often faceless and depersonalized, shot from extreme angles so that they loom menacingly over other figures (often striking workers). Such photographs of policemen undermine traditional, positive ideals of the men hired to implement the laws of the land. Officers become metaphors for a larger concept—authoritarian control of the masses through coercion and, sometimes, intimidation.

One early image by Ben Shahn (who later became a league supporter), *Sheriff during Strike, Morgantown, West Virginia*, 1935, humorously denounced the social hypocrisy of certain American political structures working to cripple the labor movement. Shahn was certainly known by Grossman; he was a peripheral associate (or "fellow traveler") of the league who, throughout its later years, consistently voiced his support of the organization (he attended the league meeting held immediately after the listing). Shahn, sympathetic to labor movements throughout his career, shot the image on his first photographic trip for the federally funded Resettlement Administration / Farm Security Administration (RA / FSA), which employed Shahn from 1935 to 1938.

This photograph illustrates the clear alliance in artistic ideals between the FSA and the Photo League—both organizations that exemplified the moral imperative of the socially conscious documentary photographer. With such emphasis on content, formal issues took a backseat. As Shahn would reflect in 1944, FSA photographers "had only one purpose—a moral one I suppose. So we decided: no angle shots, no filters, no mats, nothing glossy but paper . . . We tried to present the ordinary in an extraordinary manner. But that's a paradox because the only thing extraordinary about it was that it was so ordinary. Nobody had ever done it before, deliberately. Now it's called documentary [photography]. . . . We just took pictures that cried out to be taken."[28]

Shahn snapped a faceless, hence depersonalized, officer leaning against a mailbox while truncated figures and objects of the street surround him. He accentuated the man's broad backside by placing his camera close to the sheriff's gun and buttocks. Shahn has literally turned the policeman into an "ass" with a weapon, visually undermining any hallowed notions of noble police protection. From the title, we also know the policeman is watching striking workers, so that the symbolism refers to the potential suppression of the labor movement and fascist control of the masses. In 1935, many badly needed prolabor, New Deal proposals were enacted; in that year, for instance, the National Labor Relations Board was established to prevent any unfair labor practices by unions or employees, and the Social Security Act was introduced, providing unemployment compensation. Yet, such federal relief programs, encouraged during the Depression by FDR, caused the national debt to skyrocket, making many politicians wary of such support. Furthermore, labor unions were often associated with subversive activity, specifically Communism. Shahn's partisan, prolabor image demonstrates the documentary spirit that Grossman, and many others in the Photo League admired.

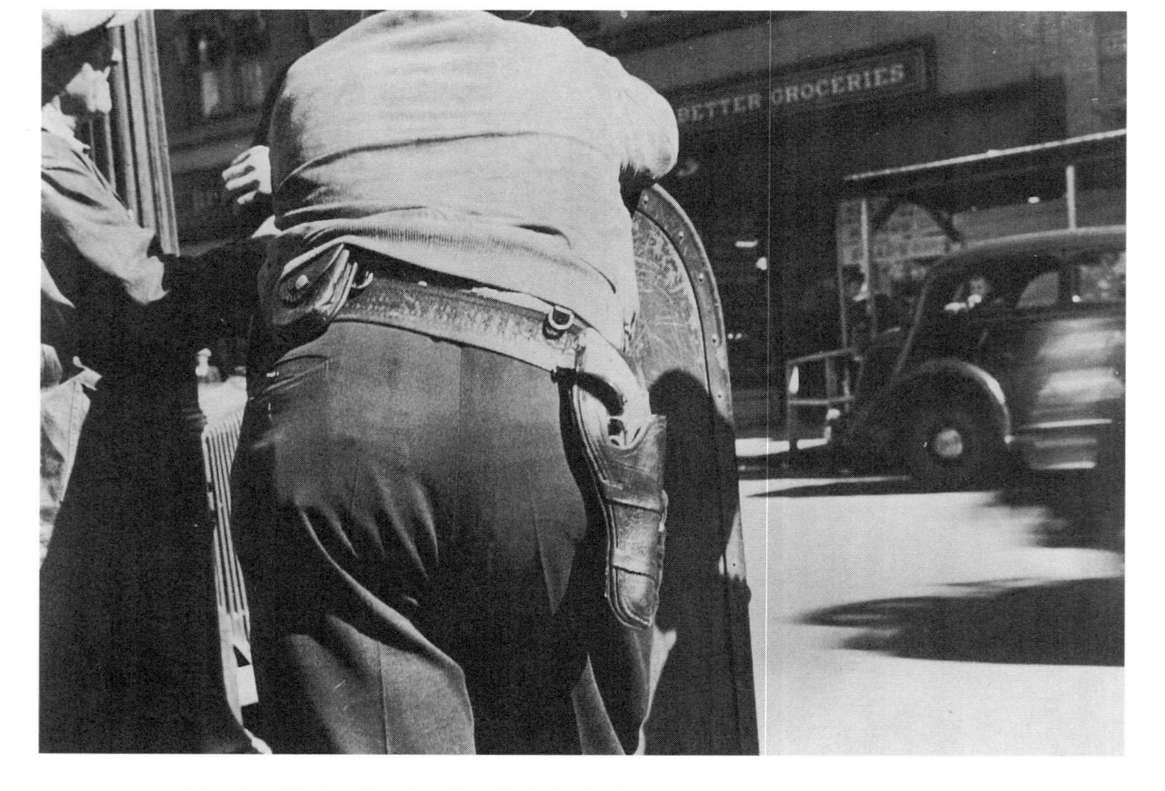

2.4. Ben Shahn, *Untitled (Sheriff during Strike, Morgantown, West Virginia), 1935.*

Ben Shahn was a painter, FSA photographer, and supporter of the Photo League. His often caustic and clearly prolabor imagery during the Depression exemplifies social documentary ideals. Courtesy of the Fogg Art Museum, Harvard University Art Museums. Gift of Bernarda Bryson Shahn.

In 1940, league member Joe Schwartz photographed *New York's Finest.* Within the elongated rectangular frame, we see the backside of a horse with an armed, uniformed rider. The low vantage point emphasizes the large haunches of the horse, leaving its head and front half obscured. On the left the photograph is framed by the columnar length of a man's backside and long coat; to the right stands a long line of sightseers watching a May Day parade against a towering backdrop of buildings and signs. Directly above the policeman on horseback, a sign reads "New York's Finest! Golden Crust Bread Fresh-Sliced!" The pun, connecting the police force with the commercial rhetoric of bread, undermines the power and omnipotence of police forces (as did the photographer's original title, *Horse's Ass, May Day*). The policeman, as with Shahn's image, is presented from behind, faceless and iconic; he is a looming, authoritarian force far larger than the background masses. Schwartz, in this brazen composition of helter-skelter street life, has visually and semantically unclothed the emperor. As the photographer noted, with laughter, "I was lucky there, I didn't get hit."[29]

Other league members also visually subverted American policemen and were leery of authoritarian figures in cold war America. In 1948, a year sandwiched between the listing and Calomiris's FBI testimony, Jerome Liebling created *Cop, Union Square Parade.* The square frame reveals, in the foreground and extremely close up, blurry views of two men in coats, one with a brimmed hat. They dominate two-thirds of the picture plane, their shapes generalized and out of focus. But just beyond them, perfectly in focus, we glimpse the familiar shape of an official police cap with insignia. No face, no body, no uniform is included. Beyond, the less focused architecture of Union Square fills the background against white sky. But the focus, gleaming and center, is the anonymous, faceless policeman's cap, facing the more formless masses to which we, through the photographer, belong. This image represents the repressive government authorities policing the public, authorities who could ruin lives and careers with the barest innuendo of suspicion provided by any source.

Liebling, a member of the league during the 1940s (who must have known Grossman and took classes with Strand), characterized his photography as "broad-ranging 'straight' photography emphasizing [its] ability to deal with meaningful recording of events in time." The vision in *Union Square* represents another "ordinary" moment in the lives of New Yorkers, yet, given the context of the times, it symbolizes the humanistic concerns in the tradition of earlier documentary photographers. As Naomi Rosenblum writes, "His camera lens has sought out the afflicted; he has photographed

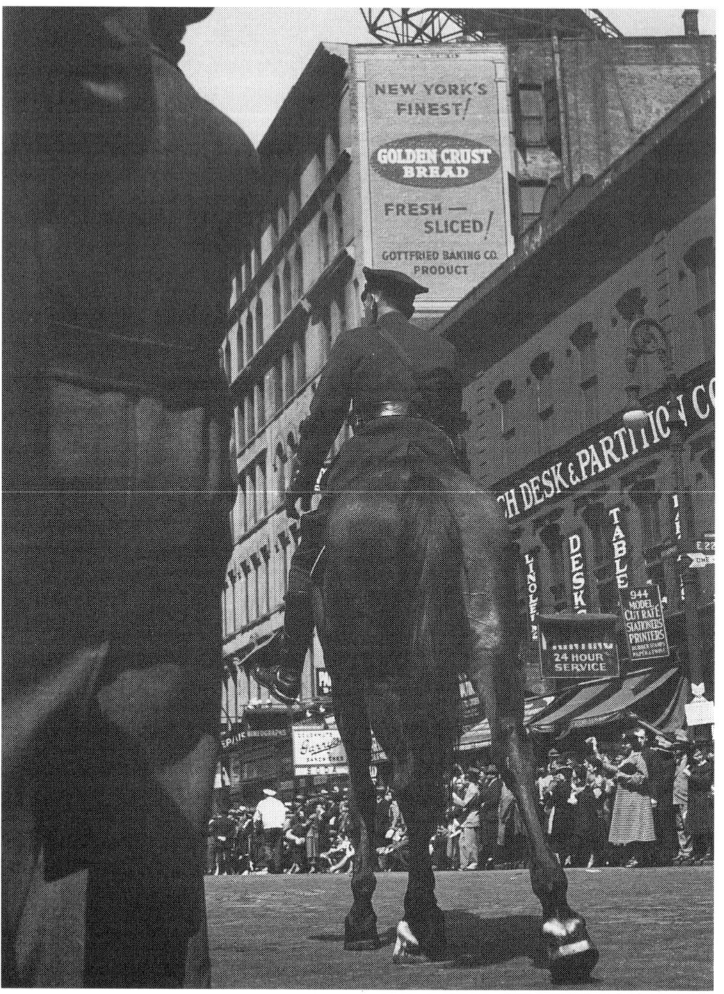

2.5. Joe Schwartz, *Horse's Ass, May Day* (or *New York's Finest*), *1940*.

Photo League member Joe Schwartz photographed this ironic image of an authoritarian police figure during a May Day parade in New York City. Courtesy Joe Schwartz.

individuals in unfathomable occupations and circumstances. . . . He uses his camera as a prod to complacency, impelling the comfortable viewer to face the unspeakable."[30]

In the March 1948 issue of *Photo Notes*, the same year Liebling shot his photograph, an article observed that two Photo League photographers, Danny Eisman and Joe Reynolds, covered a strike at the American Com-

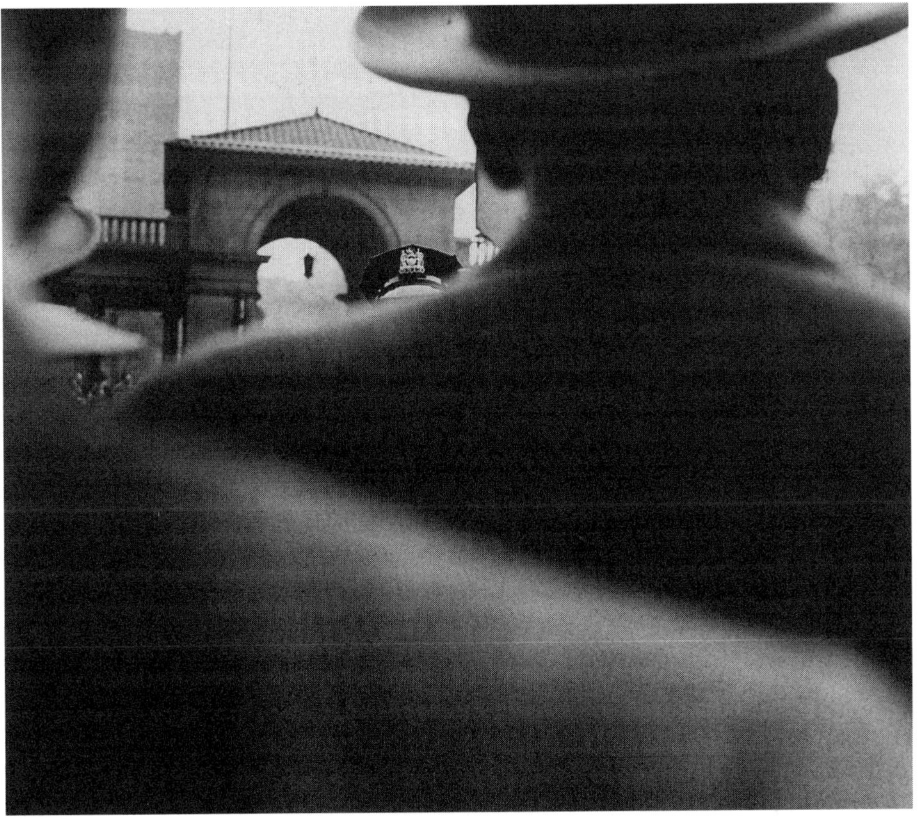

2.6. Jerome Liebling, *Cop, Union Square Parade,* 1948.

Jerome Liebling took classes at the Photo League during the 1940s; his photograph of a policeman's cap in Union Square (an active site of union agitation) creates a forceful metaphor of authoritarian control. © Jerome Liebling. Courtesy Howard Greenberg Gallery.

munications Association. The text disclosed the apprehension most league members felt toward the city police. When asked about their photographs of attending policemen at the strike, Eisman and Reynolds were quoted as saying that they did not talk to the "cops" until the second day of the strike—"sometimes it takes a cop that long to start behaving like a human being."[31] The derision and sarcasm toward the police are clear in the tone of this quotation. Liebling's image signifies a similar skepticism of the government's protective, controlling forces, a sentiment waning in acceptance during the cold war years, when "big brother" tactics dominated the machinations of the FBI and CIA.

Images of police frequently appeared in photographs of May Day events and further underscore league interest in documentary photography's capacity for evocative commentary on sociopolitical events. May Day has been celebrated as a traditional spring festival, but historically it has also been celebrated as a labor holiday.[32] Today few may remember the history leading to the celebration, but the association of May Day with labor activities was not lost on the FBI. According to Calomiris, May Day festivals and parades were a hot spot to find American Communists. During the events, she claimed she was asked by the party to photograph the festivals "for fear that the reactionary press would overlook it," but she was actually taking photographs for FBI officials. The bureau planted their own photographers at parades and collected pictures of May Day events in order to identify possibly subversive citizens.[33]

While Calomiris's testimony leaves much to be desired in the area of historical truth—considering her romantic visions of being a modern-day Mata Hari—it is difficult to doubt her words about FBI suspicions regarding the May Day festivals, since May Day had a decided historical association with labor, unions, and, following that progression, Communism. Morris Ernst and David Loth, in their *Report on the American Communist* (1952) warned readers of the tie between union activity and Communism: "The determined drive of the party to infiltrate and control key unions, which had been immeasurably strengthened by the Roosevelt New Deal, was the most successful effort Communists made in this country."[34] The mere documentation of May Day events, given the government's growing interest in leftist organizations and their participation in the festivals, illustrates a disaffected, even subversive, mood within the league.

For years, league members (as well as members of the its parent group, the Film and Photo League) photographed May Day events and typically focused on the police forces present to control the people. One typical early image, *May Day Parade* (1933), by an unknown photographer from the Film and Photo League, pictured the large form of a policeman on horseback obscuring the marching crowds beyond. The officer's form literally negates the masses so that only their placards are visible, with the words "Join the Picket Line" and "Fight Evictions." These signs demonstrate the labor and social reform interests of the crowd, although they are blocked and repressed, visually and metaphorically, by the policeman's form (a visual conceit Shahn employed as well).

Even Siskind's early work illustrates the documentary photographer's interest in symbolically communicating the power of the police at such labor celebrations. Siskind made photographs of the 1932 May Day parade just prior to formally joining the Film and Photo League. A number of his parade photographs were included in the league exhibition "America Today" (1933). As Carl Chiarenza notes of this work by Siskind, "many of [the May Day photographs] constitute the most direct propaganda he would ever produce." In one image, Siskind composed a long line of protesters carrying placards, with mounted policemen dominating the picture plane. Again, the officer in the foreground has been visually truncated so that only the massive horse's body, saddle, and dangling stirrups remain—just enough to signify "the power and authority that maintain order."[35] Another mounted official stands to the left, blocking the view of the parade participants. The background masses are visually and symbolically smaller than the forces surrounding them, although the group seems to trail endlessly into visual infinity. Further demonstrating the labor interests of the May Day Parade, the text of one placard clearly reads, "The Finnish Revolutionary Workers" and is placed centrally between the belly and foreleg of the horse. Siskind would later eschew such overtly political art so embraced within the early Photo League, but he disclosed, in this image, his strong roots in the documentary tradition, along with his own early acceptance of leftist political views.

The police and May Day parade photographs reveal a caustic, critical attitude on the part of league photographers toward authoritarian or potentially fascist figures in society, not only during the cold war years but also even earlier during the Depression. Even Strand, so associated today with aesthetics and modernism, accompanied league members to rallies and demonstrations rich with photographic opportunities. Many at the league, especially through the teaching of Grossman, were coached to concentrate on the proletariat human figure. Grossman and others collectively valued an art that could, ideally, visually educate and excite viewers on what Dan Weiner called "the central issues of our day"—such as May Day, labor reform, ethnicity, and racism, all of which were often at odds with mainstream cold war policies.[36] While the league fostered a diverse membership with varying shades of political affiliation, *Photo Notes* texts, subsequent interviews with members, and the majority of league work demonstrate that the overwhelming majority of league members were socialist, Marxist, or left-leaning humanists dedicated to the tradition of documentary photography and its concomitant ideals.

Grossman's career and pedagogical influence were interrupted by World War II, when he was shipped to Central America to work in photo labs for the U.S. Army Air Corps (1945–46). When Grossman was inducted into the army in March, 1943, the Army Intelligence Bureau investigated his political activities during his station at Atlantic City, New Jersey. According to Cohen, the army was leery of Grossman's loyalty to this country and interviewed him concerning his alleged Communist activity when he joined. During that interview he told curious interrogators that the league had stopped advertising in the *Daily Worker* in 1939—although evidence proves otherwise, as Fiona Dejardin notes.[37] Although he was eager to join the army and fight in Europe, from 1945 through 1946 he was stationed in Panama with the Air Force Public Relations Section.

Under surveillance even as a low-ranking corporal, during these years in South America Grossman's documentary aesthetics became more and more radical as he experimented with the effects of black-and-white printing, creating dynamic forms of local figures. In his own leisure time, Grossman photographed not only in Panama but also in Guatemala and the Galapagos Islands. One image of a jumping girl (1945), demonstrates Grossman's interest in pushing beyond the clear, focused "realism" of the documentary photographic tradition by allowing his camera to blur a figure in motion—here a smiling, barefoot girl in meager dress. The resultant grit and grain of the print enhances the image's mood, blending his documentary philosophy with a new, complex aesthetic. While the image focuses on another "have-not" in society, it would not, in all likelihood, be endorsed by the Communist Party, given its distortion of the figure, radical aesthetics, and narrative ambiguity concerning class issues. But this specific image was very important to Grossman; he made so many prints of it that he damaged its negative.

Such experiments related to his own exploration of camera technology. For instance, whereas he had used large-negative film and tripod cameras in the 1930s and early 1940s, he began experimenting with smaller cameras in the war years which allowed him more freedom of movement. During his stay in Central America he photographed with both a 4 x 5-inch Speed Graphic and an old 9 x 12 Voightlander, using them like the more portable and flexible 35mm cameras. He photographed the Black Christ Festival (Porto Bello, Panama, 1945) with a glaring flash as well, creating moody, almost abstracted images of seething crowds full of religious fervor.[38]

Graininess during this time (and even more so during the 1950s) was described by then editor of *Popular Photography* Arthur Goldsmith as a "hot issue" among photographers. Copious articles within the pages of that magazine also attest to the controversy concerning a photographer's deliberate inclusion of visible grain. While some photographers felt a print should be clearly focused and pristine (in the tradition of large-format camera aesthetics), others were experimenting with what Arthur Goldsmith calls a "freer, fresher style." However, he also notes that readers of *Popular Photography* "hated it" and considered graininess an artistic insult.[39] Goldsmith

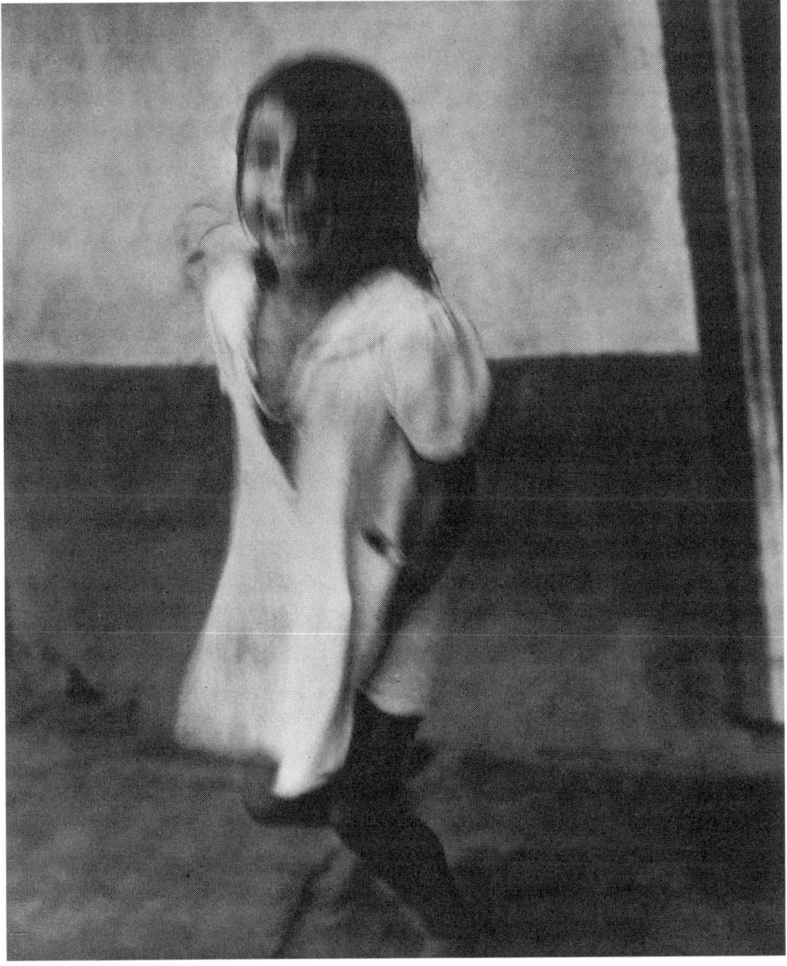

2.7. Sid Grossman, *Jumping Girl,* ca. 1945.

After his induction into the army in 1943, Sid Grossman was investigated by the Army Intelligence Bureau. Stationed in Panama with the Sixth Army Air Force's Public Relations Section in 1945 and 1946, he photographed local citizens' lives in Panama and Guatemala, developing an increasingly radical and abstract style. © Miriam Cohen. Courtesy Howard Greenberg Gallery.

credits this interest in rawer imagery among photographers to the tradition of war photography (in which photographers pushed their film to the limits, without the aid of a flash), the influence of Cartier-Bresson and European photography, and a reaction, especially during the 1950s, against pictorialism. While the inherent possibilities of 35mm aesthetics—grain, available light, and blur—have been credited as beginning in earnest in the 1950s with artists such as Robert Frank and William Klein, many league photographers (such as Grossman, Libsohn, and Rudy Burckhardt, among others) were already pursuing this style in the 1940s. Many found that graininess could visually impart a sense of realism; a feeling of immediacy ("you are there"), as evidenced in much recent war photography. The aesthetics of grain and blur maximized the visual (and emotional) impact in Grossman's work by communicating instantaneity.[40]

After Grossman returned to the United States, he enjoyed a productive period in his career as freelance assignments increased. Between 1946 and 1948, he photographed several series concerning, among other subjects, Coney Island, Mulberry Street, folk singers, and the American Legion. Of the series, only the one on folk singers was commercial work; the rest consisted primarily of New York street scenes, focusing especially on the lives of Italian Americans.[41]

According to Vestal, Grossman borrowed a 35mm camera to photograph *Mulberry Street (San Gennaro Festival)*, 1948. This annual street festival, held in Little Italy each September to mark the feast day of San Gennaro, patron saint of Naples, was visited by many a photographer seeking lively street scenes.[42] Grossman's images of the 1948 festival illustrate his radical use of 35mm technology. In this photograph, he dramatically accentuated existing light so that the image emphasizes tonal contrasts in the dark exterior of a New York street. Truncated figures crowd the tilted space, alive with active line and light. It is difficult for our eyes to rest or find any traditional focal point as we view the cacophony of a fleeting moment, characterizing life, movement, and vitality. Characteristically, too, images such as this illustrated non-WASP lives: those of Italian Americans, in this case, who maintain a sense of the old country in the midst of a dominant Anglo-American culture. The "other," those marginalized ethnic groups (reminiscent of Grossman's own Jewish background), becomes visually charged and vibrantly alive. The image is not a conventional, picturesque cliché of Italian "peasant" life, but it creates instead a near abstraction of movement and activity. Grossman succeeded in pushing the documentary tradition into modernist aesthetic territory, combining people-oriented content with daring uses of angles, viewpoints, surfaces, and light.

Some of Grossman's most-reproduced images are those in his Coney Island series (1947–48). In these photographs Grossman's off-kilter perspective and radical truncation of figures illustrates his seeming disregard for traditional composition. He used a large-reflex camera at close range and

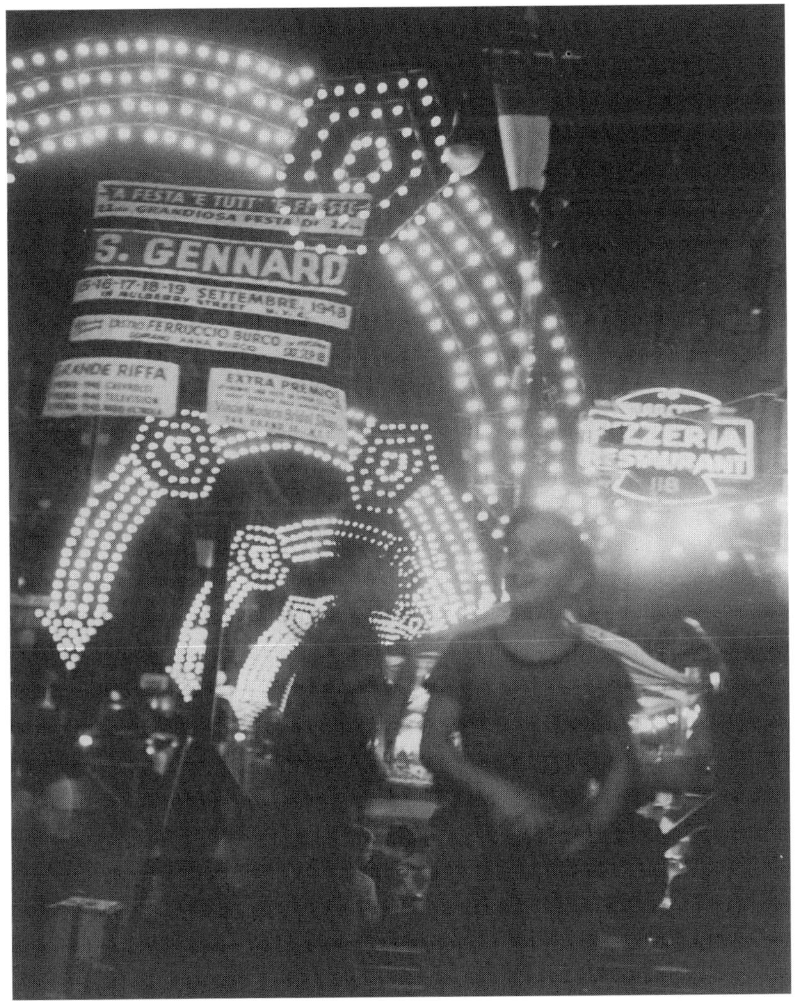

2.8. Sid Grossman, *Mulberry Street (San Gennaro Festival), 1948.*

Little Italy's San Gennaro festivals on Mulberry Street were a popular place for documentary photographers to find exciting visual opportunities. Sid Grossman's images of the 1948 festival, some of his first experiments in 35mm technology, demonstrate his radical truncation of figures and tilting point of view. © Miriam Cohen, Metropolitan Museum of Art. Purchase, the Horace W. Goldsmith Foundation Gift, 1990.

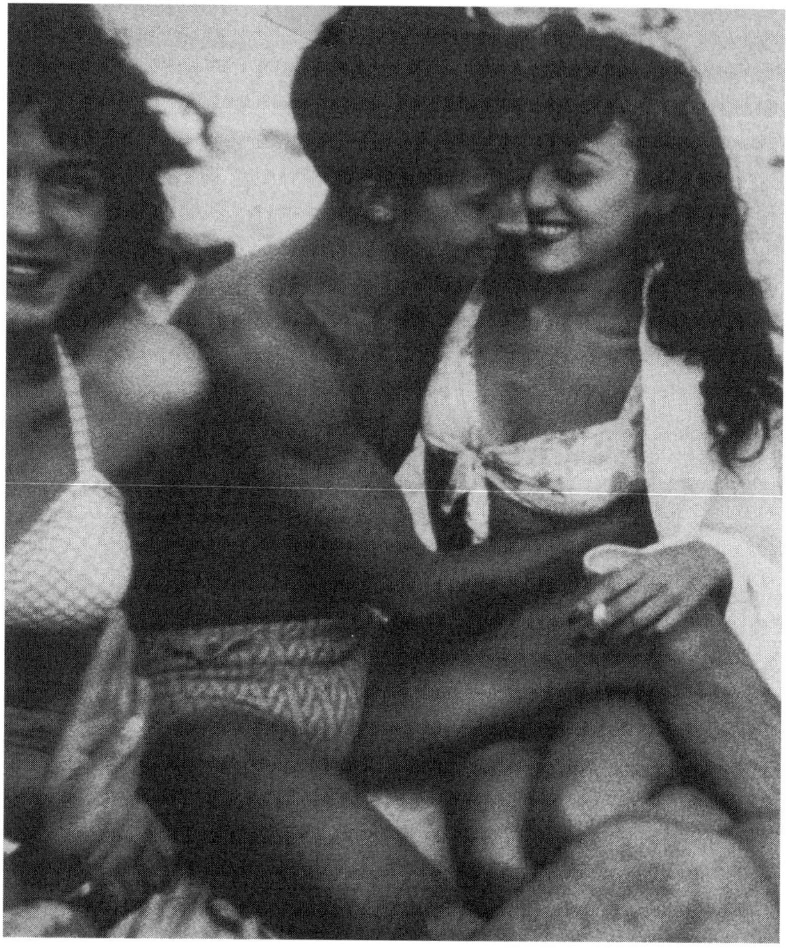

2.9. Sid Grossman, *Coney Island,* 1947–48.

Sid Grossman's photographs from the Coney Island series are among his strongest and most daring images; the radical perspectives and cropping of figures created energetically blurred and dramatically charged depictions of youth. © Miriam Cohen. Courtesy Howard Greenberg Gallery.

eye-level, in the manner of a 35mm camera, creating snapshotlike compositions of entwined figures. Vestal reports that Grossman called these resulting "blasted" forms "explosive shapes." Young people clad in bathing suits become a dramatic, energetic blur of tangled bodies with sexual overtones—hands touch skin, figures embrace and collide, while cigarettes and ecstatic smiles with white teeth punctuate shaded areas. Grossman tightened the claustrophobic borders even further by cropping the negatives he printed. Coney Island bathers, piled upon one another, become bacchanalian in their pursuit of leisure and their escape from the city and work. Miriam Grossman Cohen points out that Grossman "loved these kids" and would say "kind things" about them while printing their images. Their sensual and natural vitality celebrated youth and freedom. As Grossman said, "A photograph is not merely a substitute for a glance. It is a sharpened vision. It is the revelation of new and important facts."[43]

The sexual overtones within these images, combined with the growing societal concern for delinquent youth, provides us with a "sharpened vision" of this aspect of postwar America. A decade later, Paul Goodman would address the issue of youth in his book *Growing Up Absurd*, disparaging the alienation most American youth felt from their own country, especially as workers. He quotes the New York Governor's statement in the *New York Times* (1959) after several juvenile murders had been committed: "We have to constantly devise new ways to bring about a challenge to these young folks and to provide an outlet for their energies and give them a sense of belonging."[44] In the following decades, public concern over the seemingly wanton behavior of American youth and gang criminality would escalate into a far more serious challenge to the country. Not only do Grossman's Coney Island photographs point to daring formal issues of composition, but their subject matter also discloses a supposedly libidinous, smoking, "shameless" youth culture that many would discuss, and come to fear, in the 1950s.

Many of Grossman's students internalized and practiced Grossman's brand of documentary photography, inspired by his example. Arthur Leipzig took only two classes at the league—one with Grossman in 1942 and another with Strand in 1946—but he remained a member of the league until 1949. This exposure to documentary vision profoundly influenced his work; he has written that just two weeks into the class with Grossman, "I knew what I wanted to be"—a photographer "concerned mainly with exploring the human condition and human relationships." Grossman not only educated Leipzig in the ways of photography but also sent him to MoMA three times to expose him to ways of seeing. After Leipzig's third trip, Grossman finally told him, "Now we can begin to work."[45]

Leipzig's own background was similar to Grossman's; he had been born in Brooklyn, the grandson of immigrants, and grew up in an Orthodox Jewish household. He would also encounter the difficulties of working in a cold war climate. He was offered a job at International News Photos, a Hearst business, and for a Harlem project he was asked to photograph white students only. True to the league ideals instilled in him, Leipzig balked at such demands and photographed racially mixed groups, and as a result he was fired.[46]

Although Leipzig excelled at photographing urban children, he also turned his camera to other subjects, including the wealthy society typically ignored by the Photo League photographers. The rare images of the upper classes by league members, such as Leipzig's, were typically presented in a facetious and even sarcastic manner, visualizing the conspicuous wealth of pretentious subjects attending the opera or D.A.R. meetings. Leipzig continued the documentary tradition with new and surprising subjects centering on class, another testimony to Grossman's ability to inspire individual responses to his lessons.

Grossman's own appreciation for, and belief in, the documentary photographer's sense of social mission, as a voice of the people, was clearly conveyed in a review he wrote in the November 1947 issue of *Photo Notes* (one month before the Attorney General's listing). He reported on Edward Steichen's first exhibition since becoming director of the Photography Department at MoMA, "Three Young Photographers Exhibit." The three chosen photographers, Leonard McCombe, Homer Page, and Wayne Miller, photographed, in Grossman's eyes, "the most important aspects of people's lives." McCombe, "undoubtedly the most successful" of the group, with his images of the postwar "chaos" in Europe at the time:

> gives us in a dozen pictures, a heart-breaking reminder that a large part of the population of this world has been going through misery and a complete breakdown of their lives for many years—a reality difficult for most Americans to comprehend. . . . I get a feeling that it must be almost impossible for human personality to survive, for people to retain their sanity in this world. There seems to be no element of human security in any sense. . . . How can people have any faith at all in the value of living when there is nothing but misery—where there is no hope in sight of a direction for their lives—of a place to live, of a place to work, and of a coherent society in which they can take their place as individuals.[47]

Grossman valued McCombe's success in making him, the viewer, feel for the human condition portrayed. Seeing the images provoked Grossman's political insight and curiosity concerning the homes, work, and general security for the lives presented. Such a personal, emotional response signified artistic success to Grossman—because the images succeeded in forcing the viewer to empathize with the subjects' desperate ordeals.

Page's images of World War I Legionnaires in the MoMA show prompted Grossman to write, "I don't feel very secure for the future," a criticism echoing his concern for the subjects in McCombe's work. The specific image by

Page he was referring to involved a "boy" returning from the war and being "given the phony gladhand. . . . an attitude of 'how can we use this guy most effectively—how can we get him in.' It's a disgusting spectacle!" Grossman's dissatisfaction with the presentation of America's venerated war veterans (to him, self-serving reactionaries), combined with his sympathy for the dispossessed in Europe, led to his appreciation for photographs that pricked his leftist heart. Again, too, he demanded to be moved as a viewer, provoked into disgust, sadness, or action. Page's images, as loathsome as the content was to Grossman, had "a powerful impact because they are so alarming."

In contrast to Grossman's philosophy, Paul Strand, according to Rosenblum, "provided another dimension." While most amateur photographers in America were practicing an "out-of-date pictorialism," Rosenblum remembers, league workers were more interested in documenting "our desperate time. . . . It may be crude to say that for us art was a 'weapon,' but we hoped to strike back at a system that denied us jobs and a decent way of life." For Grossman, "the story was the important focus . . . the formal control, the sense of architecture, the aesthetics of print quality and color, were of lesser significance." However, Strand's classes and lectures at the league provided "a less doctrinaire view" and made students more aware of philosophical and aesthetic possibilities. Even so, according to Rosenblum, "a small, intractable faction" in the league regarded Strand's ideas and images as "escapist." This faction, influenced by Soviet Andrey Zhdanov's views of formalism, he wrote, questioned the purposes and values of photographing "cobwebs" when people were out of work and suffering. Miriam Grossman Cohen and others remember a cell of committed Communists at the league dedicated to agitation propaganda; but even at the organization's height, with more than two hundred members, they never numbered, she estimates, more than twenty-five.[48]

Narrow views of art with a social mission irritated Strand, who felt the true, intelligent artist could combine social ideals with formal complexity. Rosenblum credits Strand (in contrast or, perhaps, complementary to Grossman) with leading the photo league:

> beyond our limited experiences, to show us that there was more to life than the tribulations of living on the Lower East Side. . . . [but] he was certainly not an escapist. . . . The relationship of subject matter to form and philosophical content had been Strand's concern ever since Lewis Hine [Strand's teacher] had introduced him to Alfred Stieglitz at 291. If the term 'documentary photography' was to have any precise meaning, he said, it involved the relationship of the photographer to his environment. But its weakness was the tendency to rely entirely

> upon human interest while ignoring basic aesthetic problems. . . . He made it his business to see that the concerned photographers of that era were involved with the picture as well as the cause.[49]

Grossman is not remembered by league members as a champion of formalism, as is Strand, who sought balance between content and aesthetics. Grossman, especially in the early years, stressed the more traditional documentary approach, emphasizing humanistic content, even though his work proves his own technical and aesthetic sophistication. According to Tucker, Grossman "found Strand's prints too precious and his emphasis on print quality when teaching disproportionate to other values." Their ways of presenting finished works further underscore their differences: Grossman's photographs were mounted flush to Masonite board without frames or glass, while Strand's images were mounted on clean, white board with large borders framing the photograph (in the tradition of Stieglitz and "fine art" photography).[50] That the league had two such strong voices representing the possible ranges within photographic expression demonstrates the dynamic atmosphere students were exposed to.

Grossman, however, was director of the league's school. Beaumont Newhall's article "Two Schools," in the fall 1948 issue of *Photo Notes*, obliquely addressed Grossman's leadership and artistic values. The article also hinted at the changing, more broadly defined aesthetic climate within American photography of the late 1940s, when Grossman's (and the league's) brand of social realism went more and more out of fashion. In this review of a league exhibition of student work by the Department of Photography of the California School of Fine Arts and the Photo League School, Newhall noted the "air of friendly rivalry" between the two programs and, like most viewers he overheard at the show, noticed the differences more than the similarities between the two. Both schools' works were "rooted in reality," not "airless compositions, escapist sentimentalities, nor mere surface patterns," yet, in California the students attended classes full time for three years while the league, accommodating workers, offered only night sessions for shorter periods of time. Newhall's implication was that in California, photographic studies were taken more seriously, in the manner of other modern degree programs.

Newhall then compared the different instructors, Grossman representing the league and Minor White representing California. As with Ansel Adams, Newhall explained, White "demands first a thorough grounding in basic mechanics of the photographic process, on the sound theory that the tool must be mastered before it can be used with full efficiency as a medium of expression." While the California students exhibited an increased technical sophistication, Newhall continued, "the stamp of personality was missing." His hope for White's students included increased use of the miniature camera so as to "experiment more boldly," and to follow Edward Weston and Ansel Adams less literally. The league pictures Newhall credited with "more life, variety, and interest," although league members' technical levels were far below those of White's students. But then, he added, the problems faced by league students were greater: "The Photo League students take their cameras anywhere; they often push the process to technical limits. All of them feel people more strongly than nature; they want to tell us about New York and some of the people who live there. . . . there was almost a sense of desperation in the desire to convey messages of sociological import. Messages are needful, and we have learned that many of the most needful can be imparted more effectively with the camera than by any other medium." However, Newhall pointed out, other subjects "can be wonderfully said through photography." Perhaps he was tired of seeing the same old league content—the downtrodden on New York streets—as Newhall did credit the Californians with "nearly" approaching the "poetic." He said the New Yorkers, however, "have followed too closely the documentary photographer."[51]

Newhall appreciated the strong technical and formal capacities of the California school (as he did Strand's work) and called for "poetics" in photography, that is, a personal, formal approach more in tune with concurrent abstract expressionist ideals than with FSA political idealism. In this review, published almost one year after the league's blacklisting, Grossman's humanist emphasis on the documentation of people's lives was clearly positioned as contrary and, to some degree, inferior to the formalism of the West Coast school. As head of instruction at the league, Grossman was seen by Newhall as a symbolic leader of the league's interest in the documentary tradition (or, as Rosenblum called him, "a leading light at the Photo League").[52]

Minor White's work and artistic interests would prove the more influential in the next two decades of photography. In 1946 White met and was profoundly influenced by Alfred Stieglitz. White was also well educated in various philosophies (including Zen Buddhism, Gestalt psychology, and Gurdjieff) and felt, according to the rules of modernism, that the artist was involved in a task both sacred and spiritual. By 1947 he was creating series, or "sequences," of intensely personal, more formally engaged images, often with Zen-inspired titles and little to no narrative content.

Like Grossman, White, in 1939, had worked for the WPA (though as a photographer in Oregon, not a pick-and-shovel man in New York City) and also became a tremendous pedagogical influence on many photography students' lives (he taught from 1940 through the early 1970s). But White was far more formally educated than was Grossman; he had studied aesthetics and art history with Meyer Schapiro at Columbia University and had worked with the Newhalls at MoMA. He joined the faculty at the California School of Fine Arts in 1946, developing friendships there with Ansel Adams (who headed the school's photography department) and Edward Weston.[53] In the 1950s, his magazine, *Aperture*, founded in 1952, one year after the demise of the Photo League, would replace *Photo Notes* as the major photography publication in midcentury America. Like Strand's presence, White's career (with his emphasis on mysticism and the sacred, personal quest of artists) creates a polemical foil to Grossman's ideals. Increasingly during the late 1940s and early 1950s, Grossman's documentary-oriented position was questioned and, often, rejected, moving humanist ideology more into the domain of photojournalism, not "fine art" photography. Not surprisingly, given the political repercussions of Grossman's brand of social documentary work, White's aesthetic ideology would win the photographic cold war.[54]

Grossman, unlike White, suffered specific attacks within the political climate fostered by Senators Dondero and McCarthy. The 1947 listing of the league was shocking enough to members, but even more sobering was Calomiris's naming Grossman as an active, recruiting Communist in 1949. Grossman's was not even an important name within the context of the testimony—Calomiris was brought as a witness to testify against prominent Communist Party leaders before Judge Harold R. Medina. As Tucker points out, in over a week of testimony, the league was mentioned by her only twice. But even once was enough to effectively condemn the organization, and Grossman, as "Un-American."[55]

During her testimony as a paid informant for the FBI, Calomiris named Grossman as the person who had introduced her to the Communist Party and identified the league as a "front" organization. This accusation prevented Grossman from obtaining most freelance jobs.[56] His name appeared in several *New York Times* articles reporting the trials. The April 27, 1949, article, "Girl Aide of FBI Testifies of Seven Years as 'Communist,'" reported on the "new surprise witness," Calomiris, "who has a studio at 9½ Jane Street" and "specializes in animal pictures." Her work, as seen in a collection Howard Greenberg acquired, includes not only poorly printed animal and human portraits but also photographs of various union activities, crowded street scenes of May Day parades, and public events, which the FBI could use to identify potential revolutionaries; her shorthand notes on the backs of such images also testify to her secret mission. After testifying about the party's organization and endorsement of "violent" revolutionary practices, she identified four of the defendants in the trial, who were being tried for conspiracy to overthrow and possibly destroy the United States (although no overt or specific revolutionary act was cited).[57]

Calomiris, "a slight young woman with black cropped hair and an air of quiet composure," as the article described her, was also caricatured by figurative painter Alice Neel in a 1949 ink drawing Neel produced while she attended the trials. Neel recollects: "I did this wonderful drawing of Angela Calomaris [sic], who gave anti-Communist lectures on the radio. She was the stool pigeon. Medina treated her with kid gloves. At the trial they brought out the fact that Calomaris had been arrested for something in New England, but it wasn't anything like speeding. It was moral turpitude, I think. She looked just like a man, an Italian man with a hat with a little feather in it. The drawing is a marvelous satire."[58] Indeed, in the unsympathetic drawing Calomiris is transformed into a decapitated head on a wooden block, her dark features masculinized.

Neel drew another caricature of Judge Medina, which, she claimed, was reproduced in both *Masses* and *Mainstream* in 1949. Neel was no stranger to the difficulties artists such as social documentary photographers encountered during the cold war. Neel had moved to New York City in 1932; by 1933 she was employed by the Public Works Art Project and, in 1935, the WPA's Federal Art Project, Easel Division. Her paintings from this period reflect, as her biographer Patricia Hills notes, social realist concerns "about the devastating effects of the Depression on urban living." In the 1950s, Hills writes, Neel "painted older Communists, labor leaders, and community organizers at a time when it was not merely unfashionable but even professionally dangerous to do so." By then she was no longer a Communist but was still friendly with current members and read the *Daily Worker*. Her memories, like her drawings, of the 1949 trials demonstrate her strong disapproval of the government's hounding of Communist Party members: "It wasn't for doing anything. It was just for thought." The hyprocrisy of these trials irritated her into the 1980s; for instance, Judge Medina, Neel said in a much later interview, "owned a lot of slum houses. When they evicted the poor people and put their effects on the sidewalk, the Communists would carry them back in. So Medina just hated Communists."[59]

Neel's "masculinization" of Calomiris may not have been accidental. In personal interviews, a number of sources allude to the possibility that the FBI "had something" on Calomiris, some positing it was her lesbianism. Although there is no proof, some today maintain that the FBI had threatened to expose her and levy a "moral's charge" unless she agreed to spy and testify for them. There are instances, chronicled in *New York Times* articles, when

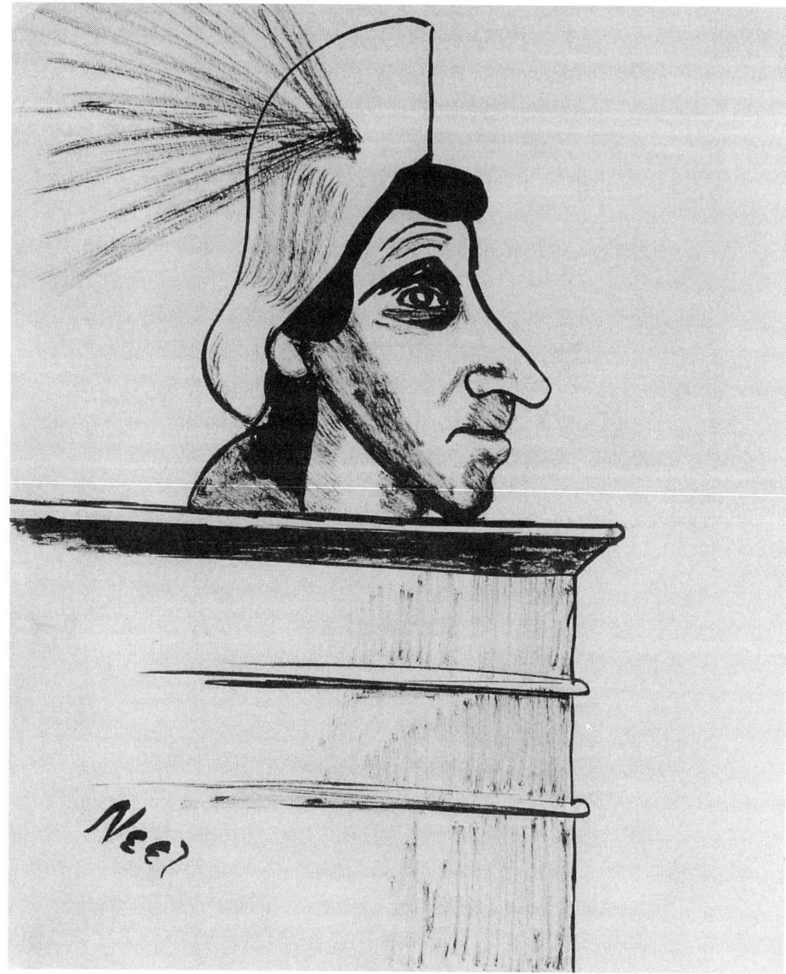

2.10. Alice Neel, *Angela Calomiris*, ink on paper, 1949.

Painter Alice Neel attended the 1949 anti-Communist trials in New York; Angela Calomiris, who testified that the Photo League was a Communist front organization and that Sid Grossman had introduced her to the Communist Party, was wickedly caricatured by an unsympathetic Neel. The Estate of Alice Neel, courtesy Robert Miller Gallery.

Judge Medina, who would not allow attempts to "discredit" his witness, stopped the defense council short of questioning Calomiris about her personal life, marital status, or lack of children. For instance: Medina stopped defense council Louis McCabe (of Philadelphia) from "a line of questioning that ended in asking the witness, who is unmarried, whether she had any children. 'No Sir,' replied the young woman, leaning forward and looking steadily at the cross-examiner. 'I think counsel should be admonished about this line of questioning,' said Edward C. Wallace of government council. 'It is the kind of thing I don't like to see,' said Judge Medina." Later, Russell Porter reported that Judge Medina again admonished defense counsel "for misrepresenting her testimony and other evidence at the trial, and again for attempts to smear her character with 'insinuations' unsupported by evidence." The irony, of course, to contemporary readers, is Medina's insistence on evidence and fair treatment when no such courtesy was extended to groups like the Photo League when blacklisted or named in court procedings.[60]

Neel's disgust toward Calomiris was not unusual; her testimony had made her a hated figure among many league members, especially in light of the generous treatment Grossman had offered her as a student. After the listing and naming, Grossman's career disintegrated, while Calomiris, Miriam Cohen recalls, was escorted to enviable job interviews at prestigious magazines by FBI agents. Cohen also remembers hearing that editor John Morris, at the *Ladies' Home Journal*, kicked the agents and Calomiris out of his office with disgust because of her background as an informant. More recently, another league source actually beamed with glee when told of Calomiris's death.[61]

Calomiris's work for the FBI destroyed the league and kept her very busy during these cold war years as an informant. Her testimony appeared in several *New York Times* articles in the following months as her undercover participation in Communist activities was investigated: "Witness Parries Red Trial Thrusts" (April 30, 1949); "Witness Swears Communists Set Up Wallace Party in 1947" (May 3, 1949); "New FBI Witness at Red Trial Here" (May 4, 1949); and "Communist Trial in Its 24th Week" (June 28, 1949), among others. Disclosed details in her testimony include not only specific names associated with Communism but also party organization and training tactics. One Communist lecturer she named, Frances Franklin, "taught the necessity of violent revolution to put socialism into effect."[62] During the trials, one *New York Times* reporter wrote, she listed the organizations "in which she attended meeings and reported to the FBI on 'the activities of persons I knew to be Communist': The American Federation of Labor, Congress of Industrial Organizations, Congress of American Women, American Labor party, Progressive party, International Workers Order, Greeks for Democratic Action, United Office and Professsional Workers of America, CIO, Joint Anti-Fascist Refugee Committtee, Photo League and the Jefferson School for Social Sciences."[63]

A year later, Calomiris detailed her experiences with the league (which she called "informal, friendly, and very badly run") and Grossman (whose name she changed to "Joe") in her book, *Red Masquerade: Undercover for the FBI*:

> Joe [Sid Grossman] ruled us students with an iron hand. We were afraid of his sarcasm but we all respected his ability. I've never known him to hold a job, although he was an excellent photographer. He had the moral drop on us because he wasn't afraid of the things that bothered us. His attitude was: to hell with the world if it "don't realise how good I am." Although I didn't realise it at the time, Joe was a typical Communist. He loved to tell how he allegedly saw his own mother starve to death before his eyes. Joe never gave any details about this family misfortune except to blame it on the "system."[64]

Her accounts read like immature right-wing propaganda, with upstanding, well-meaning FBI agents warning her of the dangers of her mission. "'Golly,'" Calomiris wrote, "'do you mean to say that the communists would get back at me by telling people that I was a communist, too?' It dawned on me that I might spend the rest of my life explaining that I was *not* a communist."[65]

This book earned Calomiris a spot entitled "Talk with Miss Calomiris" in the *New York Times Book Review* (November 26, 1950), which included her self-portrait. The review introduced readers to Calomiris, noting her small stature, her style of speech, her age (34), and other biographical items. Like Grossman, Calomiris claimed to have lived most of her life on the Lower East Side and said that she had (Greek) immigrant parents. "We were poor," the reporter recorded her as saying, "I was, I suppose, a so-called 'underprivileged' kid, but I'll tell you I didn't know I was underprivileged." When asked how she came to work as an undercover FBI agent, she recalled her membership in the Photo League in 1942: "Many of the boys in the league made no bones about their communism. They'd try to recruit me. But I kind of felt, live and let live. Everybody was on the bandwagon. After a week of thinking over the FBI job I said I would. I was recruited by the party soon after. And one week later I became executive secretary of the Photo League. Imagine! Before that I was nobody."[66] At the end of the interview, the reporter asked Calomiris about her own photography, and in the following text are clues indicating the radical politics inherent in the league's social documentary aesthetic. Citing Stieglitz and Steichen as her role models, Calomiris reportedly said documentary photography should be "an honest picture and not the ash-can school which the Photo League taught, where you weren't encouraged to shoot people if they were smiling." In contrast, however, she cited the work of Walker Evans as truly documentary: "it is fine and clean and honest work. That's what I'd like to be able to do."

From this public testimony it was made clear to readers that, according to Calomiris, the Photo League followed a didactic political platform in their partisan, even agit-prop, attitude toward social documentary. While an FBI plant in the league, Calomiris assumed her secretarial duties (keeping "the bulletin board posted with Party literature," "cultivating students who might be recruited," etc.) while taking classes. The league, she wrote, as "a cultural force," could influence millions who saw their pictures. It began to worry her that her own point of view on documentary photography "had been unconsciously influenced by the politics" of Grossman, who "had conditioned us to think that a good picture was a picture that illustrated social injustice." Her worries about the "Red slant" in photography would intrude upon countless photographers' lives in the coming months.

The league, at least in the documents left to us, angrily rallied in support of Grossman after this public naming. In one document, the writer asks, "Who is Sid Grossman?" and answers that he was a dedicated league member and director of the school. "Calomiris's smear attack is little reward for years of hard work for the Photo League. . . . And we fight now against the treachery and disgrace of such a person as Calomiris." Nine students in Grossman's workshop class in the spring term wrote a letter to the league's executive committee in May 1949 to place on record "that never at any time during the classes did he attempt to indoctrinate the students in any political ideology." Support dwindled despite such efforts; by fall 1949 league enrollment was down to thirty-three.[67]

In the early part of the twentieth century, many Americans, especially intellectuals, had either joined the Communist Party or flirted with progressive tenets. Even conservatives Morris Ernst and David Loth, in their 1952 *Report on the American Communist*, quoted Clemenceau as having supposedly said, "Any man who is not a Socialist at twenty-five has no heart and any man who is a Socialist at sixty has no brain." It is certainly no surprise that Grossman might be taken for a Communist in the cold war, whether or not he was an active member during the late 1940s. According to Ernst and Loth, the typical American Communist leader, based on FBI statistics of 1948, was foreign-born (78.4%), or with one or both parents who were foreign-born—one-third of these, furthermore, had parents who were born in Russia. American Communists also tended toward the Jewish and Catholic faiths, and they were likely to live in big cities. Aaron Siskind recalls, "You know I was a natural for a Communist because I was Jewish, I looked like a Jew and I lived in New York. I was always taken for a Communist." Even

Calomiris understood the FBI's interest in her as an informant—she could "pass" as Communist, with her Greek immigrant parents and her background of poverty and discrimination.[68]

FBI statistics concerning the actual numbers of American Communists underscore the paranoid, hysterical "witch hunt" mentality of the times: in January 1947, eleven months before the league's listing, HUAC leaders had announced their plans for an eight-point program to expose Communists and those sympathetic to Communism in the federal government and unions. By 1949 the FBI reported a probable total of 54,174 Communists in America, and by 1951 that figure had dropped to 31,608. Because these are FBI figures, the numbers were likely inflated to overstate the Communist threat. Furthermore, as Ernst and Loth note, "throughout the years, the hard core of leaders . . . has been [averaged at] about 5,000 to 8,000."[69] Despite decreasing numbers of American communists during the period 1948–49, other events occurred that intensified the fear and hatred of the party: the first Soviet atomic bomb was developed; Alger Hiss was accused of Communist Party membership by Whittaker Chambers; Mao Tse-tung proclaimed Communist rule in China; and Communists seized control of Yugoslavia, Czechoslovakia, and Hungary. Meanwhile, in order to safeguard the western world from Communist aggression, the North Atlantic Treaty Organization (NATO) was established.

The fear of Communism steadily intensified, especially with the addition of McCarthy's strident voice in HUAC courts. Many Americans' earlier, sometimes youthful and naive flirtations with the Communist Party would come back to haunt them during the cold war years (even if they had rejected its ideology by the 1940s). In fact, contemporaneous Communist violations of human rights, especially by the 1950s, disgusted many Americans in the party and its membership steadily decreased as Communist ideals unraveled with every dissenter sent to the Russian gulag.

Grossman, like these other former CPA members, was conflicted. Whether or not Grossman was an active Communist Party member in 1949, when he was named in court by Calomiris, remains open to question. Many people still will not go on the record, and others believe it makes no real difference and is no one's business, even now, more than forty years later (and over thirty years after Grossman's death). That people still fear openly discussing the matter illustrates the anxiety this period in American history can evoke. Even more recently, Grossman's acquaintances and allies have expressed widely divergent opinions on his life and work. Most league photographers remember Grossman as dedicated and sincere; others describe him as an opinionated, sometimes contentious member of the organization who adamantly professed his political beliefs to those around him. When asked whether Grossman was a Communist Party member, one photographer who studied at the league in his youth replied he didn't know; Grossman was certainly "super liberal," he said, but he just didn't know—"You couldn't quote me on that and I'd get angry with you if you did." This source still feared discussing Communism and admitted that he and Grossman didn't like each other. Furthermore, he added that it was "no big deal" when the league closed down, as "no one wanted to save" it anyway at that point.[70]

It is difficult to assess the league's demise and members' recollections of Grossman given the surrounding politics of the times. But it is possible that some former friends and students allowed Grossman's naming in court to negatively color their later assessments of his teaching and character. Helen Gee, the director of Limelight, a photographic gallery in New York during the 1950s, articulates Grossman's precarious situation as a blacklisted citizen: she said Grossman "didn't have much of a following, simply because people were afraid he was a Communist." When asked if he was in fact a Communist, she replied, "I think he was a radical. But it doesn't even matter to me whether he belonged to the Party . . . he had a very hard time. People fled and they were nervous even to be seen with him. So when I joined his class he had few students. About half of the eight were friends acting as fill-ins, so it looked as though they had a class."[71]

Rosenblum recalled Grossman as a "very dear" friend, adding "but unfortunately our friendship ended towards the end of Photo League." He admits that Grossman was "a tough guy" and that "if he didn't like you, you had great trouble. He could be devastating if he thought you were fooling around [with photography]." Their falling out, he maintains, was a direct result of the difficulty Grossman encountered during the cold war years:

> It was in 1949. [Calomiris' naming] hit him very hard because he was starting to make some money as a commercial photographer. And suddenly that disappeared. And he and I had a big argument at that time because he did something terrible. . . . He saw me one time and said, "I don't like what you are up to." I said, "What is it, Sid?" He said, and we were both devoted to the Photo League, "You're not getting me involved anymore. You're not using me at the Photo League, you're trying to take it over for yourself." We stopped talking to each other.[72]

Rosenblum sadly credits this argument to the "terrible" pressures of the times: the listing, the naming, the surveillance, the loss of a (finally) growing career.

Colin Osman pointedly asked Rosenblum, "Was Sid Grossman a member of the Communist Party?" to which Rosenblum, who is one of the strongest, most articulate sources of league history, replied, "I have no personal knowledge. It is possible but he may not have been. He was a man with all sorts of interests. He never approached me. I don't know if he ever approached Angela. . . . You see there was a danger in admitting the fact." If one did admit to being a Communist, he explained, the next question you had to answer was, "Who else was a member?" Refusing to name names incurred a contempt charge, "so that is why lots of people who were not bashful about saying 'Sure I am a member of the Communist Party' would not do so officially." More recently, Rosenblum said he doubted Calomiris's claim that Grossman recruited her into the Communist Party—"it was not the way he functioned."[73]

However, Calomiris wrote in her hyperbolic *Red Masquerade* that as soon as she became a party member "Joe" flattered her with confidences, revealing to her that the Communist Party had used his house as "a secret meeting point for comrades slipping through the blockade in 1938 to fight with the Loyalists in the Spanish Civil War." While most Americans sympathized with this cause, the Soviets, she points out, supplied the Spanish Loyalists with arms and troops in order to spread Communism. And while Calomiris "realized that many members of the Photo League were Communists," she only singled out Grossman.[74]

Another central member, who had been in the league since the 1930s, calls Grossman a "very domineering" man whose main interest was political, not photographic. When this source had formed a documentary group, he remembers: "We just refused [Grossman]. We knew if he came into our group it would become political," and that "if you didn't agree with him you were dead." Even so, this man still saw Grossman, to some extent, as an unfortunate victim: "The times were terrible. If you were left you were down. You could've been Jesus Christ and you'd be blacklisted."[75] Also recalling the tone of the times, *Popular Photography* editor Arthur Goldsmith said "Oh my God . . . I could not believe this was America, the big lie believed, people harassed because of something they thought or said. There were card-carrying members in the Photo League. . . . What [had] they actually done? There was no documentation of much of this nonsense."[76]

Siskind, on the other hand, in a personal interview, agrees that the league was a front organization and was not shy about stating his problems with Grossman: "I had lots of trouble with him. The whole organization, especially in the thirties, was very much a Communist front organization. And they had their operators in, their party people and all that. Sid Grossman was a functionary there. He was a fair photographer, but he'd always annoy me trying to convert me to Communism . . . Grossman annoyed me all the time by giving me information. So I knew what the organization was. I could tell you stories that would even stand *your* hair on end."[77] According to Siskind, Grossman's focus in photography "was so narrow it was ridiculous" owing to his strict sense of documentary purpose. Siskind's overstated interpretations, according to some league members, have actually helped perpetuate his own legacy—as he is portrayed then as the heroic outsider and competitive foil to backward socially aware photographers such as Grossman.

It is true that Grossman was a Communist. His second wife, Miriam Cohen, sees "no shame" in this fact. She also asserts that he had been trying to leave the party before the listing and the naming but it had been very difficult. Cohen met Grossman around 1947 in one of his classes when she was seventeen or eighteen. She recalls that while in the army, Grossman had learned that his first wife was living with another man, but it then had taken him a couple of years to raise $200 for a divorce. Soon after he and Cohen started living together, the league was listed. They married in 1949, the year he was named by Calomiris. Grossman, she maintains, heroically battled evil in all regards—whether it was from the political right or the political left. Cohen further remembers that during long meetings in their 7 West 24th Street loft, the party pressured him to bring league members into the Communist fold, but he refused to lure his friends and colleagues into the Communist Party. They were especially interested in recruiting the most reknowned and credible members, such as W. Eugene Smith or John Morris. Grossman was, according to Cohen, "effectively ex-communicated" from the party before the listing in 1947 because he would not use his friends at the league to help increase the party's membership or prestige. After being named, Grossman faced unsatisfying choices: he could, in order to stop the continual harassment, tell the government he had been a Communist but was no longer in the party (in which case he would be forced to "name names"); or he could become an informant, like Calomiris, and "earn" his freedom from the agents who followed his every move. Neither option offered relief or honor to Grossman. So Grossman entered what Cohen calls "limbo," rejected by the extreme left and only useful to the extreme right as an informer. Cohen, watching how the Communist Party "crucified and killed Sid" and, later, crushed the Hungarian revolt in 1956, ultimately left the party as well.[78]

Vestal, one of Grossman's favorite students and a close friend, adds wryly that Grossman was a washout as a Communist because he was too much of an individual. He believes—wrongfully, according to Cohen—that Grossman probably dropped out of the party after the naming and withdrew from the Photo League to "save himself." In any case, Grossman's voice becomes conspicuously absent from *Photo Notes* after 1948, and he resigned from the league in the fall of 1949. Cohen maintains that from 1947 until his death, in 1955, Grossman received only one commercial job—from Lord and Taylor, who hired him to photograph children in pajamas for $500. If not for the GI Bill, she continues, their lives would have been destroyed. His income from teaching private classes also sustained the family. For $50 students attended ten sessions starting at 8:00 P.M. and ending, typically, as late as 3:00–4:00 A.M. While many fled the Grossmans' company after the naming, five to ten loyal friends and students filled the classes year after year. Later, when the family moved to Provincetown, Massachusetts (where Grossman could use the GI Bill to study at the Hans Hofmann School), his private classes, and influence, continued.[79]

In later decades, upon reading Grossman's FBI files (in which almost all the names remain crossed out), his widow was amazed at the mostly innocuous contents the bureau had listed (that Grossman went to the barber, had a sandwich, attended a movie, etc.). The ultimate irony is that Grossman's photographs didn't particularly figure into the government's accusations. The FBI superficially stressed party members' recruiting and membership, not the physical or psychological danger a Communist might create in society through his or her art. Visually, Grossman's *oeuvre* is more often remembered for the radical aesthetic chances he took—the cropped figures, grain, and blur of a medium pushed to its limits. But even after his style had shifted, Grossman's subjects tended toward the working (or nonworking) class—New Yorkers haunting the streets and recreational areas of the city.

Grossman's philosophy is evidenced in the transcribed tapes of his classes around 1949–50. In these discussions with students, he admits to not having taken pictures for two years and refers to Marxist ideology tangentially in comments on art's relationship to society. He criticizes those "pictorialist" types: "they are all businessmen" who forget the negative aspects of life and instead create art as an "aspirin" of idealization. Salvador Dali receives Grossman's wrath for visualizing Spanish subjects in the midst of fascism, "disregarding completely the horror of what is going on there today." In discussions of Cartier-Bresson, Grossman accused him of being too "detached from the world," an opinion that Lisette Model spiritedly disagreed with.

On the other hand, he also disparages those too limited to find art in broader subjects, beyond the social imperative of ideology. Compared to earlier commentary, however, Grossman avoided discussing photography directed "toward the social scene." Such comments indicate, perhaps, his move away from Communist Party lines and also his acceptance of the repressive, and potentially dangerous, environment in which he lived.[80]

Jane Livingston, in her recent book, credits Grossman's mature awareness of "the greater mystery" of photography and the deficiencies of "socially aware" art idealizing the working classes as the moment marking Grossman's golden arrival within the canon of "New York School" photographers. Like the other "primal figures" she discusses, such as Lisette Model, Helen Levitt, and Alexey Brodovitch, Grossman came to reject "the often naive—or at least oversimplified—belief in the medium as an instrument for social change." Such overly polemical and biased comments, however, fail to convey the sophisticated, intellectual, and balanced approach many documentarians have toward subject and form. Thus, Livingston interprets any stylistic change in Grossman's art to "spiritual" dimensions, questioning his programmatic commitment to "socially aware" documentary photography—a change which, she claims, lost him allies in both the party and the league. Instead, Grossman found a new formal consciousness born of "wisdom, and a tolerance for ambiguity."[81] It can be no mere coincidence that such consciousness coincides with Grossman's being named by Calomiris. Does stylistic change occur only by means of intellect or, in this case, knowledge of European modernism (with which Grossman already had been familiar)? Even for a committed documentary artist such as Grossman, might repressive social circumstances encourage a new formation of style, especially given the cold war pressures of McCarthyist redbaiting?

Whatever the case, in 1949, after Calomiris's testimony, Grossman broke away from the league. Having divorced Marion Hille, he remarried, to Miriam Cohen, in 1949 and had a son, Adam, in 1954. The Grossmans went to Provincetown, but they still spent winters in New York. In New England Grossman discovered a new world of nature and photographed closeup abstractions of New England fauna and flora, as well as producing misty images of women and children. While in Provincetown he attended the Hans Hofmann School of Painting and taught photography in his own school. Emotionally damaged, and with a heart condition exacerbated by recent events, Grossman found Cape Cod a retreat, a place of rejuvenation and self-exile. His widow, Miriam, would later recall their move to the Cape as a response to a "terrible debate with the comrades," who had wanted him to continue photographing socialist realism.[82] By this time, his widow maintains, he was not using "art as a weapon" and had been accused of retreating from "the streets and the poor masses of New York." Grossman's eye certainly had turned to new subjects; he said in a taped class session: "Where do you go? I have not been photographing. I have told you that the experiences of the last year have made me absolutely frightened of what I see in faces in New York today. I came back from Cape Cod this fall expecting that I would go back to people, and I would photograph New York, but I was so frightened by what I saw that I could not deal with it. . . . I have to . . . prepare myself and strengthen myself to face these people—to face the destruction and fear which borders on insanity."[83] His message is not clear. He suggests that "the people," once his subjects, had turned against him and that the mood on the streets had turned mean. Who but Grossman might have known this feeling better?

Evidence of Grossman's later photographic work is found in *Journey to the Cape*, published posthumously by Grove Press in 1959, four years after his death from heart disease. The editors of the book included his widow, Miriam Cohen, and Sy Kattelson, Charles Pratt, and David Vestal (three of Grossman's friends and students at the league). In his biography of Grossman, Vestal wrote that the book came out the same time as Robert Frank's *The Americans*, "and it may have been the better of the two books. Neither one sold."[84] The cover of Grossman's book pictures a closeup of Henry Modgilin's hand, fingers outspread, with blue tones added. Included are images of Central America, the American Midwest, and New York street scenes. Of the thirty-seven photographs by Grossman in the book, at least twelve, at the end of the book, represent his work while living in Cape Cod.

The change in Grossman's subject matter and technique, as presented by the editors, is visually arresting. Included in *Journey to the Cape* are two color images of barely recognizable marine life. One, of a large fish eye, focuses on the compositional arrangement of formal shapes: the black circle of the open eye and linear veins on the fish's surface. The rhetoric of the text beside the image discusses "blindness" and the human capacity to sharpen vision, or understanding, in life. As humans mature, the text points out, we lose that curious vision for the ordinary, but then, "there are those who come to startle us out of our blindness, crying, *Look!*" However, considering Grossman's difficulties during the late 1940s and early 1950s, the fish's eye also could be seen more imaginatively as a wary metaphor for "who might be watching."[85]

The text of the book was written by Millard Lampell, who had himself been blacklisted for ten years. Grossman met Lampell through their common interest in folk singing. On his trip to Arkansas, Grossman had met Lee Hays, a founding member, along with Pete Seeger and Lampell, of the Almanac Singers. The interest in folk singing was also shared by Grossman's then brother-in-law, Waldemar Hille. Even in this association, Grossman's affiliations with "dangerous" people during the 1940s were clear: Pete Seeger had been blacklisted and was banned from television until 1966.[86] Lampell and Grossman continued to support each another during this difficult period in both their lives; as stated in the artists' biographies in *Jour-*

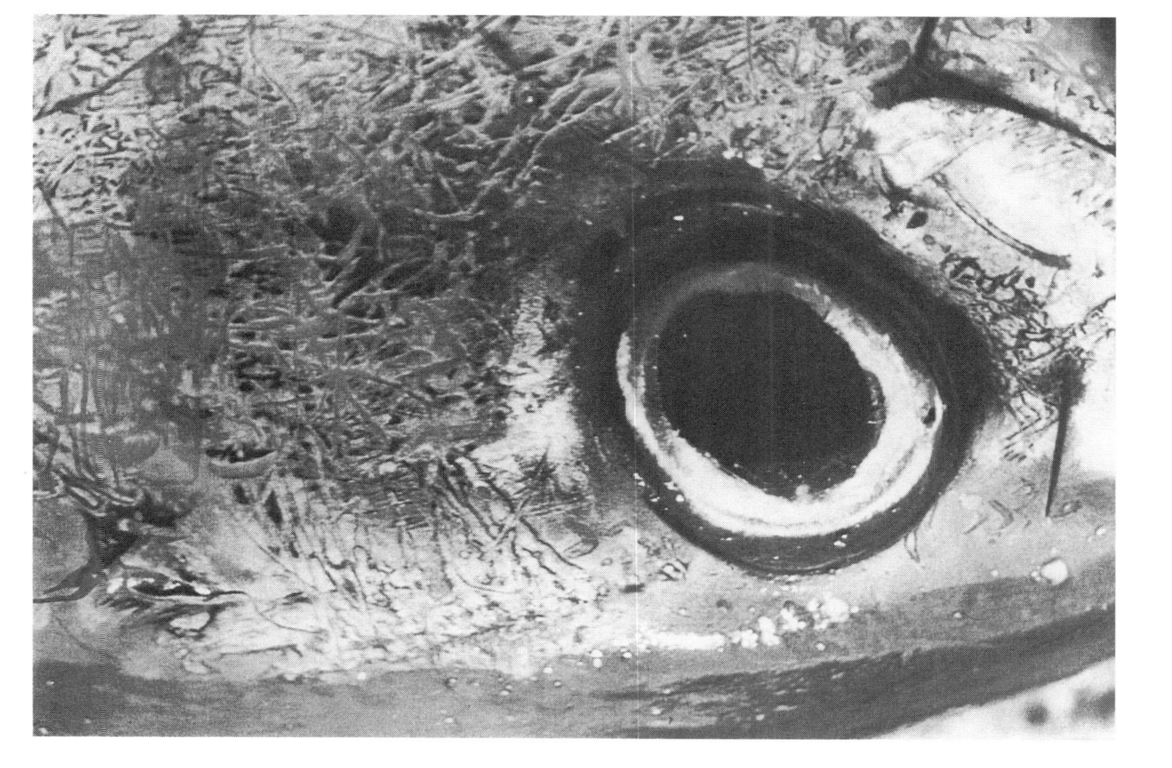

2.11. Sid Grossman, *Untitled*, ca. 1950–54.

Sid Grossman's aesthetic shifted noticeably during his time in New England, after he had been publicly named as a Communist. His abstract images increased, including closeups of marine life. © Miriam Cohen.

ney to the Cape, they had intended to collaborate on a book, but Grossman died before they could even start.

Lampell's text for the planned book accompanies the photographs in a diverse, haphazard way. Some of his text is prose, some poetry; he includes quotations by Grossman and has provided assumed dialogues between photographed subjects (as Langston Hughes did more artfully in *The Sweet Flypaper of Life*, 1955, with photographs by Roy DeCarava). In one passage Lampell writes:

> Where did the years go?
> Where
> did the years
> go?

Later he adds, as if to address obliquely his and Grossman's own lives:

> The winds change, the tides turn,
> Be patient with me,
> I have much to learn.

Such texts create a mood of poignant sadness in the face of changing times, a pivotal reminder of the stresses Grossman endured during his later career.

Other photographs presented to viewers in *Journey to the Cape* are hazy, even pictorialist, gauzy images more like those in Steichen's *The Family of Man* show than Grossman's earlier photographs—a child peering from foliage, a woman in a window, two dogs on doorsteps, a painted car, a housefront with an old man, another child, marine plants, birds in water, a fish in water, and, finally, a color image of marine plants. Most fulfill the same snapshot aesthetic Grossman enjoyed, but, in terms of content, his lens was no longer turned toward the destitute, the denizens of New York streets, or the religious celebrants of Central America. In one uncharacteristic image with an almost upbeat mood, a smiling child, practically hidden behind flora, spies upon the viewer. Grossman allowed the foreground plants to dissolve out of focus, while the white flowers of the garden are burned a bold, gleaming white, accentuating the punctuated areas of highlight.

Helen Gee is one of the few scholars to note Grossman's transition from leftist-inspired documentary work to a more abstracted, elegiac subject matter: "[Grossman] no longer felt free to photograph on the streets. Harassed by the FBI, living in fear of "the knock on the door," he sought refuge on Cape Cod, where his work changed radically. He turned from photographing people . . . to photographing quiet, contemplative scenes of sand and sea—a change that appears to be as psychological as it was geographic."[87]

Siskind had been similarly affected by Cape Cod before, during the early 1940s; during that time his work also shifted from a people-oriented humanism to a modernist-inspired art with more personal, formalistic concerns. But in Grossman's case, this later shift may have involved more dangerous motivations, considering the suspicions concerning his loyalties as an American citizen.

A comparison of Siskind and Grossman as aesthetic and political foils points to the changing artistic mood in America during the late 1940s and early 1950s. While Siskind enjoyed an increase in exposure and camaraderie among abstract expressionists in the late 1940s, Grossman's career came to a virtual standstill. Ironically, each man would look to New England as a healing source of artistic solace, even though, according to Rosenblum, the two photographers "hated each other." "To Siskind, Grossman was an anathema and Grossman couldn't stand Siskind." Siskind found Grossman an annoying Communist presence at the league who had a narrow artistic focus. Beyond their conflicts in personality, there existed a conflict in artistic vision. Grossman accentuated the necessity (or at least the possibility) of the political in art, but Siskind, by the 1940s, balked at inflexible social realist ideals. Clearly at odds with Grossman's documentary approach, Siskind was another type of pioneer in the league, extending photographic artistry into the modernist realm of personal reflection, with an emphasis on formal sophistication. Grossman might have agreed with Rosenblum's more recent criticism of Siskind's abstractions—that formal arrangements of architecture and peeling paint fail to open up a new world of experience for most viewers. From this rather strictly documentary point of view, formalism may excite the intellect, but it does not engage the heart.[88]

Grossman's later works, as shown in the last pages of *Journey to the Cape*, do not compare well to Siskind's formally engaged photographs and abstractions (although Livingston finds, in Grossman's later images, some of the strongest work of his career). After the exciting imagery Grossman had produced in New York and Central America, the photographs he took in Cape Cod seem rather forced, unexciting, and conventional. Visually, the surprises are few and the upbeat motifs rather cliché. But then, Grossman's health was failing and he was new to this rural setting, which had more beach than sidewalks. Furthermore, Grossman began his safer, more formal experiments much later than Siskind, under the added weight of having been publicly labeled a Communist.

Siskind had begun veering from the documentary ideology at the league in the late 1930s. One of his independent projects was *Tabernacle City*, a photographic essay that detailed the spiritual focus of a traditional community and emphasized structures of formal order. According to Siskind, most members of the Photo League disapproved of these experiments, but he nevertheless continued his investigations. *Tabernacle City* was exhibited at the Photo League during January and February 1941. Critical comments on the photographs included "too arty" and "Siskind has rejected the workers' cause." It was this negative criticism that caused Siskind, not surprisingly, to leave the league for good.[89]

In another project, "Chilmark" (1940), Siskind created his own still lifes, photographing the formal relationships between objects. One photograph from this series (Figure 2.12) pictures a fish head, a subject Grossman later explored. Both Grossman's and Siskind's fish head images emphasize compositional elements such as line, texture, and, in Grossman's case, color. Grossman's softly focused fish (the more abstract of the two) is presented closer up and fills the picture plane, while Siskind's occupies a clearer, sharper contextual space. Both images are enigmatic in their meaning, with less presumptions of visual narrative than earlier documentary photographs by both artists. As Chiarenza wrote concerning Siskind's photograph: "Whatever meaning one may wish to bring to this photograph from personal life experiences, it must be associated with mortality, with death, whether literal or figurative."[90] While Siskind discovered earlier what has been called a more "elegiac" or poetical relationship to subjects, Grossman certainly developed a similar artistic interest, provoked, in part, by the league's listing and his being named personally as a Communist recruiter.

Grossman's later photographs certainly point to a new aesthetic direction, away from the typical, people-oriented documentary images he printed in previous years. The "smiles" Calomiris had found so absent in league images now appeared in Grossman's work. Today we may wonder whether this direction had more to do with his own interest in artistic exploration or with his efforts to retreat from a documentary vision that reinforced notions of subversion. By 1951, of course, such issues within the league were moot because the organization no longer existed. After fifteen years of indispensable activity in the Photo League, Grossman lost his second home.

As the only member to be specifically named as associated with Communism, Grossman must have felt somewhat responsible for the league's demise, but no written record of his feelings is known to us. Instead historians have talked to his friends and his family; each source is as full of ambivalence, sadness, and contradiction as the last concerning this complex man. Certainly Grossman was a forceful and influential personality in the history of American documentary photography; he invigorated the tradition with a new radical style, affirming documentary's complex presumptions of au-

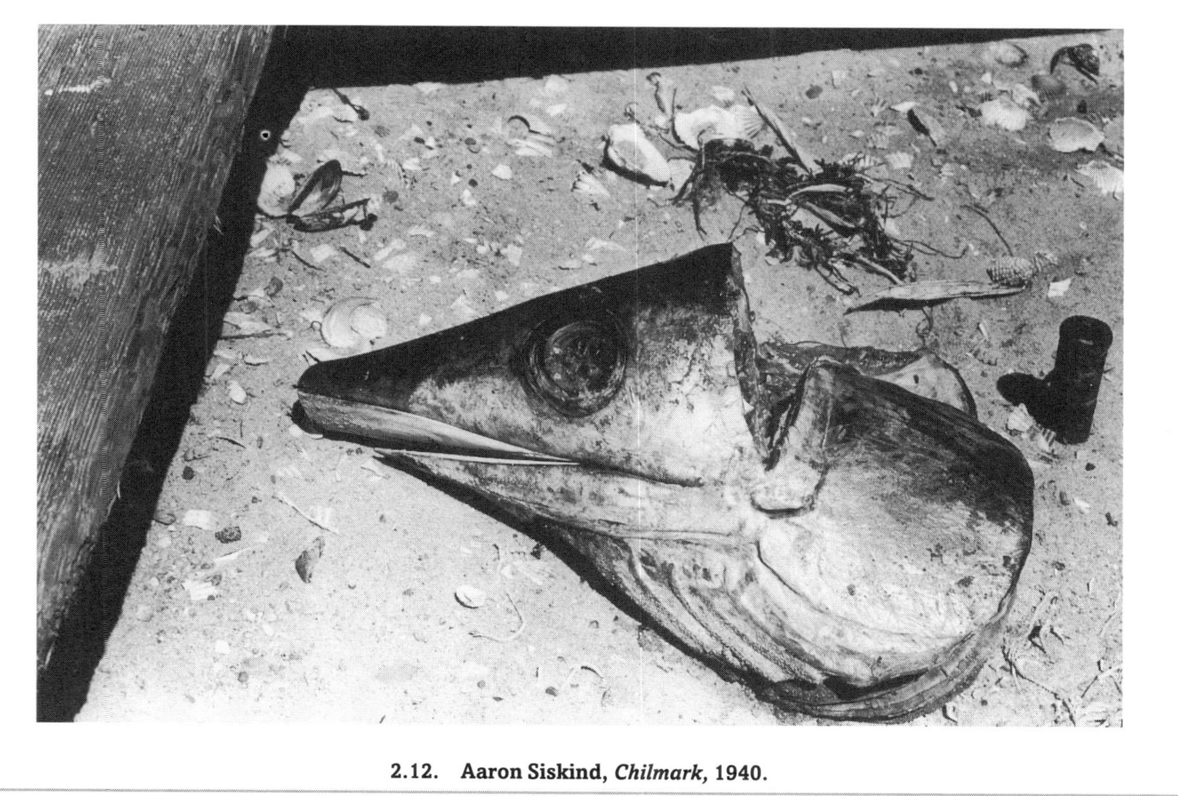

2.12. Aaron Siskind, *Chilmark,* 1940.

Aaron Siskind's interests in the dynamics of form and content are dramatically depicted in this image of a severed fish head with its eye dead center. Although clearly "straight," the image is charged with metaphoric contrasts and symbolic oppositions.

thenticity and realism. His work, in fact, denies the simplistic polarities so favored in art history analyses, as it blends documentary content with modernist aesthetics.

It is tempting to find, in some of Grossman's quotations, cautious and metaphorical hints of the tribulations he encountered as a left-wing, if no longer Communist, documentary photographer in cold war America. "The function of the photographer," he said, emphasizing the photographer's ideal role as social missionary, "is to help people understand the world about them."[91] Another quotation by Grossman, chosen for inclusion in *Journey to the Cape*, seems to signal his mature optimism toward life: "You must know that the day welcomes you, that the sun shines generously, that the rain means no harm. You must know that people can enrich you, and you them." If Grossman was bitter about his experiences, his friends rarely let on. The fury of the cold war certainly hurt Grossman, but he knew that his work would survive: "the time will come that [my photographs] will be usable and I will have won." Miriam Cohen remembers his words clearly, though differently: "The time will come when the world will want my photographs. I may not be here but they will be waiting.[92]

3

Subtle Subterfuge: The Flawed Nobility of Edward Steichen's *Family of Man*

> If you're still living, never say never,
> What is certain isn't certain.
> Things will not stay as they are . . .
>   and
> Never becomes Before The Day Is Out.
>
> BERTOLT BRECHT, "In Praise of Dialectics,"
> trans. Anna Bostock

The year following the Photo League's demise, during Sid Grossman's self-exile in New England, Edward Steichen began scouting the world for images to exhibit in the upcoming *Family of Man* show at the Museum of Modern Art. In this blockbuster exhibition, photographers and the American public were introduced to yet another, "safer" form of documentary imagery, as defined by Steichen. The show could be seen as marshaling of the last forces of documentary work as well as acknowledging that documentary photography now belonged more to the world of commercial journalism than to individual, freelance photographers such as Grossman. In contrast to Photo League photographs advocating the American underclass, *The Family of Man* celebrated the broader, mainstream culture of the 1950s.

In *The Family of Man*, Steichen diluted social documentary photography to the point of dissolving it into an all-encompassing metaphor for universal harmony. With specific partisan issues of class and race largely lost, even conservative forces could appropriate the show as their own. Documentary work came to be understood as the province of photojournalists who were, in the minds of many league members, often controlled by corporate, mass media forces in ideological collusion with cold war official policies. Even so, Steichen's *Family of Man* was, in some respects, a noble, although flawed, endeavor—with this project, Steichen tried to offset cold war fears of "otherness," Soviet aggression, and general cultural difference.[1]

The repressive context of the cold war intensified. In the early 1950s, while Steichen prepared the exhibition, Americans were enjoying unprecedented postwar prosperity. They were, as David Potter called them, a "people of plenty"; John Kenneth Galbraith dubbed them "the affluent society."[2] Perhaps the material abundance of this consumerist age helped distract Americans from worries of eroding civil liberties. Their concerns instead centered more on the specter of Communism threatening their spending and standard of living. The Korean War had begun in June 1950, adding yet another front in the fight against the dreaded "domino effect" of Communism. Domestically, such fear was reaching its peak when Julius and Ethel Rosenberg were condemned to death in 1951 for spying and executed in 1953. Dwight Eisenhower, the first Republican president since Hoover, was elected with running mate and cold warrior Richard Nixon in 1952. In 1954 the Communist Control Act deprived U.S. Communists of rights enjoyed by other citizens. Senator McCarthy's attacks on communism increased until he was censured for contempt and misconduct in the Senate. McCarthy's censure, however, did not prevent further hounding of those with "questionable" loyalties through the remaining years of the decade.

On March 9, 1954, Edward R. Murrow aired "A Report on Senator Joseph R. McCarthy" on his television show *See It Now*, which highlighted clips of the senator contradicting himself with inaccuracies. It was, as Richard Alan Schwartz writes, "the first time that network television directly addressed McCarthy's reckless demagoguery." McCarthy, during his response time the following week, attacked by calling Murrow a Communist. From April to June, the Army-McCarthy hearings (investigating Communist activity in the Army) were nationally televised. The senator's outlandish performance led to his censure by the Senate on December 2, 1954. In August of the same year, the Communist Control Act had strengthened the earlier McCarran Internal Security Act (1950) Photo League members had criticized, as Schwartz notes, "by providing severe penalties for Communist and Communist-dominated organizations that refuse to register the names of their members and supporters with the federal government." By late August, Congress outlawed the Communist Party in the United States altogether. McCarthy's censure and the penalties associated with Communist activity, however, did not prevent further hounding of those with "questionable" loyalties through the remaining years of the decade. Anyone left of Nixon was considered suspect by some reactionary officials.[3]

U.S. foreign policy became more and more entrenched in cold war policies, as policymakers shifted emphasis away from mere Soviet containment to warnings that the United States must prepare for Russian attacks and plan subsequent retaliation (leading to, for example, the construction of bomb shelters in thousands of American homes). Compounding these fears of Armageddon were the continuing atomic energy projects and racial wars on home territory as civil rights activities against segregation and discrimination intensified. An understanding of cold war rhetoric and racial policies in the United States is crucial to our appreciation of this project, as a number of these issues were addressed by Steichen in *The Family of Man*. Underscoring the difficulties Steichen—or any other arts organizer—faced was the accelerating criticism of art in cold war America. Republican representative George A. Dondero (Michigan) increased his attacks on "communistic" American art that did not "glorify our beautiful country, our cheerful and smiling people, and our material progress." Dondero continued, in his 1949 speech, "Art which does not glorify our beautiful country in plain, simple terms that everyone can understand breeds dissatisfaction. It is therefore opposed to our government, and those who create and promote it are our enemies."[4]

Artists couldn't win. Modern art was denounced and social realists like Shahn were distrusted. Even though social documentary was realistic, as Dondero preferred, it certainly did not "glorify" the lives of "smiling" Americans. Steichen faced a mob mentality from conservative, influential foes of art during the years he planned *The Family of Man*. As Eva Cockcroft has researched, even his own employer, MoMA, used abstract expressionist art from American-born artists to promote cold war ideals of democratic individuality, placing "home-grown" modernists in controversial foreign shows.[5] Uneasy relationships linking art with the propagandistic promotion of cultural beliefs exacerbated tensions during the cold war years. At least abstract "progressive" art enjoyed the museum's endorsement. In contrast, social documentary work would find fewer and fewer champions, save Steichen himself. And he would dilute those ideals considerably in order to communicate his agenda in the 1950s.

Given the show's emphasis on universality in such a splintered world, most critics and historians have commented on the exhibit's superficial and reductive attitude toward a complex humanity. They emphasize the show's mawkish sentimentality in attempting to link the world's people with the exalted American values of family unity and democracy. In subsequent criticism, W. T. Lhamon (1990) called the show "an internationalist soap opera that had the feel of a promotional trade fair." Jonathan Green (1984) likened it to a "fun house"—"reductive, pretentious and sentimental." Gerry Badger (1985) wrote that the human experience in the show was trivialized "into a series of simplistic and woolly-minded . . . platitudes . . . easily digested by a mass audience, whose presiding values it both summarized and confirms."[6] While the catalog from *The Family of Man* might make the exhibition seem the visual epitome of Eisenhower-era cultural stereotypes and middle-class myths, some images, ones often ignored, reveal ambiguity and contradiction. Images suggesting the potential subversion of universal consensus and conformity mark moments of conflict that continue the more overt, politically active documentary philosophy of the Photo League.

Steichen, who was the director of MoMA's photography department at that time, orchestrated the largest, most popular photography show to date with *The Family of Man*. The exhibition, consisting of 503 images from 68 countries and by 257 photographers, was displayed at MoMA from January 26 to May 8, 1955. As Grace Mayer recalls, the show was so packed that security guards received bonus pay.[7] A four-page press release announced that Steichen, assisted by Wayne Miller, had reviewed more than two million photographs. Poet Carl Sandburg wrote the catalog's introduction. Paul Rudolph, an architect, designed the radical installation, and Dorothy Norman researched the captions. The catalog, still in print today, accompanied the show through the 1950s and early 1960s in its tours throughout the United States, Europe, Asia, the Middle East, Latin America, and the Soviet Union. It was not just Americans who saw *The Family of Man*—so did nine million viewers across the world.[8]

The Family of Man was the brainchild of Steichen. Steichen said he came up with the title while "reading some words of Lincoln and in one of his statements he uses the phrase—the family of man."[9] Most American photographers recognized Steichen's accomplishments, as well as his power at MoMA. His personal history included working with Alfred Stieglitz to build the Photo-Secession and 291 Gallery, becoming one of the most successful commercial photographers in New York City, and commanding photographic divisions in both World War I and World War II.[10] His active tenure at MoMA (1947–62) included the supervision and organization of more than forty-five shows. In 1954 the museum publicly praised Steichen's ambitious career with a gala celebration of his seventy-fifth birthday, and *U.S. Camera* published speeches given at that dinner by his friends and supporters. By the 1950s, Steichen was venerated by many as an elder who had enjoyed a full and exciting life in photography. *The Family of Man* was considered his final crowning achievement in that medium.

The exhibitions Steichen presented at MoMA exemplified his range of interests in photography and its presentation to the public. He organized *The*

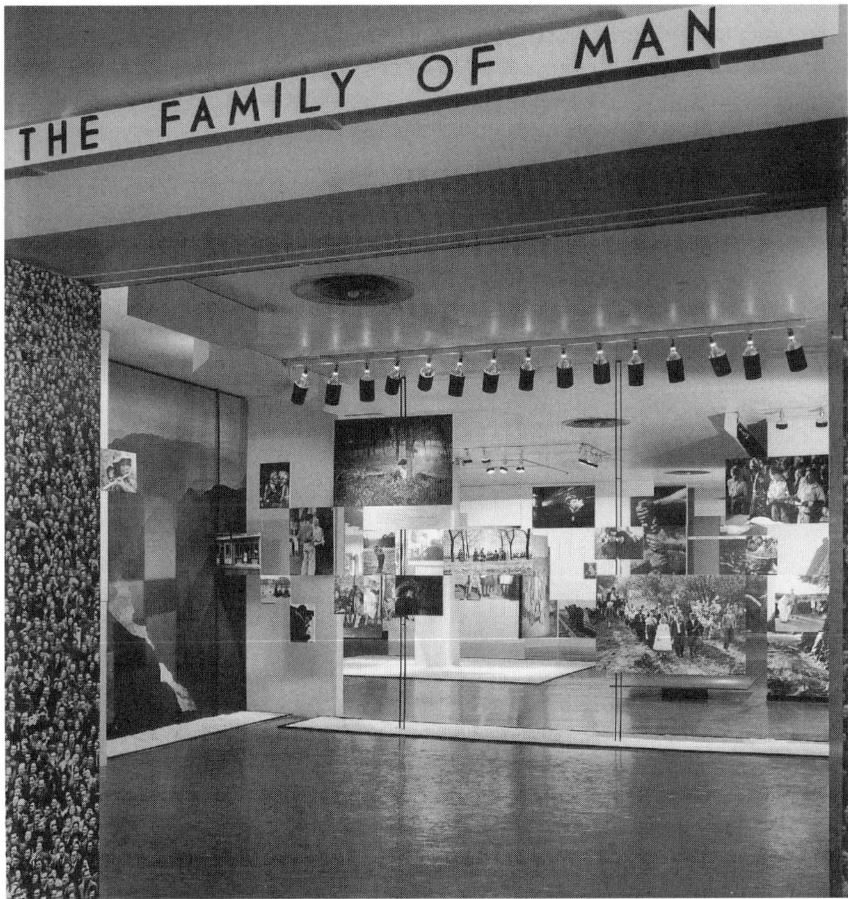

3.1. Ezra Stoller, Museum of Modern Art installation, *The Family of Man*, 1955.

Ezra Stoller photographed interior shots of *The Family of Man* exhibition, which premiered at the Museum of Modern Art in New York City, 1955. These images communicate the show's sculptural use of space, as designed by architect Paul Rudolph. Ezra Stoller, © Esto Photographics.

Road to Victory in 1942, emphasizing the lessons and images of his war experiences with documentary photography. According to Eric Sandeen's able research, Steichen's participation in two world wars had affected his understanding of photography's purpose. A decorated veteran, he had helped pioneer aerial photographic reconnaissance. Photography became, for Steichen, as well as for others imaging the war, a means of communicating

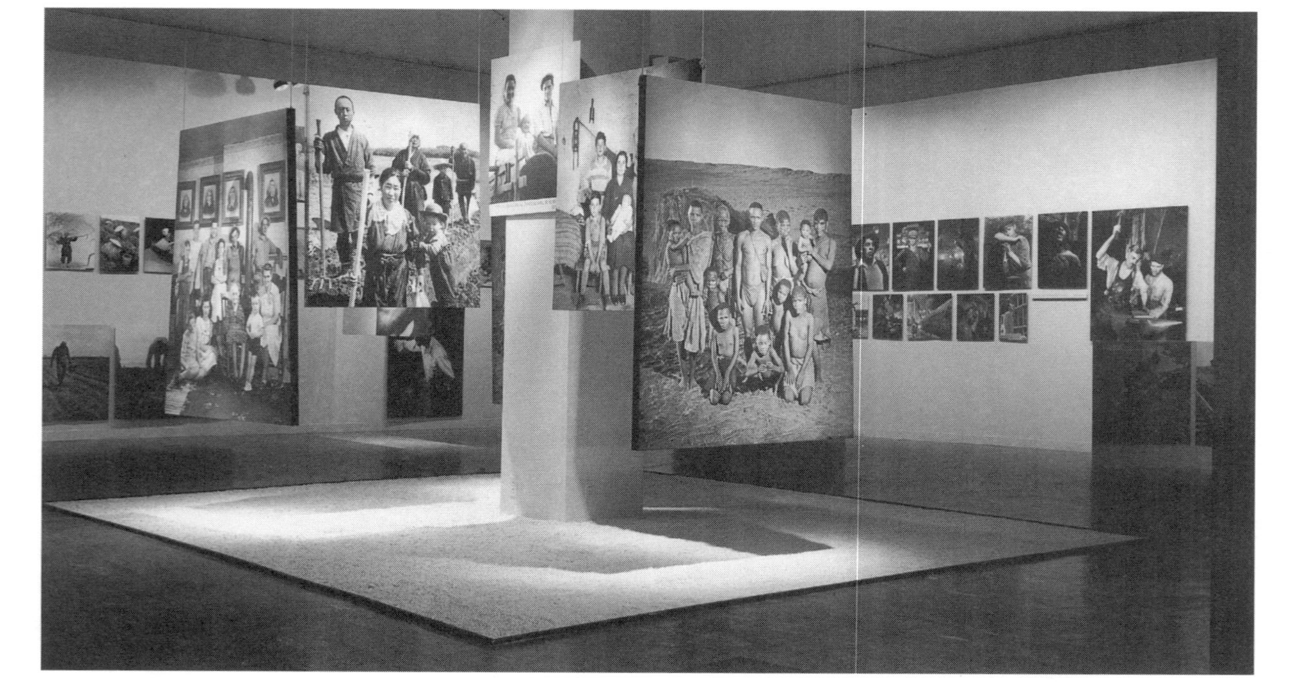

3.2. Ezra Stoller, Museum of Modern Art installation, *The Family of Man*, 1955.

Another installation image by Ezra Stoller of *The Family of Man* depicts a central section (on "family portraits" from around the world) in the thematic exhibition. A Sioux Indian quotation linked these images: "With all beings and all things we shall be as relatives." Ezra Stoller, © Esto Photographics.

the "horror": "If a real image of war could be photographed and presented to the world, it might make a contribution toward ending the specter of war."[11] *The Road to Victory* did more than announce his desire for world peace, it also illustrated Steichen's interest in modernist exhibition design. Installation designer Herbert Bayer plotted images along a path, using huge, free-standing enlargements in order to encourage a narrative structure for viewers (a technique later used for *The Family of Man* as well). This type of presentation resulted in an aggressive montage of forceful images, and Steichen came to prefer it throughout his career at MoMA. The exhibition, like most of Steichen's shows, was a crowd-pleaser—"People who ordinarily never visited the museum came to see [*The Road to Victory*]. So they passed the proposition on to me that I keep on along those lines."[12]

Steichen attempted to present an honest cross-section of photography in MoMA shows, featuring war imagery, abstractions, photojournalism, and work by young American and European photographers. It is to Steichen's credit that he encouraged and fostered new photographers such as Robert Frank, who heralded, in later decades, very different concerns and directions from his own.[13] One reviewer noted that Steichen's documentary show, which included images of the Korean War (1951), was followed by an exhibit of more self-consciously formal work, "Abstraction in Photography," illustrating that "a photograph is not only a story, it also is a graphic manifestation—a sheet of paper with forms of black and white which can be enjoyed without realistic meaning in their play of shapes, tone relations and rhythm."[14] All of Steichen's exhibitions consistently demonstrate his open-minded efforts to show various philosophies within the photographic community, both contemporary and historical, but he is best known for *The Family of Man*. This show received the most press and public attention, and Steichen himself considered it his largest, most ambitious, and all-encompassing exhibit.

Steichen's taste in photography often leaned toward the humanistic-documentary type. His four exhibits on the Diogenes theme, according to the first show's 1952 press release, displayed photographers who, like the ancient Greek philosopher, contributed "to the search for truth . . . [and] penetrat[ed] to significant meanings." For the second installment, the press release stated that photographers sought "a variety of truths . . . differently through each pair of eyes."[15]

Steichen provides an interesting foil to league members like Grossman. Steichen's optimistic faith in humanity mandated a positivist perception of hope for the world: on his seventy-fifth birthday he said, "We've got to renew our faith in ourselves. We can't go on hating and lying." However, compared to the more radical, specifically political tones of the Photo League, Steichen's rhetoric was far more generalized, philosophical, and upbeat, with an accent on hope, not despair; Steichen's did not work promote specific activism concerning current geopolitical and domestic events. His longstanding interest in organizations committed to the defense of global peace and education, such as the United Nations and UNESCO, demonstrates Steichen's broad political concerns.[16] He was, perhaps, something like the "hack writer" described by Walter Benjamin in 1934: "the man who abstains in principle from alienating the productive apparatus from the ruling class by improving it in ways serving the interests of socialism" and whose "social function" is to wring "from the political situation a continuous stream of novel effects for the entertainment of the public."[17]

Although many scholars characterize Steichen as a functionary of conservative cultural forces, he is not so easily reduced to mere liberal-conservative definitions within the photographic and political scene of the time. Bob Adelman, a photographer actively associated with left-wing and Civil Rights movements of the era, commented in 1990 that Steichen had an interest in "social concerns," which John Szarkowski, Steichen's successor at MoMA, subsequently took "off the agenda." Adelman credits Steichen as being "quite political" in his showing of forbidden topics in the 1950s (for instance, Marion Palfi's images of abused children).[18]

Steichen communicated during the planning stages of *The Family of Man* that he believed in a basic, underlying "goodness of people"; he added that "the reassuring motive we find is love." The show, he hoped, would act as a mirror, "so that people would feel they belong here." Such optimistic faith in humanity, he believed, evolved under his mother's influence: "As a small boy . . . I came in off the street one day yelling at a boy, 'dirty little kike.' My mother at that time ran a shop but excused herself from the customers, took me by the hand and for three hours she talked to me about intolerance; this was one of the big cornerstones in my life." Steichen emphasized the goodness in humanity, but he was no conservative reactionary. The overall emphasis of *The Family of Man* certainly approached a "feel-good" justification for the cold war's overprotection of American virtues and policies, but the exhibit also contained themes, texts, and images that, to varying degrees, questioned and contradicted reductive ideology. As Steichen later noted, "We are living today in a world snarled up with hypocrisy, hate and fear. It's getting out of hand. It's a much bigger danger than the atomic bomb."[19]

By the same token, Steichen was no political radical, much less a Communist, and his optimism for the future played well to both the public and MoMA officials. Apparently, given the redbaiting climate of the times, Steichen even found himself "snarled up with hypocrisy." Rosenblum recalls Steichen pledging to support the Photo League after the blacklisting but claims that support never materialized because "the pressure got too high."[20] Perhaps Steichen's philosophy of the "essential goodness" of humankind was more academic than political, a safer brand of liberalism given the repressive cold war atmosphere. On the other hand, *The Family of Man* could have represented Steichen's own way of getting even with a corrupt system that pitted friend against friend. If so, Steichen was clever, for *The Family of Man* was a mainstream success.

Steichen's generalized humanistic philosophy was rooted in a Roosevelt-era liberalism, a sentiment that was waning in America during the 1950s. In the July 1955 issue of *Picturescope*, the newsletter of the picture division of the Special Libraries Association, he wrote: "My basic interest is in people. . . . When we first talked about [*The Family of Man*] . . . the theme was to be human rights, but I decided human rights are really just a political football today."[21] Steichen avoided the "political football" of human rights that many Photo League photographers had carried so vigorously. Most of the league photographers felt artists must be personally and actively involved in helping solve the major social problems of their day. But, by the 1950s, this documentary, partisan spirit in American art was in further decline, avoided by photographers wishing to sell their images, attract corporate patrons, or exhibit.

Arthur Ekirch's *Decline of American Liberalism*, published in the same year *The Family of Man* was exhibited (1955), pessimistically chronicled the "various pressures" besetting liberals at that time. Ekirch defined contemporary American liberalism within the progressive tradition of Theodore Roosevelt's Square Deal, FDR's New Deal, and Truman's Fair Deal in the postwar era: "[Progressive liberals] regard the growth of some sort of collectivism as inevitable, and stress the need of government regulation to preserve ancient liberties and to meet the problems of modern industrial development." However, he noted, the philosophy of liberalism was difficult to reconcile with the militarism "left in the wake of two world wars." A subsequent philosophy of "vengeance and hate" produced by war, as well as war crime trials at Nuremberg and Tokyo, tested traditional liberal ideas and eroded their idealism. The collapse of liberalism had begun, Ekirch believed, in the 1930s and 1940s, "when liberals under Franklin Roosevelt seemed most strongly entrenched" but which "was actually a period of grave potential peril for traditional liberal values." As members of the Photo League would learn, it was only realized after World War II ended that "the liberal retreat was beginning to turn into a rout."[22]

From the beginning of Steichen's organizing efforts, subtle clues about the show's liberal nature were clearly articulated to the photography world. The many articles and advertisements calling for *Family of Man* entries made almost every photographer in America, amateur or professional, aware of this impending exhibition and its planned themes. European artists heard of this ambitious project as well. Jacob Deschin, photography reporter for the *New York Times*, wrote an article for the December 14, 1952, issue describing how Steichen had toured Europe searching for photographers to include in the exhibit. The article outlined Steichen's vision, as did the numerous calls for entries published in the nation's photographic journals: Steichen hoped to "portray the basic and universal elements in human relations" by "explaining man to man across the world" through photographs. Steichen had traveled, Deschin reported, to nineteen cities in eleven countries, interviewing seventy-eight photographers and looking at some ten thousand photographs (not an easy task in postwar Europe, he added, given the scarcity of photographic materials there). Deschin noted Steichen's praise for "honest" photographers who had "a wonderful feeling for people," able to show "how people live and their relationships to each other."[23] Deschin, as a former league supporter, probably welcomed Steichen's focus on humanity while questioning the exhibit's positivism—a sentiment not often communicated by league workers.

By 1954, Steichen's well-publicized message was out: he did not want any overt political content. As reported by one newspaper reviewer: "the museum is not concerned with photographs which border on propaganda for or against any political ideologies." Instead, Steichen was quoted: "We are concerned with following the individual and the family unit from its reactions to the beginnings of life and continuing on through death and burial."[24] Arnold Gassan, a young, aspiring photographer at the time, remembered all his friends in the profession madly submitting images of their own spouses and babies. (Elliott Erwitt would take the same tack in his submissions; one, depicting his wife with their newborn, was used. Photographers using family scenes included Robert Frank and Ruth Orkin, among others.)[25]

Calls for entries also stated the guidelines for submission: photographers were to send unmounted contact prints or proof enlargements no larger than 8 x 10 inches; no prints would be returned; no prizes or payment would be awarded. While photographers today might balk at such restrictions, which show so little regard for ownership and the print's integrity, these rules were not surprising given the position of photography at the time. There were few exhibition spaces, and one was lucky to receive $25 for a print. Helen Gee, who ran Limelight, the first coffeehouse and gallery devoted to photography in the 1950s, was ecstatic whenever she sold any photographs. Minor White, she notes, was "thrilled" to receive $7.50 for his *Nude Foot*.[26]

Although it was difficult to show much less sell one's photographs, many photographers recoiled at the idea of sending their work to Steichen. Rosenblum was one of many photographers who blanched at the thought of giving up control of his work. The stipulation that any picture included in the exhibition became the property of MoMA was consistent with photojournalistic practices, but that provision kept both Rosenblum and Strand from submitting photographs to *The Family of Man*. As Rosenblum puts it: "I'd never do anything where I give up the right to the photograph, under any circumstances; it's my picture."[27]

Image, the journal of photography at the George Eastman House in Rochester, also publicized the call for entries, dubbing the show "one of the most ambitious photography undertakings attempted by any art museum." By this time, the article noted, Steichen had been searching the United States and Europe for two years for amateur and professional images to include in *The Family of Man*. "When the selection has been made, the photographers will be asked for the necessary exhibition prints, or the loan of their negatives, when large mural size prints are required." The general themes Steichen desired were reiterated—universality, life, and death. Steichen added: "We are concerned with the religious rather than religions" and that the images should try to capture "essences" through "particulars." The reporter continued, saying that Steichen knew "the mood and spirit that he wants yet refuses to have specific kinds of pictures in mind." The call was open to interpretation.[28]

Infinity, published by the American Society of Magazine Photographers, included a "Last Call" for the show in its February 1954 issue, again quoting Steichen's desire for photographs "made in all parts of the world, of the gamut of life from birth to death with emphasis on the everyday relationships of man to himself, to his family, to the community and to the world we live in." The subject matter could, for instance, range from "home-made toys" to "scientific research," or from "tribal councils of primitive peoples to the councils of the United Nations." The oppositional relationship between such examples illustrates the potentially reductive, ambiguous nature of the project: children and primitives are posited at one end of the human spectrum, while scientists and the UN are situated at a "higher" human evolutionary plane. Steichen's words, as quoted in the *Infinity* article, also demonstrate the 1950s reverence of motherhood and domesticity. He asked for "photographs that reveal the selflessness of mother love"—not just "the Madonna element in 'mother' but her all embracing love, with the sense of security she gives to her children and to the home she creates in all its warmth and magnificence, its heartaches and exaltations."[29] It's no wonder so many photographers combed their own family picture files, as Gassan testified, in order to meet Steichen's demands.

The "Last Call" in *Infinity* also expressed an interest in obtaining images with negative connotations—photographs "mirroring the flaming creative forces of love and truth and the corrosive evil inherent in the lie." A hint of anarchy, an acknowledgment of destructive forces, is found in Steichen's allusion to the *lie*, a term not clearly defined in the article but which may refer to totalitarian and fascist regimes Steichen had encountered during World War II. Steichen seemed to have some personal notion of the "truth" and "universals" of the human condition, although he did not clearly state them. *The Family of Man* would convey more obliquely his humanistic philosophy to millions of viewers. Whether this understanding was translated visually to viewers is a subjective matter and depends on each viewer's own background. As Arthur Goldsmith said, "you were never really sure whether it was the family of man or one man's family."[30]

Aperture, the newest, most avant-garde of the photography journals (under the guidance of editor Minor White) also announced the call for entries, laboring in a 1953 article to define what Steichen wanted. It was reported that Dorothea Lange had called a conference of photographers of the San Francisco region "in order to make known the nature of *The Family of Man* show." Unlike typical photojournalistic assignments, wherein a photographer had little to no control over which images were used and how, this time, the article noted, a photographer had the "opportunity to make and submit the kind of picture he believes belongs." In this way, the exhibit would allow photographers to prove that they "can think for themselves, interpret for themselves; produce visual images that communicate the inner spirit of man with the outer facts."[31] Described in this way, such a project probably would have appealed to most Photo League photographers, with its emphasis on the documentary philosophy of realist images that could convey important sociological facts in an artistic manner. Most documentary photographers and photojournalists of the early 1950s, as Gee observes, "still believed . . . in 'truth'"—the ability of a picture to illuminate the human condition.[32] The problem was, whose truth? Steichen, as auteur of *The Family of Man*, would ultimately decide.

The populist orientation of the show already had been decided, as *The Family of Man* targeted a large cross-section of the population. *Aperture* warned photographers to "remember the audience" when submitting work; "the photographs are for laymen . . . remember the general level of training and match it with lucidity." The message to photographers was to send images with easily perceived content and narrative that a general audience could appreciate. Steichen further communicated that the "exhibit should concern itself with the likeness of men. Their brotherhood is to be stressed, though their hatreds are not to be omitted." This plea demonstrates that Steichen already had a broad audience in mind, one that desired a generally positive, or pleasing, outlook on humanity. But, again, Steichen did not ignore the negative aspects of this "inner man" and sought images concerning all aspects of "his soul," including "his cruelty, his hate, compassion, fears, virtues, foibles, and vanities, struggle and suffering." Steichen's primary focus was a positive humanism, but, at least verbally, he tried to include less idealized human experiences, the contradictions and moments of antagonism inherent to all lives.[33]

The *Aperture* writer knew Steichen's call for entries would appeal most to documentary photographers: "the faces of those to whom this theme is a challenge light up; the faces of those who find a ready made sympathy for the kind of work they have been doing for years without either outlet or recognition light up; the rest get a vacant stare as they try to remember if they have a picture that might get included in a famous exhibit." In the final analysis, the writer questioned presumptions of narrative content: "perhaps the only soul a photographer can reveal is his own." Sounding more and more like *Aperture*'s editor, Minor White, the writer believed that Steichen "is asking for the highly activated approach, the penetrative approach to both life and photography. This has not been asked in a very loud voice since Stieglitz stopped publishing *Camera Work* in 1917." Associating Steichen's call for work at this time with the venerated "high art" tradition of Stieglitz during the early years of the twentieth century might cause some art historians to wince, but *Aperture*'s writer was anticipating a broadly interpreted definition of contemporary photography beyond the confines of conventional documentary or photojournalism.[34]

After Steichen had spent three years reviewing thousands of photographs in magazine picture files, personal portfolios, and historical collections, *The Family of Man* was finally presented to the public, with resounding success. As Helen Gee remembers thinking triumphantly, "photography had arrived!" MoMA accorded it the publicity and space appropriate to any ambitious art exhibition. Far from being relegated to the basement area near the ladies' room that Gee describes as the typical exhibition space for photography at the museum, the show took up the entire second floor. Guides to the show, such as one published in *Popular Photography*, illustrate the carefully orchestrated, narrative themes viewers were routed through as they walked the serpentine path of the show. Photographs and captions were mounted on overlapping, freestanding walls that were arranged to guide the audience in a particular direction. For those who have not experienced the show's calculated narrative in person, sources describing the layout of images are crucial to understanding the exhibition. Following such accounts, while referring to the catalog (which follows the show's design quite closely), can approximate but not fully re-create the walk through the script of images, flowing from lovers to childbirth, from loneliness to war. While some viewers, like Gee, were skeptical of universal "oneness," the dramatic display was unquestionably moving. As Gee writes, "It no longer mattered that the show was overdesigned, or that I had reservations about the theme. There I was, like everyone else, agog as I traveled man's journey through life."[35]

Before analyzing specific images, it is important to understand the general tenor of the exhibition. The "essential oneness and goodness of man" that Steichen sought to portray was communicated in scenes of basic labor, entertainment, learning, playing, and gender relationships, among other subjects. The final passages culminated in a humanist crescendo. The rear section, as the museum's press release noted, pointed out "the way in which death is a great leveler," displaying images of a dead baby, soldier, and chieftain. Other photographs sought to "reveal the sometime cruelty of a majority to a minority," with a decided emphasis on hope and the dignity of humankind. The section with group portraits even included a mirror, so that viewers themselves were literally part of "the family." The climax of the show, picturing a hydrogen bomb explosion, called attention to "one of the greatest challenges of our time—the hydrogen bomb and what it may mean for the future of the family of man."[36]

The last gallery, just after the bomb image, contained photographs of couples, accompanied by a line from Ovid, "We two form a multitude," and juxtaposed to a sixteen-foot mural of the United Nations General Assembly and its charter. The show, as stated in the press release, closed "on the theme of the eternal hope that lies again and again in the magic of childhood with a series of gay, lilting, tender photographs," emphasizing the positive aspects of human life. It was this optimism toward the human condition which provoked Robert Frank to sarcastically nickname *The Family of Man* the "tits and tots" show.[37] The criticism of its sentimentality is understandable, yet the hints of negativity Steichen included must be addressed as a vital aspect of his vision during the cold war.

Potentially critical documentary images, however, could be ignored within the positive whole of the exhibition or safely appropriated by conservative forces. *The Family of Man*'s preview address, on January 24, 1955, was given by Nelson Rockefeller, special assistant to the President of the United States, who, in 1939, had become president of MoMA. Rockefeller left the following year to join Roosevelt in Washington as coordinator of the Office of Inter-American Affairs and later became assistant Secretary of State for Latin American affairs. He resumed the presidency of MoMA in 1946. According to the research of Eva Cockcroft, the Rockefellers were instrumental in involving MoMA with American foreign policy and CIA operations. As an elite, powerful family who moved in the most influential policymaking circles of the 1940s and 1950, the Rockefellers helped coordinate a "cold war cultural offensive" by showing American art as a symbol of democracy and freedom in international exhibitions.[38]

Rockefeller's adulatory address at the opening of *The Family of Man* probably would have been heckled by the more radical, progressive photographers of the Photo League's earlier years for its pandering to the bourgeois values and dominant conservative forces in American politics at the time. Rockefeller joyfully embraced the universality of basic experiences: laughter, family, food, play. He praised "Captain" Steichen's ability "to communicate his deep sympathy and love for man, his contagious zest for the flowing stream of life, and his undeviating respect for the inherent dignity of the human spirit."[39] After stating his hope to increase global communications so that such positive sentiments could be shared, Rockefeller concluded with a quotation by President Eisenhower that called for hope, not fear, in these cold war years. These were admirable thoughts, certainly, but they ring hollow today considering the escalation of conflicts in Korea and Southeast Asia and the repressive political climate at the time.

The list of guests invited to the opening of the show reveals an interesting cross-section of artists and celebrated political figures, including Eleanor Roosevelt and ambassadors from many countries. Magazine editors, critics, and photographers included in *The Family of Man* were also invited: Mrs. Edna Woolman Chase, *Vogue's* editor emeritus; Margaret Bourke-White; Mr. and Mrs. Robert Frank; Helen Levitt; the Newhalls; Mr. and Mrs. Irving Penn, Mr. and Mrs. W. Eugene Smith, the Shahns, and others.[40] As even this brief list shows, a broad array of photographers was included in the show, representing many different types of photography: documentary, commercial, fashion, and "fine art."

Steichen did limit the types of images in *The Family of Man* to straight, representational photographs and selected no purely abstract images. But choosing the photographs, Steichen said, was "heartbreaking." Huge volumes of work had arrived at MoMA, and Steichen and his assistant Wayne Miller combed the files of *Life*, the Library of Congress, and picture agencies such as Magnum. Both contemporary and historical photographs were researched and viewed. Steichen did not emphasize individual work or champion any single aesthetic; he was more interested in conveying his message of world peace and reconciliation. He clearly envisioned the major themes for the final product during this preliminary research period. For such an ambitious ideal, one image per theme would not be sufficient. He mentioned his disappointment that no one picture in the show's first section, "Lovers," captured "ecstasy," but Steichen felt "where one photograph cannot do this, groups of photographs will and can do this."[41] Reminiscent of the Photo League's interest in documents, series of images by multiple photographers on a single theme, Steichen imagined photographs working together, not stressing individual personality but collectively representing his own larger agenda of humanistic optimism.

Discussing individual themes and photographs within *The Family of Man* creates troubling methodological problems, as the show was designed so that images were plotted along a master narrative, like sentences and chapters within a novel. Choosing one image as representative of the entire exhibit would be like choosing one word out of a book's chapter as representative of the entire text. Communicating the show's original thematic and visual intent within such a limited scope is almost impossible. Furthermore, viewers today must rely on the catalog in order to re-create this visual experience, which cannot precisely approximate the actual viewing experience of walking through the exhibit in 1955. The catalog does, however, outline the thoroughly planned, sometimes ambiguous, mixture of images and text.

The contributions of venerated poet Carl Sandburg (who was also Steichen's brother-in-law) to *The Family of Man* were often praised in articles reviewing the show. His prologue in the catalog begins with the observation that all babies' first cries say, "I am! I have come through! I belong! I am a member of the Family!" but these words are curiously placed next to Wynn Bullock's image of a small, naked girl lying inert and facedown, eyes closed, in a forest covered with ivy. Although the text argues for the unity of all humankind, the photograph is upsetting, even existential, in its ambiguity. Out of all the images available, the photograph seems a surprising choice to illustrate Sandburg's notion of "one big family hugging close to the ball of Earth for its life and being." The child certainly could be interpreted as "hugging the earth," but her small, harsh, white form, alone in a sea of vegetation, looks dead, a body overwhelmed by nature.[42]

Though Sandburg displayed an upbeat, universalist tone within the catalog essay, extolling the "drama of the grand canyon of humanity, an epic woven of fun, mystery and holiness," the writer himself had encountered his own share of difficulties with American politics. The recipient of Pulitzer prizes in both poetry and history, Sandburg had been highly praised for his popular biography, *Abraham Lincoln: The Prairie Years and the War Years*. Not as well known was the poet's history of political activism, which contributed to his Army intelligence file, dating back to 1918, as well as a heavily censored FBI file (researched in later years by his friend Herbert Mitgang). Mitgang found "it was hard to imagine that such a quintessentially American author would be the subject of a government dossier. Yet what he had said and written were considered dangerously liberal, or worse, by the Federals." Sandburg's history, however, explains why the government was so interested in him as a possibly subversive citizen. As a younger man, Sandburg had worked for left-wing causes: he had been a Social Democratic party organizer, had known John Reed and his wife, had supported Eugene Debs, had been a Roosevelt New Dealer, and had campaigned for his friend Adlai Stevenson. As Mitgang writes, "Now and then, [Sandburg] would feel free enough and angry enough to take a crack at such as Hoover and McCarthy as well as others who violated his libertarian views about 'the people.'"[43]

Like Grossman, Sandburg endured surveillance. Army Intelligence, Mitgang noted, never did "forgive and forget" Sandburg. Having accused Sandburg at one point of being a courier of revolutionary literature, they maintained a file on him even twenty years after his death. The FBI, in 1941, noted his "unfriendly attitude" toward the bureau, and, in 1947, they added to his file an article from the *Daily Worker* mentioning Sandburg's association with a CBS documentary on Lincoln. The *Daily Worker* also quoted Sandburg that year as saying that the "hate Russia" campaign must end. Even though many of these allegations reflect the government's tendency to confuse Carl Sandburg with Dr. Karl Sandburg, by 1948 his FBI files included a memorandum calling Sandberg "a well-known Communist in Chicago."[44]

Such reports continued into the 1950s. Sandburg's past associations with "Communist fronts" were chronicled. In 1954, another FBI memorandum noted that Sandburg had praised "Russian courage" in World War II and had saluted, alongside Charlie Chaplin, "our Russian ally" at a Chicago rally. By 1958, three years after *The Family of Man* premiered at MoMA, the FBI upgraded Sandburg's status in their records to "Internal Security-C" (for Communist) because of his plans to write an introduction for a suspect book. Even when Sandburg was in his eighties, during the 1960s, the FBI continued to add to his file.[45]

Like his friend Steichen, Sandburg considered himself a realist; yet for all his occasional pessimism concerning human struggles, in the end he affirmed "the enduring strength of people." His poem of 1935, "The People,

Yes," reflects his hopeful vision of humanity and touches on universal themes similar to those found in *The Family of Man*. Sandburg's poem honored the disenfranchised people of the Depression, evoking an image reminiscent of FSA or Photo League documentation:

> The unemployed
> without a stake in the country
> without jobs or nest eggs
> marching they don't know where . . .
> they fall into a dusty disordered poetry.

Sandburg was no reactionary friend of McCarthyist forces, but he did not publicly rail against them either. However, when Edward Murrow asked him what the worst word in the English language was, Sandburg replied, "exclusive," as it "shut out a more or less large range of humanity from your mind and heart."[46] Sandburg saw *The Family of Man* exhibit as a full and logical expression of his long-held beliefs in liberal humanism, which transcended specific political dogma and reached a more spiritual, philosophical dimension—beliefs he held in common with Steichen.

Many, however, viewed Sandburg's (and probably Steichen's) liberalism with suspicion. Later, when *The Family of Man* toured the Soviet Union in 1959, criticism of Sandburg's liberal attitude toward that country surfaced in articles that called the poet "a good Russian" and contrasted him to McCarthy, who "fought to the death enemies and ideas that Sandburg endorses." Meanwhile, other wire stories reported his praise for "Red Exhibits."[47] Steichen also supported increased understanding of the Soviets, whom most of America regarded as enemies. In 1959 he wrote: "I personally like [Khrushchev] and recognize that, if he is sincere in his peace proposal and is willing to accept the necessary give-and-take to achieve universal disarmament, he will go down in history as one of the greatest figures of all times."[48]

Steichen's ideology did not reinforce right-wing fears of Soviet aggression, and some recent critics have even come to consider his optimistic political beliefs somewhat naive. In 1955 *Infinity* published a transcript of an NBC broadcast on Steichen. In that show he again addressed his conceptions of the exhibit, including the idea of "oneness," or "brotherhood," words "that like so many others [have] become meaningless." The "element of love" must dominate, he said, in an age of politicians telling us daily "how bad things are." Steichen admitted to being an optimist, "and optimism means faith in ourselves, faith in the *everydayness* of our lives."[49]

To critics today, and to some in the 1950s, Steichen's equation of "you, me, somebody from Tibet" simplistically reduced human tragedy to a common denominator and belied an ignorance of imperialist political motives in the world.[50] This is an important criticism. However, some of these images and quotations in *The Family of Man* were nevertheless effective in undermining the status quo and questioning the cohesion of governments that did not try to understand one another. Critics on the far right bemoaned Steichen's concept of international brotherhood, which linked Communists with freedom-loving Americans. An American public affairs officer saw the show in Mexico City and noted that Communists might spread the same propaganda in *The Family of Man* to advertise their appeal to the masses. The show's inherent ideals, he warned, encouraged dangerous notions: the "opening" of borders and the perception that America is not "front and center" but, instead, one of many nations.[51] In short, his message was: Don't make Communists part of *my* family.

Eric Sandeen's recent research on the social and political context of *The Family of Man* forces readers to appreciate Steichen's effort to visualize unity within a fractured world. He argues that Steichen *chose* to generalize the human condition in order to bridge all perceptual barriers between "us" and "them." Steichen also "assumed that emotion, kindled by the fire of sentiment, could move people to action," to effect change in the present world.[52] In this sense, Steichen's show presumed political motivations, especially in the eyes of cold war officials busy watching subversive citizens like Sandburg. Looking at the images today, however, beyond the suspicions of the 1950s, modern viewers get a diluted sense of the show's power and cannot glean specific historical references. Unfortunately, then, over time, the show loses its specific political significance and becomes simply a manifestation of mainstream values in a consumerist, imperialist, and prosperous America.

Upon deeper reflection subversive cracks in the supposedly ideal surface of *The Family of Man* appear. In a few instances, both visually and philosophically, Steichen took risks with the show. He succeeded in bridging diverse ideological branches in an exhibition that enjoyed endorsement by socialist as well as conservative journals. Furthermore, the show appealed to the bourgeois masses in unheard-of proportions. The director of the Des Moines, Iowa, Art Center expressed his delight over record attendance at the museum when the exhibition was shown there: "I find that only two months ever topped this March 1956 attendance, one in June 1953 with a Rose Show and one in September 1951 with Grandma Moses."[53]

The popular success of *The Family of Man* was related to the fascinating and diverse array of artistic, documentary, commercial, and photojournalistic images. Referring to the catalog (which includes all but two of the images in the original show), we find that Steichen's assistant, Wayne Miller, had the most images, with twelve; next was Henri Cartier-Bresson, with ten; then Dorothea Lange and Homer Page, each with nine; followed by Alfred Eisenstaedt, Dmitri Kessel, and Nat Farbman, with eight. Margaret Bourke-White and Robert Frank were each represented by seven images. The show included some of America's best-known documentary and photojournalistic photographers, most notably Lange and Bourke-White.

Steichen also included commercial fashion photographers in the show, such as Diane Arbus, Richard Avedon, and Irving Penn, and photographers from the West Coast school, represented by Ansel Adams and Edward Weston. Steichen did not neglect younger artists like Robert Frank—who, in the following years, would receive more attention—and others such as Wynn Bullock, Harry Callahan, Roy DeCarava, Louis Faurer, and Garry Winogrand.

Even though the Photo League had disbanded, league photographers were represented in *The Family of Man*, and many of their images communicated the subjects typical to documentary taste—urban children, the poor, and African Americans. Ed Feingersch had two images of black musicians in the show; Consuelo Kanaga provided two images of black women. Barbara Morgan's photograph of an African American woman on her knees scrubbing a floor, which was in *This Is the Photo League*, appeared again in *The Family of Man*. Other former Photo League members in the exhibition included Lou Bernstein, Arthur Leipzig, Leon Levinstein, Sol Libsohn, Lisette Model, Ruth Orkin, Marion Palfi, and Dan Weiner.

The photographs chosen also indicate Steichen's reliance on picture files such as *Life* magazine's, which Miller had reviewed. Miller himself had three images in the show from *Life*'s files (and one from the *Ladies' Home Journal*); Eisenstaedt's photographs were culled from *Life* files, as were all of the photographs by Kessel, Bourke-White, and Farbman. Out of the 503 images in the show, more than one hundred, in fact, were *Life* photographs. (A distant second was *Vogue*, with only ten images.) Steichen said, in 1961, that his shows at MoMA, for the first time, put photojournalism "in the sacredness of an art museum."[54] He was right; however, some critics would disparage the inclusion of journalistic imagery in the show, which blurred distinctions between commercial, illustrative photography and "fine art" photography. In choosing work for *The Family of Man*, as Steichen noted, "it was the content of the photograph that took first place. We discarded many fine photographs just because of lack of content."[55] According to Steichen, photojournalistic images narrated specific and persuasive documentary subjects more successfully than personal, creative images could.

Many of the *Life* images Steichen included in *The Family of Man* were familiar to some viewers. *Life* magazine had begun in 1936 under the direction of Henry Luce, who employed German émigré editors such as Kurt Korff (previously the editor of *Berliner Illustrierte*) and hired some of the best-known documentary photographers.[56] *Life* emphasized the photographic essay, with narrative sequencing of images, and revolutionized layout design. The magazine was a huge popular success. Bourke-White and Eisenstaedt, who were so prominently represented in *The Family of Man* by their *Life* images, were two of the four original photographers hired for the magazine.

Life's general philosophy, with executive editor Wilson Hicks at the helm, was a documentary one. Luce wanted high-quality printing, big news stories, and special features. The aim of the magazine was "to watch the faces of the poor and the gestures of the proud; . . . to see man's work . . . to see things a thousand miles away; the women that men love and many children; to see and take pleasure in seeing; to see and be amazed, to see and be instructed." *Life*'s photo essays pictured broad human interest stories, mixing a single photographer's images with explanatory text for a popular audience. Its picture stories were similar in presentation to Photo League documents, which provided multiple images on a single theme (although the league's documents were far more partisan and critical in their overall content and commentary). By the mid-1950s *Life* magazine enjoyed a mass circulation of 6 million copies annually and supported mainstream, middle-class values (or what Sandeen calls "conservative populism"). Many of the *Life* photographers' works clearly satisfied Steichen's own populist expectations for *The Family of Man*, and the magazine's files proved a fertile source of visual images.[57]

The large number of *Life* photographs in *The Family of Man* underscores Steichen's ideological compatibility with aspects of the magazine's vision and also demonstrates the show's categorical blurring of documentary work and photojournalism. Such images indicate that Steichen did not have a preference for new, original material, since many of these photographs were not new in 1955 but had been used in earlier *Life* issues. For example, John Phillips's image of an Arab boy at a blackboard in Palestine in *The Family of Man* dates back to his 1943 assignment in that country.[58]

Steichen and Miller also raided photography agency files during their search for material. Magnum was the agency represented with the most photographs, more than thirty-five credits. This cooperative photo agency, in which photographers chose the staff and editorial policies while sharing profits, had been founded in Paris in 1946 by Henri Cartier-Bresson, Robert Capa, David Seymour, George Rodger, and Bill Vandivert. In 1947 a New

York office had opened.[59] From Magnum's files, Steichen drew images by Eve Arnold, Werner Bischof, Robert Capa, Henri Cartier-Bresson, Elliott Erwitt, Burt Glinn, Ernst Haas, and others. Many of these agency images provided scenes of distant countries Steichen wanted to include. So while African, Asian, and Middle Eastern subjects were included in the show, they were most often seen in photographs taken by Americans or Europeans.

Sixteen images from Black Star were also chosen. This New York–based agency, founded in 1936, represented freelance European and American photographers, including W. Eugene Smith (who had signed on in 1938). Like *Life*, Black Star had been affected by the immigration of German photography editors, such as Kurt Kornfeld, who managed the agency with a "common concern for humanity." Black Star often hired their photographers out to *Life*, splitting all editorial fees fifty-fifty with the photographer. In fact, many Black Star photographers went on to become *Life* staff photographers, and *Life* provided 30 to 40 percent of Black Star's business.[60]

Other agencies Steichen culled images from include Rapho Guillumette (which counted among its photographers Brassai, Izis, Sanford Roth, Sabine Weiss, and Robert Doisneau, among others), Guy Brackman (which employed Garry Winogrand and Dan Weiner), Pix (representing Ed Feingersch and others), Scope, and Three Lions. In addition to the files of photography agencies, Steichen also had at his disposal images from U.S. government agencies such as the Farm Security Administration (which included work from Ben Shahn, Dorothea Lange, Jack Delano, and Russell Lee), and miscellaneous newspaper files.

The breakdown of images by country illustrates the international diversity represented in *The Family of Man*, although, as mentioned, most images were taken by American or European artists. The majority (over 200 of the 503 images) were photographs taken in the United States, mainly by American photographers. The reason for this, as Steichen pointed out in interviews, was that Americans had not endured a recent war on home ground, and so there had been no interruption in the flow of available photographic technology.[61] Images of America's foreign enemies, past or present, were not neglected, although most picture the subject as "other" and few are by photographers from that country. Germany was represented by more than twenty images (many of the war). There were about ten of Japan, ten of China, and six of Korea (though most of these are of American soldiers in the war). The Soviet Union and Eastern European nations (Romania, Hungary, Czechoslovakia, Yugoslavia, and Poland) were represented by more than twenty photographs. The approximately twenty images of Africa and twenty of Latin American and Mexican countries were taken (in most cases, again) by American and European photographers.

As a case in point, of the thirteen images of the Soviet Union in *The Family of Man* catalog, eight were taken by Russian photographers (four are by anonymous photographers from the Russian agency Sovfoto, two by named artists of Sovfoto, and two more by photographers in the Moscow Journalists' Club). These images pictured Kirghiz horseback riders, a Siberian mother and infant, two scenes of children playing "ring-around-the-rosy," a boy playing a horn while children run, a smiling couple with a newborn and nurse, figures playing instruments in a small band, and a man and boy exercising. Of the images shot by non-Soviet photographers, one is by Bourke-White (of priests, in the religion section of the show), another is by Thomas McAvoy, from *Life*, (of three grinning teenage boys), and three are by Robert Capa (who was born in Hungary but worked in the United States). Capa's images (from the *Ladies' Home Journal*) included two scenes of labor (a woman working in a field and a couple building a roof) and a photograph of a family eating.

Despite the tremendous tensions between the United States and the Soviet Union, not one of the Soviet images was situated within any "negative" section of the show. Instead, they were used in the sections on children, birth, music, fatherhood, youth, and eating. Only Bourke-White's image of priests might be deemed overtly controversial, given the Soviet bans on organized religion. On the one hand, Soviet citizens were made to fit within idealized American democratic social models (work ethic, family unity, and community). On the other hand, such reductive values, ironically, could be considered communist ideals as well. Establishing a conceptual compatibility between Americans and Soviets undermined the very essence of the separatist cold war mentality—without fears of Russian aggression perpetuating the economy and political machinery of the time, how could Americans justify their actions? During the 1950s, the concept of a "Red Menace" helped define American goodness. Steichen made a potentially inflammatory statement during the cold war years by linking Americans and Soviets as part of the same "family," and in doing so he demonstrated his liberal efforts to integrate otherness into oneness: Steichen maintained that "of all the people I have visited the Russian people is the one that most resembles the American people."[62]

The optimistic, mainstream themes in the show have been exhaustively discussed in recent scholarship, yet examining the visual moments of anarchy offers a deeper look into the changing nature of documentary photography in the 1950s. Ambivalent but critical photographs were presented within a majority of palatable, favorable, and positive images, revealing a subtextual effort to counter and sometimes contradict the conservative myths and stereotypes of the time. The show was not completely, in every moment, optimistic about humanity. Some themes and images in *The Family of Man* conflict with modern stereotypes of the 1950s American dream—photographs included scenes of the dead, the unempowered, racial discrimination, and gender conflicts, among other potent issues.

While the catalog cannot reconstruct exactly the physical experience of the exhibit (for instance, it cannot show each image's relative size), it does follow Steichen's general thematic narratives. The first theme, on family, covers the opening sixty pages of the catalog. Beginning with scenes of lovers, the section continues with images of marriage, pregnancy, mothers with children, and fathers with children, culminating in photographs of whole, extended families from Italy, Japan, Bechuanaland, and the United States. The 1950s cult of domesticity pervaded images of mothers with children—a group of images that fills over twenty pages, while fathers received four. Steichen believed that "all the beauty of human existence reaches its peak" in pregnancy and childbirth.[63]

Yet, sandwiched within this section are unsettling, nonidealized images, all from the United States: Yasuhiro Ishimoto's girl tied to a tree; Homer Page's two boys fighting; George Heyer's boy with a stick, about, it seems, to hit a woman; and W. Eugene Smith's image of a boy tormenting a girl.[64] On the next page viewers find more unsettling images of children—in front of a weather-beaten home, poor and dirty on the streets. Only one pictures a well-dressed boy: Lange's shot of a small child, head down, walking behind a fashionable woman who ignores him.

The photograph by Smith of a tormented girl appeared in *Life* magazine, September 21, 1953, in a picture essay, "My Daughter Juanita." Eight-year-old Juanita, in a Mexican hat, graces the magazine's cover as well. The text admitted that Smith's snapshots of his family reveal "more love than art." The next page quotes Smith's description of Juanita's party with dolls and stuffed animals: "Suddenly a streak of male, her older brother, lost in the frustration of having three sisters, swept her guests into chaos and kidnapped Bong-Bong the monkey." Smith's daughter screamed and rescued the toy, "but the magic was broken, the calm dispelled by the human intruder. Defiant, defeated, she fled into the house."[65] This "streak of male," as symbolized in Smith's photograph by a boy child, violently intrudes upon female space in other nearby images as well, documenting the gender conflicts in one specific family and in Steichen's more broadly defined family. The conflict, as presented in *Life* (or in *The Family of Man*) is not neatly resolved with an image of the two siblings making up but ends with Juanita's tearful departure and retreat. Such images point to moments of dissonance and ambiguity rather than tidy resolution in human relationships, a punctuating effect Steichen clearly desired from the show's inception.

The family section begins with images of lovers (such as one of Robert Frank and his wife, shot by Louis Faurer), including African American lovers (dancing, by Roy DeCarava, and embracing, by Wayne Miller). However, there are no biracial couples; whether Asian, black, or caucasian, the races do not mix. Scenes of pregnancy follow (by Frank and Manuel Alvarez Bravo, among others). In a critical review of 1955, Phoebe Lou Adams points out that the majority of the women represented in *The Family of Man* were too idealized and pleasantly "not-too-pregnant." Indeed, in many of the images the state of pregnancy is not visually observable (as in Frank's photographs) or is sentimentalized (Erwitt's woman and kitten). Only Bravo's fully rounded female figure counters Adams's criticism. To picture pregnancy at all around 1955 was somewhat risky, as pregnancy was still a taboo subject in the popular media. Lucille Ball was not even permitted by TV censors to use the word *pregnant*.[66] Such images of pregnancy, as "clean" as they are, would have been visual surprises to a mid-1950s audience.

Miller's picture story of his wife giving birth follows: two photographs show her face in pain, another shows the slippery new child hanging, its sexual organs dark and bloated, from the hands of a doctor. The umbilical cord connects to sheeted areas below. Grossman had already reviewed these images for *Photo Notes* in 1947. The photographs, he reported, when shown at MoMA, had caused a "sensation" among viewers (indicating the contemporary sensitivity to pregnancy and birth). As a partisan social documentarian, Grossman, unlike those who felt such pictures were in poor taste, thought "this to be a very wholesome and wonderful project" but added that it was an "oversimplified approach to a basic emotion."[67]

After other scenes of mothers, babies, and nursing infants, a quotation, "She is a tree of life to them," (Proverbs 3:18) accompanies former league member Consuelo Kanaga's social documentary image of an African American mother with two children in 1950. The woman is shabbily dressed and emaciated, and she stares into the distance. Behind her stands a blank white wall. The text evokes the idealized notion of "mother" in the 1950s, an ideological constraint many, such as Betty Friedan, found hard to break away from. But the image introduces poverty as an issue for some mothers, countering the bourgeois media representations of mothers like Harriet Nelson and June Cleaver. The image on the next page, of a blond white woman ly-

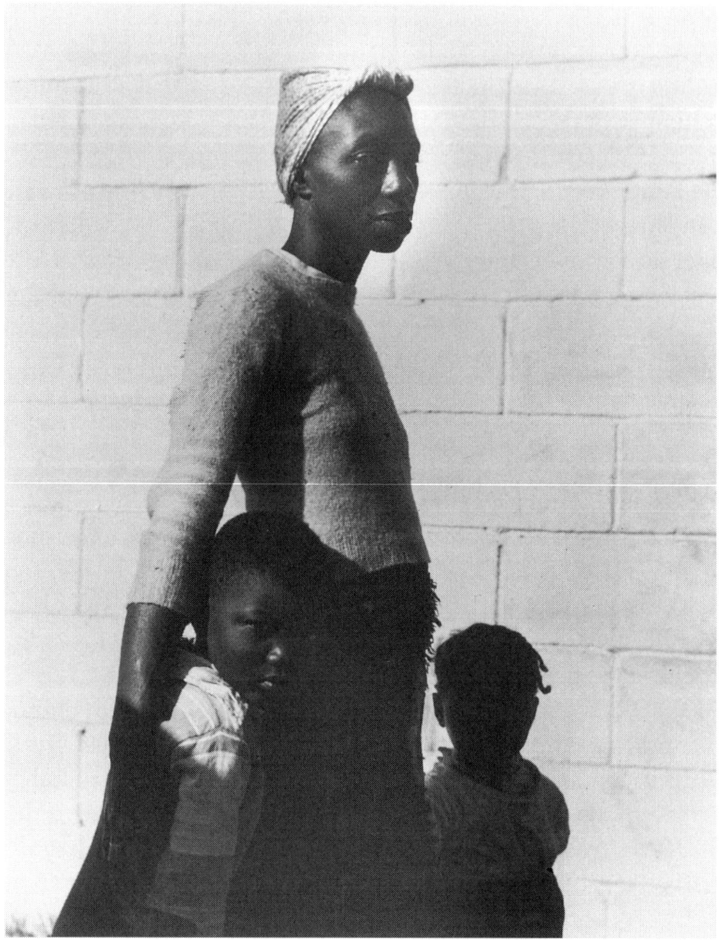

3.3. Consuelo Kanaga, *She Is a Tree of Life to Them,* 1950.

Consuelo Kanaga's iconic image of a sheltering mother figure, photographed in Florida, was accompanied by the quotation "She is a tree of life to them" (Proverbs 3:18) in *The Family of Man*. Kanaga, who produced dynamic documentary work, especially in portraits of children and African Americans, also had been included in the 1948 show *This Is the Photo League*. The Brooklyn Museum of Art, Gift of Wallace B. Putnam for the Estate of Consuelo Kanaga.

ing on a bed, looking at a small child holding a baby, perhaps fulfills such ideals more effectively.

Simone de Beauvoir cogently addresses issues of motherhood and gender in *The Second Sex* (1952). She describes how women have been perceived only as mothers and wives: "humanity is male and man defines woman not in herself but as relative to him: she is not regarded as an autonomous being." In actuality, unprecedented numbers of women were entering the work force at this time, calling into question the ideal of domesticity. For African American women, as pictured by Kanaga, the American dream of domesticity was more complicated—statistically, the most impoverished Americans in the 1950s were black women living in the south.[68]

Consuelo Kanaga (1894–1978) internalized documentary ideals during the course of her photographic career. She was a reporter and photographer for the *San Francisco Chronicle*, joined the *New York American* in 1926, and in 1934 became a contract photographer for the *Daily Worker* and the *New Masses*. Her career in the WPA ended in the 1930s, and she became a freelance photographer for *Woman's Day*. In 1948 her work was included in *This Is the Photo League*.[69] Her hopeful sense of photography's social mission is realized in the 1950 image of a destitute woman in Florida included in *The Family of Man*. Thin and exhausted, impoverished but alive, she shelters her small charges, in an image that suits Steichen's own vision of the world's extended, persevering family.

Less attention was given to fathers. Images included a Jamaican man lovingly caressing an infant, a youth looking into a mirror with an adult, and a Soviet boy exercising with a man. On the previous page, in one of Nat Farbman's images of Bechuanaland, a boy observes an adult male spear an animal. Also included: a tearful child whose crying soldier father hugs him and Diane and Allan Arbus's image of a bourgeois father and son reading newspapers (a fitting photograph from the files of *Vogue*). Such interest in fathers, as brief as it was in *The Family of Man*, was timely. As Wini Breines's research of the 1950s has shown, the rise of the bureaucratic "organization man" in a "gray flannel suit" provoked anxiety concerning the role of fathers, who were largely absent and invested in corporate jobs. Many sociologists and writers in the 1950s worried that working men were not only physically but psychically distanced from their families. Consequently, feminine and masculine sex roles converged, as men were encouraged to take more interest in domestic activities.[70] Although *The Family of Man* catalog included only four pages on fatherhood, the images point to a contemporary concern for paternal involvement—perhaps men, in fear of losing power, initiated a more active role both outside *and* inside the home.

In the following sections Steichen focused on an eclectic assortment of work and labor pictures. Most feature male workers, but a few illustrate female "labor" (sorting nuts and bolts, a pair of gnarled hands, sewing, gossiping at a fence, and washing). Ansel Adams's *Mt. Williamson*, which was blown up to huge proportions in the show, envisioned a pristine, clean vision of wilderness alongside environmentally destructive industry scenes criticizing the consequences of labor. Images of anonymous organization men in clean, urban corporations concluded this theme.

Steichen then turned to recreational themes, as a balance to the labor and monotony of work. These images concentrated on general activities such as eating, playing ring-around-the-rosy, enjoying music, and dancing. But following this upbeat section, the thematic narrative becomes ambiguous: nuclear experiments; a bombed German city; alienated couples. The darker mood was later alleviated by images depicting happy couples.

After a few general and genial street scenes, however, the show reverted to images of death, including: a boy in a cemetery (France, Izis); a dead child in a coffin (Spain, Leonti Planskoy); a dead soldier (United States, Mathew Brady); a funeral (New Guinea, Arnold Maahs); a Korean woman crying over a coffin (Bourke-White); and women in mourning costumes. Such images alluded to recent wars, including the Civil War fought on America's own soil. But, again, the photographs following these subverted any hopeless pessimism—Fifth Avenue, congested with bustling people, and images of children with grandmothers. Next came scenes of desolation and alienation (such as Robert Frank's isolated Peruvian peasant with head down), again continuing the flip-flop syncopation of positive-negative imagery.[71] Lest we become too optimistic, Steichen seems to say, remember instances of cruelty. Conversely, lest we become too pessimistic, remember the human spirit.

The "Inhumanities" section reinforced such recognition with images of famine, deprivation, and adversity (starving Indians, mourners at funerals, soldiers crying, rural poverty). Two iconic documentary FSA images are found here as well: Shahn's image of a woman holding herself and Lange's *Migrant Mother* (Figure I.1). Next to this well-known image we also find Frank's *Near Victoria Station, London*, 1951—a dark and brooding image of a street musician as isolated in his world of music as Lange's mother appears to be in her world of economic distress and maternal responsibility. Poverty and deprivation exist in all corners of the global family (although America's are found most often in the past, not present, tense).

Not all images of the poor were warmly received or easily interpreted. George Silk, a photojournalist and staff photographer for *Life* during the years 1943–72, spurred debate. Silk's photograph in *The Family of Man* (Figure 3.5) pictures a poor Chinese boy holding out an empty bowl. As Sandeen notes, Silk took the image for *Life* in 1946, well before Mao Tse-tung's rise to power and the Communist takeover there which formed the People's Republic of China in 1949. But by the 1950s the photograph had generated so much controversy that it was removed from *The Family of Man* exhibition in

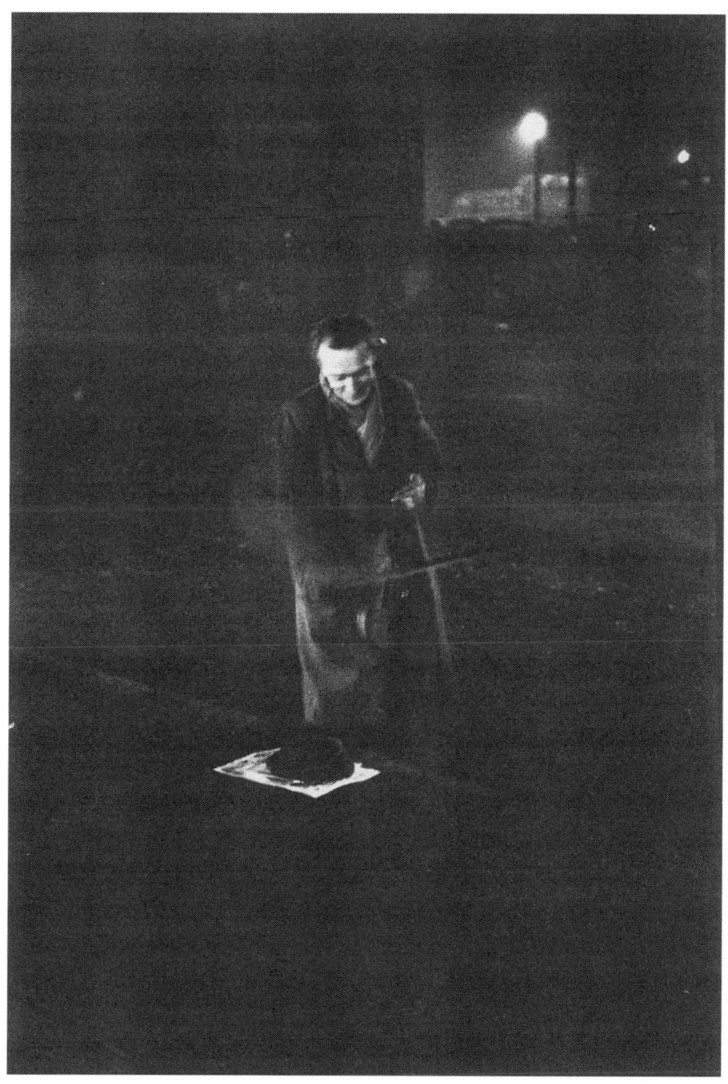

3.4. Robert Frank, *Near Victoria Station, London,* 1951.

Robert Frank helped Edward Steichen choose work to be included in *The Family of Man* and was one of the most represented photographers in the show. His image of a street musician in London was made during one of several trips he took to Europe between 1951 and 1953. It was included in the catalog alongside Lange's *Migrant Mother*, with Virgil's line: "What region of the earth is not full of our calamities?" Robert Frank Collection, Gift of the Herbert and Nannette Rothschild Memorial Fund in memory of Judith Rothschild, National Gallery of Art, Washington. Copyright Robert Frank, courtesy PaceWildensteinMacGill, New York.

Moscow (1959) "in response to Soviet objections." Even though Steichen saw the image as "a universal symbol of hunger," Soviet Union Chamber of Commerce president M. S. Nesterov convinced officials that a picture from the famine-stricken Hunan province did not belong in Moscow. "Famed Rice Bowl Photo Withdrawn," proclaimed an Associated Press story in the *Sioux City Journal* of 1959. The *Denver Post* reported "A Little Child Is Cast Out!" and used the fiasco to denigrate Russians, who, the story stated, saw this image as "a general slap at their Chinese allies": "The incident gives us some hints about the Communist mind, different from those we may glean from the Eisenhower-Khrushchev visits. The Communist mind cannot imagine the expression of truth for truth's sake, without an ulterior political motive. The picture *had* to be propagandistic—why else was it exhibited? So the Communist reasons." The reporter appropriated the image for his own agenda, just as the Soviets had. Communists, unlike citizens of democracies, he wrote, cannot "admit faults." This "blind spot in the Communist mind," furthermore, "makes it very tedious to try to exchange ideas with a Communist. We might as well realize this before the age of international conversation goes any further."[72] Such text demonstrates the precarious nature of American-Soviet relations; the controversy over this one image was enough to provoke this writer to call for an end to virtually all relations and negotiations with the USSR. The controversy also shows that Steichen's liberal efforts to create a unified world family were no more appreciated by some Soviets than they were by some American critics.

After *The Family of Man*'s section on famine, a more hopeful tone returned with photographs of different religions and forms of worship alongside a quotation, "Behold, this dreamer cometh," from Genesis (37:19). The next section quoted Anne Frank ("I still believe that people are really good at heart"), which accompanied images of international youth. The juxtaposition of this murdered girl's words with banal teen pursuits such as girls gossiping and couples courting strains Steichen's positive ideology. But other images of youth (speeding in a car, dancing, smoking, "making out," and one of two tough-looking, "delinquent" young women) are less "agreeable." The ever-optimistic humanist Steichen reflected that "some of those pictures of teenagers show some pretty rough-looking characters but there are also some lovely ones. I really think the human race is all right."[73] Many sociologists and parents in the mid-1950s would disagree; teen alienation, rebellion, and crime concerned many and were reflected consistently in movies such as James Dean's *Rebel without a Cause* (1955).

After this section on youth, Steichen included images confronting war

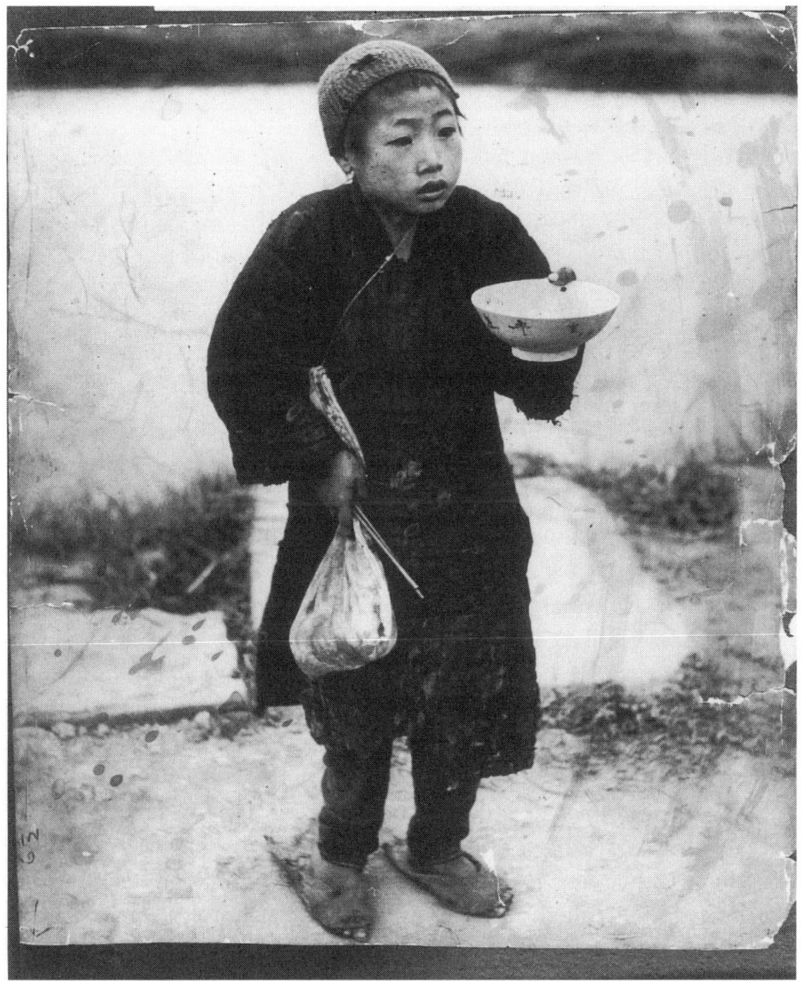

3.5. George Silk, *Chinese Boy with Bowl,* ca. 1945.

George Silk's image of a hungry Chinese boy entered the charged cold war world of politics during the 1950s. In *The Family of Man* it was surrounded by images of famine (from India, Holland, and the Arctic) and accompanied by the text "Nothing is real to us but hunger" (Kakuzo Okakura). George Silk, Life Magazine. © Time Inc.

and injustice. A World War II photograph of Jewish prisoners in the Warsaw Ghetto accompanied a hopeful quote by George Sand: "Humanity is outraged in me and with me. We must not dissimulate nor try to forget this indignation which is one of the most passionate forms of love." Consistently, such historical instances of murder and cruelty were undercut with positive and optimistic rhetoric. While the images' content strains one's ability to believe in generous human impulses, such photographs of outrage, hate, injustice, and revolt provide some of the most interesting evidence of political dissent and contradiction in a cold war world.

For instance, we find illustrations of the "restless" mind, "turbulent, strong and unyielding" (Bhagavad-Gita) in images of an unhappy, struggling baby photographed by Wayne Miller and a forlorn child trapped behind a makeshift fence photographed by ex-league member Marian Palfi (Figure 3.6). The photograph was in Palfi's *Suffer Little Children* (1952), which visualized abandoned, impoverished, and neglected children in the 1940s and contradicted the idealized American dream of equality, justice, and prosperity. Palfi, whom Steichen had already shown at MoMA, called herself not an "artist" but "a social research photographer" determined to change society. Like Hine's work, her photographs had been used before Congress and the Senate to illustrate various problems involving children in America. She also photographed other marginalized groups such as African Americans, the elderly, and Native Americans. Steichen celebrated her collective work on the marginalized, calling it "a magnificent crusade" of social content which ignored aesthetic considerations in favor of documentary intent.[74] Like many Photo League members and other social documentarians, Steichen had respect for pedagogical, humanistic messages that could activate viewers' feelings.

The theme of injustice and conflict continues with the text "Who is on my side? Who?" (2 Kings 9:32). Homer Page's photograph of a black South African living under apartheid pictures the proud man from below, a heroic figure against a sun-filled sky.[75] John Floria's *Life* photograph shows an Indonesian trolley sporting American-inspired graffiti—"All people are created equal." Such images reflect American democratic ideals but, again, are undercut by photographs of rebellion and authoritarian police forces (reminiscent of the police photographs by Photo League workers discussed in Chapter 2). Bob Schwalberg, an American Pix photographer, depicted the amorphous black form of an American cop, the buttons of his coat and cap insignia proclaiming his allegiance. Although the MoMA press release said this figure was "photographed from above as if he were literally the pillar he is figuratively," the image, like those from the Photo League, is more ambiguous. This is no proud declarative symbol of American values; instead the officer is an unindividualized blur of clothing taken from a bird's eye angle, faceless against concrete.[76]

In the catalog, facing the policeman on the opposite page is *Judge Learned*

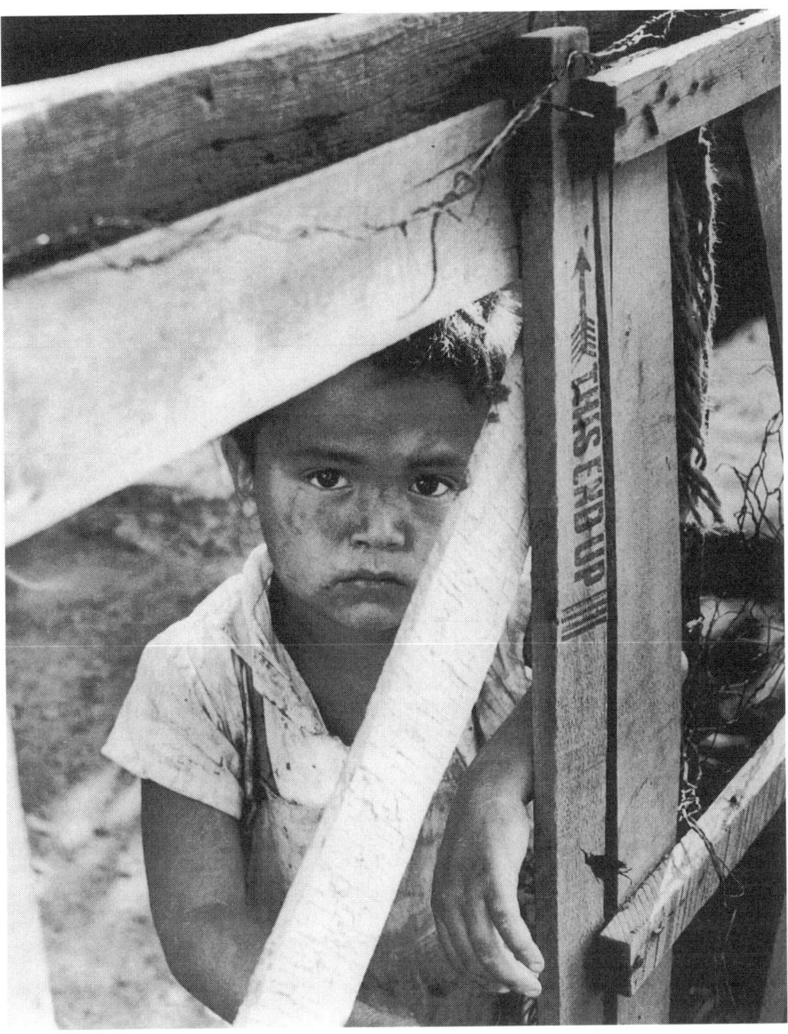

3.6. Marion Palfi *Los Angeles,* ca. 1946–49.

Former Photo League member Marion Palfi's image of a caged child in *The Family of Man* was from her earlier series on impoverished and neglected children, *Suffer Little Children*, (1952). Beside this image in the catalog is that of a distressed baby (photographed by Wayne Miller) who struggles, trapped between chair legs; in the catalog, to its right, Korean women protest behind barbed wire. Text from the Bhagavad-Gita explains: "the mind is restless, turbulent, strong and unyielding . . . as difficult to subdue as the wind." © Martin Magner. Collection Center for Creative Photography, the University of Arizona.

Hand by Dan Weiner (1952). The stern judge, to most modern viewers, seems the archetypal authority image in his robes, surrounded by open books. But Judge Learned Hand was critically involved in America's controversial purge of Communists in the trials of the 1950s. In one trial of January 1953, he held a dissenting opinion in the testimony of Ann Moos Remington, a woman who had been called to discredit her ex-husband, William Remington, a Commerce Department employee accused of passing secret government documents to Elizabeth Bentley.[77] As judge of the U.S. Southern District of New York (1909–24) and the U.S. Court of Appeals (1924–51), Judge Learned Hand had earned a reputation as an outstanding and eloquent liberal. In 1952 he published *Spirit of Liberty*, defending freedom against extremists such as McCarthy. Including Judge Hand within this section of *The Family of Man* speaks of Steichen's own liberal views toward the climate of persecution and fear. Sir Talfourd's text reinforces this message: "Fill the seats of justice / With good men, not so absolute in goodness / As to forget what human frailty is."

Steichen, as a "safe" liberal in a repressive context, does not go any further than to comment obliquely on current, general injustices that reflect not only on American politics, but also on the world. Such instances of Steichen's questioning the mainstream values so many Americans held dear are more numerous than viewers today may perceive. The narrative of the catalog and, by extension, of *The Family of Man* exhibition, does not simply reflect the cold war status-quo. The images at times explode one against another in a seesaw of liberal versus conservative values. Following the Judge, for instance, are four decontextualized images of French, Japanese, Chinese, and Turkish voters at ballot boxes, a symbol of Anglo-American democracy, and ironically supported by a Sioux Indian quotation: "Behold this and always love it! It is very sacred, and you must treat it as such."

Now approaching the end of the show's narrative, and after the images of death, loneliness, grief, pity, hard times, famine, and "man's inhumanity to man," viewers faced the most fascinating image in the show: a dramatically lit color transparency of an H-bomb explosion. According to the museum's press release, this 6 x 8 foot image was lit from behind, making it the only light in a small gallery that was painted black. The press release discussed this picture, and its implications, more than any other photograph in the show.

While the H-bomb image was not published in the catalog, it served an important function and received critical attention. Steichen, in the press release, said the image raised "one of the greatest challenges of our time—the hydrogen bomb and what it may mean for the future of the family of man."

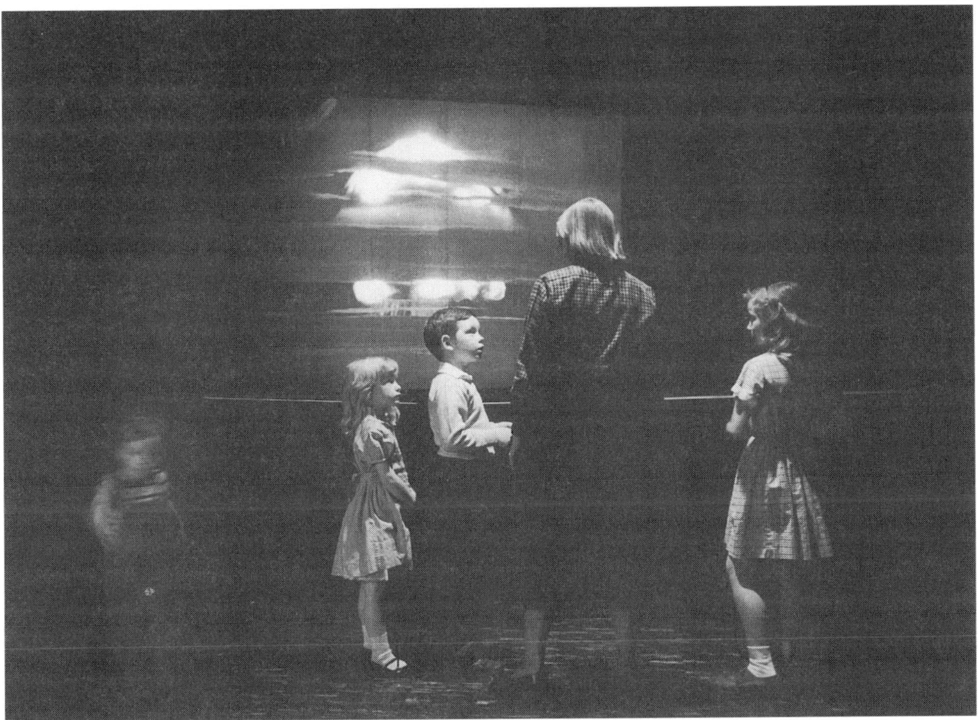

3.7.

Wayne Miller's photograph of his family in front of the H-bomb transparency in *The Family of Man* provides a look at this culminating section of the show (it was not included in the exhibition catalog). Courtesy Wayne F. Miller.

Many praised his inclusion of this image; an NBC broadcast on Steichen, *Infinity* reported, commended "the atom-bomb shot," an act that took, Wayne Miller added, "Steichen's sort of courage." The image must have been impossible for viewers to miss, since, according to Arthur Goldsmith, it was "illuminated from behind in a darkened room just before the exit." In a *Photovision* review, Ira Latour noted the "threat of total destruction now upon us" as seen in the bomb image, which he referred to as "the climax of the show." Judith Crist, in the *New York Herald Tribune*, called it, simply, "terrifying."[78]

Inclusion of this image was timely. Other images in *The Family of Man* alluded to the current scientific community's experimenting with nuclear weapons, such as Andreas Feininger's *Life* image of a glowing test tube, Farbman's *Radiation Laboratory, University of California*, and Alfred Eisenstaedt's images of the Institute for Advanced Study, Princeton. The development of the bomb increasingly preoccupied American imaginations during the cold war. Under the leadership of Robert Oppenheimer, the Manhattan Project, a secret program started in 1942 after it was learned that German scientists had split the uranium nucleus in 1939, endeavored to develop an atomic bomb for the United States. The first device was detonated on July 1945, in New Mexico, and led to the atomic bombs used in Nagasaki and Hiroshima the following month. The American monopoly on nuclear weaponry lasted four years, until Soviet scientists tested their own atomic bomb in 1949. The fear of retaliation and a nuclear war increased federal demands for the development of the H-bomb, one thousand times more powerful than the atomic bomb.

Given this cultural context, Steichen's inclusion of photographs alluding to atomic weapons signified the destructive potential of cold war policies. By the 1950s, experiments in nuclear weaponry were intensifying. Oppenheimer, regretting the monster he had unleashed, was stripped of his security clearance in 1954 after arduous court trials analyzing his communist sympathies and criticism of nuclear weaponry. That same year America committed itself to escalating cold war tensions by testing the first "super" (H-bomb) at Bikini Island in the Pacific. It is, to date, the largest hydrogen bomb ever exploded, and the blast wounded some three hundred Americans and Japanese. The "age of anxiety" intensified; admissions to mental hospitals nearly doubled between 1940 and 1956, and in 1956 Americans consumed over a billion tranquilizer pills.[79]

Federal leaders deflected public fears. President Eisenhower spoke to the UN, encouraging the use of atomic energy for "peace": in areas of industry, agriculture, medicine, and energy.[80] As hopeful as such sentiments were, Americans feared nuclear annihilation enough to construct thousands of bomb shelters in their homes during the decade. The *U.S. Camera Annuals* of the 1950s often included special sections on photographs of atom bomb tests. One spread in the 1954 issue showed stills of a film illustrating what would happen to "a typical American home in an atomic bomb test at Yucca Flat, Nevada. . . . It was not a cheerful scene." This devastating image of a typical suburban home, obliterated, was circulated in *Life* (1953). While today, as Sandeen observes, Steichen's "faith in humankind's ability to be shocked by a single mushroom cloud [may] seem naive," the photograph proves an attempted critique of his times.[81]

Steichen's bomb image must have sparked concern for the future by forcing viewers to concentrate on its visual impact. Following about five hundred images of the "human family," the rhetoric of the bomb spoke of the potential waste of human life in the face of such technology. Steichen clearly distrusted the bomb's presence in this world, calling attention to this presence and describing its destructive capabilities. The constructive potential of atomic energy, increasingly advertised to the American public during the 1950s, was not championed by Steichen or other liberal intellectuals of the era, such as I. F. Stone, who called out in 1954: "If there is still a peace movement left in America, this must be its platform. As a first step away from mutual destruction, no more tests."[82]

Steichen used the image as a documentary photographer would; the image of the atomic blast, as a key representation at the end of the show, encouraged viewers to consider their lives—and what they had just seen of other humans' lives—more deeply and with an element of feeling. On the NBC broadcast, Steichen asked: "How can anybody be satisfied [with] . . . photographing the horrible monstrosity we call 'war'? . . . I don't see how any artist can be satisfied. I couldn't be satisfied with a photograph of a cup and saucer. . . . People look at the pictures; they are exciting pictures; and occasionally they shed a tear at some tragic thing, and they tell me it was a wonderful job, and then they go out and have some drinks. That is a negative approach."[83] Steichen encouraged viewers to think and respond by *experiencing* a dramatic visualization of atomic bomb energy; his placing the large color transparency in a darkened room, in fact, put people within the very space of the symbolic "blast."

Steichen broadly generalized the issue of atomic energy by not including images of nuclear devastation or its consequences on human lives (as, perhaps, Photo League photographers, with their more specific social documentary interests, would have done). In Steichen's safer presentation, the potential of annihilation simply existed, with no culpable government or country. As noted in the MoMA press release, surrounding images of "questioning faces" and a quotation by Bertrand Russell immediately preceded the bomb image: "The best authorities are unanimous in saying that a war with hydrogen bombs is quite likely to put an end to the human race. . . . There will be universal death—sudden only for a fortunate minority, but for the majority a slow torture of disease and disintegration."

Even though Steichen's presentation of the nuclear bomb topic was distanced, safe, and general, not every viewer was sympathetic to Steichen's message. Historian and writer Lewis Mumford, in a letter to Dorothy Norman (1955) called the image "inanely bathetic: I have seen infinitely better black-and-whites that give one a sense of lonely terror, and not a bad Victorian chromo."[84] Mumford accused the bomb photograph of excessive sentimentality and triteness, but this criticism was related to its aesthetic presentation as a large, nondistinct color transparency, unable to communicate the "lonely terror" black-and-white photographs could convey. However flawed the show may have been in presentation, Steichen wanted *The Family of Man* to contribute to world peace in an age of division and fear. The image following the blast continued this general theme.

The next gallery in the show included a large sixteen-foot mural of the UN General Assembly by Maria Bordy, which is reproduced in the catalog as a two-page spread. The UN charter was quoted ("to save succeeding generations from the scourge of war"), and the viewer was confronted by a sea of women and men of many nations and colors. The pictures leading us to this grandiose vision of a united world included the bomb, a seemingly dead soldier (from Eniwetok, one of the islands where nuclear bombs were tested), and seven couples from different nations placed at right angles to the mural. Steichen created a forceful visual narrative arguing for world communication and world peace through the intervention of organizations such as the UN. While this was, perhaps, as some critics say, a ploy emphasizing democracy as a salvation to the world's ills, Steichen nevertheless used a liberal method of persuasion. Conservatives during the 1950s did not care to imagine a world in which all humans were basically similar. According to Rosenblum and others, such a world vision would not have fueled the cold war economy.[85]

The Family of Man finale, as orchestrated by Steichen, hinged on this large image of the UN, a symbol of potential salvation for warring humankind. The term *united nations* was first coined during the early years of World War II by FDR to describe countries fighting the Axis, and, in 1945, replaced the League of Nations. The UN, headquartered in New York since 1952, maintains peace and also has broader responsibilities concerning international human rights and trade. Despite right-wing fears of a "one-world" government, the UN came to symbolize the potential of international peacekeeping and cooperation among nations.

During the cold war years, some politicians, such as the progressive liberal Henry Wallace, felt that a strong UN committee could preserve the precarious peace in that era, specifically that between the US and the Soviet Union. Such notions of a united world were not always welcome. As Richard Pells points out, many conservatives were unenamored "with the Soviet Union or the vaporous notions of 'one world.'" In 1954, I. F. Stone linked the UN, the cold war, and the bomb. Discussions of disarmament between the United States and the USSR at the UN, he maintained, were "insoluble. For there is no way to convince either side that any system of inspection and control may not be evaded or abused by the other."[86] Clearly, Steichen, champion of the UN, communicated his own liberal message of hope to the masses of viewers by means of the size and prominence of this photograph in *The Family of Man*.

This message was not lost on most reviewers of the show. In 1955 O. N. Solbert, in the George Eastman House journal, *Image*, remarked that *The Family of Man* "most importantly is a contribution to the understanding of world peace. It is a document that speaks the same language to all people by all people the world over in their longing and striving for security."[87] Cognizant of cold war tensions, even superficial reviews often praised the potentially healing aspects of the show in regard to the unstable contemporary political climate.

The image of the UN was followed by photographs of Steichen's hope for the future—children (in the catalog these pictures of children fill the final three pages). Most are positive images that include nature—children playing, exploring, interacting—but some are not. They also include images of a one-legged boy in Morocco and poor children on the streets. The final catalog image, the one most often used to describe the naive sentimentality of the exhibition, is by W. Eugene Smith, which pictures two children walking in the woods. It is accompanied by a text, "A world to be born under your footsteps" (St.-John Perse).

Smith's photograph, *Walk to Paradise Garden*, 1946, captures his own son Patrick and daughter Juanita from behind, walking out of a darker area of woods into sunlight, while gentle arboring tree limbs frame their small forms on a path. Steichen had worked with Smith in the naval photography unit during World War II; Smith's commitment to documentary photojournalism was said to have turned "old Steichen to jelly." As Jim Hughes points out: "In a world of hydrogen bombs and the increasing nihilism of intellectuals," this image epitomized Steichen's belief in "affirmation and hope." It became, for Steichen, "a twentieth-century icon."[88]

The concept for this image grew from Smith's careful consideration of artistic and philosophical choices. The day Smith took the image, he recalled, was revelatory, "a day of spiritual decision," during a time when he was recovering from war wounds in 1946:

> It was a spring day. . . . We walked along, these my children—and I. We were in different worlds, for the children were exultant in exploring their new world, and I was desperately trying to regain my powers from a past world. . . . The children remained unaware of my struggle to control the wracking turbulence of my mind as I pushed against the physical and mental handicaps that were hampering my photographic speech. . . . as I watched I knew again that in spite of all of it, and in spite of every war, and of every setback, that today, now, I wished to speak out

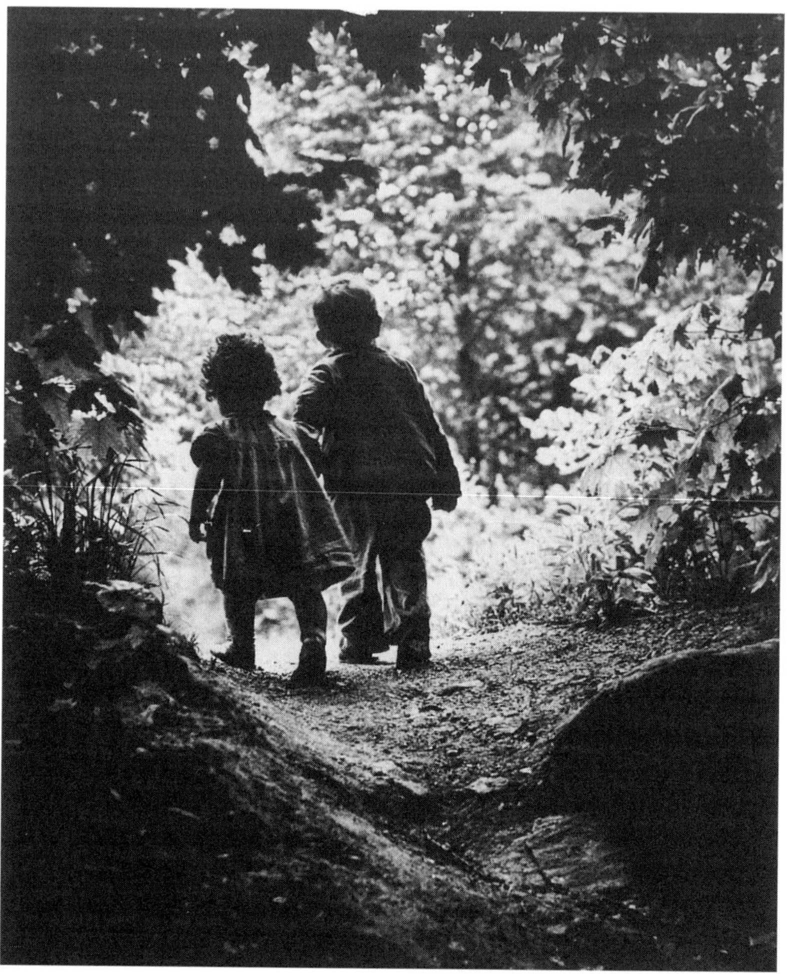

3.8. W. Eugene Smith, *Walk to Paradise Garden,* 1946.

W. Eugene Smith photographed his children walking in the woods (symbolizing the future) after he returned, depressed and despairing, from the war in 1946. A final, crowning image in *The Family of Man* exhibition and catalog, it symbolized for Smith and Steichen "affirmation and hope." St.-John Perse's text reinforced the photograph's optimistic appeal: "A world to be born under your footsteps." © W. Eugene Smith, Courtesy Blackstar Publishing Co., Inc.

a sonnet for life and of the worth of continuing. . . . The reaction was immediate. I knew the photograph, though not perfect, and however unimportant to the world, had been held. Shock waves of feeling released through me, breaking damply out of my flesh. Mist hazed my eyes, I began to tremble, nearly sick; I

> turned away that my children who had continued on might not turn and discover I was crying—crying out from the agony of my relief.[89]

As much as this image meant to Smith, Hughes maintains that *Life* turned it down at the time because the figures were walking away from the viewers. However, the image did appear in *Life's* picture essay mentioned earlier, "My Daughter Juanita," although it was reproduced only as a small insert photograph.

The popular appreciation for this image made it a potent advertising tool; the Ford Motor Company used *Paradise Garden* for an advertisement (1952), as did the Mutual of New York Insurance Company, Kodak, and the International Ladies' Garment Workers Union. Smith received letters from international admirers of the picture who appreciated its narrative. In a story for his local newspaper, the *Croton-Harmon News*, Smith said the photograph was taken to counter the horrors of World War II and that its message was "for freedom, for justice, for human rights. . . . It was a good day on which to try. A beautiful, warm spring day to cradle a man's efforts to reclaim himself."[90] Photo League members, following Hine's lead, also had often turned to children as subjects (though, typically, they focused on poor, urban ones) in their efforts to communicate larger societal issues to viewers. A legacy of the documentary tradition continued in this image from *The Family of Man*.

Steichen called *Paradise Garden* "the perfect closing" photograph, which "best tell[s] the story of humanity around the world. . . . Why perfect? A good answer, I think, lies in the words of Robert Frost, which were printed on this page not long ago. When a reporter asked him what he thought about life, Frost replied, Vermont-fashion, in just three words. He said, '*It goes on!*' . . . Hand in hand, they are marching into the future on confident feet—symbols of a fear-free faith, of the strength and dignity of man, of the rich promise of tomorrow."[91] Given the difficult images preceding *Paradise Garden* in *The Family of Man*, viewers ultimately were given a liberal dose of Steichen's political optimism. As Steichen said, "that is our real faith—children."[92] One of Steichen's three images in the show even pictured his own children, Mary and Kate, as members of the universal family.

The photograph by Smith, the H-bomb transparency, and the UN scene sum up the critical complexity of the show. Together these elements prompt two questions: Are we to ignore individual images' artistic intent and content in *The Family of Man* in favor of the show's message as a totality, or can certain photographs be said to undermine that totality in their contextual relationship to the political scene? Was Steichen a soft, armchair liberal trying to challenge the contemporary state of affairs, or was he, in more current slang, a right-wing reactionary in politically correct sheep's clothing?

Steichen, in theory, wanted to expand and challenge viewers' minds with *The Family of Man*, but apparently he had to capitulate to certain societal norms. In the *Picturescope* essay of July 1955, Steichen mentioned a mysterious image that had disappeared from *The Family of Man*—a photograph of a black man, lynched and chained to a tree, called *Death Slump at Mississippi Lynching*, (1937, photographer unknown). The image had been included in the opening of the show, but had been removed after that. A few early articles on the exhibition, including one in *Life*, reproduced it as an illustration. Steichen mentioned the image in the 1955 essay: "We tried to be very honest in this exhibition. The lynching photograph has hurt many people—and many don't like it in the show—but I feel it plays an important part. It is an expression of our honesty—we admit that we are not always right or good." He nevertheless soon followed the quotation above with his idiosyncratic optimism: "I really think the human race is all right. If we weren't all right then we would have messed ourselves up long, long ago." Sandeen points out that the image probably provoked too much controversial attention and detracted viewers from the overriding theme.[93]

When *Life* published the lynching photograph, it was surrounded by three others from the show under the heading, "Tensions turned to dread and hate": *Playtime Torment in Chicago Park* by Yasuhiro Ishimoto (a small girl, her hands tied behind her to a tree, with a fearful expression), *Son's Rebellious Fury on Connecticut Lawn* by George Heyer (a small boy lifts a plank of wood almost as big as he is while a woman, in a position of fear, puts her arms out in a protective thrust), and, finally, *Panic as Communists Approach Shanghai* by Cartier-Bresson (a huddled mass of Chinese people with various facial expressions are tightly boxed within a claustrophobic space).[94] In *The Family of Man* catalog the Heyer photograph appeared with the Ishimoto while the Cartier-Bresson was reproduced with other visualized instances of political repression (in the United States, Germany, South Africa, and Indonesia) alongside the aforementioned biblical caption, "Who is on my side? Who?"

The lynching image, however, was not included in the catalog. As Steichen mentioned, the image was important to him, a shocking, repugnant image of truth concerning his own country's racism; specifically how and why it was removed remains a mystery. Goldsmith recalls seeing the image in the first days of the show, a "powerful aspect" of the exhibit. For Goldsmith, the image provoked him to understand more fully the negative aspects to the "family of man." Rollie McKenna's review in the *New Republic* (1955) also mentioned this photograph, which "sears the mind." The brutal scene may have distracted viewers because of its specificity to American racism; it may have been too violent in its political reverberations. Perhaps, too, it was deemed insensitive to African American viewers, who would be witnessing what may be a so-called trophy shot taken by the subject's murderers. Whatever the case, clearly Steichen's "family" could, at times, be inhumane.[95]

Steichen expressed general concern for the plight of African Americans. Even earlier, in outlining his plans for MoMA, he mentioned having a "new project in mind on the subject of the American Negro . . . that will reveal the Negro simply as a human being, just like everybody else."[96] However well-intentioned, the project never came to fruition. More recently, scholars such as bell hooks have noted that diluted liberal ideals will "often give lip service to a vision of diversity and plurality while clinging to notions of sameness."[97] By removing the lynching image, Steichen also removed the most specific, repulsive image of oppression and the dehumanizing aspects of white supremacy.

The hazy history of the lynching image underscores the troubled state of documentary within the emerging cold war climate; whereas subject matter critical of American democracy was sought by Photo League photographers, by the repressive 1950s such content was discouraged. Yet social documentarians never simply sought to expose the negative, or "depressing," social factors in American culture; they also sought to portray the underclass with dignity, to inspire hope for social change. The horrifying lynching image, within the context of *The Family of Man*, was not developed enough as a theme to join seamlessly with the totality of the show. That image may have ruptured the optimistic discourse too deeply by betraying the black subject, not as a safely objectified or noble fetish, but as a justifiably angry victim of racism.

Owing to such highly controversial images and the show's popularity, *The Family of Man* was reviewed in many magazines and newspapers throughout the United States. While most of the popular press reviews applauded the show, others voiced criticisms which have followed it to this day. Some praised its popularity and ability to draw nations together; others found fault with Steichen's philosophical dominance and vision; still others disliked the design and the way photographs were printed and presented.

Popular Photography, a magazine devoted more to technical issues in photography than to aesthetics or critical debate, published a long, favorable article on the show in May 1955, including many installation shots and championing the "spectacular" exhibition. The installation shots recreated the passageways designed for the show, while the article's minimal text described the visual effects. An essay by Goldsmith discusses the "gargantuan" show, which "will be praised, damned, criticized, and discussed for a long time to come." He notes the variety of human experiences pictured and the tremendous attendance numbers. Goldsmith also observes that Steichen drew heavily from journalistic and documentary photographs and was "guided by story-telling content as much as by the artistic merit of each picture." The design of the show, Goldsmith admits, sometimes "lapsed into the melodramatic or overly clever" but overall enhanced the photographs. A diagram of the show's layout was included, alongside a listing of the various themes. This drawing helps recreate the designed environment viewers wove through in the "interplay of overlapping, three-dimensional forms."[98]

Goldsmith knew *The Family of Man* viewers would react with a variety of responses. Some would see this show not as art, he notes, but as "a social and anthropological document" belonging to the Museum of Natural History. Others, he writes, would question the theme—"an optimistic assumption of the 'essential oneness and goodness of man.'" Finally, still others might criticize the way "some pictures are linked . . . as superficial." In any case, "it is Steichen's hope that *The Family of Man*, with its message of brotherhood spoken in the universal language of photography, may in some measure help ease the tensions afflicting mankind today." Not all *Popular Photography* viewers sympathetically accepted Steichen's universal theme in *The Family of Man*. One letter-writer castigates the "trite" concept of the show, which he claims was "based on ignorance if not a lie." Mr. E. L. Gates, an editor of the *General Semantics Bulletin*, suggests that a better title might have been "The Family of Mammals" due to the "excessive concentration on man's procreation, pregnancy, and childbirth."[99]

The *Photovision* review by Latour noted that "even Russia is represented. . . . It would be a fine thing if the exhibition could be sent to the people of Russia in a token of friendship and as a reminder that, after all, we are all brothers." Latour's short essay appreciated the more global, political implications (and applications) of the show, taking into account contemporary American fears of Soviet atomic weaponry and aggression. Latour's ideals were not realized, as far as we know. In 1959, when the show toured the Soviet Union at the American Exhibition (also the site of Nixon and Khrushchev's "kitchen debate"), it was viewed as a decisive political statement and event. Reporters often used the show as an opportunity to discuss Soviet aggression; headlines included "Red Feet Crumble US Exhibit Floor" and "Is US Fair 'Converting' Russians?"[100]

The propagandistic appropriation of *The Family of Man* by writers or agencies during the show's international travels calls for further study. From 1955 to 1962, five versions of the show traveled throughout thirty-eight foreign countries (underwritten by the United States Information Agency). Although Steichen's participation in these uses of the show has not been established, *The Family of Man* was used by several political and ideological forces to further the cold war discourse and "sell" American values overseas; it became, as Eric Sandeen notes, a "commodity in cultural diplomacy."[101] Rave reviews flowed into the museum from Bombay, Havana, Stockholm, Jerusalem, Paris, and many other points across the globe. Lange, writing to Steichen from Saigon on September 25, 1958, said: "I hear of [*The Family of Man*] all over, and in unexpected places—for instance, in a tiny Chinese fishing village . . . in a Philippine barrio. . . . I think that if ever you were to visit the Philippines, and they heard of it, you would receive a Heroe's [sic] Welcome, a public celebration, and a big parad [sic]. In fact, I have been so informed."[102]

Because of *The Family of Man*'s wide-ranging appeal, organizations rarely associated with the artistic elite embraced the show for their own purposes. The *UAW-CIO Ammunition*, a union labor magazine for the International Union of United Automobile, Aircraft and Agricultural Implement Workers of America, lauded *The Family of Man*, seeing their own members as part of the family. The reviewer commended the show's themes, such as "The Bitter Problem of Unemployment," "The Many Sides of Political Action," "Fighting for More Than Themselves," and, lastly, "Building a Better Life for the Family of Man." That this union publication would spend so much space on the exhibit reveals the populist interest in the show. The periodical also presented its own version of union workers photographed as a "family" of workers: on the job, at recreation, pursuing "progress with the community" (handing out pamphlets). One caption, under an image of a crowd of men and women, black and white, read "The Union Is People."[103] The editors connected, with ease, Steichen's view of a global humanity with their own progressive labor concerns.

Edwin Rosskam, who had been an FSA documentary photographer and Photo League member, positively, yet cautiously, reviewed the show for *Artnews*. He calls Steichen "a kindly man, with an almost innocent faith in the essential goodness of life," who "seems to shy away from the cruelties and stupidities so amply demonstrated by men of all kinds." The show, he notes, did not avoid conflict (displaying, as it did, images of the bomb, the Depression, and Hitler), but it treated such conflict too gently. As a whole, Rosskam states, the exhibition "ends up as a fervent and undisguised plea for immediate world unity and co-operation." This review points to differences between earlier documentary ideals and Steichen's show; whereas the FSA and most Photo League photographers made efforts to visualize difference (the specific effects on lives considering class, race, and gender), Steichen diluted social conflict by presenting humanity as a generalized totality without any culpable force (such as capitalism) at fault. Furthermore, according to Rosskam, in combination with Paul Rudolph's rather trivializing, gimmicky design and presentation, Steichen "occasionally defeats his own ends."[104]

Rosskam's critical and even-handed article, however, was poorly summed up when reprinted in a bibliography published by *Aperture* (1955) on the show's reviews. The *Aperture* writer, probably Minor White, argued that Rosskam "excuses all the lapses of taste because he has caught the white hope of this show, to unite people, no matter how little, at a desperate time when separation may mean a crippling of civilization."[105] *Aperture*, as the premier symbol of formally engaged photographers who were more akin to abstract expressionists than social documentarians, derided Steichen's effort (and, in their eyes, failure) to "unite people" and noted that his lack of "taste" crippled the exhibition.

Of all the photo magazine reviews, *Aperture*'s response was the most stinging. The issue excerpted numerous reviewers' comments in a large section called "The Controversial Family of Man," which included pieces from: Jacob Deschin and Aline B. Saarinen for the *New York Times*; Dorothy Norman; a bibliography of newspapers with articles covering the exhibition; a "re-enacted" conversation on the show by George and Cora Wright; and one by former league member Barbara Morgan. Read together, these articles touch upon almost every critical issue associated with the show to this day. Despite the variety of reviews, the journal's overall sense of aesthetic superiority and disdain for the show's philosophy and popularity is communicated.

Aperture's disapproval of the show was manifested in various sarcastic blurbs. One paragraph gleefully noted reviewer Phoebe Lou Adams's "kid[ding] the daylights out of the sentimentality with which apparently any show must be loaded that is aimed at today's juke box and TV stunned public." Another section facetiously asked how photography would change once "the hobbyist" turns "this powerful magnificent all-dignity theme into drivel." While *The Family of Man* proved "how quickly the milk of human kindness turns to schmaltz," *Aperture* worked hard to distance itself from populist mass media and mainstream kitsch.[106]

The debate between freelance writers George and Cora Wright criticized the show with cynical humor. George, as "Devil's Advocate," defended the show to his wife, Cora, mimicking situation comedy dialogue. The biting humor raised critical questions: Cora asks, "Is it legitimate . . . to overlook . . . powerful expressions and use individual photos only as bricks to build up a different theme?" George then wonders if whether, instead of splitting up images originally planned in groupings, they had been left contextually intact, the photographs "might have gotten across a deeper and truer glimpse of reality." Furthermore, he says (sounding more and more like the individualist editor and arch-modernist, White): "When we see a group of pictures made by [a photographer], we enter his subjective world to look at reality through his eyes. But mixed up with others in a show, he surrenders this individuality—just as a writer might if he gave permission for single paragraphs to be quoted by an editor in any sequence and in any context." He also adds: "Here is the crux of all the criticism, isn't it: should Steichen be announcing to the public that all men are brothers, or should he be educating it that photographers, like painters, have powerful, individual, personal statements to make?"[107]

This dialogue examines the polarities and ambiguities between individual expression and documentary or journalistic vision, and the more inner-directed, heroic visionary is lauded. *Aperture* readers were encouraged to grapple with the thorny issue of artistic independence in a medium often defined by outer control (from newspaper or magazine editors and even museum directors). Like George Wright, the magazine lamented this "Century of the all-too-damned-Common Man," which collectively degraded photographers as "faceless." The most biting blurb criticizing the show, and Steichen in particular, followed a quotation from the catalog's introduction ("the art of photography is a dynamic process of giving form to ideas and of explaining man to man"): "The ideal department head of a museum would be expected to take a larger view of the art of photography." In other words, *Aperture* considered Steichen a narrow, provincial arbiter of populist taste who did not reflect the broader, deeper concerns of fine art photography. According to *Aperture*, the photographer should be more like the ideal abstract expressionist painter—heroic, mythic, searching, formalist—the existentialist individual few in the masses would ever truly understand.

Dorothy Norman's historical claim to fame was her close association with Stieglitz. In her *Aperture* review she discusses his traditional disinterest in mass photographic reproduction and popular exhibitions—traits that Steichen was known for. Her article compares Stieglitz to Steichen, in oppositional terms that call to mind the Strand-Grossman polarity critics often constructed. Norman reconciles Stieglitz's and Steichen's work, while also defending each man's artistic vision. She admired Steichen for his attempt "to project his own vision of life," his "passionate concern" for humanity. Remembering the two mens' tender reunion a few week's before Stieglitz's death, she harmonizes the opposite tendencies each man represents to her: "Is there not room for both traditions—that of Steichen and that of Stieglitz—plus every other approach that is alive? . . . The one thing that cannot be held against the Steichen exhibition is that it is not in the 'purist' tradition of Stieglitz. It does not pretend to be. It must be judged according to its own merits; for its own lacunae. It cannot be judged for what it is not."[108]

It is no wonder that Adams's scathing review, "Through a Lens Darkly," in the *Atlantic Monthly*, is mentioned favorably in *Aperture*. Adams wrote that Steichen had failed miserably (in regard to both content and presentation). She condescendingly noted that humankind, as displayed in the show, had not stepped "beyond the Stone Age" and that the show itself "is arranged as a piece of sympathetic magic." Steichen tried to prove that "mankind is all good" by excluding "deliberate evil." Certainly most of the images in *The Family of Man* were optimistic; however, a number of photographs clearly alluded to "deliberate" human evils (World War, atomic weapons, male aggression against women, racism, poverty, and famine, for instance). These negative images were, apparently, ignored by Adams, who had been overwhelmed by the positive. Adams was particularly disgusted by idealized visions of women nursing ("very décolleté") and the aforementioned "not-too-pregnant girls." She added, disparagingly, as if such classical Freudian conditions were as absolute as Steichen's own sense of a universal family, that "there are no Oedipal shadows in this sharply focused world." Perhaps for this reason, Adams did appreciate "the photographs representing loneliness," a "true" human condition according to her existential definition of modern humanity. After the H-bomb image, "looking like any other splash of orange fire," Adams continued, "encouragement" was provided by the UN picture while "consolation" was found in photographs of romping children: "mankind is back in the second grade and enjoying every minute of it" (even, one presumes, the one-legged boy).[109]

Adams ends by pointing out that Steichen "neglected to conjure the intangible beliefs and preferences that divide men into countries and parties and clans" (a difficult anthropological task to complete, given the size of MoMA's second floor). She does not mention the fact that Steichen deliberately tried to unite those clans, countries, and parties in an effort to unify dissenting groups and foster understanding. Adams ignored individual images of conflict and ambiguity, overwhelmed instead by the positive totality of the experience. Ideologically, Adams was like the alienated "outsider" described by Marxist Ernst Fischer in 1959, who refused to commit to anything, was free from all social obligations, and sought redemption of the existential "I." She rose "above the world of commons" to "gaze down with sarcastic superiority upon the clumsy efforts of [her] 'committed' brethren."[110]

An important criticism for Adams and others, however, was the show's aesthetic failure. In addition to his social myopia, Steichen was posited as an antimodernist who "tolerates . . . no nonsense with symbolism, distortion, combined images, or anything else that might suggest an individual point of view behind the camera." The elitist, aesthetically snobbish tone continues with Adams's comment that "creative seems not quite the right term for this style. Transferred to writing, for instance, it would put a news reporter in the same line of business as a novelist." The logical conclusion of Adams's argument is that intellectually valid art is fragmented, complex, and difficult to understand (paralleling Clement Greenberg's praise of "important art" like abstract expressionism). Ironically, Adams herself was a writer for a magazine; but then, the *Atlantic Monthly* was a literary publication, over a century old, Boston based, with an elite and illustrious cadre of contributors.[111]

Others in the American intellectual, photographic, and artistic communities cynically chafed at Steichen's *Family of Man*. While the reductive, idealized concept of a global family was certainly challenged by many critics, many other negative reviews also stressed the show's aesthetic weaknesses in photographic reproduction and presentation of images. The show did not reflect the growing trend toward overtly personal, individual, and non-narrative photography reflective more of the image maker than society's ills at large.

The traditional documentary paradigm had shifted and fluctuated as photography became more entrenched in cold war politics. That any social "truth" existed and could be communicated to viewers was increasingly questioned by many critics. Subsequent scholarship on *The Family of Man* perpetuates the point of view that Steichen simply upheld the American status quo of the 1950s and disdains his illustrative, popular, "low-art" tactics.[112] In numerous secondary sources we are told that the show was a culturally and aesthetically embarrassing moment in the course of American art. Such sources trace the further collapse of social documentary ideals in following decades, as well as the rise of a postmodern sensibility. As Colin Osman notes, "later reaction against *The Family of Man* ushered in the period of truly contemporary photography."[113] From Adams's article to more recent criticism, readers can trace the decline of the intellectual left as it fell prey to elitist, aesthetic arguments which, in the end, silenced the voices of many documentary-oriented artists.

In *On Photography* (1973), Susan Sontag took the show to task, comparing it to the later work of Diane Arbus (who was represented in *The Family of Man* by one image from *Vogue*). Sontag wrote that the exhibition was "the last sigh of the Whitmanesque erotic embrace of the nation but universalized and stripped of all demands." In contrast, tourist-voyeur Arbus, in a more sardonic and existentially attuned manner, illustrated in her art of the 1960s that "everybody is an alien, hopelessly isolated . . . crippled."[114] Sontag's depressive criticism tells us more about the state of the intellectual left in the 1970s than *The Family of Man* in the 1950s. The "anti-humanist" Arbus reflects the critical taste of following decades, whereas Steichen, in the evolutionary course of art, represented a dying breed of humanistic dinosaurs.

The exhibition signaled, for many critics, a detour from the modernist course of American photography toward inwardly directed aesthetics and the disintegration of "truth" embraced by documentarians of earlier years. John Szarkowski, who had inherited Steichen's position as Director of Photography at the museum in 1962, called the show (in *Mirrors and Windows*, 1978) one of the three most important events in photography of the 1950s (alongside the founding of *Aperture* and Frank's *The Americans*); otherwise, it received scant attention from him. In a statement reminiscent of the dying dinosaur analogy, Szarkowski wrote that *The Family of Man* "was perhaps the last and greatest achievement in the group journalism concept of photography—in which the personal intentions of the photographer are subservient to a larger, overriding concept." The show, he maintained, "ran counter" to the decade's younger, "original" photographers and "had little perceptible effect on the subsequent directions of American photography."[115] Szarkowski dismissed *The Family of Man* because it could not and did not presage the important aesthetic directions of the future. Instead, it represented the last dying breath of documentary dominance in photography and became inextricably linked with the "inferior" category of journalism.

Christopher Phillips grappled deeply with the philosophical issues surrounding the "family of man," noting its violation of "high art" aesthetics and artistic individuality in order to create a subjective, orchestrated meaning (outlining, for example, how Steichen reprinted photos using his own darkroom operators and included captions of his own choosing). In Steichen's hands, then, the show resembled a huge mass media magazine layout, wherein the "photographer's eye" was deemphasized in favor of design. The fine art tradition of photography was further undermined by the fact that photographs were flush mounted (as Hine and Grossman had preferred), not matted and displayed under glass (as Stieglitz and Strand had preferred). While Steichen gained a large following and audience through his tactics, the "price exacted at MoMA," according to Phillips, "was the eclipse of the individual photographer and the subordination of his or her work to the more or less overtly instrumental demands of illustration."[116]

These comments reveal the distance between the post-1970s apotheosis of photographs as museum collectibles and Steichen's populist enterprise.

Gerry Badger, in *American Images* (1985), aligned *The Family of Man* "firmly . . . on the right" and accused "humanist documentary photography" of "self-deceit," as it acquiesced, affirmed, and promoted "mass cultural values." Critics such as Badger distrusted the show's popularity—a sure sign of artistic incompetence, since mass appeal can only signify aesthetic or even ideological inferiority. Modernist views of the artist often reject any hint of popular appeal. Like most studies of *The Family of Man*, Badger's did not isolate specific images (and risk, perhaps, decontextualization) in order to glimpse moments of contradiction or conflict. Instances of charged images, such as the photograph of the bomb, demonstrate that, more broadly speaking, *The Family of Man* was not a completely passive, delightfully holistic, and positive humanistic statement. In reducing the exhibit to a knee-jerk reactionary response to cold war policies, many scholars have, in a sense, been guilty of the very crime they accuse the show of—simplistic reductivism. If one focuses only on these generalities, *The Family of Man* more easily becomes archetypal of the stereotypically conformist 1950s. Badger also criticized the show's lack of resolution concerning "the thorny issue of meaning" and credited "the shift towards personal, interior concerns" to the belief that "in so doing a more honest, heartfelt, meaningful and relevant form of photographic expression might be attained."[117] Meaning, then, is *truer* when directed inwardly, not outwardly toward the world of social concerns. Such interpretation allows Badger's text to move deftly on to a modernist artist whose works ably illustrate the artistic and ideological disintegration of "truth"—Siskind, a premier example of the formally engaged photographer of this century.

Siskind himself dismissed *The Family of Man* as a show "for journalists" only. Magnum photographer Burt Glinn, who had one image in the show (culled from *Life* files), described it as "sentimental," the preferred adjective among many other photographers in recalling the show. Helen Gee, however, acknowledged that the show affirmed photography in the eyes of the public and provided a huge showing of contemporary work. While Gee was somewhat skeptical of Steichen's theme, which she said "subordinated the work of the individual photographers," she also claimed to have been "deeply moved by it": "I think this Steichen-bashing phenomenon is sort of like toppling the gods. Whether you approve of *The Family of Man* or not I think his performance as a whole at the Museum was extraordinary. Nobody else was doing anything like it. Photography was then in the basement and he finally got it upstairs. And this contribution has almost been ignored. You don't want to sound like one of those old fogies who believe that everything in the fifties was wonderful but it was a powerful, moving exhibition."[118]

Sandeen, whose book on *The Family of Man* represents the most fully contexualized research to date, would later agree; he notes that the argument accusing Steichen of a lack of understanding in "fine arts" presentation misunderstands the show's purpose. Steichen, he writes, "ignored Manichean cold war ideologies and entrenched canons of taste" deliberately; his purpose was not "to fight high culture or pander" to vulgar taste but to craft a show excluding categories of class.[119]

In a way, critics such as Szarkowski have not *allowed* documentary work in *The Family of Man* to have any effect; photographs with political content have been repeatedly dismissed and effectively silenced by the critical, intellectual community of later decades. Or they were appropriated by conservative forces, such as Rockefeller or the United States Information Agency, who molded particular images to their own propagandistic ends. Again, this transition and growing distrust of documentary photography must be considered parallel to the repressive political climate of America in the 1950s, when overtly "political" art and activism could land you in a HUAC court (as it did for Shahn) or, in combination with personal progressive ideals, could initiate FBI surveillance (as in Grossman's case). Furthermore, in the cultural chaos of the late 1950s, with its Beat literary movement and civil rights activism setting the stage for the 1960s, fewer and fewer thoughtful Americans could complacently accept a positivist, objective concept of "truth" when the very myths upon which such a concept stood were unavoidably crumbling.

In 1957, Roland Barthes, the French semiotician, disdained the show's flimsy moral assumptions of a universal "man" born of God. This shallow, sentimental presumption, he wrote, suppressed "the determining weight of History" and prevented penetration into "this ulterior zone of human behavior where historical alienation introduces some 'differences' which we shall here quite simply call 'injustices.'" Barthes then went for the American jugular: if you want to posit a universal humanity, "why not ask the parents of Emmett Till, the young Negro assassinated by the Whites what *they* think of *The Great Family of Man?*"[120] Unfortunately, Barthes wrote without having known of the removed image of the lynched African American man; it would be interesting to read his reaction to its overt referencing of American racism. Even so, the inclusion of the anonymous photograph would probably not have satisfied Barthes' charge of reductivism, as he investigated the multivocality and unfixed nature of visual "meaning."

Barthes' intelligent review of *The Family of Man* presages key issues in contemporary criticism of the show. Its "sentimentality" was derided by Barthes, as were the myth of human "community" and the theory of "human essence." Like Adams, Barthes was more pessimistic about the existential cold war world; the show's grandiose themes rang hollow. For instance, Barthes dissected the theme of death in *The Family of Man*, noting that nothing was said about its prevention, instead its "essence" was celebrated. Similarly, he stated, "work is 'natural' just as long as it is 'profitable.'" Barthes, sickened by the show's hopeful sentiment, argued persuasively for a historicist examination of the sign systems Steichen presented as "natural." He also, as Sandeen points out, probably saw "signs of unwelcome Americanization of European experience." Colin Wilson noted in *The Outsider* (1956), with words that could apply to Barthes: "the Outsider is a man who cannot live in the comfortable, insulated world of the bourgeois, accepting what he sees and touches as reality."[121]

Later, in *Camera Lucida* (1981), Barthes would write that "photography cannot signify (aim at a generality) except by assuming a mask."[122] Steichen wore such a mask; during the cold war, could he have achieved his critique any other way?

Steichen never professed to represent all humanity in *The Family of Man*; as he said, the show "only barely indicates the universe." He tried to present an exhibition that might help heal a splintered world verging on nuclear war. He called it "an article of faith—an antidote to the horror we have been fed from day to day for a number of years."[123] Like documentary minded artists, he felt that liberal, humanist views (articulated in photographic imagery) could indeed inspire and improve humankind or could even be "true." In order for the show to succeed and win the approval of a vast audience, he cautiously presented the photographs from a safe, capitulating stance, even removing offending images when necessary.

The analyses of a few specific images expose contradictory forces, or subtle subterfuge, within the narrative totality of *The Family of Man*. In its time, this exhibition, in small part, countered right-wing, isolationist, imperialist rhetoric and aspired to a documentary language of humanistic inclusion, a point of view in contrast to the splintering of national and racial groups into enemy camps. But any hint of contradiction has been buried under forty years of hostility toward the show. The criticism has emphasized the oppression of "otherness" (not American) while ignoring the ideological sources for such a philosophical position and difficult cultural conditions under which the show was realized.

Given the suppression, even destruction, of documentary photographers such as Grossman during the cold war years, Steichen's effort at communicating traditional social documentary ideals, as diluted as they were in *The Family of Man*, might be seen as a survival tactic within the repressive sociopolitical context of the 1950s. Steichen's critique of mainstream, conservative American ideals can only surface through the study of individual photographs that counter cold war rhetoric of the times.

4

Robert Frank: The Only Game in Town?

All alone in the night I had my own thoughts and held the car to the white line in the holy road. What was I doing? Where was I going? I'd soon find out.

Jack Kerouac, *On the Road*

Out of the thousands of photographers during the cold war, Robert Frank has emerged as the defining voice of his generation.[1] His ironic, deliberately anti-aesthetic visions of American life in the 1950s undermined traditional ideals formed during the heyday of social documentary. His ascendancy is as ironic as his images; while he assisted Steichen during the formation of *The Family of Man* and displayed numerous images in that show and others, he increasingly rebelled against the elder man, much like a son rejecting the lessons of his father. Since the publication of his profoundly innovative and influential collection of images, *The Americans* (1959), Frank has been heralded as the premier bohemian photographer of the 1950s—an isolated genius misunderstood by the popular press and persecuted for his satirical, unidealized images of American society. In reality, Frank was hardly isolated, and, while a "bohemian," he successfully worked for popular presses. Such dialectical complexity and mythmaking in Frank's career signify the complex shifts in American photography during the cold war years as a more modernist (even prepostmodernist) artistic style began to overshadow documentary ideals. Analyses of his life, images in *The Americans* involving African Americans, women, and cars, the critical reception of this book, and subsequent histories of his *oeuvre* illuminate how Frank both used and modified traditional social documentary ideals in the 1950s.

Frank was an outsider when he arrived in the United States in 1947 at the age of 22. He was born in 1924 to a bourgeois Jewish family in Zurich. He was no outsider to photography—during the war he had apprenticed with several film companies in Switzerland, eventually immigrating to the United

States with an impressive portfolio in hand.[2] That he was soon hired by Alexey Brodovich at *Harper's Bazaar* indicates the high quality of his work and his enthusiastic European letters of introduction. Those early photographs (including shots of pristine, highly focused still lifes which rival Edward Weston's photographic clarity) demonstrate his technical skill. While studies of his life and work have neglected Frank's early years as a European photographer, the student prints he brought with him prove his sophisticated technical ability and multiple visual interests, ranging from skewed perspectival studies, landscape scenes, and still life studies to street scenes and skiers.[3]

During his employment at *Harper's Bazaar*, Frank photographed accessories for both *Harper's* and *Junior Bazaar*. Like Andy Warhol, Frank had a "rags to riches" career that started with department store window design and advertising shots of women's belts and shoes. But Frank was not comfortable in fashion photography; while he admired Brodovitch's interest in going beyond the stereotypical fashion photograph, he noted, "I was never any good at fashion photography. I had no interest in clothes."[4]

Frank independently pursued his own interests in photography by documenting local peoples during his trips to Peru and Bolivia in 1948. These images were later collected in the book *Indiens pas morts* (1956). In 1949 he traveled to Europe with friend Elliott Erwitt, where he photographed France, England, and Wales and, as he had with the South American photographs, created a unique, monographic book of his Parisian photographs. Such handmade books would become a frequent source of creative pleasure for Frank. Even as early as 1946 he bound images without any accompanying text and entitled the series *40 Fotos*.[5]

By the late 1940s, Frank's freelance assignments had accelerated. Not only were many of his photographs pictured in the pages of *Harper's* and *Junior Bazaar*, but he also had been published in *U.S. Camera 1949* and *Camera* magazine. Letters to his family demonstrate his growing awareness of American society as he pursued his photographic career. In a letter from 1947 he noted the difficulties of adjusting to the fast-paced, materialist life in New York City: "I can only tell you this: you have to see for yourself. I would not want to live here forever. For older people who do not have much $, it is terrible here. Nobody has any consideration for anybody else. Old or young, man or woman, here it is everyone for himself. . . . And nevertheless, the people are much nicer and kinder than in Switzerland." He also wrote of another lesson learned about the "American character:" "There is only one thing you should not do, criticize anything. The Americans are extremely proud of their country!"[6]

Frank was clearly ambivalent toward his new home, as he would be throughout his career. Despite his skepticism of the consumer capitalism of the United States, in the early 1950s its prosperity helped launch his career as he entered into the publishing and exhibition culture of the country. He joined established photographers Aaron Siskind, Harry Callahan, David Vestal and Frederick Sommer (as well as fellow newcomer and friend Louis Faurer) in Steichen's *51 American Photographers* at MoMA (1950), which earned him favorable mention in several reviews. Although he was accepted as "American" within this exhibition context, Frank's work (consisting of Parisian scenes) was shown within the category "International Photography" in the 1951 *U.S. Camera Annual.* Frank's immigrant status helped accelerate his career by allowing him to publish in both American and European contexts.[7]

In 1951, Frank showed his work alongside Ben Schultz and W. Eugene Smith at the Gallery Tibor de Nagy. He was also included in MoMA's *Abstraction in Photography* and *Photographs as Christmas Gifts* (both curated by Steichen). The *Universal Photo Almanac 1952* and, again, the *U.S. Camera Annual 1952* also published his work. This time, the *U.S. Camera Annual* not only included his images of "Indians of Peru" but also a brief commentary on the artist. Frank continued photographing fashion scenes for *Harper's Bazaar* and also made his way into other periodicals, such as *Time* magazine (which published his portrait of Wright Morris) and *Life*. Frank's work in *Life* (May 1951) included his photographs of chairs in Parisian parks. In one, a single, isolated folding chair, like an existential figure by Giacometti, teeters on small legs in desolate surroundings.[8]

Despite a growing penchant for individual expression, Frank's forays into the photojournalistic world of the popular picture magazine continued; in November 1951 Frank won second prize ($1,250) in *Life*'s "Young Photographers Contest" under the category "Individual Pictures." That his patron and friend, Steichen, was one of the judges probably helped him to win. Other winners included his friend Elliott Erwitt and Photo Leaguers Ruth Orkin and Louis Stettner (who came in third and fourth, respectively).[9] That year, Frank also enjoyed increased press coverage in a *Photo Arts* magazine article entitled "Robert Frank: Swiss Mister," which discussed his alternating "European approach" (focusing on composition) and "American approach" (stressing "mood and tempo").[10]

No longer an outsider by the early 1950s, Frank had clearly benefitted from endorsements in both the journalistic and artistic worlds of American photography. Frank's success was all the more remarkable considering that other photographers, like Grossman, had been laboring at photography far longer than Frank had but barely made money from their work and rarely exhibited. The mainstream success Frank enjoyed in New York at this time emphasizes his talent, hunger, and interest in the competitive realm of commercial photography. Several events and relationships at this time profoundly influenced Frank and his photographic direction. These influences included: his associations with MoMA and Steichen; the abstract expressionist painters; Beat writers; existentialist philosophy; and, eventually, his rejection of photojournalism. Combined, such issues encouraged Frank to assume an increasingly personal, ironic stance as photographer of the cold war social scene, one that questioned prevailing documentary, fashion, and photojournalistic photography. Later interviews revealing his disparagement of commercial and narrative work either represent a truthful account of his increased sophistication in the arts or, possibly, a reconstruction of his past to suit post-1950s ideals concerning "art photography."

Martha Rosler points out that the 1950s witnessed a period of "the most deeply enforced artistic passivity and withdrawal into a phantasmic universe"; documentary turned "from an outward-looking, reportorial, partisan, and collective [enterprise] to a symbolically expressive, oppositional, and solitary one; the lionizing of Robert Frank marks this shift from metonymy to metaphor."[11] Frank's ascendancy into the modernist canon parallels this shift in style and taste, as his vision of personal fragmentation triumphantly replaced documentary presumptions of truth and social action. In histories of American photography written over the past three decades, Frank is critically transformed, like a compliant shape shifter, in response to each decade's aesthetic demands, while the Photo League is neglected, like a fossilized relic. The most obvious example of Frank's altered sense of artistic purpose during the 1950s is his rebellion against his elder friend Steichen—a rebellion that enabled him to begin this shift toward a more private, insistently personal voice in photography.

Steichen had helped Frank greatly in his early photographic career when he arrived as a relative unknown in the New York scene. Steichen included Frank in MoMA shows such as *PostWar European Photography* (1953), *The Family of Man* (1955), *70 Photographers Look at New York* (1957) and *Photographs from the Museum Collection* (1958). He also used a Frank photograph for a MoMA bulletin cover in 1952. That same year, Frank dedicated one of four known versions of a self-published book of 34 photographs, *Black, White, and Things*, to Steichen, with the inscription, "With much respect and gratitude to Mr. Steichen. R. Frank. Paris, Novembre 1952."[12]

Frank had much to be grateful for. In addition to having judged the *Life* contest that earned Frank second place and $1,250, Steichen also juried (alongside Irving Penn and W. Eugene Smith) a 1953 international picture contest for *Popular Photography* in which Frank earned fourth place (and a $500 bond). A photographer was lucky to receive $25 for an original photograph during this time, so Frank's prize money was considerable and unusual, especially for a new European immigrant. That Steichen had been on all these juries and advocated Frank's work certainly helped in forming Frank's increasing list of accolades and accomplishments during these years.[13]

Likewise, Frank helped Steichen greatly during the formative phase of *The Family of Man* by introducing Steichen to European photographers.[14] Steichen's inclusion of seven photographs by Frank in that show reveals his interest and support of the younger photographer's work.

In later interviews, Frank downplayed Steichen's direct influence and even derided the old man's philosophy of global unity and documentary's ability to make viewers feel sympathetic to the collective human condition. Frank admitted in 1988: "Steichen liked me a lot and he was very good to me. I just didn't agree with his sentimentality about photographs any more. I had used up the single, beautiful image. I was aware that I was living in a different world—that the world wasn't as good as that—that it was a myth that the sky was blue and that all photographs were beautiful."[15] By the mid-1950s Frank had come to question much of the earlier work he had done, as well as the potentially reductive humanistic ideology that Steichen and others espoused. Frank rejected Steichen's aesthetic to the point of deliberately ignoring his ninetieth birthday fête at the Plaza Hotel: "I did not go; I do not like the adoration of old men. Besides, I think that Steichen's influence on photography is a rather mediocre one. Ken Heyman [whose book on Leonard Bernstein Frank called "worthless, pretentious shit"] and Steichen have similar tastes in photography—sentimentality and moral [statements]."[16] Frank's shift, from opportunistic support of Steichen's projects to subsequent disdain, reflected the intervening modernist ideals of the cold war art scene, involving existential philosophies, the Beat generation writers, and abstract expressionism.

Frank later emphasized instead the influence of abstract expressionist painters whom he befriended in the mid-1950s. His photographic portraits of artists Franz Kline (1956) and Willem de Kooning (1957) document these acquaintances.[17] Frank's wife at the time, sculptor Mary Frank, attended the Hans Hofmann school and moved in the expressionist art circle, enabling him to meet such artists. He has said that their "lifestyle" impressed him at the time: "It was like a political stand. . . . They were having a hard time. And they totally believed in what they were doing. They were a really strong group. All that photographers talked about at that time was how to make money, how to get into magazines. It was a relief to go into a group that was not interested in that way."[18] Whereas some historians, like Serge Guilbaut, have accused the abstract expressionists of safely retreating from obvious forms of content because of the cold war chill, others maintain that their abstract art was an ultimate form of rebellion during an age of consensus. Defenders note that these artists' spiritual search for profoundly personal and, perhaps, ultimately universal content reached far beyond the grasping arms of material reality. Frank embraced the abstract expressionists' modernist ideal, insisting on the private realms of subjective experience and rejecting the overt political, realist themes developed during the social realism of the 1930s. Robert Motherwell summed up the abstract expressionist school as "apolitical, like cats."[19]

Frank's relationship to the abstract expressionists deserves further research, as even in this capacity he experienced ambivalence to "group-think." In later publications Frank criticized the cold formalism of Helen Frankenthaler and said Harry Callahan's work (which is more compatible with abstract expressionist ideals of the time) was "deadly . . . It's the aesthetics of tombstone photography."[20] During the late 1950s, Frank was in a critical limbo, caught between the individualist formalism of contemporary painting and the "proto-pop" aesthetics of artists such as Robert Rauschenberg and Jasper Johns. He certainly challenged all preconceptions concerning documentary photography—spurred, in his own memories, by abstract expressionist and modernist ideals.

And yet, Frank's work is adamantly not abstract, as is most of Siskind's, who more closely developed an abstract expressionist aesthetic in his photographs. Even so, Frank increasingly began to share ideological similarities with contemporary New York Scene painters. He believed that the individual, by rejecting the popular, majority views of the time, could be personally political. "I was like an action painter," he has said, in a "solitary journey" as a photographer. Frank even admitted in 1988: "I think it's a little embarrassing because I only deal with my own personal problems, I mean I'm not politically motivated that way. . . . But I always felt that the way you live—that's my political statement, that's what I am; that's who I am." When later questioned about his political awareness of McCarthyism and the hearings on television at that time, he responded, "Well, I was so concerned with making my photographs—I was on a different track. . . . I didn't think politically that way. I was certainly aware. . . . But I didn't want to make propaganda. I wanted to say it in a subtle way." His admission that he has never voted hints, perhaps, to his own rebellion against Swiss bourgeois values, which require all citizens to vote.[21]

Being "political," of course, is a difficult and slippery trait to assess in any artist, depending on his or her own social circumstances in time (whether Bruegel during the Reformation or Grossman during the cold war). As Frank said, "political is a big umbrella, and you shove anything under that word, 'political.' I don't know what it means."[22] Art historian Lucy Lippard has tried to define various shades of political art. Following her definitions, Frank could be called, broadly speaking, a "political artist": "someone whose subjects and contexts reflect social issues, usually in the form of ironic criticism." "Activist art," Lippard contends, "tends to be socially *involved*" rather than "socially *concerned*," which would apply more aptly, though still uneasily, to photographers such as Grossman (before his public naming in the HUAC trial) than to Frank. Lippard also notes that activist, community-oriented artists "have most often shunned and been shunned by the high art world," a statement that does not apply to Frank.[23] However Frank is categorized, he has, historically, come out on top of the photographic heap in photohistory texts and critical anthologies of American postwar photography.

Jan-Christopher Horak is one of the few writers to have devoted critical attention to this issue of "political" content in Frank's films. Horak maintains that Frank disallows "any political intrusions into his films" by denying "the interrelationship between the personal and the political in modern life." Thus, Frank turns "highly political topics . . . into highly personalized apolitical discourses." In a taped conversation, Horak said to Frank: "You want it both ways: you want to be apart from the market and maintain your artistic integrity, and yet at the same time you are continually commodifying yourself through the books, through the films, which even though they might be on Broadway, they are in the academic market, the art appreciation market—because that's how you live."[24]

As Rosler points out, Frank has been canonized as both political *and* artistic, having straddled successfully numerous categories in the visual spectrum. But during the early 1950s, his work was still easily interpreted as traditional social documentary. Two images that he had taken during self-financed trips to England and Wales were part of a series on British society and Welsh coal miners; both were included in *The Family of Man*. The first depicts a street musician in England, isolated in night's darkness; highlights define his face, a street lamp, and the surface of a paper under his open hat, ready to catch coins from passers-by (Figure 3.4). Frank's image of the fiddler pushed the available light of the dark scene to its limits so that the photograph displays the grainy quality of much 35mm street photography of the time (as in the works of William Klein and Louis Faurer, who were pushing their film to similar limits). This image lent itself well to the ideological aspects of Steichen's show and was surrounded in the catalog by FSA images by Shahn and Lange as well as a line from Virgil: "What region of the earth is not full of our calamities?" While Frank's image was grainier and darker, the photograph was visually linked with the classic documentary tradition of previous decades and, in the catalog, sits right next to that icon of the Depression years, Lange's *Migrant Mother*. Of course, such placement is more indicative of Steichen's aesthetics, not Frank's, as *The Family of Man* allowed photographers little to no control of their images. But the juxtaposition of Frank and these iconic, even stereotypical, documentary photographs indicates how easily his work fits into that tradition.

Another image in *The Family of Man* focused on a Welsh coal miner, accompanied by a quotation from Genesis, "behold, this dreamer cometh." Here, too, Frank imaged the disenfranchised, as had Hine years before him in his photographs of child laborers in coal mines. The solitary face of one man, his white eyes dramatically highlighted against sooty skin, looks upward, while more softly focused figures populate the darkened space around him. Frank may have professed verbally not to be overtly "political" in his search for more subtle signifiers of social issues, but his early images from these trips abroad certainly (perhaps to Frank's disgust) lent themselves to Steichen's vision of the world's "family of men."

Many others in the New York scene shared Frank's growing frustration and ambiguity toward the art and politics of the cold war years. Members of Frank's circle acknowledge the lack of organized activism by most artists. Another photographer who had befriended the New York painters, when asked whether Frank and others in this art group were "political," responded, "We ain't got no politics, lady. Just a nasty bunch of kids. We were not a political bunch of kids." Faurer, who shared a studio with Frank for a time and explored small-format street photography in the early 1950s, also maintains that this New York scene of photographers was "absolutely not" political.[25] Bob Adelman echoes that Frank was "not at all political." Adelman, as an active, socially aware artist who documented the civil rights movement, believes that "unless there are social forces afoot there are not politics, there are [only] attitudes, perspectives."[26] In other words, the lack of revolutionary organization created, according to Adelman, a conspicuous lack of political awareness in American art of the 1950s. And yet, Frank's camera often turned to highly charged "political" subjects, such as delinquent outcasts in motorcycle gangs, African Americans in the South, or Jasper Johns's own ironically undermined American icon, the national flag.

Frank's work in the 1950s blurred categorical distinctions in American photography. Whereas one could emphatically state that most FSA and

Photo League photographers were engaged in more deliberate political realms in their documentary photography (by endeavoring to ennoble the disenfranchised or move viewers to some form of action or awareness), Frank's images are more difficult to define within traditional genres. His work in *The Americans* presented subjects that were, at the time, politically charged with racial, class, and gender difference. But Frank did not work within a collaborative team, he did little (if any) sociological research on an area, and he did not add editorializing captions. Distrustful of photographic clarity and meaning, he subverted his potentially controversial subjects by emphasizing formal relationships of light and shadow. Frank stated that "a message picture is something that's simply too clear"; and, in 1961, "For the thousandth time, it must be said that pictures speak for themselves, wordlessly, visually—or they fail."[27] This was why he disliked most photojournalism (except for images by W. Eugene Smith, whose courageous values he admired)—its pretension to communicate objective reality and truth was extremely flawed from his point of view.[28] Of *Life* magazine, he said: "I wanted to sell my pictures to them, and they never did buy them. So I developed a tremendous contempt for them, which helped me . . . as an artist . . . you have to be enraged . . . not to make any concession—not make a *Life* story. That was another thing I hated. Those god-damned stories with a beginning and an end."[29] Like White, he followed the Stieglitz tradition of high art modernist photography and grew profoundly disinterested in and contemptuous of supposedly superficial, clear, narrative content. No wonder, then, that *The Family of Man*, with its majority images from primarily photojournalistic sources, so irritated Frank later in his career.

Frank's shift in aesthetic ideals is documented by the ambiguous labels attached to him during his early career in the United States; increasingly the labels describing his style become flaccid, meaningless indicators of his content and intent. For instance, Frank was categorized as a fashion photographer, documentarian, and, increasingly, high art "poet." In one review of MoMA's *Post-War European Photography* (1953), Deschin called Frank "a photojournalist who works in New York as well as in Europe," noting that his work was the most comprehensively exhibited. *U.S. Camera*'s review of the same show noted Frank's "enviable reputation" as a photographer in New York. In 1954, *U.S. Camera* magazine featured Frank with the subtitle, "The Photographer as Poet."[30]

The notion of "poetic photography," a term of artistic praise used frequently by Minor White and other *Aperture* writers, involved the belief that true artists should not be so didactic or obvious in their manipulation of content and should explore internal, spiritual realms beyond the mere "retinal world" Marcel Duchamp had so disparaged years earlier. The notion of the "poet-photographer" in the 1950s deserves more attention, since this term signified a more personal orientation toward the phenomenal world and indicated some works' connotative depth and sense of spiritual possibility. According to White, "Mirage and metamorphosis open the way for the photographer to work with the truth of metaphor. Once freed of the tyranny of surface and textures, substance and form, he can use the same to pursue poetic truth . . . poetry (whether visual, verbal or musical) . . . is far better fitted to the elucidation of the inner world than documents. Paradoxically again, poetry is the name for documents of the inner world."[31] In an earlier issue of Aperture, Nancy Newhall expanded on the formal implications of the poetic photographer: "What is it to be a poet in photography? Basic to it, perhaps, is the power to make music of light and shade; to make a shape sonorous and a detail sing. It is a power that transcends the purely visual." That same year, Myron Martin delineated between poetic artistry and documentary work: "The poet-photographers do not hold the mirror up to man as the documentarieans do because they feel that, for them at least, such an approach is futile . . . Unlike the documentarian who asks that the photograph be life itself, they only ask that it evoke an experience in the beholder."[32] Few of these writers and critics were serious poets themselves, indicating the possibility of their idealizing and oversimplifying the craft, discipline, and history of poetry in general. Poetry becomes, then, rather reductively presupposed as antinarrative and enigmatic, as opposed to the "clarity" of narrative verse.

The word *poetry* was often used in critical discussions of Frank's work of the 1950s to differentiate his art from documentary; such criticism served to lift his art into transcendent (and literally superior realms). Ironically, Helen Gee remembers Frank hating the phoney-sounding label, "poet of the camera." But Frank was attracted to the ideals behind the label; he has called T. S. Eliot's poetry "really absolutely remarkable," expressing "something so deep and without explaining, so mysteriously, about life—it moves me. And maybe that's what I'm trying to do in what I do."[33] Thus, as Frank moved toward this understanding of the function (or nonfunction) of art, he was increasingly prasied as "poetic." Such rhetoric demonstrates the move of many artists and critics toward inner goals during these difficult cold war years.

Frank was not alone. As Dave Heath later wrote, concerning the 1950s: "Disenchantment, strife and anxiety enshroud our times in stygian darkness. Pressed from all sides by the rapid pace of technical progress and increased authoritarian control, many people are caught up in an anguish of alienation."[34] Along these lines, one influence Frank does admit to is existentialism. He claims to have read all the early books by Sartre and to still enjoy Camus. Such interest in existentialism only served to strengthen his belief in the freedom of individual, not collective, action and responsibility. Frank's memories of the 1950s emphasize individuality over the mainstream or group-organized ideals of that decade: "I went to some political meetings but I didn't become involved. I didn't want to give up anything for a group. . . . I'm suspicious of groups and rules and authority. I'd like to not be bound by rules."[35] Most art historians interpret such intense, artistic individualism as a sign of heroic rebellion during an age of cold war conformity; others find this retreat from overt political action a sign of seeking safety and even cowardice. Frank often escaped such polemical scrutiny by verbally denying politics in his work, even while his photographs signified the opposite.

In the end, his images, Frank maintains, demonstrate his own personal response to the world around him rather than any higher political cause (as opposed to, for instance, Grossman, whose agenda was decidedly leftist if not, early on, Communist). Rosler writes: "More and more clearly, the subject of all high art has become the self, subjectivity, and what this has meant for photography is that all photographic practice being hustled into galleries must be reseen in terms of its revelatory character not in relation to its iconic subject but in relation to its 'real' subject, the producer."[36] Thus Frank becomes, in histories of photography, satisfying to all ideological camps; those seeking political satisfaction are visually excited by the anti-authoritarian inclusion of class, race, and gender issues, while those interested in modernist aesthetic ideals enjoy his deliberate formalism in photographs full of blur, odd angles, and idiosyncratic perspectives. The categorical polemics continued, even if tastes changed.

Andy Grundberg's criticism of Frank, emphasizing the problem of defining political content in photographs, substantiates Rosler's scheme on the rise of "high art" typologies in photography. Grundberg finds Frank's work "less political than personal . . . it is political only in the context of its concern for the individual." The themes in Frank's work, existentialism and alienation, often praised as "incisive social criticism," are truly reflective of "the disaffected artist. . . . caught up in the romance of the existential dilemma."[37]

Certainly this modernist ideal was internalized by Frank; in October 1954, he felt confident enough to apply for a Guggenheim Fellowship proposing to explore the United States and his own vision of the nation—eighty-three photographs taken by Frank during his Guggenheim-sponsored trips would become, three years later, *The Americans*. Frank presented a strong case for the grant, communicating his serious photographic intent and a list of accomplishments. In 1954 alone his work was included in one traveling group exhibition from MoMA (*Post-War European Photography*), a Christmas show at the small Limelight Gallery run by Helen Gee, and a published photographic essay in *U.S. Camera 1955* (on the Welsh miners), while he also produced photographs for *McCall's*, *Aftonbladet*, *Vogue*, *Infinity*, *Leica Photography*, and *U.S. Camera*.

His essay for the Guggenheim reflects Frank's interest in pursuing individual artistic interests, not the more narrowly defined, manifest sense of purpose one might presume to encounter in social documentary or photojournalism. His language in the application betrays elements both documentary and artistic, indicating his own suspicions of (or ambivalence toward) narrow definitions: "I am submitting work that will be seen to be *documentation*—most broadly speaking," he wrote, of "the American nation." But the project, he admitted, "is only *partly documentary* in nature: one of its aims is more *artistic* than the word *documentary* implies" (all emphasis mine). He stressed that such images would record the observations of "one naturalized American" of a "civilization born here and spreading elsewhere." After emphasizing his "European eye," Frank listed possible visual images he might seek: "a town at night, a parking lot, a supermarket, a highway, the man who owns three cars and the man who owns none, the farmer and his children, a new house and warped clapboard house, the dictation of taste, the dream of grandeur, advertising, neon lights, the faces of the leaders and the faces of the followers, gas tanks and postoffices and backyards."[38]

Such subjects do not sound, in theory, very different from volumes of images found in FSA files; they all center on human experience in American society, with a nod to class and economic difference (though in a mobile, seemingly affluent postwar society rather than the Depression). The ultimate uses of such a project, Frank insisted, "would be sociological, historical and aesthetic." Like FSA work, Frank continued, the file "should be deposited in a collection such as the one in the Library of Congress" (his collection is now, like Stieglitz's archive, at the National Gallery). Frank's language evoked the rhetoric of documentary. He even added that the study "will include caption notes" (which *The Americans*, ultimately, according to his own desires, did not). Frank textually created a case for his own brand of personal documentation of the social landscape, with no direct mention of political orientation. He did not mention disenfranchised workers, blacks, migrants, immigrants or any other specific, economically impoverished group of peoples, although he would explore such lives during his photographic trips. Instead, Frank alluded to the differences in American ownership, class, and cultural distinctions within this text more enigmatically.

Frank was awarded $3000 for one year, June 1955 to June 1956, and became the first European honored with a Guggenheim.[39] It is no wonder he earned the fellowship—Frank's list of references on the application reads like a who's who list of contemporary photography: Alexey Brodovitch, from *Harper's Bazaar*; Walker Evans; Alexander Lieberman, from *Vogue*; Meyer Schapiro, an art history professor at Columbia University; and Steichen (still Director of Photography at MoMA). Frank knew Brodovitch and Lieberman from his freelancing and fashion photography assignments, and he had maintained a relationship with Steichen through their numerous encounters. A photograph of Schapiro with Frank's son, Pablo (1953), indicates the two had a friendship of at least one year.[40]

But it was Evans, in particular, whom Frank most admired and praised: "I'm bored with the aesthetics of photographs but then Walker's photographs are like jewels." To the young Frank, Evans also represented a photographer with "class and style." They certainly came to share some attitudes; Frank recalled that Evans "couldn't stand Steichen." They even worked together in 1955 for two *Fortune* magazine picture essays, "Beauties of the Common Tool" and "The Congressional" (a train carrying businessmen between New York and Washington, D.C.).[41] A number of Frank's photographs in *The Americans* would directly recall Evans's own images in *American Photographs* (1938).

Their professional relationship and friendship deepened, as shown in a copy of a memo written by Evans to *Fortune* magazine editor Ray Mackland. In it, Evans praised images Frank took during his Guggenheim trip as among the best he'd ever seen, and Evans encouraged Mackland to take note of this new, outstanding talent. His accolades in this memo would make any young photographer ecstatic, as Evans enthusiastically endorsed Frank's work as ground-breaking. Such an encouraging endorsement by the venerated Evans could not hurt; when Frank embarked on his personal odyssey in his 1950 Ford, he went forth knowing he had strong, substantial contacts and champions, such as Evans, throughout the New York photographic scene.[42]

Frank took to the road in 1955 and 1956 (he was awarded another Guggenheim to continue the project). The pictures from this trip, which Evans so highly praised, were taken in all parts of the United States, in the South, through the Southwest to California, and across the Northwest and Midwest. After returning to New York in 1956, he moved to Third Avenue near Tenth Street, where there was a tight community of painters and poets, such as Alfred Leslie and Willem de Kooning.[43]

While traveling, Frank continued to publish his work in periodicals and exhibitions, most notably *The Family of Man*; his seven images made him one of the ten most represented photographers in the show. He also exhibited (as a "Swiss photographer") in Zurich's *Photographie als Ausdruck* (*Photography as a Means of Expression*), which earned him favorable mention in friend Gotthard Schuh's *Camera* magazine review. He continued publishing in periodicals such as *Vogue*, *Popular Photography*, the *New York Times* (which announced the Guggenheim Fellowship winners), *Fortune*, *Intro Bulletin: A Literary Newspaper of the Arts* (which mentioned Frank as one of the "greats" in photography because of his work at the Limelight Gallery in Greenwich Village), and even, although he claimed they rejected his work, *Life* magazine, which obtained Frank's photographs indirectly through the Gamma photo agency.[44]

In 1956, Frank's work appeared in the mainstream and artistic periodicals of America and Europe, including *Du*, *Modern Photography*, *Popular Photography*, *U.S. Camera*, and *Leica Photography*. His South American work was included in *Indiens pas morts* (edited by Robert Delpire in Paris) alongside photographs by Werner Bischof and Pierre Verge (the American version was entitled *From Incas to Indios*).[45] During the mid-1950s, then, Frank was not only recording his visions of American society, but he was also publishing earlier images of other cultures to which he was an outsider. In contrast to later reviews of *The Americans*, many critics found his earlier photographs, of the "lonely descendants of the Peruvian Incas, as they scratch out a meager living amid silent poverty and rich traditions," quite moving, and, according to Tom Maloney, "beautiful."[46]

Many of these South American images contain isolated figures, evoking feelings of alienation and loneliness (not unlike Frank's even earlier project, single, isolated, spindly chairs pictured in the large voids of Parisian parks). One, taken in 1948, had already been shown in *The Family of Man*; it depicts a solitary Peruvian, faceless, head down and obscured by a large-brimmed straw hat. Cloaked in modest clothing, the figure reaches out to a wall on the right. A dramatic white area beyond is drenched with exposed sun, while the figure is darkened and drooping with age or fatigue. These images enjoyed positive criticism; their sense of alienation was more palatable to critics. But once that mood entered photographs of *American* subjects, the response was not as kind. Perhaps feelings of existential distress are more attractive in outside cultures rather than one's own.

The images Frank chose to publish in *The Americans* have a similar sensibility and style to his South American shots. Frank's eye gravitated to charged, seemingly banal moments when content and form merge to create enigmatic and often profoundly moving visions. He has been noted for his talent in capturing what some have called *indecisive moments*, an ironic inversion of the French photographer Cartier-Bresson's "decisive moment" (the moment in time when content and form merge in the most psychologically penetrating split second). Increasingly, during these formative years, Frank came to question conventional concepts of beauty. Later he would note: "I don't believe in it anymore—beauty, aesthetics."[47]

Frank did not immediately publish the work he had accomplished during the two Guggenheims. He sorted the hundreds of rolls of film and chose just eighty-three images for inclusion in his book, *The Americans*. Frank sought interested and sympathetic publishers who would reproduce the images according to his own specifications (without journalistic text explicating a narrative). At the same time, Frank continued to publish photographs in major periodicals although his interests centered on his more personal, creative work. Frank benefited from increased exposure and some acclaim from 1957 through 1958: *From Incas to Indios* continued to enjoy positive criticism; he was included in *Seventy Photographers Look at New York* (MoMA, November 1957–March 1958); and Evans praised him very publicly in a *U.S. Camera Annual 1958* essay.

The *U.S. Camera Annual 1958* also provided a "sneak peek" at a number of Frank's Guggenheim-sponsored images, spurring comments on his vision of the United States. Tom Maloney, editor of the annuals, called Frank's photography, ironically, "a throwback to the documentary that was so important to photography in the thirties" and reported that Steichen found this work "excellent." Maloney added that Frank "adds an eye that knows what is effective and reaches a climax in picture after picture that mounts to a penetrating whole." Maloney admitted, however, that "Frank's vision of America certainly isn't everyone's picture of the country we live in. This is hardly the inspirational school of photography."[48]

The words used in these quotations are intriguing: clearly Frank's work was linked ideologically with social documentary work of past decades, with its focus on disenfranchised human lives in society—those moving moments when the rhetoric of democracy becomes tainted by the reality of hypocrisy and inequality. Either Frank's work was forced falsely into an incompatible but acceptable stylistic category, or else there is some truth to these observations. Frank's photographic metaphors of American society critically bridge documentary and personal modes of expression—a feat testifying to his talent as a photographer in the cold war.

Walker Evans's essay in the same *U.S. Camera* demonstrates the elder photographer's profound appreciation for the young, Swiss-born artist. He lauded Frank's rare and ironic detachment, convinced the young photographer was heaven-sent: "Assuredly the gods who sent Robert Frank, so heavily armed, across the United States did so with a certain smile." Evans derides *The Family of Man* by contrasting its ideals with Frank's: "[Frank's work] is a far cry from all the wooly, successful 'photo-sentiments' about human familyhood."[49] Textually, then, Evans's essay champions Frank while undermining contemporary notions of documentary and photojournalism. His words differentiate Frank from inadequate, unsophisticated peers; Frank becomes (ever-so-gradually) the isolated visionary whose images, Evans predicted, would probably not be accepted by the public.

The annual also includes Frank's seminal essay, "A Statement," in which he asserts his philosophy of photography, which germinated from documentary ideals but pushed such interests further, into the individual realm of the personal. To many critics, it seemed Frank had created a new form of *personal* social documentary. Although many of the Photo League photographers certainly felt their social documentary was as "personal" as Frank's, the images in *The Americans* were read as more ambiguous, bitter, and ironic. Reiterating his Guggenheim essay, Frank writes of his desire to create "an authentic contemporary *document*" (emphasis mine) that should "nullify explanation." "The view," he continues, "is personal and, therefore, various facets of American life and society have been ignored." He admitted that he had been "frequently accused" of "deliberately twisting subject-matter to my point of view." But he defended such individual vision as criticism born "of love. It is important to see what is invisible to others—perhaps the look of hope or the look of sadness."[50]

Frank's statement has become a rhetorical icon of the committed photographer who settles for nothing less than his own personal commentary in a materialist world that is oppositional to and lacks understanding of such higher vision. He clearly differentiates himself from the photojournalist, which he calls the "hack writer" or "commercial illustrator," by belittling the editors' and magazines' control of photographic vision and editing. Later, Frank then neatly posits himself, despite his successful career in magazines and periodicals, as the defiant outsider making *art*, not kitsch: "I have a genuine distrust and 'mefiance' toward all group activities. Mass production of uninspired photojournalism and photography without thought becomes anonymous merchandise. The air becomes infected with the 'smell' of photography. If the photographer wants to be an artist, his thoughts cannot be developed overnight at the corner drugstore."[51] The language of this statement defines Frank as different, as having higher ideals, as an inspired artist, the heroic outsider whose vision, as Frank quoted André Malraux in his statement, "transform[s] destiny into awareness." And yet, given the history of photography at the time, Frank had very clear influences from and similarities with documentarians of the past while enjoying a successful commercial career (even if he derided such successes). Frank might be called the perfect cold war photographer—his work walked the tightrope between social consciousness and political awareness while it remained invested with enough irony to obscure any didactic political clarity. No one named Frank in court, as they had Grossman, for Frank's rebellion was one of spirit and personal alienation from contemporary society; there was no organizational or "communist" effort to his brand of disenchantment.

An interesting parallel to Frank's photography—an example illustrating the difference between more direct politicization as opposed to more subtle forms of aestheticized persuasion—can be found in Allen Ginsberg's seminal poem *Howl*, written the same year Frank was on the road (1955). *Howl* contains numerous references to the escalating dangers of cold war policies (such as nuclear weaponry and the Korean War). But as Ginsberg's biographer, Michael Schumacher, points out, despite such "tirades against the system," *Howl* is not a political poem compared to many of Ginsberg's later poems, which focus on "individuals, the mass of whom, he implies, constitute a repressed society."[52] Similarly, Frank's images in *The Americans* do not specify political platforms by including descriptive texts or persuasive rhetoric that would lead the audience to a passively absorbed understanding of specific instances of repression or hypocrisy. Instead, viewers face ambiguous and subjectively personal visions in his aestheticized, ironic, and mordant views of the United States (with considerably less overt, personal passion than Ginsberg's *Howl*, it might be added). *The Americans* also universalized the alienating effects of capitalism and cold war policies on groups of people (whether elderly, African American, glamorous Hollywood women, teenagers, or politicians). There is no causality or specific blame in the book, as one might expect from classic documentarians.

Frank was, as many historians like to point out, thrown in jail on two occasions during his transcontinental photographic trips—indications, it is assumed, of his peripheral, avant-garde position within cold war society. Such accounts also reinforce the idea of provincial attitudes outside New York City, as the arrests took place in the South and Midwest. The mass media mythology surrounding trouble with the law often implies that the person arrested recognizes and internalizes his or her outsider status as a socially disruptive dissenter or outlaw (witness the "holy" con artists Kerouac championed, a rhetorical ideal handed down in American society from Jesse James to gangster figures). In other instances, being arrested signifies moral integrity and bravery (as in the case of civil rights activists such as Rosa Parks). In regard to his arrests, however, Frank was not associated with specific, organized, social or criminal activity in any way—he was not in the South marching to end segregation, nor was he in Michigan defending auto workers' rights.

A brief account of these arrests serves to underscore Frank's marginalization in the United States during the cold war as a Jewish immigrant. In July 1955, he was arrested in Detroit for having two different license plates.[53] He wrote, in a letter to wife Mary dated July, 1955: "My night in jail was not so funny as it might have sounded. It was depressing and I got scared. I was ready to give up when they let me out and maybe it is my Swiss-Background that helps. (Don't laugh)."[54] His ironic allusion to his native country indicates his awareness of its reputation for neutrality during World War II, a capitulating attitude that probably helped in these paranoid times.

Later, in November of that year, he was detained again. This time the letter from the Department of Arkansas State Police discussed the grounds for suspicion: Frank had been "shabbily dressed," in need of "a shave and haircut, also a bath." Even more importantly, however, the letter noted his "foreign accent" and cameras. Frank, the officer noted, was "smart-alecky" and "uncooperative" in answering questions. The officers consulted a counterintelligence specialist. Frank's accent, cameras, and attitude led to the officers' suspecting him of spy activities; like the Rosenbergs, he was Jewish, and he was from an urban northern city. As the officer noted, "we are continually being advised to watch out for any persons illegally in this country possibly in the employ of some unfriendly foreign power and the possibility of Communist affiliations." Frank was fingerprinted and information was sent to the FBI.[55]

Frank immediately wrote his influential (he hoped) friend Evans for help. His letter communicates his fear upon being locked in a cell for seven hours and threatened "that if I would not be quiet they would teach me how to be quiet." Officers interrogated him for four more hours, Frank recalls: "the most humiliating experience I had so far." The dialogue included questions concerning the Guggenheim, being Jewish, and having liquor in his car, among other topics. Especially of interest was how Frank had obtained clearance to photograph the Ford Motor plant and New Orleans refineries. Frank even tried to name-drop in an effort to seek help; he mentioned Steichen and friends of people the policemen might have heard of in government. But finally the officers' questions hit home: "'Are you a commie?' I said no. He said, 'Do you know what a commie is?' I said yes." Frank admitted to Evans that the "fury" he felt after being released had dissipated forty hours after the event; his real concern was having the fingerprint records "destroyed or annulled," as they could jeopardize his naturalization process. He signed off,

"À nous la liberté!" By the following December, Frank's lawyer had worked to recover the fingerprints from the FBI and warned Frank to "be in communication" with him if he planned to travel in the South, so as to keep him aware of "risks."[56]

Frank's hatred of Southern racism was reinforced by this personal history. In a later publication (*The Lines of My Hand*) he included four images of white teenage boys, captioned "in front of high school, Port Gibson, Mississippi," 1955. Alongside an image of the boys lounging outdoors amongst cars, he included the following account:

> KIDS: What are you doing here? Are you from New York?
> ME: I'm just taking pictures.
> KIDS: Why?
> ME: For myself—just to see . . .
> KIDS: He must be a communist. He looks like one. Why don't you go to the other side of town and watch the niggers play?[57]

While we cannot know whether this exchange actually took place between Frank and the boys, it underscores his potential identification as outsider and bohemian. The image also alludes to Frank's sensitivity to the general problems of racism without addressing them within a specifically historical context (such as documenting a "whites only" sign or other material evidence). Furthermore, the title, *Mississippi*, sets his experience in one of the most racially troubled states of the time. However, Frank's brand of rebellion and social criticism is more broadly considered, without the polemics of either of his documentary predecessors, the FSA or Photo League photographers. Perhaps this photograph of racist teenagers was *not* chosen by Frank for inclusion in *The Americans* precisely because of its specific content and reliance on the accompanying text. It more closely approached earlier documentary ideals, wherein text and image worked together to alert viewers to social concerns.

Emphasizing Frank's metaphorical political content does not position him as a timid or hypocritical artist in the cold war world. There are numerous ways for artists to engage in radical social commentary, and no one way is necessarily superior to another. But Frank has, in subsequent histories, been championed as "the first," "the best," and other hyperboles that tend to reduce him to the mythologized, heroic ideal while ignoring scores of other photographers engaged in similar, or even more radical, photographic experimentation during the 1950s. It could be said that critically, Frank had his cake and ate it too—he created an original, ambiguous photographic language that allowed him access to all photographic worlds, whether photojournalistic, documentary, commercial, or artistic. Specific influences affecting his work have been neglected in light of such hagiographic historiography.

For instance, few scholars have linked Frank with the documentary tradition, preferring, perhaps, to bestow on him that ultimate modernist compliment, "original." Yet this lineage is crucial to understanding Frank's vision in *The Americans*, in that he sustains documentary ideals while subverting, extending, or enriching them within a new historical context. The one connection to past documentary work that most historians allow is, of course, Frank's mentor and friend, Walker Evans. As an FSA photographer, however, Evans had been criticized by Stryker as overly formal. In many later histories of the FSA, he, like Frank in the 1950s, is described as "superior," "committed," and "ironic." But there are similarities between Frank and the other FSA workers. Like Frank, these photographers often left urban cultural centers to photograph rural, agricultural, even destitute places in the United States. However, FSA photographers, unlike Frank, were beholden to a potent patron, a federal agency funded by the U.S. government and under the opinionated direction of Stryker; they were accountable to forces beyond individual, personal ideals. Frank's freedom, thanks to the Guggenheim money, was enviable.

Frank frequently turned to the documentary subject matter of FSA and even some Photo League photographers—the rural American scene—and added a new stylistic twist, as his champions note. He created, so many writers have stated, more personal, ambiguous, or, the preferred adjective, *ironic* images critical of cold war American society, subverting traditional ideal visualizations of the United States in the 1950s.[58] His *Georgetown, South Carolina* is one image very close in style and content to classic FSA shots (such as Lange's *Migrant Mother*, Figure I.1), yet it displays profound differences as well. In Frank's picture, we find three generations with no specific focal point: a middle aged woman, a young woman, and a child sitting on a threadbare sofa against the raw wood of a structure. No face engages our gaze—all eyes are directed downward, the women's faces toward the child, who also looks down to his lap. The oldest woman smiles slightly while holding in her hand, with fingernails grimy and short, a cigarette. The younger woman attempts a modicum of glamour by posing in a floral halter dress with the shiny accent of a black patent leather belt.

In contrast, the children in Lange's photograph touch, blend with, and frame the central woman, forming a powerful triangular solidarity of figures. Her serious, penetrating gaze looks beyond the photograph's frame and her hand gesture signifies anxiety and thoughtfulness. Compared to Lange,

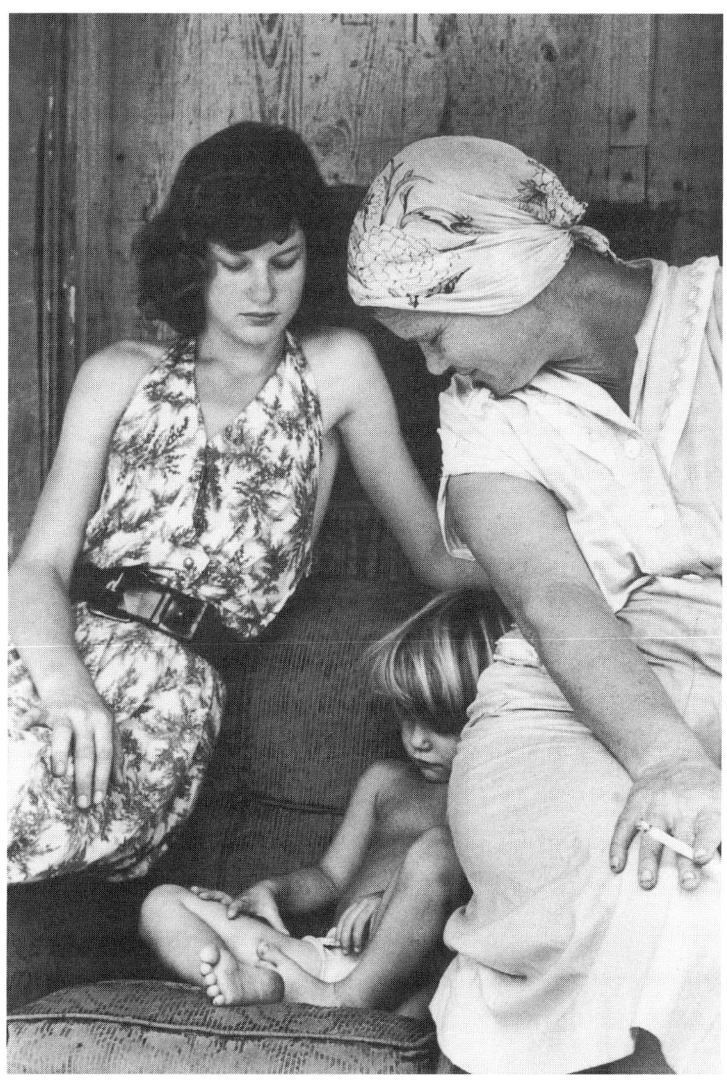

4.1. Robert Frank, *Georgetown, South Carolina,* 1955.

Robert Frank's images selected for *The Americans* included some photographs of the rural South, including this one from South Carolina which evokes, but ultimately subverts, traditional FSA documentary style and ideals. The Museum of Fine Arts, Houston, Museum purchase. Copyright Robert Frank, courtesy PaceWildensteinMacGill, New York.

Frank did not accentuate the humanistic ennobling of surviving victims of social inequity; instead we focus on the ambiguous trinity of alienated figures, close but barely touching one another. Frank's content seems to focus more on lower-class Southern "white trash," not noble workers.

In another foray into FSA subject matter, Frank's *The Americans* included images of roads, all of which reflect his taste for ironic ambiguity in the car culture of America in the 1950s. *U.S. 285, New Mexico* depicts a long stretch of desolate highway dissolving into the distant horizon while a single black automobile in the distance heads directly toward the viewer. The no-passing lines recall the monotony of driving. As Kerouac wrote, "The white line in the middle of the highway unrolled and hugged our left front tire as if glued to our groove."[59] The landscape has no observable vegetation or human habitation; the vast sky is cloudless.

The photograph's sequencing in *The Americans* is crucial, as is the case for all of Frank's images, so carefully chosen for their overall filmlike orchestration. In the two previous pages, viewers face *Covered Car, Long Beach, California*, a pristine and clearly focused photograph of a car, as American fetish, protectively sheathed by glistening white material. The next page, just preceding the photograph from New Mexico, documents an accident in Arizona: bodies lay covered by rough cloths while four onlookers stand, dispassionately staring at the amorphous pile. In concert these images encourage a thoughtful narrative emphasizing the unnaturally elevated position of the car in American society (protected more elegantly than the dead bodies by the road). The long stretch of highway, then, takes on an ominous quality, with the risks accentuated by the potential of a head-on collision with the oncoming car. Later, in another section of the book, we find *Crosses on Scene of Highway Accident, U.S. 91, Idaho*, depicting three crosses alongside a road marking more deaths from car travel; a heavily burned-in, unearthly light glows from the heavens. Other images in *The Americans* similarly display cars and highways, leading us toward deeper introspection of automobile technology in contemporary America.

Many documentary photographers, such as Evans, sought similar content concerning the American automobile culture in previous years, critiquing the potential dangers of highway travel. Although Frank's work reflects popular concerns of the time, many scholars characterize Frank as having looked at such scenes with a new eye, a sardonic detachment born of intense personal (and European) vision. Ulrich Keller maintains that Frank's immigrant status allowed him an increased appreciation for America's contradictions:

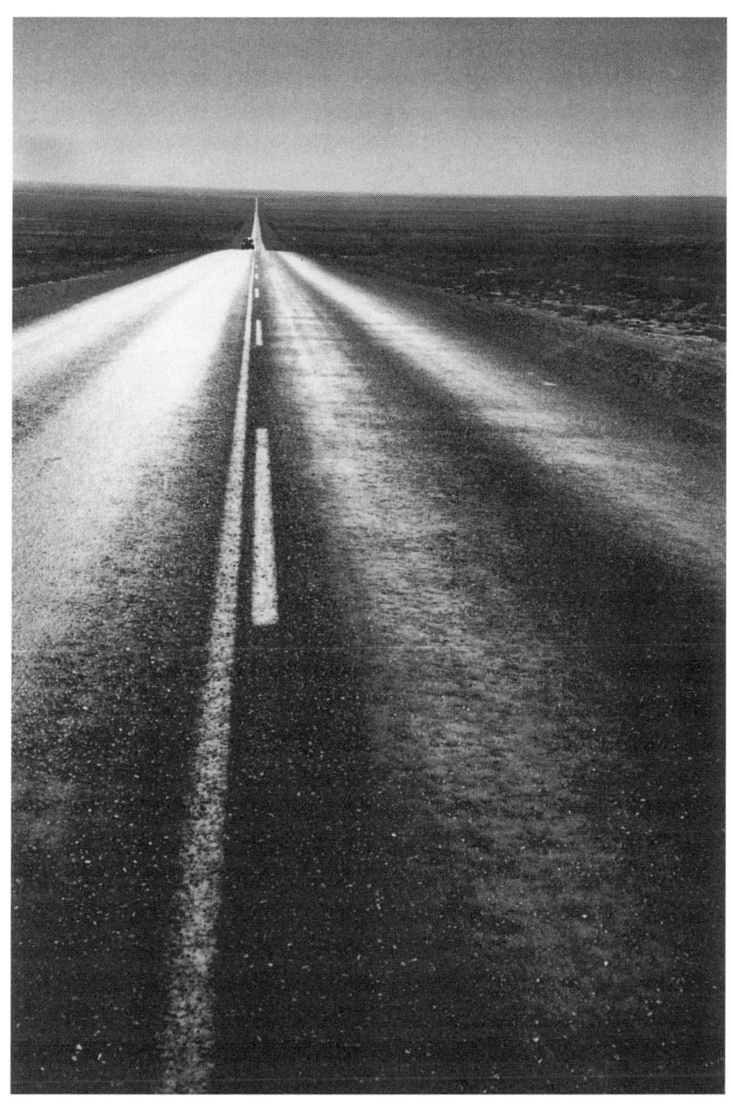

4.2. Robert Frank, *U.S. 285, New Mexico,* 1955.

This is just one of many photographs in *The Americans* taken by Frank documenting the dominant and capitalistic American "car culture" in the 1950s. The Museum of Fine Arts, Houston, Museum purchase with funds provided by Charter Banks and Mr. and Mrs. Jerry E. Finger. Copyright Robert Frank, courtesy PaceWildensteinMacGill, New York.

> With the car as cult object and the car as killer—images placed next to each other in his book—Frank marked the poles of American automobile culture. In between he found little relief. His uncompromising reliance on his own easily irritated and, in turn, rashly provocative subjectivity, and his refusal to aim at a fair and balanced view of America, were novelties in the arts spectrum of the time. With one impatient sequence of irreverent photographs the complacent horizon of the 1950s was broken open to a whole range of controversial issues that are still with us today.

Frank, Keller continues, unlike Americans, who were "enveloped in a haze of conformism," was better equipped "to break [the] spell" of American postwar prosperity.[60] What *was* particularly unique was Frank's ability to sustain this discourse in book form, allowing the luxury of a developed sense of personal vision. He could create more complex metaphorical relationships in this comprehensive view, funded by the Guggenheim and dictated by his own sense of content, narrative, and style.

American car culture had been explored by countless other photographers in previous years. The subject of the American road was hardly new and offered many photographers the opportunity to communicate the vastness of America's west in particular. In comparison to earlier images of the American road, Frank's images demonstrate his critical emphasis on personal alienation, isolation, and danger. Russell Lee's *Highway East of Midland, Texas*, 1947, also depicts a long stretch of road bleeding into the horizon. Lee, a former FSA photographer employed by Stryker's administration of the Standard Oil (New Jersey) photography project, like Frank, had stood in the center of the road for his shot—but the highway in Lee's photograph is more clearly focused, more detailed, and brighter. The Southwestern landscape is also desolate, but Lee captures evidence of human life: power lines and fence posts punctuate the space. Furthermore, there is no oncoming car or no-passing lines creating a tension of impending confrontation with an automobile. Lee's highway is well-lit and divides an inhabited landscape.

Lange also captured the lonely landscape of western cross- country travel in *New Mexico Desert Highway No. 70*, 1938. She, too, had stood in the middle of the long road, and the pavement in her image is stopped, abruptly, by the distant peak of a mountain range. The horizon, as in the other images, is in the top half of the composition so that this length of road is accentuated. No signs of human habitation exist in the vast landscape other than the road itself, so that, again, the viewer shares the photographer's sense of alienation and utter solitude. In comparison to Frank's *U.S. 285, New Mexico*, Lange's image (like Lee's) is more reassuring, with brighter, sunlit highlights and no oncoming car facing us. Her sky is light and cloudless; Frank's is cloudless,

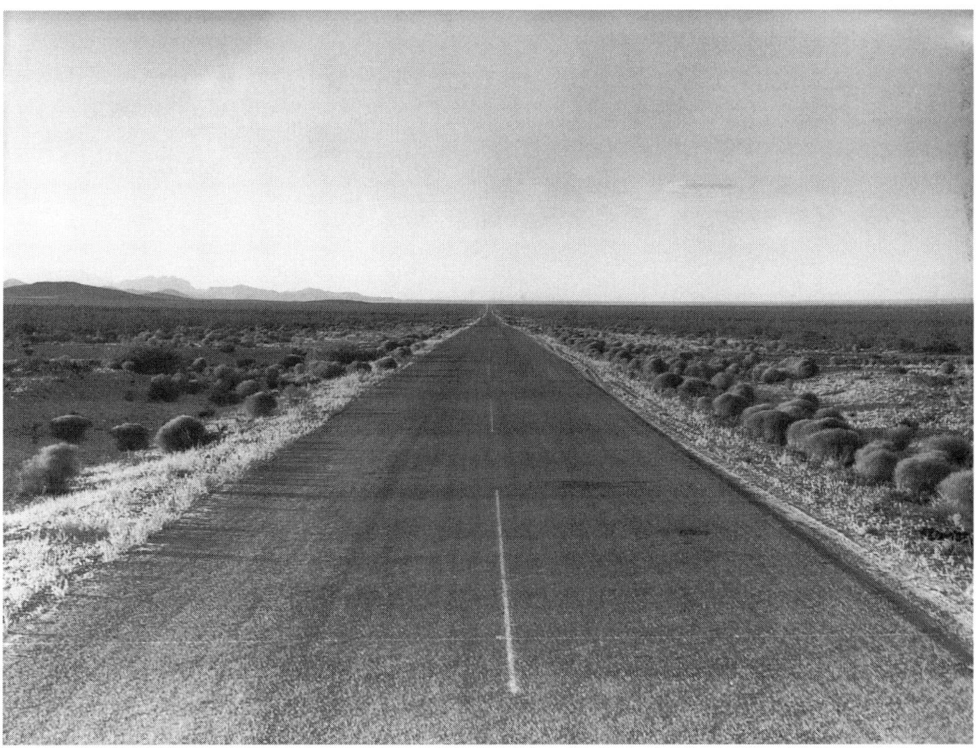

4.3. Dorothea Lange, *New Mexico Desert Highway No. 70, the Route Many Refugees Cross*, 1938.

Dorothea Lange, like other photographers of the 1930s, often photographed the dramatic perspectival lines created by long stretches of American highways. U.S. Farm Security Administration, Prints and Photographs Division, Library of Congress.

too, but the glow of the horizon seems unnatural, even ominous, owing to the heavy black tones in the upper region signifying the liminal moment of dawn or dusk. Nevertheless, without the accompanying images in *The Americans* of car culture in the United States, his highway shot might seem like one of many in the history of documentary photography.

Frank's preoccupation with American automobile culture reflects European stereotypes of the United States. The nation's emphasis on the car, Keller writes, was well-known by European visitors, who "felt that the highway habitat was not just one among countless other parts of American culture, but an essential and emblematic one, a part that could stand for the whole." As Keller notes, French visitor Georges Duhamel, in the early 1930s, criticized the United States in *America the Menace* by highlighting the tragic consequences of a culture whose technology had been inundated with the automobile. All his encounters with wrecks and accidents led him to denounce the American automobile as "a sinister symbol of the future world." Frank approached similar criticism with his highway photos in *The Americans*. The images by Lee and Lange are, in purer documentary fashion, more objectively descriptive of scenes (perhaps deceptively so), whereas Frank's grainy, dark images more clearly evoke feelings of desolation, danger, and loneliness. In contrast, Lee and Lange's brightly lit, focused images could be interpreted as more reassuring. They could more easily affirm, as Keller puts it, "a good culture . . . worth defending."[61] Not all photographs taken by American photographers at the time simply served to uphold chauvinist national values; however, to maintain Frank's status as visionary, all other artists, in comparison, must be seen as reifying collective American values while Frank deconstructs them. This is simplistic and reductive but makes a stronger case for Frank's uniqueness and originality.

The fact that many photographers, including Frank, focused on the road reinforces the materialist history of America's car culture in the 1950s; it was a source of pride to most in the nation and added to America's sense of achievement and power. After World War II, automobiles and highway travel became an ever-growing, predominant aspect of suburban American culture. Construction of roads and highways escalated, culminating in 1956 with Congress's authorization of a nationwide interstate system of highways covering 41,000 miles. This new network of highways was financed by the defense budget, with the justification that they would allow efficient transportation in the event of a nuclear attack, clearly indicating the car culture's alliance with the cold war. By 1957, *Time* magazine called road building "*the* American art" and a "true indicator of our culture." Even *Popular Photography* articles of the 1950s reflected a national obsession with road photography.[62]

Accents on the car culture existed in less popular publications of the time as well. Kerouac's *On the Road*, like Frank's *The Americans*, also looked to American highway travel as a source of spiritual revelation and inspiration. While Kerouac had begun writing the book during the late 1940s, following journals he'd kept of observations made during his travels, like Frank, he did not immediately publish it; his book was finally published in 1955 after numerous publishers had rejected it. The efforts of both artists bear telling similarities—like Frank, Kerouac "insisted he wanted nothing to do with politics" (even though his chronicles of Beat escapades often lead readers to think otherwise). Kerouac, who also wrote a short, impassioned essay for the American edition of *The Americans*, similarly eschewed the obvious political orientation of artists during the cold war. He supported McCarthy in 1954, although his own art certainly would not have passed McCarthy's artistic litmus tests. Kerouac was, in fact, according to Tom Clark, "adamantly antileft," refusing, like Frank, group-organized political activity and instead searching for individual liberation.[63] This ambiguous political orientation may seem odd or even contradictory to those living in the current polemicized world. Both artists denied overt politics in their art, yet their images and words certainly encouraged in viewers and readers a deeper understanding of the social mechanisms dictating cultural norms. Both also traveled the same road afforded bohemian artists of the cold war years—a retreat into personal politics.

Kerouac, like Frank, critiqued capitalist America's quick and easy money made from the prosperous automobile culture in *On The Road*: "Americans are killing themselves by the millions every year with defective rubber tires that get hot on the road and blow up. They could make tires that never blow up." The unnamed culprits, "they," become the materialist enemy but remain unspecified. The buyers of inferior, cheap goods become generalized duped citizens. The nation's misguided materialism is further undermined by the alternative populations inhabiting Kerouac's world as well as Frank's; *On The Road* is vitalized with the inclusion of the poor, African Americans, the working class, the criminal, and so on, who punctuate the spiritual emptiness of this vast, seemingly prosperous country and give it life: "The only people for me are the mad ones, the ones who are mad to live, mad to talk, mad to be saved, desirous of everything at the same time, the ones who never yawn or say a commonplace thing, but burn, burn, burn like fabulous yellow roman candles exploding like spiders across the stars."[64] The Beats, too, then, become heroic nonconformists defying American norms through experimentations with bisexuality, drugs, and nonwestern religions during the cold war years. As Gary Snyder has pointed out, Beat detachment from mainstream society was a general form of protest paving the way for more organized protests of the 1960s: "In the fifties we really did have to protect, defend, and nurture our freaks because they were valuable people."[65]

While Kerouac and Frank were anti-authoritarian nonconformists, Frank was not as radical in his own life as some bohemians. He enjoyed mainstream employment and accolades in the photographic world while supporting his wife and two children. He admits to feeling peripheral to the Beats, indicating, again, his aversion to belonging to any group. Frank could still be called a Beat "fellow traveler," given his hip visual syntax imaging cold war American culture: "I don't think that I traveled on the Beat's path, . . . but it seems we've heard each other."[66] Beyond similarities in Kerouac's and

Frank's bleak vision of cold war America, both artists' reputations also have been affected by the subsequent myth-making and lionizing of bohemian artists. Whereas popular notions dictate that *On the Road* was spontaneously written, it was in fact edited and reworked for a number of years, belying Kerouac's own literary background and discipline for craft. *The Americans*, too, often perceived by unfriendly critics as a rather careless work of spontaneity, was also carefully, seriously thought out and premeditated. However, neither artist demonstrated, in later years, any desire to correct the mythology of their "spontaneous genius," and many writers, typically, have not emphasized either their lineage or their serious devotion to craft.

Images of African Americans, as symbols of spirit, figure prominently in both *On The Road* and *The Americans*. Approximately eleven of the eighty-three images Frank chose for inclusion in *The Americans* focused on African American subjects and provoked one *Popular Photography* critic, Charles Reynolds, to remark that the "only slight vestiges of nobility left in this wasteland of vehicles, jukeboxes, and American flags are possessed by Negroes and small children."[67] During the mid-1950s, escalating battles over civil rights issues for black Americans—such as desegregation, voting rights, and justice for the murders of Reverend George Lee and Emmett Till, among others—were critical topics in American mass media and politics. In 1955, the year Frank began his travels, the Supreme Court ordered public school desegregation to begin; two years later, federal troops were needed to enforce desegregation in Little Rock, Arkansas. The same year saw the beginning of the Montgomery, Alabama, bus boycotts, which gained national prominence, while Martin Luther King gathered support as a leader of the civil rights movement.

Photographs such as Frank's much-reproduced *Trolley, New Orleans* herald Frank's sensitivity to contemporaneous racial issues. In *Trolley* we find the ultimate aestheticized expression of racial discrimination—a perfect blend of formal organization and explosive content. Frank focuses on the windows of a trolley, while the sitters inside reflect the social strata of American society: in the two windows toward the front of the car sit whites; in the middle, two white children; behind them, an African American man looks toward the camera; and finally, in the back, an African American woman. The image evokes histories of resistance, from the bravery of Rosa Parks to the boycotts organized by King.

Frank's *Trolley* is contained within a formal construction as tight and classically pure as the architecture of the Parthenon or Josef Albers's squares. The planes of windows mimic the frames of the photograph. The grit and grain of his 35mm camera, a crucial aspect of Frank's aesthetic in discussions

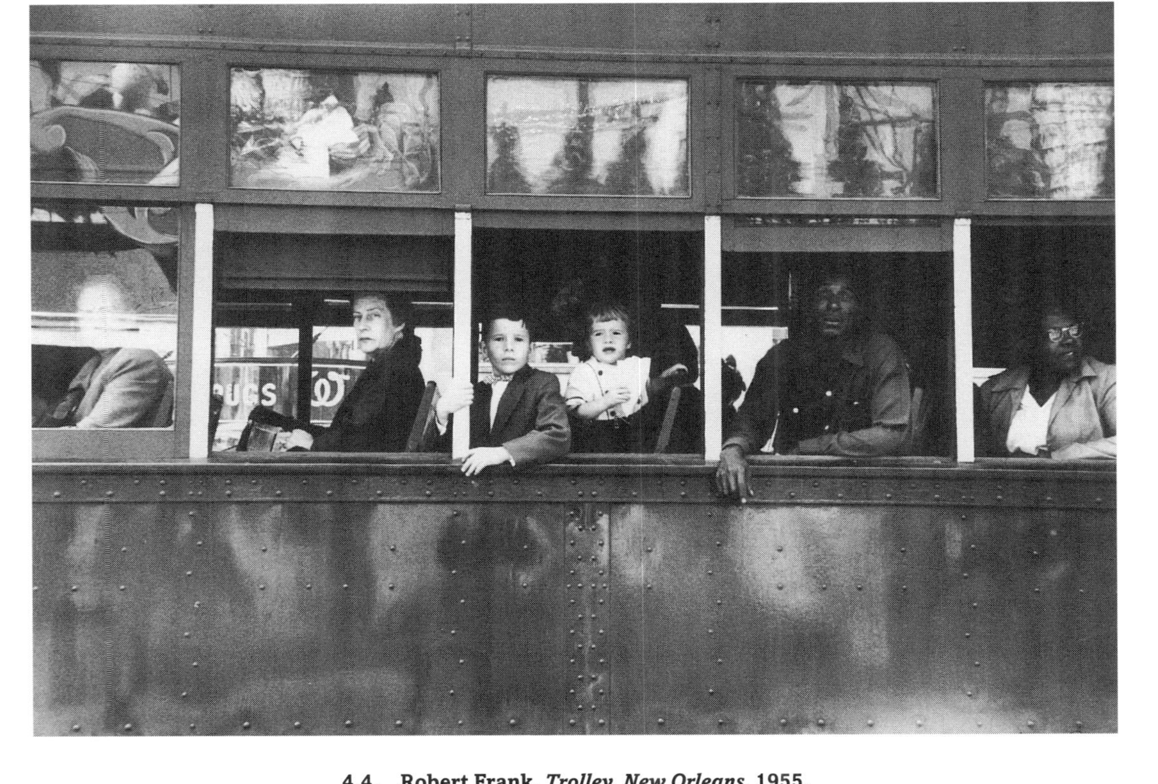

4.4. Robert Frank, *Trolley, New Orleans,* 1955.

In one of Frank's most acclaimed photographs from *The Americans*, this trolley in New Orleans visualizes the social stratifications in 1950s American culture. The Museum of Fine Arts, Houston, the Target Collection of American Photography, museum purchase with funds provided by Target Stores. Copyright Robert Frank, courtesy PaceWildensteinMacGill, New York.

of his work, is negligible here because of the high focus clarity of the image. On a technical level, Frank has created a photograph that satisfies understandings of discrimination while containing such metaphors within a sophisticated formal arrangement, suggesting the permanence of racial segregation in the structures of American culture.

Unlike other, more openly socially engaged photographers, such as Weiner or Palfi (both of whom were Photo League members), Frank does not enter the bus or chronicle the specific historical events of material culture; his camera is pointed toward allegorical realms alluding to the alienating effects of a hypocritical American democracy. Viewers, given no explicating text or didactic visual clues, must participate in the creation of content over the course of the book. In general, his images of African American life and spirit offer some of the most positive, even celebratory, aspects of possibility in the barren culture presented in *The Americans*. Their iconographical significance in relation to specific events in the contemporary history of the civil rights movement deserves much more attention.

Comparisons between racially charged images by Frank, Weiner, and Palfi differentiate Frank's personal style of documentary work from the other two artists' sense of documentary photography and political purpose. Weiner's image of a bus's interior is specifically entitled *Bus Boycott, Montgomery, Alabama*, 1956, and the *absence* of African Americans in the photograph signifies their refusal to capitulate to segregationist forces. Instead, a white woman sits midcenter, alone among the rows of gleaming, empty seats. Weiner was working for *Collier's* at the time (on an article about "the dilemma of the moderate in the South") and felt dissatisfied by their use of his images from the South: "There was a larger issue at stake. . . . My point was to show the great forces struggling here in one area. I felt that this was an historic occasion which I must try to record with my camera."[68] Weiner was engaged in a specific historical event, was sympathetic to that historical specificity and racism in general, and sought to communicate, in the fashion typical to social documentary and sensitive photojournalism, a sense of place and time as well as more metaphorical, ideological realms.

Palfi's earlier photograph of a city bus is entitled *Somewhere in the South*, ca. 1946–49. Palfi not only entered the bus but also moved to the rear, entering the very explosive space of the segregated blacks, and focused on the back seat, where we find a man and woman with infant. While Frank might eschew such didacticism (with its emphasis on content, not aesthetics), Palfi included the text above the figures, which appears to have been retouched so that it is strongly darkened and legible: "This part of the bus for the colored race." The metaphorical, or "poetic," possibilities are deadened by Palfi's al-

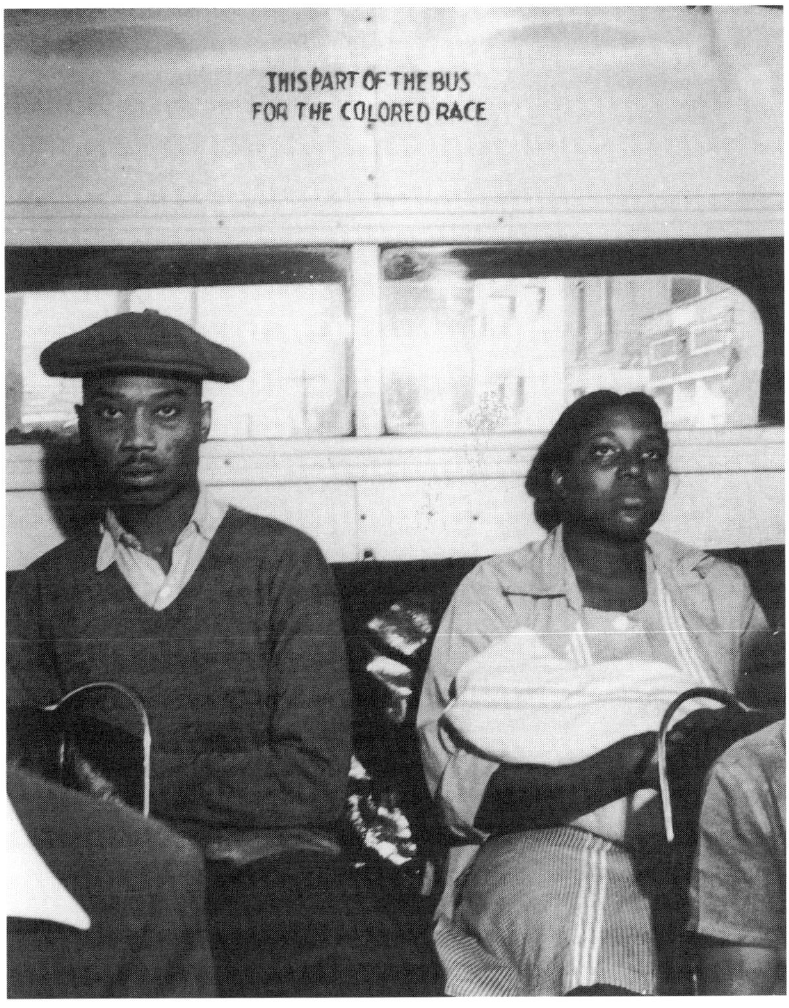

4.5. Marion Palfi, *Somewhere in the South,* ca. 1946–49.

Photo League member Marion Palfi also documented racism during her travels to the South in the 1940s. With typical social documentary force, she entered the back of the bus and documented the lives of segregated African Americans. © Martin Magner. Collection Center for Creative Photography, the University of Arizona.

legiance to clarity and narrative, emphasized so that no viewer can miss her distinctly political message. Viewers are, perhaps, expected to be less active as decipherers of the scene, as there is no mistaking her political agenda. Palfi turned frequently in her career to signs of discrimination and civil rights issues, especially in the series "There Is No More Time," (1949) and "That May Affect Their Hearts and Minds" (1963–64).[69] Her images, including such material manifestations of American racism, were culled from other areas in the United States, not just the South, as she found instances of injustice a national, not regional, phenomenon.

Frank's *Charleston, South Carolina* also explores racial inequality in the South (in fact, most of Frank's images exploring African American life come from his travels south—at least those that most overtly illustrate repression). In this image, Frank focuses on a black woman in what appears to be a white uniform, holding an extremely white baby, its bald globular head contrasting starkly with the darkness of the woman's skin. Purse-lipped, the figures barely interact, isolated against the vanishing point of a long stretch of washed-out white sidewalk. Kerouac, in his introduction to *The Americans*, clearly understood the deeper implications of this image, as he wrote it should be "blown up and hung in the street of Little Rock showing love under the sky and in the womb of our universe the mother." However, *New York Times* critic Gilbert Millstein was more blunt: "Robert Frank is above all a harsh social critic. The implications of that photograph of Negro nurse and white infant are plain."[70] That American parents could look to African Americans for care of their children while not allowing them the same basic civil liberties afforded to their white charges was an immediate example of discrimination and hypocrisy in the United States. Ironically, Millstein compared Frank's "distaste and distrust" of humanity with Grossman's "compassion" and "understanding and acceptance" of the human subject, citing this photograph as the one instance of Frank's similarity with the earlier social documentarian.

This photograph is perhaps the closest Frank comes to an open acknowledgment of traditional documentary ideals; he may have even surpassed the masters at the league with this complex and moving image. However, as Stange points out, Frank intensely questioned the notion of photographic realism, which he maintained could "proliferate distortion and falsification as readily as transparency and verisimilitude." Instead he "spurns" such "long cherished aspirations to immediacy and transparency" in his metaphorical investigations of American life during the cold war years.[71] Frank's complex orientation toward photographic vision involved the undermining of valued documentary aesthetic ideals while embracing the sophisticated tradition of complex, formal organization.

Almost half of the images in *The Americans* include female figures that address and evoke, to varying degrees, a diversity of key issues surrounding women in the 1950s. The book includes photographs of a broad cross-

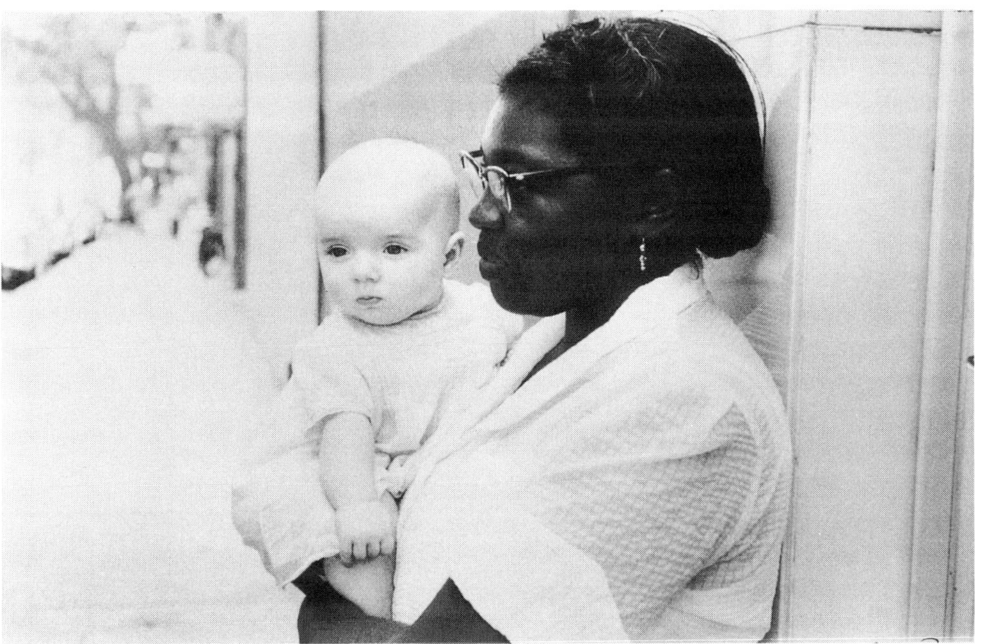

4.6. Robert Frank, *Charleston, South Carolina,* 1955.

In another image of South Carolina included in *The Americans*, Frank photographed this African American woman and white baby, an image one *New York Times* reviewer found "harsh" in its implied social criticism. The Museum of Fine Arts, Houston, Museum purchase with funds provided by Charter Banks and Mr. and Mrs. Jerry E. Finger. Copyright Robert Frank, courtesy PaceWildensteinMacGill, New York.

section of American women: African American women, working women, teenage and elderly women, mothers, and glamorous stars. Although Frank avoids an explicitly political or feminist stance, his is not the profoundly sexist gaze of some male photographers at that time. Nor does he merely reinforce the 1950s domestic ideal that provoked Betty Friedan's response, *The Feminine Mystique*. Instead, Frank's images touch on the paradoxes surrounding the public and private lives of women in the 1950s. Frank's photographs often demonstrate his distance from the more didactic documentary photographic tradition, in that they more broadly reflect the mood and ambience of cold war America; one cannot conveniently pinpoint specific, historical events or document famous faces with his images. Yet his images of women provide an undeniably rich commentary on American women of the 1950s (as had many images by women in the Photo League, such as

Lisette Model, Marion Palfi, Erika Stone, Ruth Orkin, Rosalie Gwathmey, Dorothea Lange, or Helen Levitt).

Women's lives during the Eisenhower years have suffered from consensus theory histories and studies centering on the male-dominated arenas of politics and war. Many essays, then and now, point to the issue of white, middle-class conformity, as if white collar, grey-flanneled businessmen with pill-popping suburban wives were the only reality. Women, long submerged in historical essays on the cold war years, are now resurfacing in the research of scholars such as Eugenia Kaledin, who tries to "modify the dominant myth of their victimization."[72] Frank's images of women, compared to other contemporary popular images, more often suggest conflict, not consensus. Three of Frank's images in *The Americans* address the issue of glamorized beauty in the 1950s by picturing young blond starlets who participate in the movie or television media. These photographs do not simply reduce glamorous blonds to their sexually stereotyped forms but instead provoke a dialogue concerning mass media and its influence in creating a myth of beauty. Ideals of "youth and beauty" were expensive for women in the 1950s; as George Lefferts pointed out in 1961, in just one year "American women spent over two billion dollars for beauty aids, . . . spent 943 million hours in beauty salons, . . . [and] 100 million dollars for deodorants." He added: "The implications are clear. If you are young and beautiful, you will automatically enjoy happiness, fulfillment and love."[73] Amid the persuasive, media-inspired standards of beauty of the time, Frank's images often subverted popular images of women in what Marjorie Rosen has called the "mammary mad" 1950s.

In one image in *The Americans*, *Movie Premiere, Hollywood*, Frank's focus centers not on the young, blond woman participating in this unspecified movie premiere but on the faces of the women beyond. As with all three of his images directly concerned with this glamour ideal, the blurred woman in the foreground is young and blond—like Marilyn Monroe, Mamie van Doren, and Jayne Mansfield, who were all successfully exploited as ideal objects of male desire in the mass media. Frank could have easily focused on the blond, but his concern is for the background faces who stare and smile at the vision before them. The blurred face, so unlike the faces beyond, represents an ideal they internalize. The image parallels Annette Kuhn's study of glamour and the male gaze; she writes that women have been forced to look through the eyes of men, "to see woman, to see herself, as an object of desire." The centerfolds, fashion models, actresses, and women of cosmetic advertisements created a standard of beauty few could ever achieve. This desire to identify with such ideals, Kuhn continues, is "displaced into desire for the products they advertise or connote."[74]

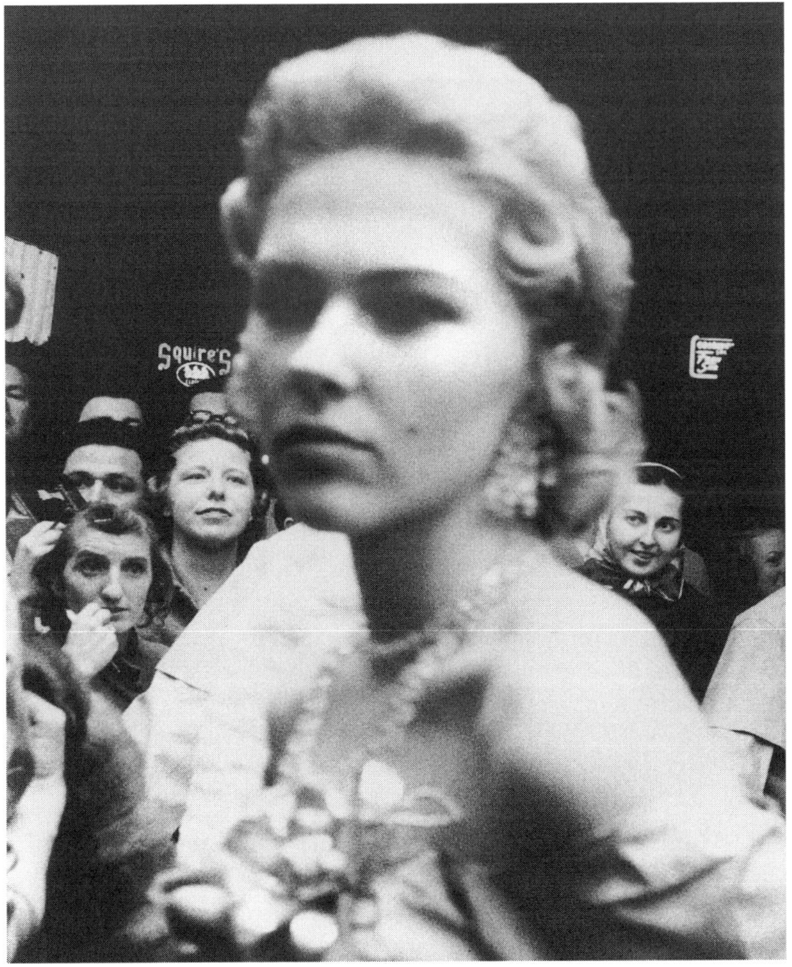

4.7. Robert Frank, *Movie Premiere, Hollywood, ca. 1955–56.*

Some of Frank's most dynamic and innovative images in *The Americans* are found in photographs of the mass media, as seen in this example of avid fans at a movie premiere in Hollywood. The Museum of Fine Arts, Houston, the Target Collection of American Photography, Museum purchase with funds provided by Target Stores. Copyright Robert Frank, courtesy PaceWildensteinMacGill, New York.

Frank, in this image, denies viewers the satisfaction of deriving sexual or aesthetic pleasure from the blond by distorting her beauty with a lens. Instead he forces us to focus, finally, on the more common, everyday women beyond. In distorting the blond he also creates a visual symbol for the ideal beauty the starlet represents: she is like a vision, an apparition, insubstantial and nonconcrete compared with the focused faces beyond. Frank's image, by focusing on the hopelessness of female spectators drinking in America's ideal of beauty, critiques gender-specific expectations of these consumerist years. As Simone de Beauvoir commented in *The Second Sex* (1953), the glamour girl "yields Woman over to the dreams of man, who repays her with wealth and fame."[75]

In *Television Studio, Burbank, California*, another young blond woman sits before the camera, an enigmatic black male form truncating the lower portion of her body. Her face, with eyes looking off-camera and a fixed smile, is reflected again in the television to the right. Frank calls attention not to her physical features but to the fact that she is posing, aware of the mass media gaze of faceless TV watchers. The woman here is a passive object of male-controlled mass media; she is literally boxed and packaged, a product for mass consumption.

In his images of glamorous women in *The Americans*, Frank accomplished the subversion of popular and traditional expectations by undermining the descriptive function (or metonymy) of photography. Frank's photographs do not fulfill a more manifest political (or mainstream) agenda as did many photojournalistic or documentary photographs of the time, but instead they look at more broadly conceived, metaphorical realms of social behavior. It is this element of symbolic *possibility* of meanings, rather than presumptions of clear meaning, that most viewers value in his work. His ironic parodies of mass culture norms and expectations position Frank clearly as the avant-garde voyeur looking with disdain at popular culture tastes. Yet, the subtlety and ambiguity inherent in his images may also be seen as a suitable response within a McCarthyist social terrain, wherein manifest political content might alert government officials of suspect or even subversive intent.

Not surprisingly, some Photo League photographers looked upon Frank with suspicion. Certainly Frank was no stranger to the Photo League. Walter Rosenblum remembers him participating in a few activities, and Frank spoke at the league in 1950 with Ed Feingersh, a 35mm photographer who has received little attention.[76] William Johnson adds that Frank lived close to the league's headquarters, met Lou Stettner there, and might even have showed his works under their auspices. Frank only recalls, cryptically, "I may have had a little speech there."[77] In any case, Frank does not include the league in his litany of influences, indicating, by his silence, little regard for the organization or any effect on his work by its members.

Former league members Lou Stettner and David Vestal, in later reviews, discuss Frank's distance from the league's sense of photographic purpose.

Their critical writings do not support subsequent "lionizing" histories of Frank and offer another, less popular point of view in regard to Frank's personal form of documentary.

Stettner's review in *Camera 35*, "Speaking Out: Politics of Despair" (1973) begins with criticism of 1960s photographer Diane Arbus's "nausea with people," proving "that humans were really innately monstrous beings, not beautiful." Her champions, including critics A. D. Coleman, Hilton Kramer, and John Szarkowski, he maintains, confused such despair toward humanity with profundity. More specifically, "Szarkowski's statement that her photographs 'deal with private rather than social realities' is romantic mysticism." He then traces Arbus's aesthetic back to what he perceived as its source, *The Americans*, "whose photographs are the epitome of alienation, despair and futility." Stettner continues: "But Frank's 'disgust with life,' is based on two fundamental assumptions that are not true: one, that the values of our society are permanent and can never be changed for the better; and two, that the majority of people are inane zombies incapable of bettering their situation (also an elitist position)." In contrast to this new aesthetic of despair, Stettner recalls Ruth Orkin's *Summer Afternoon in the Slums* (Figure 1.12), which follows "the humanist tradition, which is to say that she believes that human beings have great potential." In comparison, the work of "despairing" artists such as Frank and Arbus "leads nowhere but backwards. History will prove I am right."[78]

Stettner's text invokes the rhetorical tradition of Marx, alluding to the "mysticism" of high-art language and the social purpose of art to ennoble the masses or undermine the capitalist culture at large. Frank's work could not, for him, enter into these loftier dimensions of intent—it undermined the very forces of potential change by focusing on the negative without offering alternative visions of hope (or revolution). To some today, Stettner sounds like a theoretical dinosaur, with his presumptions that art can alter or at least affect history through meaning and interventions in the visual discourse of power.

In another article, "Speaking Out: On the Windshield of My Mind" (1973), Stettner again blasts Frank's photographs as he reviewed Time-Life's recently published book *Documentary Photography*. This time he began with memories of Grossman's "Dialogues," the unpublished talks the Photo League teacher gave. Stettner appreciated Grossman's open engagement with the visualizing of material reality that was never "absolute" but hoped to "eventually lead to a better understanding of what the object is really like." He again praises Orkin's profound and subtle image of the urban sandstorm, with its "compassion for the horror of the city ghetto under the heat." He further underscores Orkin's commitment to the league and her bravery in cold war America, demonstrated by her "staunch support of the Photo League during the McCarthy era."[79]

Frank does not fare as well as Orkin in Stettner's review. He mentions Frank in the context of Frank's many followers, who were also included in this Time-Life anthology of documentary photography and who, like Frank, were "hopelessly alienated from society and one another" and were never "really together or related in any positive way . . . [instead remaining] completely detached from their environment and one another." Stettner admits that Frank shows "pity and compassion" for the human subject, but ultimately such subjects become, in Stettner's eyes, "helpless pawns, incapable of ever throwing off their lethargy and bettering their condition."[80] To this social documentary critic, Frank could not be called humanist, as he dwelled on *de*humanization in his deconstructive analyses of alienation and defeated souls. His negativity, Stettner feels, was not directed toward the specifics of revolutionary change, and in this way Frank failed to take a decided, actual stand in the face of such societal "despair." Stettner does not appreciate the visual power Frank's work offered a new generation of alienated viewers eager to expand photography's discourse.

David Vestal, another critic who had been an active member of the Photo League, in a review of *Lines of My Hand*, 1973, took a similar route in attacking Frank's work. A "cleanly done, sensitive, truthful book," *The Americans*, Vestal maintains, "was neither that bad nor that good." It did, however, make Frank "into a legendary, mysterious, overrated figure." Vestal remembered having known Frank since 1948: Frank was "one of those artists who carefully live in a constant elegant mess—financial, aesthetic, and psychological. I always figured he was working to live down his Swiss middle-class background." This comment indicates another key difference between Frank and many Photo Leaguers—that of economic background. Whereas many in the league had come from poor immigrant families, Frank had come from a decidedly bourgeois home. This privileged background, Vestal implies, influenced the development of his more ironic, personal, and less bombastic indictments of the "system." It is telling, as well, that Vestal's professed favorite images by Frank are most consistent with the critic's appreciation for more traditional definition of documentary photography: for instance, *Elizabethville, North Carolina*, which Vestal calls "an echo, but not an imitation, of Ben Shahn at his best."[81]

A letter Frank wrote in 1981 to a Japanese colleague further demonstrates the depth of difference between Photo League aesthetics and Frank's understanding of social change. In that letter Frank articulates his sympathy for the underprivileged in society but also admits he can't believe in the romantic notion of justice.[82] Frank cannot, within his generational context, assume that society will triumph in its empowerment of the "other." Instead, he is jaundiced and leery of documentary ideals proclaiming humanistic intent. Cold war hypocrisy, fears of nuclear annihilation, and Frank's own existential angst, perhaps, make such idealism impossible.

The articles above articulate the key differences between the increasingly outmoded humanist documentary ideals, as evidenced in Stettner's and Vestal's texts, versus Frank's more ambiguous depictions of subtle, personal realms of human interaction. The history of photographic criticism involving Frank allows us an even better glimpse into the evolving tastes and aesthetics during the post–World War II years. Ultimately, Frank has been subsumed completely into the high-art canon, through the auspices of Szarkowski at MoMA and other photohistorical critics, until, phoenix-like, he has risen as the avant-garde bohemian leader who changed the entire course of photography's history.

This historiography of Frank's lionization is also detected in the present-day popular conceptions of Frank's abuse and calumny in press reviews following publication of *The Americans*. The book was not immediately published after the Guggenheim Fellowship ended, and its history from 1956 to 1959 offers an interesting look into Frank's career during this three-year period. Frank continued to publish in mainstream popular presses, doing advertisements for Leica and the *New York Times*, enjoying press coverage of his photos in books such as *Incas to Indians* and assorted annuals, and participating in exhibitions. In 1958 the Guggenheim-sponsored images were collected and published by Robert Delpire in Paris as *Les Américains*. This publication apparently troubled Frank, as it included copious text in the form of quotations concerning American life and history by the likes of Simone de Beauvoir, Erskine Caldwell, William Faulkner, Abraham Lincoln, Henry Miller, FDR, Walt Whitman, Richard Wright, and Alexis de Tocqueville, among many others.[83]

In the next year, 1959, however, Frank found an American publisher—Grove Press, in New York, which published the literary magazine *Evergreen Review* as well as books by Alain Robbe-Grillet, Samuel Beckett, and Eugene Ionesco. The press and editor Barney Rosset were more interested in cutting-edge contemporary work than blockbuster sales. The clothbound Grove edition of *The Americans* was finally released on January 15, 1960, with approximately 2,600 copies at $7.50 each (only half of these sold). Despite the relegation of first editions to remainder shelves, the book has been reprinted several times to accommodate the ever-increasing interest of subsequent generations in Frank's work; it is still in print.[84]

This time the photographs were accompanied by short place-name captions and a six-page introduction by Kerouac. Kerouac's participation in *The Americans* has been clarified in later interviews. Green writes that Frank met Kerouac in 1958 and asked him to write the introduction.[85] While Frank "didn't want it to come out with any text," Barney Rosset at Grove Press wanted to publish poetry with the images. Finally, "Kerouac came along and everything fell into place," Frank remembers. He further recalls meeting Kerouac at a party and showing him the French edition. Kerouac "liked the photos" and agreed to write "something for it." "He wrote it twice, which was very unusual for him. He objected very much, he never did rewrites for anybody. But I thought the first time was too short and so he wrote a little longer version. I liked it right away. We stayed friends." But Frank still maintains a disinterest in text; "often I find words are pretentious, false, phony and posturing. I know pictures can be the same, can be false. But I just trust it more. I trust *pictures* more."[86]

The popular point of view today is that Frank was reviled, rejected, and suffered devastating critical blows after the publication of *The Americans*. The reviews most often cited are those published in *Popular Photography*, which devoted space to multiple reviews from their editors and writers, indicating the force that *The Americans* had on their viewers. It was in this magazine and another mainstream popular photographic periodical, *Modern Photography*, that Frank endured the harshest criticism, not only for his "anti-American" content but also for the "sloppy" 35mm technique born of his Leica. "P. C.," reviewing *The Americans* for *Modern Photography* (June 1960), noted that the negative book should have been entitled, "My Americans," or "Why I Can't Stand America." This reviewer also noted that "Frank has rejected the obvious layout as an editorial aid, but he editorializes just as effectively, if more subtly, by simple sequence." The most biting criticism was not Frank's negativity overall, the reviewer wrote, but that "he is not *for* anything. His outlook seems just as disorganized, just as totally destructive—and frankly, just as adolescent—as that of the beat school of writers with whom he is associated."[87]

The multiple reviews reprinted in *Popular Photography* (July 1960) have been overused as the representative criticism Frank encountered while serving as examples of his alienation from commercial, mainstream photography. Comments often cited, like media sound bytes, include: "his book is an attack on the United States" (Les Barry); "the book seems to me to be a mean use to put a camera to" (Bruce Downes); "a wart-covered picture of America" (John Durniak); and "a sad poem for sick people" (James Zanutto). Indeed, many of these short reviews voice hatred of the book and its view of

American life. But not all of the reviews are completely negative; indeed H. M. Kinzer praised the book's "sharp perception" and "sheer power." Even negative reviewers admit to liking certain aspects of *The Americans*: Durniak says there are "many beautiful pictures"; Arthur Goldsmith writes the book is "worth seeing"; and Charles Reynolds feels "an artist with a strong viewpoint, however limited, is better than one with no viewpoint at all."[88] In short, these critical reviews certainly demonstrate a xenophobic cold war fear of dissent and social criticism, but they deserve a closer textual reading in order to more fully appreciate their points.

Critiques were often based on style, not just content. Some of the most belabored criticism involved Frank's use of 35mm photography, a technical debate that raged throughout the 1950s in *Popular Photography* articles. The following headlines demonstrate the fear of this new aesthetic Frank and others (such as Grossman, Klein, and Faurer) explored: "The New Clichés" (on 35mm subjects, December 1957); "Is It Too Easy?" (on available light photography, January 1958); "Is 35-mm Producing a Generation of Sloppy Photographers?" (August 1958); "Midget into Monster" (on 35mm work, August 1959); "The Photo Bohemians" (October 1959); "Alexander King Blasts Today's Photography" (on "the small-camera boys," November 1959). Ed Grazda, who printed for Frank in the 1970s, points out that Frank was certainly cognizant of technique to the point of being downright "fussy."[89] The critical, aesthetic distinctions between the clearly focused, "successful" photograph, as dictated by *Popular Photography*, and the grain and blur encouraged by the growing number of 35mm photographers of the 1950s (an aesthetic frequently pursued earlier in the Photo League), certainly deserves more attention. It may be that Frank's dedication to this "anti-aesthetic" has been overstated.

However, some overwhelmingly (and some begrudgingly) positive reviews indicate that many viewers took *The Americans* very seriously indeed. Few photographic books of the time earned so much attention, although *The Americans* was not a popular success. Given the sorry state of photographic criticism in the 1950s, the attention that the book did receive indicates Frank's high-profile position within the arts as well as his book's general impact on surprised American viewers.

Reviews of *The Americans* dating from 1960 are found in diverse sources, ranging from *Popular Photography*, *Modern Photography*, and *Aperture* to *Dissent*, the *New Yorker*, *Library Journal*, and the *New York Times Book Review*, among others. The assumption often communicated in later histories of Frank is that his book hit the photographic community with the ideological force of a gale wind, forcing an explosion of commentary. Yet there is less acknowledgment that he was an already known and respected force in the photography scene of that time and that his book was all the more surprising for its alteration of assumed visual codes and presumptions. Such interpretations, then, reinforce the view that Frank was an original in style and content, despite his many predecessors in 35mm photography. This interpretation also underscores the exalted image of the maligned individual coping within the grey-flanneled decade of organization men.

Yet when one reads the primary critical reviews, one finds they did not all disparage his "anti-Americanism" to the degree we have been led to believe in subsequent histories of this photographer. Dorothy Nyren, in the *Library Journal*, calls it "a fine collection" of "biting pictures" and recommends it "for any library that can afford it." Gilbert Millstein, in the *New York Times Book Review*, ironically reviewed *The Americans* alongside Grossman's *Journey to the Cape*, published around the same time. He proclaimed Frank "much the better photographer, although both are superior," and wrote that "their contrasting intelligences . . . produce results poles apart." The *New Yorker* critic called *The Americans* a "beautiful social comment."[90]

Not surprisingly, Donald Gutierrez, writing for the leftist publication *Dissent*, found that Frank's photographs reveal the alienating effects of capitalism on American society in images that most would like to repress if not suppress. Ultimately, the book reinforces Gutierrez's agenda: "Americans, like any people engulfed in a corrupt social order, go on living, if only by inertia. The mark of a good civilization, however, is that through its institutions it transforms this instinctual will to exist into an elaborate sense of beauty and meaning." The America in *The Americans* finally fails, then, as "a place of impetus without direction," evoking Stettner's sentiment that revolution cannot be achieved with the inertia exhibited by Frank's figures. Nonetheless, the overall tone of Gutierrez's text is positive.[91]

Minor White's highly selective periodical, *Aperture*, in 1961, included an impressively long portfolio of Frank's work and a sympathetic essay by Edna Bennett entitled "Black and White Are the Colors of Robert Frank." In it, Bennett emphasizes Frank's desire to go beyond traditional expression of "meaning" by combining realism, "the humanity of the moment," with vision, "where matter ends and mind begins."[92] Such quotations echo White's own understanding of photography: that the true artist can transcend the material world in favor of more spiritual, but not didactically political, realms of the mind or individual "soul"—the site of genius and potential revelation. Frank's talents, according to *Aperture*, realized these lofty aspirations.

The Americans elicited overwhelming responses and was favorably reviewed by more critics than historians have sometimes admitted. While many may like to think the book was a critical disaster, it was, in fact, taken very seriously in the press and accorded a good deal of space in periodicals, especially considering the peripheral place of photography in arts criticism in the 1950s—an indicator that Frank was certainly in the public eye compared to many others working at the time.[93] A reevaluation of Frank's critical reception, commercial success, and popularity (within the New York photographic scene) forces us to challenge historiographies reifying Frank as the lonely, radical, alienated avant-garde artist after World War II. Whereas his work could be called "documentary" by many reviewers in the early to mid-1950s, by 1960 it transcends what seems, increasingly, an awkward and limiting label.

Traditional social documentary as a form of political and artistic expression declined in high-art circles as a viable form of viable photographic practice. One of photography's most influential tastemakers, MoMA curator John Szarkowski, in *Mirrors and Windows: American Photography Since 1960* (1978), describes Frank's book as one of three crucial events in American photography of the 1950s (alongside Steichen's *The Family of Man* and White's *Aperture*). Unlike Steichen, whose show was the only "popular" success of the three, Frank and White were "uncompromisingly committed to a highly personal vision of the world. . . . Neither pretended to offer a comprehensive or authoritative view of the world, or a program for its improvement." Szarkowski notes the "shock" Frank's book caused (citing *Popular Photography* quotations only) with its "fragmentary, intuitive, and elliptical" images.[94] With Szarkowski's written blessing, Frank's unique body of photographs was elevated to almost divine status (and higher economic worth) within the twentieth-century canon.

In contrast, social documentary, a tradition crucial to Frank's imaging of the cultural world of America, became a dim and distant light in the past, irreparably damaged by the increasing taste for personal, individually engaged photography of self-anointed artists of the medium. That documentary also involved personal aesthetics and sophisticated choices became less and less obvious over time as the more formally engaged photographers became the beacons of artistry. Social documentary, as evidenced in the major books of the time, loses a sense of stylistic individuality (as the league members had understood) and becomes increasingly subsumed within photojournalist territory. Frank, however, has become the aggrandized father of modern photography, defying traditional aesthetics and political didacticism—to the point that today it is difficult for most students of photography to conceive of a world without his influence.

Frank has continued to elaborate seductively upon his mythology as well, especially in the movie he directed with Rudy Wurlitzer, *Candy Mountain* (1987), in which a Franklike character, pursued by ravenous disciples, heroically rejects American capitalist ideals by working and living in Mabou, Nova Scotia (Frank's present-day home).[95] Perhaps the film character's rejection of the self-serving followers indicates that Frank, too, tires of teetering on such a tall pedestal. But writers and historians continue to substantiate Frank myths in subsequent histories, which obstruct or deny the photographer's sense of lineage and inspiration in past documentary and photojournalistic photography. The focus on Frank—as with Arbus, the Sylvia Plath of American photography—has resulted in numerous exhibitions, bibliographies, and dissertations, to the detriment of other photographers of the era who experimented in 35mm street photography and social documentation. Unfortunately, among studies of cold war photographers, Robert Frank has often been the only game in town.

Postscript: The Triumph of American Photographic Expressionism

> Unlike explicitly informational pictures, such as the photojournalist favors (and which can be read directly), the expressive / creative photographs have to be read cautiously . . . [and] may act, for the viewer, like a kind of daydream. . . . Is a wise photographer offended at another man's dream?
>
> MINOR WHITE, *Aperture* (1957)

In April 1956, a notice for a workshop at Indiana University, Bloomington, was advertised in the *New York Times.* The announcement signaled new, energetic directions in American photography that diverged greatly from earlier documentary concerns as evidenced in the history and aesthetics of the Photo League, Sid Grossman, and *The Family of Man*. The goal of the four-week "intensive" program, directed by Henry Holmes Smith, was to instruct those photographers interested in mastering "the language of photography" through the teachings of Minor White, Aaron Siskind, and Harry Callahan. Program topics included image interpretation, photographic fact versus fiction, photography's limitations, reading the photograph, photograph as sign and symbol, iconography and iconology, and abstract photography in communication. Instruction was also provided in "formalism versus naturalism," "uses of stereotypes in photographic communication," and "applications of visual clichés in communication."[1]

This workshop is one of many examples indicating the growing acceptance of photography in academic programs that fostered abstract or personal directions in the photographic arts of the late 1950s. In the advertisement's accompanying text by Deschin, still writing as the *New York Times* photography critic, the collapse of presumptions of clarity and purpose in photography was clear: "On the assumption that a good photograph contains for different observers more meanings than the mere record of a fact, a photography workshop and seminar to explore 'ways of reading photographs' is announced at Indiana University."[2]

Concern for "truth," meaning, and narrative was as crucial to these workshop teachers as it had been to earlier documentarians of the Photo League or even Steichen in his search for universal human values. However, the notion of truth, as explored in the work of Robert Frank, took on, by the late 1950s, expanded and serious intellectual dimensions. Truth no longer necessarily involved documentary issues of social class and cultural inequity but instead suggested more personal realms in this sophisticated understanding of formalism, multivocality, and reader response. By the late 1950s, Frank, Siskind, and especially White, among others, undressed the emperor that had been documentary photography. With the rising intellectual appeal of art photography, as complex and aesthetically complicated as painting or sculpture, the photography market grew, as did the medium's inclusion in art collections and university curricula. That this gradual shift from "metonymy" to "metaphor" occurred during the cold war years underscores the effects of this oppressive decade on the work of artists in general. As Martha Rosler states, "Allegory and aestheticism become attractive or even imperative in times of repression or despair."[3]

Battle lines between the two camps were frequently drawn throughout the cold war years, with champions of "clarity" and social purpose increasingly perceived of as less intellectual or as amateurs in the medium. In a letter to the editors of *Popular Photography* in 1958, J. A. Vaughn of Atlanta, Georgia, wrote that "a good photograph must be clear, sharp, correctly composed, harmonious, free from distortion, and above all, pleasing to the eye."[4] Vaughn's opinion reflects the mainstream, conventional, and positivist values many in the public realm held toward art in general. The Photo League photographers, or even Steichen, were not so blinded by normative values as to agree with such reductive reasoning, and indeed they discussed complex issues of photographic clarity themselves. However, they were also driven by the conviction that photography could have a higher sense of purpose above and beyond the personal, modernist mystifications identified with abstraction or even Frank's brand of personal realism. Clemens Kalischer's 1957 letter to *Aperture* asked: "Why cannot *Aperture* explore *all* artistic achievements in photography instead of retreating within the limits of 'artiness?'"[5] While at an earlier time, perhaps within the pages of *Photo Notes*, Kalischer's words would have been in agreement with many Photo League members' critical beliefs, in *Aperture* they were distinctly minority concerns and seemed oddly out of place and rather old-fashioned.

Although Frank frequently had been identified with the documentary tradition, he probably felt more comfortable with the new league of personally engaged photographers, who expanded the medium's metaphorical possibilities with their emphasis on theoretical models incorporating psychological, expressive, and spiritual symbolism. This new vision, apparent in the growing recognition of artists such as Minor White, Aaron Siskind (see Figure 1.7), Harry Callahan, Walter Chappell, Clarence John Laughlin, Frederick Sommer, Syl Labrot, and Carl Chiarenza, among others, forced the burgeoning number of critics specifically engaged in the medium's criticism to confront assumptions of photographic clarity. This coincided with the rise of structuralist textual readings and a more rigorous theoretical climate in general—especially in the French philosophical community of the 1960s. Michel Foucault, Roland Barthes, and others investigated the deconstruction of shared signs, attacking notions of textual clarity. Naturalistic, realist, or documentary photographs might pretend to convey a photographer's intent, but, according to the new philosophies, such meaning would lie. For Barthes, the only truth a photograph asserts is that "the thing has been there"; a reality once existed but is now "a reality one can no longer touch." By the 1960s, as John Tagg writes, "whatever sense or necessity such a critical appropriation of the term 'documentary' might have had at the time, its earlier currency was strained to the point of breaking. The unlikely and paradoxical mixture of social and psychological 'truths' . . . was contradictory and inherently unstable."[6]

The criticism of Henry Holmes Smith, as published in *Aperture*, concerning an abstract photograph of wall graffiti by Siskind, certainly signals an increased awareness of complex, structuralist systems of theoreticized visual discourse: "The letter's intellectual function has been twice dismissed, once by whoever abandoned the sign . . . and second by the photographer who pictures only a fragment of a single letter. The trite sweeps of the letter have been transformed and given new life."[7] Siskind's image inspired serious response concerning his abstract representations of complex forms. Whereas the photograph discussed by Holmes could be called "straight," or realistic, it was shot so close to the source that any original context is obliterated. Smith's explication of this image reads as a modernist's hope for transcendence and so champions increased awareness of form and signification. In short, he writes, Siskind "redeems the letter R." Other volumes of *Aperture* include similar topics, signifying the increase in intellectual, critical rigor: Beaumont Newhall's "Photographing the Reality of the Abstract" (1956), "Avanindranath Tagore's Concept of Aesthetic Universality" (1959), and an article on semantics and the art of Paul Caponigro (1959). New signs, now emblematic of intellect, individualism, and metaphysics (not Depression-era social awareness), emerge.

Historiographically, then, this period in American photography has taken on a critical meaningfulness not unlike Irving Sandler's triumphant rise of abstract expressionist painting. American photography during the 1950s seems to shake off its documentary shackles, dominating the international photographic scene (despite the crucial influences of European artists and movements) and becoming more theoretical, academic, and avant-garde in orientation. The rise of less popularized or less understandable critical language in periodicals of the time, notably *Aperture*, marks for many a new, higher plane in the history of American photography, one critics today can be proud of, with its serious discourse of sophisticated criticism. The artists exemplifying such ideals, such as Frank or White, become heroic versions of Greenberg's Pollock; documentarians such as Grossman and Rosenblum fade into the past.

The influence of abstract expressionist ideals on the rise of more personally engaged photography of the 1950s was considerable, not only in the case of Frank but for others as well. Siskind's work, although rooted in the early Photo League, became, by the 1950s, a signal of new "sophisticated, completely urban, and profound" work.[8] One must question why, historically and stylistically, Grossman, for example, is *not* considered as "sophisticated," "urban," or "profound" in comparison. Such criticism implies that any photographer engaged in more specifically social and political realms is less attuned to philosophical and aesthetic constructs, either by choice or by a narrower intellectual curiosity in his or her consideration of the incipient class structures in society. In contrast, artists such as White are interpreted as being committed to loftier artistic goals and ideals—"the *advancement* of photography" (emphasis mine).[9]

A book of Siskind's photographs, *Aaron Siskind: Photographs* (1959) includes a short introduction by abstract expressionist critic Harold Rosenberg, in which he applauds the parallels between Siskind's work and "advanced contemporary paintings": "Siskind's photos are inseparable from painting. Yet they have nothing to do with that movement in photography, abetted by professional vanity, that seeks to establish the photograph as 'fine art' to be hung alongside the canvas on the walls of museums and galleries. These magnificent black and whites disdain 'interpretation' and the devices—blurring, angle shots, foreshortening, double exposure—by which 'creative' photography attempts to simulate the effects of modern modes in painting." Instead of superficially mimicking paintings, Siskind's works, to Rosenberg, "ARE paintings," and, like the best of paintings, they are authentic and original.[10] Siskind further enjoyed the endorsement of Minor White, who called him a photographer "with all three eyes on the subject and none on the grandstand."[11]

Siskind's command of formal issues especially impressed Rosenberg: "It is in his wonderful grasp of surfaces by the modulations of his greys that Siskind almost makes us forget that these are not paintings." Siskind provides, Rosenberg says, the "intellectual pleasure in recognizing them [his photographs] as extensions of our esthetic tradition [modernism]." Rosenberg also disparages the supposed legibility of photographs, that ghost of "truth" haunting photography through the decades since its invention: "This assumption of intrinsic significance is a fallacy that photography shares with its twins, the newspaper and naturalistic literature. The fact is that most photographs . . . simply stare back at you with the dumb stare of physical fact." White corroborates Rosenberg's questioning of photographic truth in *Aperture*, 1955: "Truth is an extracting abstraction to be in pursuit of and slippery. Just as one reaches for the hammer to nail it down in one dimension it escapes in a fourth."[12]

Another quotation from Rosenberg's introduction further underscores the growing distance and differentiation between popular taste and high art photography in contemporary American criticism: "With the instinct of a master for the philosophic basis of his medium, [Siskind] has comprehended the camera as an instrument turned outward to variety rather than as a tool for inscribing a signature. As a group and separately, his images evoke a commonly accessible world—though one which . . . has as its strict entrance requirement an educated sensibility."[13] Much of the work subsumed under the broad rubric of American "new vision" involves the development of elite "entrance requirements" and "educated sensibilities" in order to fully appreciate the richly layered multivocality of complex formalistic and personal symbology. In this respect, perhaps many in the photographic community felt that shows such as *The Family of Man* had done more harm than good; while bringing the medium to the eyes of the masses, it also fostered false perceptions of critical passivity and simplicity by narrating the visitors' understanding of the complex issues presented.

Rosenberg and Siskind's alliance was an uneasy one, since the fit between photography and abstract expressionism was not perfect. As Tagg notes, the "assimilation of photographic practices to 'Fine Art' models was fraught with difficulties, and that precarious generalisation Photography did not sit well in the modern museum of Art." Nevertheless the formation of photographic hierarchies within high arts practice intensified during the postwar decades, a situation Tagg finds ironic: the history of photography "cannot be reduced to a unity and assimilated to the very canon [the history of art] it has, practically and theoretically, called into question."[14] The calcification of photographic categories (documentary versus art, for example) also intensified in relationship to the medium's increased market value.

Ideally, photohistorians, critics, and viewers of photography should apply Rosenberg's "educated sensibilities" to the reading of *any* image, whether art, magazine advertisement, or newspaper photograph. However, to argue that all representations are visually complex undermines the formation of market-inspired hierarchies. And during the 1950s the assumptions among the new disciples of complex personal photography seemed to dictate that "good" photographs require more thought, taste, discrimination, and general "educated sensibility." Over time, in response to these hierarchies of photographic expression, photohistorical scholars have responded with volumes of texts devoted to those very practitioners of more sophisticated, high art aesthetics, such as Frank. Popular mainstream successes (or "kitsch," as Clement Greenberg might call them) such as *The Family of Man* seem, in comparison, too legible, too accessible, too popular with uneducated masses, and suffer, consequently, from oversimplification and reductive criticism themselves.

Unlike the photographer who assumes purpose and clarity, those engaged in deeper levels of multivocal signification are lauded as superior. White writes in rhapsodic terms that the mature photographer (or "poet-photographer") goes beyond the immediately observable: "Having learned how to be lucid, he has now only to move upward, ever upward, a little bundle of flaming excelsior in his hand to fire each wayside station on the way. We can trace his progress up the mountain by the lengthening string of bonfires until he disappears in a sunset of snow at the summit."[15] Such rhetoric reinforces the hierarchical categories that differentiate photographers with social purpose from those with visionary purpose by creating standards of excellence. By the cold war, those standards increasingly favored the retreat into personal symbolism based on the lessons of, in White's case, Zen Buddhism, general non-Western aesthetics, and other anti-establishment, avant-garde theoretical models of the time. Jonathan Green notes that White sought "a continual affirmation of expansion and consciousness" in contemporary photography, beyond the "superficial" or "pictorial."[16] And Frank becomes, according to Joel Meyerowitz, "the hinge on which photography swings."[17]

The subsequent critical privileging of these new trends, corresponding with a lack of attention to the history of the Photo League and *The Family of Man*, heralds a broader cultural disenchantment in the 1960s. By this decade, sardonic images more broadly visualizing aspects of American culture (the Vietnam War, civil rights, consumerism, and gender inequity, among other social factors) were frequently considered, by tastemakers like Szarkowski, more intellectually and conceptually astute compared to much of the social realism of the 1930s (which, in the more jaded 1960s might have seemed hopelessly "corny"). Even though many of their images concerning American political life were devastatingly negative, a position many radicals in the 1960s could embrace, most Photo League photographers took a positivist critical stance that was fundamentally humanist; their essential assumption was that change and improvements were needed, and they were *possible*—humanity could be rescued from consumerist capitalism.

In art history texts of the 1970s, earlier documentary and photojournalistic works by such revered artists as Walker Evans and W. Eugene Smith were increasingly subsumed into higher art categories, differentiating them from the "rabble" of other commercial or federally sponsored photographers who could not so easily fulfill myths and values concerning personal expressionism, existential angst, fragmentation, anti-authoritarianism, and irony. In a 1957 review, an *Aperture* writer (probably White) wrote that "certainly the objectivity of the FSA photographers has been long absent," assuming, as many do, those photographers believed in objectivity or presumed to attain it.[18] This supposed stance was rejected by the rising pool of subjectivist photographers and replaced by a new presumption—that the photographer could translate a more authentic, interior reality: the soul.

Photography has tried in the decades past, sometimes in vain or with overzealous clumsiness, to rise to the perceived high art standards of painting. This course should be questioned in regard to our histories, standards, and canon-formation, as we cannot afford to leave crucial documentary figures out of the collective picture of American photography. The history of taste and its formation in the historiography of photographic criticism has created an almost impermeable canon of photographers who fit neatly within modernist ideals of originality and postmodern ideals of ambiguity, even if such categories necessarily ignore the importance of lineage in the formation of careers and styles.

The Photo League and artists such as Grossman have suffered in the literature from lingering cold war taboos and a postmodern critical climate dictating contemporary taste. Thus, through time, the league has become an obscure, arcane reference in photohistory texts, and Grossman, a ghost of the cold war; *The Family of Man*, regarded by many as a historical embarrassment, seemingly so transparent an ideological ruse, has been critically dismissed and simplified; and Robert Frank has become the textbook godhead of the 1950s—the epitome of the alienated artist and avant-garde genius of his age. Whereas Frank, like Grossman, successfully straddled the simplistic polemics between "art" and "document," Grossman, unlike Frank, endured the McCarthyist years more directly and descended into forty years of obscurity and neglect.

Documentary's dominance has declined in critical and historical prestige over the last fifty years, but its attitude never disappeared, despite the many writers and photographers who questioned its earlier ideals. In fact, today we may be witnessing a renaissance of social documentary photography, as seen in the increased interest in socially engaged artists of the past, recent exhibitions on documentary styles, and new magazines such as *DoubleTake*. In reality, "documentary photography" is but another flawed and imprecise category presuming to define styles, purposes, and content far richer and more complex than the words used to describe them. Its presumptions of truth, narrative function, and social purpose imply a photographer's passionate commitment to the communication of cultural subjects in any era.

All documentary inspired photographers bring with them a vast agenda of beliefs, assumptions, and intellect, as is the case with all artists of all media—in short, documentary photography is as narrow, or as broad, as the photographer behind the lens. Analysis of American photographic expression during the cold war years can be viewed as a cautionary tale warning us against the dangers of simplistic interpretations. As photography, so solidly identified with mass appeal and mass use since its birth nearly 200 years ago, approaches the aestheticized and entrenched realms of categorical hierarchies haunting painting and sculpture, it often retreats from engagement and risks becoming divorced from life. Even so, the social documentary tradition continues, in all its rich complexity, resisting the tide.

Notes

Introduction: What Is Documentary Photography?

1. Beaumont Newhall, "A Backward Glance at Documentary," in *Observations: Essays on Documentary Photography*, ed. David Featherstone (Carmel, Calif.: Friends of Photography, 1984), 2–3. Newhall discusses these often contradictory and ambiguous categories: "No one thinks of Alfred Stieglitz as a 'documentarian'; he would snort at the thought." Yet his early work, such as *The Steerage*, "is in every sense a document of a highly important aspect of American culture." Newhall believes that "most of the work done under the name *documentary* can best be described . . . [as] *humanistic*." Finally, he admits confusion: "One of the puzzling things about *documentary* is that it has been used so often in an exclusive, categorical way," applied easily to Farm Security Administration images, yet not to the "brilliant *Life* photo essays by W. Eugene Smith."

2. William Stott, *Documentary Expression and Thirties America* (Chicago: University of Chicago Press, 1973), 11.

3. Abstract, personal styles have existed throughout the history of photographic expression to varying degrees, a historical aspect that cannot be fully addressed in this context. During the first decades of the twentieth century, the modernist photography Stieglitz promoted at 291 and in *Camera Work* heralded this movement within American photographic circles. Historiographically, the Stieglitz school has been championed as a "triumph" of modernism in American art. To scholars raised on historiographies praising the rise of European-inspired modernism in photography, claims of documentary hegemony during the Depression may seem questionable; however, the balance was tilted in realism's favor during the 1930s, aided by the Works Progress Administration (begun in 1935 and renamed the Work Projects Administration in 1939), a New Deal agency employing artists engaged in many creative endeavors (art, sculpture, murals, theater, music, etc.). Before it was disbanded in 1943, the WPA "brought the American artist and the American public face to face for the first time. It created a mass audience for what had been privileged entertainment" (Stott, *Documentary Expression*, 104). While modernism coexisted with social realism or documentary photography during the Depression years, realism clearly dominated in texts, criticism, and exhibitions of the time.

4. For more on the formation of photographic categories, see Allan Sekula's key essay, "On the Invention of Photographic Meaning," in *Photography in Print*, ed. Vicki Goldberg (New York: Simon and Schuster, 1981), 452–73. This essay, originally published in *Artforum* (1975), is also reprinted in *Thinking Photography*, ed. Victor Burgin (London: Macmillan, 1982), 84–109.

5. This book does not belabor ambiguous distinctions within artistic hierarchies

and presumes visual creators such as FSA photographers were *artists* with a documentary focus.

6. Maren Stange, *Symbols of Ideal Life: Social Documentary Photography in America, 1890–1950* (Cambridge: Cambridge University Press, 1989), 90–92, 105. Stryker's problematic role as auteur within the FSA is a crucial consideration in studying the production and ideology of the images that were made and circulated. Maren Stange maintains that Stryker constructed representations with "the appearance of seeming social fact in order to express what was currently appropriate and even attractive" about new the liberal ideology he and others (such as Dewey and Tugwell) espoused in the 1920s (99, 105). She adds: "To show the inevitably modernizing American, but in a style credibly humanitarian and artfully individualizing, would be Stryker's task at the FSA. It was, of course, a task made easier because the New Deal government was both the agent of change and the sponsor of representation" (105).

Stryker's allegiance was to documentary photography. Later he visited the Photo League (on March 22, 1940); *Photo Notes* reported, ironically, that he "closed with a word of good cheer. The outlook for government subsidization of documentary photography, he said, is very hopeful."

7. Newhall, "A Backward Glance," 4–5; Stange, *Symbols of Ideal Life*, 107–8.

8. Stange, *Symbols of Ideal Life*, 90–107. The organization of the RA and FSA was far more complicated than indicated in this introduction; Stange's book traces the background and evolution of the FSA in more detail. Stange likens the organization to a corporate business, with an interest in the legitimation of New Deal policies such as "expansion, rising productivity," and "mass consumption economy." To Stange, then, the FSA was an example of a federal agency manipulating public opinion "to sustain the national rate of consumption" (89). Her research on the FSA describes the organization as an ideological front for bourgeois American values (and "utopian" progress) rather than a "well-meaning" program formed, ideally, to alleviate human suffering. Yet this useful collective picture of the FSA neglects many independent photographers' views, ideals, and beliefs toward documentary photography.

9. Anne Wilkes Tucker, "Photographic Facts and Thirties America," in Featherstone, ed., *Observations*, 50. Arthur Rothstein, in another of many similar statements by FSA photographers, said he wanted "a factual and true scene" (Stott, *Documentary Expression*, 61).

10. Stott, *Documentary Expression*, 21. It is this definition of *social documentary* that this book uses to define American documentary work of the 1930s through the 1950s. Stott's book still offers the longest, most in-depth cross-disciplinary analysis of the history of 1930s documentary.

11. Stott, *Documentary Expression*, 56, 49. Today, the politics of representing the "other"—ethnicities and classes outside the photographer's own personal experiences—have become more critically scrutinized than in the past. For more information on this subject in the context of the FSA, see Nicholas Natanson, *The Black Image in the New Deal: The Politics of FSA Photography* (Knoxville: University of Tennessee Press, 1992).

12. There have been many analyses of the relationship between form and content throughout the history of art; discussions of this topic are ably demonstrated in the post–World War II era writings of Ben Shahn and poet Robert Creeley. In a let-

ter to Charles Olson at Black Mountain College (ca. 1950), Creeley noted that "form is never more than an *extension* of content." *Charles Olson and Robert Creeley: The Complete Correspondence*, vol. 1, ed. George F. Butterick (Santa Barbara, Calif.: Black Sparrow Press, 1980), 79. In his essay "Projective Verse," Olson wrote the same line in bold letters: "FORM IS NEVER MORE THAN AN EXTENSION OF CONTENT." *Selected Writings of Charles Olson*, ed. Robert Creeley (New York: New Directions, 1966), 16. The literature of the time was witnessing a similar parallel to the rise of abstract expressionism in painting with the evolution of New Criticism, a more formal approach to literary criticism wherein content and biography were deemphasized.

Ben Shahn also addressed the growing tensions between form and content in art in his Charles Eliot Norton Lectures at Harvard University (given in 1956–57 and published as *The Shape of Content* in 1957). In his discussion of the rise of increasingly abstract, formal art on the American scene, Shahn argued that "form is the shape of content. . . . Form could not possibly exist without a content of some kind." Much abstract, formal art, he wrote, alienates the public: "Worth itself inheres only in the special few, the initiate" (60, 61). Earlier in his career Shahn had felt "the long artistic tug of war between idea and image." He perceived both the "subjective" and "objective" in his art as inseparable: "The challenge is not to abolish both from art, but rather to unite them into a single impression, an image of which meaning is an inalienable part." However, he later noted, "Such a nostalgia for content and meaning in art goes counter to the creed as it is set forth by the true spokesmen for the new doctrine" (abstract expressionism, in its "race against content"). Shahn, who identified with social realist ideals, was dissatisfied with contemporary trends that dictated form over content; he missed other artists such as Thomas Eakins, with his "complete dedication to comprehending something, someone outside himself," his "intensity of honesty." Abstraction is not without content to Shahn (it "admits of content"); however, he noted, in a repressive climate it represents conformity, "the retreat from controversiality." Contemporaneously, Shahn was forced to attend HUAC court trials concerning his own political past; his writings forcefully indicate the decline in documentary or realist agendas in comparison to abstract ideals. See Ben Shahn, *The Shape of Content* (Cambridge: Harvard University Press, 1957), 36, 45, 57–58, 62, 91.

13. Newhall, "A Backward Glance," 5. The group never learned Lange's own answer, as she died just two months later. A key aspect to appreciating the role of documentary before 1960 involves understanding that many of the photographers themselves differentiated between their photojournalistic work and their "purer" documentary work. The latter was (more or less) freer of outside editorial controls and involved less strict adherence to the inclusion of a text written by others. Many Photo League photographers, in particular, maintain a far more specific definition when discussing their documentary work in contrast to paid commissions from picture magazine editors. Documentary images, then, were often more overtly politically engaged and more descriptive of unequal class distinctions, and they allowed more freedom in general for the photographer. However, these distinctions are seldom delineated in contemporary photography today.

14. Stott, *Documentary Expression*, 281. Evans's work, according to Stott, was

"generally thought idiosyncratic, old-fashioned, cold, [and] insufficiently reformist," which led to his being fired by the FSA photography unit in March 1937 (222). Oddly enough, Lewis Hine did not fare much better with Stryker, according to Stange. Hine sought FSA work during the 1930s, but, as written in a letter by Stryker to Tugwell, "it was impossible to make the type of arrangements which would be satisfactory to him." Stange also adds that Hine's photographs after World War I "showed no interest in portraying the benefits of the new management sciences" that Tugwell and Stryker endorsed (92, 93).

15. Paul Taylor, "Migrant Mother: 1936," in *Photography in Print*, ed. Vicki Goldberg, 355–57. Taylor, professor of economics at the University of California, Berkeley, teamed with Lange in 1935 to document migrant housing in California. Their efforts helped persuade government officials to provide federal funds for housing. As the *San Francisco News* reported on March 10, 1936: "Ragged, ill, emaciated by hunger, 2,500 men, women and children are rescued after weeks of suffering by the chance visit of a Government photographer" (quoted in Taylor, "Migrant Mother," 355). Lange had brought the photograph *Migrant Mother* to the attention of news bureaus, and the *San Francisco News* editor sent it to the United Press for release. The UP then contacted authorities, who sent representatives to the women's camp in Nipomo, California, and informed the migrant workers that food was on the way. The rhetoric of the *San Francisco News* caption addressed the central hope of documentarians, that of change and improvement for the masses.

16. As Newhall has noted, "Documentary seems . . . a matter of intent, not only on the part of the photographer, but of the viewer as well. It is as much a matter of how the picture is used as how it is taken" (Newhall, "A Backward Glance," 6). The "audience of millions" for FSA images was varied and extensive; Stryker supplied the growing file of FSA photographs free to publishers, and by the end of 1936 he had placed them with numerous periodicals and also prepared twenty-three exhibitions of the work (one of which was at MoMA, another at the 1936 Democratic National Convention). By 1942, the number of published books with illustrations by FSA images approached a full dozen (Stange, *Symbols of Ideal Life*, 107, 108–9, 111). However, difficulties began to arise because of the mass circulation of FSA photographs; Shahn recalled that by 1937 children he met in the field had become "sophisticated" enough to assume commercial motivations. Furthermore, disagreement over the images' circulation created tensions, especially within the pronounced middle-class audience Stryker sought. Stange notes that the most popular traveling exhibit on migrants was requested over eighty times in three years, but none of these requests were from the states with the highest migrant populations (Oklahoma, Arkansas, and Texas). Lange wanted to use her negatives in regional publications with little to no national circulation, but mass-circulated periodicals were given top priority, a disagreement that led to Lange's dismissal from the FSA, Stange maintains, in 1939 (128, 129, 114). Despite such difficulties, the FSA photographs were widely circulated and enjoyed a more popular audience than most other previous photographic movements in the history of the medium. The New Deal arts projects, as written in a 1937 *Fortune* magazine article, witnessed "a more immediate contact with the people" and "a greater human response than anything the government has done in generations" (quoted in Stott, *Documentary Expression*, 105).

17. Stott, *Documentary Expression*, 9–10, 11–12; Newhall, "A Backward Glance," 3.

18. Stott, *Documentary Expression*, 9–10, 21.

19. Ibid., 23. For another expanded discussion of propaganda in the 1930s, see Estelle Jussim, "Propaganda and Persuasion," in Featherstone, ed., *Observations*. While Stott re-creates the contemporary dialogues and arguments over the notion of propaganda (whether it was perceived of as "art," associated with totalitarian regimes, or seen as negative or positive by various intellectual camps in the 1930s), Jussim explores the ideological realms of viewer perception of propaganda, as well as how documentary work succeeds in persuading and influencing public opinion. Jussim rightly notes the perceptual activity of "cognitive dissonance," wherein information that does not support that which the viewer thinks it should is rejected, so that visual data only verifies or legitimates a viewer's opinion, which had been formed before the image was presented. She also cites the critical writings of Jacques Ellul, who maintains that "the idea of stimulating action as a result of persuasion is a relatively new one" and that responses to propaganda are no mere result of "cause and effect" (108).

20. Stott, *Documentary Expression*, 18–25, 56. Documentarians and social realists of the 1930s were driven by a humanitarian desire to empower the human subject; Shahn recalled the art he had created during the Depression: "I found the qualities of people a constant pleasure. . . . There were the poor who were rich in spirit, and the rich who were also sometimes rich in spirit" (Shahn, *The Shape of Content*, 40–41).

21. Stott, *Documentary Expression*, 30. See also Judith Mara Gutman, *Lewis W. Hine and the American Social Conscience* (New York: Walker, 1967), 19; and Maren Stange, "The Pittsburgh Survey: Lewis Hine and the Establishment of Documentary Style" in Stange, *Symbols of Ideal Life*. Hine's quotation alludes to the critical relationship in documentary photography between image and text as the two work, ideally, in concert to convey the information desired. Hine may have focused on content, but his sophisticated designs forcefully convey those powerful meanings.

22. Steven W. Plattner, *Roy Stryker: USA, 1943–1950* (Austin: University of Texas Press, 1983), 16–17.

23. John Tagg, "The Currency of the Photograph," in Burgin, ed., *Thinking Photography*, 117. Tagg's critical writings include key poststructuralist questions on the constructions of meaning relevant to this discussion.

24. Stott, *Documentary Expression*, 14, 29.

25. Roy Stryker, "The FSA Collection of Photographs," in Goldberg, ed., *Photography in Print*, 350.

26. Stott, *Documentary Expression*, 26.

27. Stryker, "The FSA Collection," 352.

28. Stott, *Documentary Expression*, 119. Stott also touches on writer Theodore Dreiser's reaction to the times. From the beginning of the Depression until the bombing of Pearl Harbor, Dreiser wrote less fiction than he had previously in his career: "How can one more novel mean anything in this catastrophic period through which the world is passing? . . . No, I must write on economics" (119).

29. *In the Presence of Walker Evans*, ed. Alan Trachtenberg and Isabelle Storey (Boston: Institute of Contemporary Art, 1978), 5.

30. Edward Steichen, foreword and commentary, *Memorable Life Photographs* (New York: Museum of Modern Art and Time, 1951).

31. Andreas Feininger, *Successful Photography* (Englewood Cliffs, N.J.: Prentice-Hall, 1954), 225.

32. Beaumont Newhall, *Photography at Mid-Century* (Rochester: George Eastman House, 1959), n.p.

33. Beaumont Newhall, *The History of Photography: From 1839 to the Present*, rev. ed. (Boston: Little, Brown; New York: Museum of Modern Art, [1937] 1982), 246.

34. Shahn believed that "In such a climate [with Republican Congressman Dondero and "civic crusades" against art] all art becomes suspect." He also added that formal art ("paint-alone métier"), while under attack itself, "is on the whole a safer category to be in than is the more communicative kind of art. In paint alone there are at least no daring commitments to the future, no indiscretions, no irreverence toward relatively sacred individuals, or toward their manners, emblems, or favored slogans. The aesthetic of line, color, and form, like any other way of painting, may always grow in the hands of a gifted painter; but today it has become the norm and the model of conformity" (Shahn, *The Shape of Content*, 90). Shahn recognized and condemned "paint-alone" art for escaping the repressive political climate more than could realism. "Our national fears, too," he added, "affect the evaluations of art. Soviet Realism, for instance, tinged as it is with the official Soviet stamp, cannot be evaluated by critics according to its competence, nor be in any way dissociated from its political overtones" (105).

35. The historiography of these later decades, as FSA photography moved into high-art contexts (or as it was ignored in such contexts) is out of the scope of this book. In 1962, however, MoMA curator of photography Edward Steichen introduced FSA work to new generations in *The Bitter Years, 1935–1941*, an exhibition dedicated to Stryker. Stange notes that the "FSA photographs quickly achieved the status, as Tugwell told an interviewer in 1965, of 'an art form.'" (Stange, *Symbols of Ideal Life*, 133, 130). However, in 1978 MoMA curator John Szarkowski rather dismissed FSA documentary photography in his essay for the exhibit *Mirrors and Windows*, since "the general movement of American photography during the past quarter century has been from public to private concerns," John Szarkowski, *Mirrors and Windows: American Photography Since 1960* (New York: Museum of Modern Art and New York Graphic Society, 1978), 11. While he discusses picture magazines and photojournalism, the FSA is not included at all in Szarkowski's brief survey leading to present-day photography (except under the caption of a Lange image, *Refugees from Abiline, Texas, 1936*).

36. Ansel Adams, "The Profession of Photography," *Aperture* 1, no. 3 (1952): 32. Minor White, "Editorial," *Aperture* 2, no. 3 (1953): 3.

37. Beaumont Newhall, "Photographing the Reality of the Abstract," *Aperture* 4, no. 1 (1956): 32.

38. Minor White, "Editorial," *Aperture* 4, no. 2 (1956): 48.

39. *International Center of Photography Encyclopedia of Photography* (New York: Pound Press and Crown Publishers, 1984), 150–52.

40. Szarkowski, *Mirrors and Windows*, 14.

41. Ernst Fischer, *The Necessity of Art*, trans. Anna Bostock (New York: Penguin

Books, 1986), 219. Fischer was one of many critics, like Shahn, who criticized the dominance of more formally engaged aesthetics in contemporary art.

42. Shahn, *The Shape of Content*, 41.

43. Michel Foucault, "The Political Function of the Intellectual," *Radical Philosophy* (summer 1977): 13; quoted in Tagg, "The Currency of the Photograph," 129. Tagg's influential essay delves more deeply into the theoretical dimensions of American documentary photography during the Depression years and the photographers' and images' relationship to issues of power and the tradition of realism. His essay crucially links assumptions of "realism" with the "privileged status" of the photograph as signifier of visual "truth," while it also explores the cultural, ideological, and political determinants promoting such presumptions within a given time (such as the Depression). Such discussions, however, sometimes neglect to provide the contextualization of beliefs held by the photographers during their own times.

Chapter One: "Where Do We Go from Here?"

1. Robert Justin Goldstein, *Political Repression in Modern America from 1870 to the Present* (Boston: G. K. Hall, 1978), 298, 299, 295. See also Richard Alan Schwartz, *The Cold War Reference Guide: A General History and Annotated Chronology with Selected Biographies* (Jefferson, N.C.: McFarland, 1997).

2. Goldstein, *Political Repression*, 287. Oliver Larkin, *Art and Life in America* (New York: Holt, Rinehart and Winston, 1949, 1960), 467. Larkin, who was a professor of art at Smith College, also wrote a very encouraging letter to the league complimenting the organization's "splendid" and "excellent" magazine, *Photo Notes* (spring 1949). *Photo Notes, 1938–1950*, ed. Nathan Lyons (Rochester: Visual Studies Workshop, 1977).

Page numbers for *Photo Notes* citations, when identified, are according to the Visual Studies Workshop reprint pagination for the series. The editor for this Visual Studies reprint, Nathan Lyons, in "Notes and Acknowledgments," explains that copies of *Photo Notes* have disappeared or are scattered and that no complete set exists in any collection or library. The periodical originated in 1938 as a one-page mimeographed bulletin, but it grew steadily in size and quality to longer monthly issues. The fall 1948 league editors announced a "new format" as *Photo Notes* "tries on its first full dress suit." This new issue promised "broadened scope" and included higher quality offset reproductions and a neater, double-page layout, and it became a seasonal quarterly organized by editor Rosalie Gwathmey ("Introduce You to the New Photo Notes," *Photo Notes* [fall 1948]: 1). However, given the league's blacklisting, subsequent financial problems, and demise by 1951, very few of these newly formated issues were published.

3. Frances K. Pohl, *Ben Shahn: New Deal Artist in a Cold War Climate, 1947–1954* (Austin: University of Texas Press, 1989), 73–74, 37. William Hauptman, "The Suppression of Art in the McCarthy Decade," *Artforum* (October 1973): 48–52.

4. Neil C. Trager, "The Curators," in *The Photo League, 1936–1951* (New Paltz: College Art Gallery, State University of New York, n.d.; New York: Gallery Association of New York State and Photofind Gallery, n.d.), 5. For crucial background, see Leah Ollman, "The Photo League's Forgotten Past," *History of Photography* 18, no. 2

(1994). Other sources in this special issue of *History of Photography* include: Fiona M. Dejardin, "The Photo League: Left-Wing Politics and the Popular Press"; Anne Tucker, "A History of the Photo League: The Members Speak"; and William S. Johnson, "*Photo Notes, 1938–1950*: Annotated Author and Photographer Index."

5. Anne Tucker, "The Photo League," *Ovo Magazine* 10, no. 40/41 (1981): 3, 5. "League News" in the January 7, 1935, issue of *Photo Notes* boasted of members' photographs in the following publications: the *Daily Worker*, *Freiheit*, *Der Arbeiter*, *Labor Unity*, *Labor Defender*, *Better Times Magazine*, *Fortune*, and the *Jewish Daily Bulletin* (12). The word *Nykino* was an acronym for "New York Cinema," *kino* being a Russian word for cinema (Trager, "The Curators," 5).

6. Trager, "The Curators," 5.

7. Ute Eskildsen, "Germany: The Weimar Republic," in *A History of Photography: Social and Cultural Perspectives*, ed. Jean-Claude Lemagny and André Rouillé (Cambridge: Cambridge University Press, 1987), 147, 149.

8. According to Rosenblum, the League received the Hine collection in 1937 or 1938 from Hine's son (Hine died in 1940). Walter Rosenblum, interview by author, tape recording, Long Island City, N.Y., June 16, 1992. Later, when the league needed money and knew they could not afford to properly preserve Hine's work, they offered the collection to Edward Steichen, Director of Photography at MoMA, who turned down the offer. Beaumont Newhall accepted the Hine collection for the George Eastman House, where it remains today.

9. Ibid. A quote from Elizabeth McCausland in the January 1939 issue of *Photo Notes* further illustrates the League's reverence for Hine's documentary integrity: "To Lewis Hine, who thirty-five years ago was making photographs of child labor in sweat shops and textile mills, the vague tenets of pictorialism or the even less useful purposes of the 'photogram' or 'rayograph' must be incomprehensible" Elizabeth McCausland, "Documentary Photography," *Photo Notes* (January 1939): 6. She also defines documentary photography within the selfless Hine tradition: "[The photographer's] purpose must be clear and unified, his mood simple and modest. Montage of his personality over his subject will only defeat the serious aims of documentary photography" (9). Another verbal display of respect for Hine is found in a May 1940 *Photo Notes* article that articulated "Hine's Credo," and proudly noted a recent "all-League show" based on this credo. "An All-League Show Based on 'Hine's Credo,'" *Photo Notes* (May 1940): 5.

10. The league photographers were not naive, unquestioning, or unsophisticated concerning such matters of visual "truth" and debated its existence frequently. In the June 1948 issue of *Photo Notes* a symposium speech on photographic journalism that was to be given by W. Eugene Smith (who was delayed in Pittsburgh and unable to attend) was printed. In the speech, Smith articulated his own belief that photography was never objective but should seek honesty, since "truth [is] many things to many people" W. Eugene Smith, "Photographic Journalism," *Photo Notes* (June 1948): 4. Model also questioned the thorny issue of "truth" in photography as well as the viability of documentary work. She avoided such categories for her own work, but the league never insisted on any one photographic vision and instead discussed and exhibited many types of artistic expression. Model held an exhibition at the league in 1941 which enjoyed an enthusiastic review by

Elizabeth McCausland. See Ann Thomas, *Lisette Model* (Ottawa: National Gallery of Canada, 1990), 93–94.

11. Rosenblum, interview by author, 1992. Mike Weaver, "Dynamic Realist," in *Paul Strand: Essays on His Life and Work*, ed. Maren Stange (New York: Aperture, 1990), 207. Strand's commitment to the league and photographic expression cannot be overstated. In the March–April 1940 issue of *Photo Notes*, Strand reviewed *An American Exodus* by Dorothea Lange and Paul Taylor, calling it a "valuable document . . . of integrity and honest feeling." Paul Strand, "An American Exodus by Dorothea Lange and Paul S. Taylor," *Photo Notes* (March–April 1940): 2–3. Strand's praise is, however, uneven; "For if books like this are to have their maximum value, then it is clear that the basic material, the photographs, must be more than documentary records" (meaning the photographs needed more "unity and intensity of expression which give all works of art their impact"). He then defines this thorny term: "documentary is I believe a certain definite approach to the realities of the world we live in. But this must not be understood as mere record making" (2).

12. Edward Hunt, "The Photo Magazine Craze," *Photo Notes* (August 1938): 2.

13. Carl Chiarenza, *Aaron Siskind: Pleasures and Terrors* (Boston: Little, Brown, 1982), 25, 32, 34. Also see Aaron Siskind, *Harlem Photographs, 1932–1940* (Washington, D.C.: National Museum of American Art, 1981). Another league article, "Harlem Document Goes on View," *Photo Notes* (February 1939): 1, names all of the photographers who worked on this feature group: Lucy Ashjian, Harold Corsini, Beatrice Kosofsky, Richard Lyon, Jack Mendelsohn, and Sol Prom, as well as Aaron Siskind (who, in most histories of the document, receives more than his share of credit).

14. Aaron Siskind, interview by author, tape recording, Providence, R.I., June 23, 1989. See also Lili Corbus Bezner, "Interview: Aaron Siskind," *History of Photography* 16, no. 1 (1992): 28–33.

15. Chiarenza, *Aaron Siskind*, 27, 17–19.

16. McCausland, "Documentary Photography," 9.

17. Ibid., 6–7. Dejardin notes that McCausland was "earmarked" as a CPA member and occasionally used Communist language in references such as "art as a weapon" (Dejardin, "The Photo League," 161–62).

18. Colin Osman, "Biographical Notes," *Creative Camera* no. 223/224 (July/August 1983): 1027. "Sol Libsohn," *Documentary Photography* (New York: Time-Life Books, 1972), 90. Sol Libsohn, telephone conversations with author, May 1998.

19. Elizabeth McCausland, "The Chelsea Document," *Photo Notes* (May 1940): 4.

20. The American Artists' Congress was founded in 1935 and represented art workers fighting fascism during the Depression. The Artists' Union (which published *Art Front* magazine), grew out of John Reed Club meetings during the early years of the Depression and sought federal relief work for unemployed artists. The Artists Equity Association was formed later, in 1947, and also endured political difficulties (see Pohl, *Ben Shahn*, 33). Magazines published by these organizations frequently commented not only on issues of artistic employment but also on historical events, elections, war activity, and other concerns. See Gerald M. Monroe, "Art Front," *Studio International* (September 1974): 66–70; Gerald M. Monroe, "The Artists' Union of New York," *Art Journal* (fall 1972): 17–20; numerous articles in

"Poverty, Politics and Artists: 1930–1945," *Art in America* special issue (August/September 1965); *Artists Against War and Fascism: Papers of the First American Artists' Congress*, ed. Matthew Baigell and Julia Williams (New Brunswick, N.J.: Rutgers University Press, 1986).

21. Walter Rosenblum, review of *The Image of Freedom!*, Museum of Modern Art exhibition, *Photo Notes* (December 1941): 4.

22. *Documentary Photography*, 92. In my interview with Rosenblum, he verbalized his respect for the subjects he photographed: "If you are photographing someone, you owe them a print . . . someone would say to me, why are you taking my picture? . . . I would say, 'I think you look terrific, that's why I'm taking your picture,' . . . So, I always gave out pictures to the people I photographed on Pitt Street" (Rosenblum, interview by author, 1992). Providing a print to the subject is not required, typically, and could be interpreted as a gesture of courtesy. For more on Rosenblum, see *Walter Rosenblum* (Dresden: Verlag der Kunst, 1990).

23. Rosenblum, interview by author, 1992. Rosenblum's recollections of the league include meeting a "who's who" assortment of twentieth-century photographers, who all opened their homes for print critiques, dialogues, and parties. The structure was very loose, open, and based on volunteerism. There were few opportunities to make a living from photography at the time, Rosenblum recalled, so most photographers had day jobs or, during the 1930s, worked for the WPA.

24. Ibid. Jane Addams (1860–1935) was a Chicago social worker who devoted her life to improving the lives of American children and immigrants, and Jacob Riis (1849–1914) photographed and wrote for social reform in New York City.

25. Ibid.

26. "Premiere of Fine Film," *Photo Notes* (May 1942): 3. Also see the following essays in Stange, ed., *Paul Strand*: John Rohrbach, "*Time in New England*: Creating a Usable Past," 174; William Alexander, "Paul Strand as Filmmaker, 1933–1942," 156–59; Anne Tucker, "Strand as Mentor," 126.

27. Victor S. Navasky, *Naming Names* (New York: Viking Press, 1980), 187–88; Joe Schwartz, telephone conversation with author, April 27, 1998; Martin Duberman, *Paul Robeson* (New York: Knopf, 1988): 316–21, 360–62, 364–66. Robeson and the league crossed paths again in 1949 when he attended the Foley Square trials in New York, during which Grossman was named (Duberman, *Paul Robeson*, 337).

28. Schwartz, telephone conversation with author, 1998. Henry A. Wallace was vice president during FDR's third term; under Truman he was appointed sectretary of commerce in 1945. He resigned in 1946, however, after publicly protesting U.S. policy toward the Soviet Union. By 1948 Wallace was campaigning as the candidate of the newly formed third party. "Co-chaired" by Robeson, the Progressive Party protested the Marshall Plan, called for disarmament, and maintained a pro-Soviet platform. The party failed to carry any state in the election, and in 1952 Wallace published a statement titled "Why I Was Wrong." See also Joe Schwartz, *Poems I've Never Written* (San Luis Obispo: California Polytechnic State University, 1994).

29. I. Rice Pereira, "Artists' Equity," *Photo Notes* (May–June 1947): 6. "Report on April 18th Meeting," on the same page, also hinted at an issue any Republican senator, like Dondero, might have chafed at—aid to the suffering people of Greece: "The Photo League took the positive action of sending a resolution to President Truman

urging that food and clothing be sent to the people of Greece, but no help in the form of military supplies to a fascist Greek government." Some league members felt that helping the nonmilitary citizens of a potential enemy constituted humanitarian aid, not complicity. But this, too, could be construed as a sensitive area of political debate considering the conservative climate at the time.

30. Anne Tucker, "The Photo League," *Creative Camera* no. 223/224 (July/August 1983): 1013.

31. Elizabeth McCausland, "Camera and Brush in Service of Humanity," *Photo Notes* (May–June 1947): 8–9. This was a reprint of the third article in a series of three she wrote in 1942 for the *Springfield Republican* newspaper.

32. Serge Guilbaut, *How New York Stole the Idea of Modern Art: Abstract Expressionism, Freedom, and the Cold War*, trans. Arthur Goldhammer (Chicago: University of Chicago Press, 1983). See also *Reconstructing Modernism: Art in New York, Paris, and Montreal, 1945–1964*, ed. Serge Guilbaut (Cambridge, Mass.: MIT Press, 1992); David Shapiro and Cecile Shapiro, *Abstract Expressionism: A Critical Record* (Cambridge: Cambridge University Press, 1990). Assorted helpful essays in *Pollock and After: The Critical Debate*, ed. Francis Frascina (New York: Harper and Row, 1985) include: Max Kozloff, "American Painting during the Cold War," 107–24; Eva Cockcroft, "Abstract Expressionism, Weapon of the Cold War," 125–34; and David Shapiro and Cecile Shapiro, "Abstract Expressionism: The Politics of Apolitical Painting," 135–52.

33. Nancy Newhall, "Ben Shahn," review of Museum of Modern Art exhibition, *Photo Notes* (November 1947): 3. Newhall (1908–74) studied art at the Museum of Fine Arts in Boston and Smith College, graduating in 1930. In New York, she continued her creative studies at the Art Students' League. She filled in for her husband, Beaumont, as curator of photography at MoMA while he was in the army (1942–45) and later served as a consultant for the George Eastman House. Her publications include books on P. H. Emerson, collaborations with Ansel Adams, Edward Weston's *Daybooks* (vol. 1, 1957), and *Time in New England* (with Paul Strand, 1950), among many others.

34. Beaumont Newhall, *The History of Photography: From 1839 to the Present*, rev. ed. (New York: Museum of Modern Art; Boston: Little, Brown, 1982), 246. Newhall's text is the fifth revised and expanded edition, first published as a catalog of the exhibition "Photography 1839–1937" for MoMA in 1937. Newhall earned an AB and MBA fine arts at Harvard, then went on to study in Paris and the Courtauld in London as well. In the 1930s and 1940s he was a curator at MoMA and, later, at the International Museum of Photography at the George Eastman House, in addition to teaching at institutions such as Black Mountain College in North Carolina.

35. Rosenblum, interview by author, 1992; Mary Street Alinder, *Ansel Adams: An Autobiography* (New York: Henry Holt, 1996), 242–44, 291–92.

36. Richard Whelan, *Robert Capa* (New York: Ballantine, 1985), 364–65. Louis Stettner, "Cezanne's Apples and the Photo League: A Memoir by Louis Stettner," *Aperture* no. 112 (fall 1988): 34. Given the reality of reprisals against those belonging to listed organizations, it is hard to fault those who left the league. Rosenblum paraphrased the Newhalls' excuse for leaving, expressing their unease with the organization: "'We know the Photo League. . . . They helped many of us get started.

However, it may be possible that there are some things happening that we don't know about and since we don't know' . . . No evidence and that's the way things went, little by little. Adams resigned with some. Weston didn't. Weston was terrific. . . . Strand hung on; [Leo] Hurwitz [a contributing editor of *Photo Notes*] hung on. But the Newhalls left, Barbara Morgan left. . . . And they were corresponding with each other . . . so there is documentation." This documentation is in Nancy Newhall's letters to Morgan, which outline their suspicions of Communist activity in the league, housed in the Getty Archives in Malibu, California (Rosenblum, interview by author, 1992). David Vestal adds that Adams was upset when he lost his security clearance for the U.S. Navy because of his membership with the Photo League, adding, "You have to save yourself" (David Vestal, telephone conversation with author, July 1996). Others felt forced to quit, too, such as Marion Palfi, who would later regret her fears (see interview by Anne Tucker, personal collection of Anne Tucker, Houston, Tex., n.d.). Adams maintained that he resigned because he "refused to be associated with Communism, even in the name of freedom of choice." In a letter responding to Adams's fears, Gene Smith wrote that he had no doubt the League had some Communists, but that did not "make it a subversive organization" since few members were inclined "to overthrow the government" (Alinder, *Ansel Adams*, 291, 292).

37. Walter Rosenblum, "Some Thoughts about the Photo League," *Photo Notes* (November 1947): 6–8; Tucker, "A History of the Photo League," 174.

38. Goldstein, *Political Repression*, 322.

39. Lewis Wood, "90 Groups, Schools Named on US List as Being Disloyal," *New York Times*, December 5, 1947, sec. 1, pp. 1, 18.

40. "Discussion from the Floor," *Photo Notes* (January 1948): 1, 5; Walter Rosenblum, "For Immediate Release," December 5, 1947 (personal collection of Anne Tucker).

41. Walter Rosenblum, "Where Do We Go from Here?," *Photo Notes* (January 1948): 7.

42. Ibid., 8; see also "Discussion from the Floor," which outlined the germination of the idea that became *This Is the Photo League*. The exhibition grew from Barbara Morgan's suggestion to assemble photographs with captions, including those by Riis and Hine, in order to trace "the historical development" of documentary photography. These images could then be "submitted to some national magazine reaching all kinds of readers. A further motion was made that reprints of this article might be sent with the league's brochure to social institutions throughout the country" (6). The league proposed a publicity campaign, in effect, to offset the Attorney General's listing it as a disloyal organization.

43. "Walter Rosenblum," interview by Colin Osman, *Creative Camera*, no. 223/224 (July/August 1983): 1019–20. Also Rosenblum, interview by author, 1992.

44. Siskind, interview by author, 1989.

45. Dejardin, "The Photo League," 159. Dejardin researched the specific reasons for the FBI's attentions toward the league, citing numerous left-wing or Communist periodicals associated with league writers and photographers and including commentary on the nature of the FBI documents themselves. She notes: "It is not believable that they were unaware of the coverage they were receiving in the publications. . . . It would take a great leap of faith to believe that they were so politically naive as not to know of the radical nature of most of the publications in which they

placed their photographs, press releases and advertisements" (170–71). Tucker's research indicates that the FBI had been compiling "damaging reports" since 1940, after Grossman's trip to the Midwest (Tucker, "A History of the Photo League," 182). In an interview with Anne Tucker, Cornelia Cotton remembered a Photo League benefit for the CPA at Bee Pancoast's apartment (personal collection of Anne Tucker, n.d.).

46. Paul Strand, "Address by Paul Strand," *Photo Notes* (January 1948): 1, 3.

47. Anne Tucker, "Strand as Mentor," in Stange, ed., *Paul Strand*, 123; Walter Rosenblum, "A Personal Memoir," ibid., 140.

48. Rosenblum, interview by author, 1992.

49. "A Platform for Artists," *Photo Notes* (fall 1948): 14. This article stated that "for the first time in this country's history, a political party has adopted a plank which aims at helping the artist" and included excerpts from the Progressive Party's platform. Such a party would extend enjoyment of the arts to a broader cross section of American society while employing artists, the article said, in the manner of the WPA and FSA. *Photo Notes* abounds with such references to previous federally funded arts projects.

50. Rosenblum, interview by author, 1992. Strand had sponsored the New York City Council campaign of black Communist leader Ben Davis, as reported in the April 10, 1945, issue of the *Daily Worker*. By 1949, Davis had been convicted under the Smith Act of 1949 in the Foley Square trial of the Communist Party's top leaders. Strand then sponsored a conference focusing on a denunciation of their prosecution. See Mike Weaver, "Dynamic Realist," in Stange, ed., *Paul Strand*, 200, 290.

51. Tucker, "Strand as Mentor," 135. Tucker paraphrases Sam Mahl, who remembered Strand saying "he could no longer work in the atmosphere that prevailed in America; he was moving to France to begin a new book." Strand left in the summer of 1949 but continued to support the Photo League and correspond with league members.

52. Rosenblum, interview by author, 1992. Also see Pohl, *Ben Shahn*, concerning Shahn's career with the National Council of the Arts, Sciences and Professions (NCASP). This organization supported the 1948 presidential campaign of Progressive Party candidate Henry Wallace. The NCASP was attacked by Representative Dondero in 1949 as a "Communist affiliation" of Shahn's (also included in Dondero's list were the John Reed Club, the American Artists' Congress, and the Artists' Union) (Pohl, *Ben Shahn*, 65, 73–74). Republican officials such as Dondero viewed both modern and social realist art as dangerously leftist (the social realists were attacked more vehemently, however, in HUAC trials).

53. "Discussion from the Floor," 5–6; see also "Letters and Telegrams Received and Read," *Photo Notes* (January 1948): 4. This issue of *Photo Notes* reprinted telegrams and letters from Leo Hurwitz, Eliot Elisofon, Dorothea Lange, Ben Shahn, Henry Lester, Jack Levine, Philip Evergood, Edward Weston, Robert Gwathmey, and Ansel Adams.

54. Milton Brown, "Badly Out of Focus," review of Museum of Modern Art exhibition entitled "In and Out of Focus," *Photo Notes* (June 1948): 5–6. David Vestal's rebuttal to this review was featured in the fall 1948 issue. Vestal took exception to the review because Brown had "dismissed summarily" or declared "criminal" every photograph without social significance. The show, Vestal wrote, did indeed lack the typ-

ical league "philosophic or photographic concept," but he claimed that following this concept had not been Steichen's aim. In short, Vestal declared that Brown's review smacked of "bigotry" with its provential and narrow standards: "There is room and need for healthy polemics: but also there is too much thoughtless invective abroad these days, as Photo League members have been made aware. We are our own enemies when we add to it" David Vestal, in "Letters to the Editor," *Photo Notes* (fall 1948): 39.

55. Elizabeth Timberman, "Aaron Siskind," *Photo Notes* (June 1948): 10; Rosenblum, interview by author, 1992.

56. Siskind, interview by author, 1989; *Documentary Photography*, 117; Ruth Bernhard, telephone conversation with author, March 1996. Bernhard added, with good-natured humor, that she "felt so rejected" but "was not the Ashcan type."

57. Jacquelyn Judge, "FSA Attacked," *Photo Notes* (fall 1948): 5–6. Judge later became a writer and editor for *Popular Photography*. Her *Photo Notes* article included a reference to a Hearst newspaper, the *New York Journal-American*, which had viciously attacked the FSA picture files on May 18, 1948. William Randolph Hearst (1863–1951) is widely known for his use of yellow journalism in the many newspapers and publications he owned (and, later, in his motion picture and radio companies).

58. Osman, "Walter Rosenblum," 1021). One of many examples of the league's reverence for FSA work is found in McCausland's 1939 article "Documentary Photography," which extolled the FSA as "the strongest precedent for documentary photography." Unfortunately, since league membership was not documented, it is impossible to trace the exact years of each FSA photographer's interaction with the Photo League. Surprisingly, after the blacklisting Stryker promised to support the league–however, no such support materialized (Rosenblum, "A Personal Memoir," 146).

59. Morris L. Ernst and David Loth, *Report on the American Communist* (New York: Capricorn, 1952), 142–43. For a more complete understanding of the U.S. government's conception of Communism, see *Report on the Communist Party of the United States as an Advocate of Overthrow of Government by Force and Violence*, Investigation of Un-American Activities in the United States (Washington, D.C.: Government Printing Office, 1948).

60. Goldstein, *Political Repression*, 303.

61. Margaret Walker, *Richard Wright: Daemonic Genius* (New York: Warner, 1988), 355, 176, 177.

62. Ernst and Loth, *Report on the American Communist*, 145–46. The report adds, "[Negroes] have been attracted principally by the hope of improvement, and have not been convinced that they can get it through the party"; they had instead, the report claims, confronted "patronizing attitudes" of white Communists who still kept the top leadership positions.

63. Walker, *Richard Wright*, 179.

64. Tucker, "The Photo League," 1983: 1014. Tucker maintains that the publicity from the exhibition *This Is the Photo League* was "fruitless," as the government did not regard the league's interest in art as that group's primary purpose but instead viewed the league as a front for a political organization. Although Rosenblum maintains that FBI files of league activity are practically useless (most of the text is blacked out or inaccurate), Tucker (like Dejardin) has apparently read portions of these files and asserts that the FBI "neither discussed the photographs made and exhibited at

the League, nor related its photographic events to those activities regarded as political. . . . The FBI was also interested in those activities and alliances alleged to be politically motivated, such as any involvements that its members and officers had outside of the League, and also political actions that the League supported or opposed" (especially when such actions corresponded to the Communist Party's platform; 1014–15). But given the blacked-out texts, it is hard today to judge the FBI's specific motivations.

65. Strand, "Address by Paul Strand," 3. To postmodern eyes, many of the images may seem nostalgic and romantic, imbued with the social realist conceit that art could effect change if only to uncover, visually, injustices inherent in the American system. Rosenblum addressed this social emphasis in league photography: "We have developed a tradition based on social realism because our members concern themselves deeply with the world they live in . . . you make the best photograph of that which affects you most strongly. We feel deeply about the people we photography [*sic*], because we aren't tourists spying on the quaint mannerisms of the people" (Rosenblum, "Where Do We Go from Here," 7–8).

66. "Discussion from the Floor," 6.

67. Nancy Newhall, *This Is the Photo League* (New York: The Photo League, 1948), n.p. The last page of this catalog lists the league's executive committee, including then president W. Eugene Smith (Smith had hoped his name and reputation would lend credibility to the organization), vice president Rosenblum, executive secretary Dan Weiner, and *Photo Notes* editor Rosalie Gwathmey. Other member contributors included (among many others): Rudolph Burckhardt, Eliot Elisofon, Morris Engel, George Gilbert, Marian Hille, Sol Libsohn, Lisette Model, Barbara Morgan, Arnold Newman, Marion Palfi, John Rawlings, John Vachon, Todd Webb, and Edward Weston. Even a partial list displays the enormous range of photographers involved in the league, a variety the league hoped would offset the Attorney General's accusations that they were subversive and politically oriented. Indeed, membership soared right after the listing as photographers joined in shows of support, but it significantly tapered off after the late 1940s as the climate became more repressive (leage members' job security was threatened, and passport procurement and other areas of their lives became more difficult).

68. Model's career in the Photo League illustrates the degree to which some photographers rallied support for the organization in its time of need. An active member, she had a league exhibition of her work in 1941 (prepared with the help of Elizabeth McCausland, who also reviewed the show). Model also attended classes at Sid Grossman's house during the time he was under surveillance for alleged subversive activity, as a show of support for him as well as for the league. By the 1950s she was encountering direct attacks born of McCarthyism: "It was terrible," she said, "You didn't know *what* to photograph." Model was investigted surreptitiously by officials who questioned friends and neighbors about her activities. It may have been this repressive climate, Ann Thomas contends, that led Model to turn away from human subject matter to more sculptural, abstracted forms (Thomas, *Lisette Model*, 86, 94–95, 131).

69. Osman, "Biographical Notes," 1027. Quote from Emily Goldstein and Jeff Rosenheim, "A Converstion with Rosalie Gwathmey," in *Rosalie Gwathmey: Photographs from the Forties* (East Hampton: Glenn Horowitz, 1994), 5.

70. Goldstein and Rosenheim, "A Conversation with Rosalie Gwathmey," 7–9; Rosalie Gwathmey, phone conversation with author, tape recording, October 19, 1997. Gwathmey's interest in left-wing issues and publications continued; her 1951 article on Charles Coburn appeared in the *Daily Worker.*

71. Leo Hurwitz, "This Is the Photo League," *Photo Notes* (spring 1949): 2–4.

72. "Press Notices on 'This Is the Photo League' Exhibition," *Photo Notes* (spring 1949): 7, 9, 20. The reviews by all sources were reprinted in this issue.

73. Herbert Mitgang, *Dangerous Dossiers: Exposing the Secret War against America's Greatest Authors* (New York: Donald I. Fine, 1988), 82, 155–56, 161, 278. Dejardin's article "The Photo League" summarizes the professional ties between the Photo League and the *Daily Worker.*

74. Russell Porter, "Girl Aide of FBI Testifies of Seven Years as 'Communist,'" *New York Times*, April 27, 1949, sec. 1, pp. 1, 10. The front page story read, in part, as follows: "A girl photographer from Greenwich Village testified at the Communist trial yesterday that she had spent the last seven years in the New York Communist movement as an undercover agent of the Federal Bureau of Investigation. . . . Miss Calomiris said she became a member of the Communist Party in 1942 as a result of her membership in the Photo League. She was asked to join the Party, she said, by Sidney Grossman, then director of the Photo League; Leona Saron, Communist branch organizer in the Tenth Assembly District, and Marion Hills [Marion Hille, Grossman's wife]." This article is reprinted in Anne Tucker, "Sid Grossman: Major Projects," *Creative Camera*, no. 223/224 (July/August 1983): 1041.

75. Angela Calomiris, *Red Masquerade: Undercover for the FBI* (New York: J. B. Lippincott, 1950). Excerpted in *Creative Camera*, no. 223/224 (July/August 1983): 1054–55.

76. Ibid.

77. *New York Times*, April 30, 1949, sec. 1, p. 6. "The Red Menace" (advertisement) *New York Times*, Saturday, June 25, 1949, sec. 1, p. 9.

78. "For Immediate Release," Photo League press release, April 28, 1949, Howard Greenberg Gallery, New York.

79. "Minutes of [Photo League] Meeting," July 14, 1949, Howard Greenberg Gallery, New York.

80. "That Statement Still Stands," n.d., Howard Greenberg Gallery, New York. This undated, anonymous essay was accompanied by a copy of the letter the league had earlier sent to the Attorney General detailing their outrage over the listing. The essay then adds that the statement still stands after Calomiris's testimony of May 1949. The words used in combating these events were strong and angry as the author quoted Calomiris's testimony and the innuendo needed in order to implicate the league in subversive activities.

> It is not too difficult to see that the Photo League is being used as one of the scapegoats in the current attacks upon the civil liberties of the American people. . . . These dangerous attacks upon civil liberties have made themselves felt in every part of our country and to Americans in every walk of life. . . . The trial of the twelve Communist leaders, at which Calomiris testified, is an invasion of the constitutional rights of all Americans, for they are on trial for 'teaching and advo-

cating' an unpopular political doctrine, although they are not charged with committing any overt act.

Here too the writer linked broader-reaching legislation of the time with the trials facing the Photo League, such as the attacks on FSA material, the Mundt and Ferguson bills, the banning of "liberal magazine" the *Nation* from New York City schools, and the Feinberg Bill (making "any teacher belonging to a so called 'subversive' organization subject to immediate dismissal"). The writer summarized, "These are tense times. . . . We must not allow ourselves to be made one of the victims in the witch-hunt against civil liberties which is now being waged by the forces of reaction in this country."

81. "Gene Smith," interview by Beverly Bethune (1976), *Creative Camera*, no. 223/224 (July/August 1983): 1055. Smith's involvement in the Photo League demonstrates the paranoid mood of the time. Arthur Rothstein's images of the Soviet Union, which appeared in a 1947 issue of *Look*, had outraged Smith. Rothstein had reversed his sympathetic view of the Soviet Union after a visit to the country. His subsequent picture essay of Soviet life infuriated Smith, who saw it as yet another reactionary way of creating fear and mistrust of the USSR. Rothstein said, "When this was printed, everybody who was a member of the Photo League, which was a rather radical organization and which I was a member of myself, was horrified that I could make such an anti-Soviet statement." The Photo League wrote Rothstein to inform him that they intended to print Smith's criticism of the photo essay and ask if he wanted to write a rebuttal. He did not, but he did ask that they "edit it carefully to omit all references to me either actual or implied." Smith had been a member of the league for one month prior to the publication of the letter, dating his membership to about six months before the December 1947 listing. As Jim Hughes points out, Smith's joining the league was seen as a coup, given his status as a staff photographer for *Life*; evidently he had been pressured not to join. Smith offered to become president of the league after the listing because, he recalled, "I felt they [the attorney general's office] were wrong, and I was clean enought to be practically untouchable." But finally, Rosenblum said, Smith "decided he couldn't go on with it any longer—he was just having too difficult a time" and had drifted away by the time of the league's demise in 1951. See Jim Hughes, *W. Eugene Smith: Shadow and Substance* (New York: McGraw-Hill, 1989), 207–13.

82. Osman, "Walter Rosenblum," 1055; Rosenblum, interview with author, 1992. It is rumored by multiple sources that Calomiris' work for the government and subsequent testimony was prompted by a "moral's charge" held against her (in regard to lesbianism).

83. Mary Engel, *Ruth Orkin: A Retrospective* (New York: International Center of Photography, 1995), 39; Turner Browne and Elaine Partnow, *Macmillan Biographical Encyclopedia of Photographic Artists and Innovators* (New York: Macmillan, 1983), 466; see also *Documentary Photography*, 105.

84. Sandra Weiner, "Personal Recollections," in *Dan Weiner*, ed. Sandra Weiner and Cornell Capa (New York: Viking Press and International Center of Photography Library of Photographers, 1974), 92–93. Dan Weiner had taught at the league school, but, according to Sandra Weiner, the Photo League had gone out of existence by the early date of 1947 (93). In fact, the league actually limped on for four more years.

85. Arthur Miller, "Dan Weiner," in Weiner and Capa, eds., *Dan Weiner*, 10.

86. Quoted in *Documentary Photography*, 90; "Max Yavno," interview, 1977, Oral History Project at George Eastman House, *Creative Camera*, no. 223/224 (July/August 1983): 1018; Rosenblum, interview by author, 1992.

87. Ansel Adams, "A Letter from Ansel Adams!," *Photo Notes* (June/July 1940): 5.

88. Lester Talkington, "Ansel Adams at the Photo League," *Photo Notes* (March 1948): 5. Within this forum of discussion in the magazine, Adams also questions the viability of documentary reportage ("Photography shows up untruth quicker than any other medium") while also condemning escapist abstractions.

89. Talkington, "Ansel Adams at the Photo League," 5–6 (includes quotes from Rosenblum at the discussion). Crucial to Adams's conception of photography was his association with the San Francisco Bay area group f/64 in the 1930s, which typically emphasized the use of larger-view cameras in order to produce pure, straight photographs without manipulated and soft-focused effects. See Michel Oren, "On the 'Impurity' of Group f/64 Photography," *History of Photography* 15, no. 2 (1991): 119.

90. Rosenblum, "A Personal Memoir," 17; Rosenblum, interview by author, 1992. Adams's letter of support, sent to the league after the listing and reprinted in the January 1948 issue, reflected his disgust, at that time, with the current political scene.

91. Larkin, *Art and Life in America*, 470.

92. "Special Photo League Meeting," October 6, 1950, Howard Greenberg Gallery, New York. The specific authors and the use of these notes is unknown at this time, but the events identified within them deserve futher explication in order for their inclusion in the notes to be appreciated. The Taft-Hartley Bill was a crucial piece of legislation passed by Congress in 1947 over Truman's veto. The law concerned the regulation of unions and included a requirement that union leaders take an oath stating they were not Communists. Perceived by many workers as antilabor, the act included a large range of restrictions. Indeed, strikes dropped 40 percent after its passage (Goldstein, *Political Repression*, 290). Why this law was deleted from the league's notes involves speculation; mentioning it was, perhaps, deemed among members too controversial or ideologically dangerous.

The jailing of the "Hollywood Ten" occured in October 1947, when the HUAC heard testimonies from actors, writers, producers, and directors against Communist activity in the movie industry. Ten witnesses refused to participate or answer HUAC questions concerning their involvement, past or present, in political organizationsy; they were then charged as Communist Party members and jailed for contempt. This encouraged the movie industry to initiate loyalty programs by not employing anyone associated with Communism (Goldstein, *Political Repression*, 307–9).

The Mundt-Nixon Bill was passed by the House in 1948, authorizing the use of camps to detain possible subversives and control the immigration of radicals. Republicans Karl E. Mundt (South Dakota) and Richard Nixon (California) coauthored this legislation in the wake of HUAC investigations of accused Communist Alger Hiss, a former state department official and head of the Carnegie Endowment. On August 3, 1948, Whittaker Chambers testified before HUAC that he had been a Communist Party member with Hiss in the 1930s. Hiss was found guilty in 1950, and the successive trials intensified the fear of Communist activity within the government. In March 1949, Judith Coplon, a worker in the Justice Department, was arrested, tried, and convicted of anti-American espionage (the case was eventually overturned when it was revealed that she had been illegally wiretapped by the FBI).

The McCarran-Wood Bill refers to one of many acts intiated by Senator Patrick McCarran (who was head of the Senate Internal Security Committee in the late 1940s). The Senator was especially keen to bar from the United States any immigrants with "dangerous" political beliefs. Ultimately, the Internal Security Act, or McCarran Act, was passed over President Truman's veto in 1950 and required the registration of all Communist organizations. It also prohibited the employment of Communists in defense work, required labels on publications that originated from a "Communist organization," and denied entry into the United States to anyone associated with Communist or totalitarian organizations. Goldstein calls this act "clearly one of the most massive onslaughts against freedom of speech and association ever launched in American history" (323). I. F. Stone, in an essay concerning the act's further refinement in the Senate, said "This bill may prove fateful for liberty in America." In I. F. Stone, *The Haunted Fifties, 1953–1963* (Boston: Little, Brown, 1963), 46.

The reference in the league draft to the Korean War is timely; this war started, officially, in June 1950, after Communist forces in North Korea invaded American-occupied South Korea. The war, lasting through 1953, ignited fears of an escalating World War with China and the Soviet Union. To the author of the league draft, the conflict signified another indication of unreasonable fear and cold war paranoia.

93. For instance, Rosalie Gwathmey's subject for an image in the 1953 *Photography Annual* was a pair of lovers; Ed Feingersh's images in various issues of the *Photography Annual* were movie stars (1953, 1954, 1956), a self portrait and woman on horseback (1954), and a parade scene (1958); Leon Levinstein was represented in the 1955 *Photography Annual* by images of a picnic, a child, and a man with a cat; Louis Stettner had fashion photographs (1954) and a landscape (1956). Such examples abound. While other images more representative of earlier (pre-McCarthy) subjects still appeared occasionally (especially in the work of Dan Weiner, Clem Kallisher, and others), during the 1950s many of the photographs produced by former league members do not have the more critical social or documentary content of previous years. These photographers, to varying degrees, may still have chosen subjects such as the lower classes, but these images are not as readily found as they once were—indicating the preference, by editors of the growing number of popular magazines and annuals in the 1950s, for a more "positive" imaging of the nation at large.

94. Osman, "Walter Rosenblum," 1020.

95. Minor White, "What Is Photography?" *Photo Notes* (spring 1950): 16, 19.

96. Homer Page, "A Photo League Symposium," *Photo Notes* (spring 1950): 17–18.

97. Navasky, *Naming Names*, 333.

98. John Tagg, "The Currency of the Photograph," in *Thinking Photography*, ed. Victor Burgin (London: Macmillan, 1982), 111–12, 125, 139.

99. "A Statement from the Executive Committee of the Photo League," August 1951 (personal collection of Anne Tucker).

Chapter Two: Coming in from the Cold

1. Anne Tucker, "Sid Grossman: Major Projects," *Creative Camera* no. 223/224 (July/August 1983): 1040. David Vestal, "Sid(ney) Grossman," in *Contemporary Pho-*

tographers (New York: St. Martin's Press, 1982), 391; *Documentary Photography* (New York: Time-Life Books, 1972), 95. Miriam Grossman Cohen, telephone conversation with author, May 9, 1998. Sources vary on whether Grossman's father deserted the family or died; Cohen knew the family intimately and maintains that the father deserted the family while Grossman's mother was pregnant with him. More information on Grossman's biography is located in the personal collection of Anne Tucker, Houston, Tex.

2. "Walter Rosenblum," interview by Colin Osman, *Creative Camera*, no. 223/224 (July/August 1983): 1019. Rosenblum says "Nobody had any money. Sid had a terrible time . . . I don't know how he survived. He had a mouth full of rotten teeth which gave him terrible trouble. He had migraine headaches that used to drive him up the walls." Later he also had heart problems, which caused his early death from a heart attack. Walter Rosenblum, interview by author, tape recording, Long Island City, N.Y., June 16, 1992. Tucker, "Sid Grossman," 1040–41. Grossman's widow notes that they had no money; they paid $35 a month for the Chelsea apartment after 1948 or 1949 and lived by then on $105 a month. Although Grossman did not like to, he did do commercial work, she says, including portraits, weddings, and other small jobs (Miriam Grossman Cohen, interview by Anne Tucker, personal collection of Anne Tucker).

3. Anne Tucker, "The Photo League," *Ovo Magazine* 10, no. 40/41 (1981): 7; Walter Rosenblum, "A Personal Memoir," in *Paul Strand: Essays on His Life and Work*, ed. Maren Stange (New York: Aperture, 1990), 139. The syllabus has been discussed by Fiona Dejardin, who notes Grossman's encouragement for students to show "what is being done to bring about a better life." The accompanying reading list contains lectures, reprints, articles, and a bibliography. Marxists such as F. D. Klingender as well as other radical writers like Paul Strand and Elizabeth McCausland, are represented alongside more traditional art texts, betraying the league's leftist leanings. A new and short-lived periodical, *Photo History*, a quarterly produced by the Communists' Progressive Book Shop, was also praised and included in the reading list. Fiona M. Dejardin, "The Photo League: Left-Wing Politics and the Popular Press," *History of Photography* 18, no. 2 (1994): 160, 162–63). As Dejardin notes, "It is easy to see this literature as collectively reflecting and complementing the ideology of many, if not all" league members. She stressed that "the important role photography could play in the class struggle would have confirmed the FBI's suspicions that the League originated as a communist front organization."

4. "Photo League School," *Photo Notes* (spring 1949): 14; Hal Greenwald, "The Photo League School," *Photo Notes* (February 1947): 2–3. Reprinted in *Photo Notes, 1938–1950*, ed. Nathan Lyons (Rochester: Visual Studies Workshop, 1977). As stated, page numbers for *Photo Notes* citations, when identified, are according to the Visual Studies Workshop reprint pagination for the series.

5. Barney Cole, "Photo League School," *Photo Notes* (fall 1948): 22.

6. "Louis Stettner," interview by Colin Osman, *Creative Camera* no. 223/224 (July/August 1983): 1021. Osman, "Walter Rosenblum," 1019; Rosenblum, "A Personal Memoir," 139.

7. Arthur Leipzig, "Introduction," *Arthur Leipzig: A Retrospective* (New York: Long Island University and Hillwood Art Gallery, 1989): 2. Ida Wyman, telephone

conversation with author, June 25, 1996. Anne Tucker, "A History of the Photo League: The Members Speak," *History of Photography* 18, no. 2 (1994): 181.

8. Helen Gee, *Limelight: A Greenwich Village Gallery and Coffeehouse in the Fifties* (Albuquerque: University of New Mexico Press, 1997), 24–25, 150.

9. Cohen, telephone conversation with author, 1998. Ironically, Model herself was criticized for her demanding teaching methodology, as her "strongly expressed criticisms . . . had an alienating effect on students whose work was quieter and less directed toward subjective experience" (Ann Thomas, *Lisette Model* [Ottawa: National Gallery of Canada, 1990], 121). Lisette and her husband Evsa Model were very poor and often, Cohen remembers, joined the Grossmans for dinner. Once as they were leaving Lisette said, Cohen recalls, "you know Sid [pronounced *Seed* given her thick accent], you do too much for people; they will hate you for it." Later, after so many had fled their company in the advent of the HUAC naming, the Grossmans would appreciate Model's perceptions.

10. Les Barry, "The Legend of Sid Grossman," *Popular Photography* 47, no. 5 (November 1961): 51, 94. *Photo Notes* (April 1942): 3.

11. *Journey to the Cape*, photographs by Sid Grossman, text by Millard Lampell, eds. Miriam Cohen, Sy Kattelson, Charles Pratt, and David Vestal (New York: Grove Press, 1959), n.p.

12. Walter Rosenblum, interview by author, 1992.

13. Vestal, "Sid(ney) Grossman," 391. Vestal was right about the FSA's influence on Grossman. In a later taping of classroom dialogue, the transcription of Grossman's discussion includes praise for the organization; its contribution, he said, was "the introduction, on a national scale, of the idea that the photographer could play a real part in effecting the lives and history of the people of America. . . . Whether great art emerged . . . is a slightly different question." But, he continued, FSA work told viewers "that one-third of the people of this country were living in ways that were completely unknown to us" (versus "what we were told by Hollywood"). "It is a great lesson on what can happen with a more intelligent and functional use of photographers." Sid Grossman, transcription of tape recording, n.d. [1949–1950], Howard Greenberg Gallery, New York.

14. Walter Rosenblum, review of *The Image of Freedom!*, Museum of Modern Art exhibition, *Photo Notes* (December 1941): 5. As Carl Chiarenza points out, in the same month that Rosenblum's review extolling the power of the photograph to influence ideology and reform appeared, Pearl Harbor was attacked and the United States declared war on Japan: "Within a very few years the same people who had called for photographs depicting the evils of American capitalism were calling for images heralding the wonders of American democracy: both calls were in the service of the good of the greater masses of humanity" (Carl Chiarenza, *Aaron Siskind: Pleasures and Terrors* [Boston: Little, Brown, 1982], 51–52). Herein, he writes, are the dangers of documentary claims, as any one image could be used to propagandize for or against something.

15. William Stott, *Documentary Expression and Thirties America* (Chicago: University of Chicago Press, 1973): 11, 21.

16. Tucker, "Sid Grossman," 1040. Anne Tucker, "The Photo League," *Creative Camera* no. 223/224 (July/August 1983): 1013–14. As Tucker has reported, Gross-

man traveled the Midwest with both his future wife, Marion Hille, and his future brother-in-law, Waldemar Hille who was collecting folksongs as head of the music department at Elmhurst College in Illinois. In Mena, Arkansas, they visited Commonwealth College, which Marion had attended and where Waldemar had met folksingers Lee Hayes and Emma Dusenberry (Tucker, "Sid Grossman," 1040). It was through these two musicians that Grossman contacted the Southern Tenant Farmers' Union and the Farmers' Union Local 576. Later, in New York, he did a series of portraits of folksingers at $5 a job for People's Songs (including Woody Guthrie, Leadbelly, Big Bill Broonzy, Pete Seeger, and Billie Holliday). Vestal says *Mademoiselle*, "strangely," published this portfolio in the late 1940s (Vestal, "Sid[ney] Grossman," 392). When asked why he went on this trip, Grossman's second wife points out that the country was hurting economically and environmentally, given the effects of the Depression and dust bowl; "Where else," she asked, "would a photographer with social conscious go?" (Cohen, telephone converstation with author, 1998).

17. Vestal, "Sid[ney] Grossman," 391. Grossman explored many photographic technologies during his career: large-negative film and a tripod-held camera (in the Midwest), a hand-held press camera (in Central America), a twin-lens reflex camera (1947) and a 35mm Contax (to capture San Gennaro Festival scenes) *International Center of Photography Encyclopedia of Photography* (New York: Pound Press and Crown Publishers, 1984): 235.

18. Tucker, "The Photo League," *Creative Camera*, 1013–14. Supposedly the postmistress in Oklahoma City reported the Grossmans to the FBI, doubting "the patriotism of both Grossman and his wife" since she had "noted several photographs of poor people in tents and shacks as well as negatives of oil well pumps and equipment" (personal collection of Anne Tucker).

19. Sid Grossman, "12,000,000 Black Voices," review of *12,000,000 Black Voices: A Folk History of the Negro in the US*, text by Richard Wright, photographs by Edwin Rosskam, *Photo Notes* (December 1941): 2.

20. Dejardin, "The Photo League," 165. Herbert Mitgang, *Dangerous Dossiers: Exposing the Secret War against America's Greatest Authors* (New York: Donald I. Fine, 1988), 155. A so-called close list (naming those "extremely close to the Communist Party in recent years") included Lillian Hellman, Dashiell Hammett, Clifford Odets, and Richard Wright. Hellman's anti-Nazi play, *Watch on the Rhine*, although denounced in *New Masses* in 1939 (the time of the Hitler-Stalin pact), was cited in court hearings as suspect literature in the early fifties when Hellman was brought to trial. She chronicles her fascinating life in Communism during the cold war in *Scoundrel Time*. In this book she outlines the seductive lure of Stalinist Communism in the early thirties and how "children of timid immigrants" were often attracted to its claims. She also recalled the anger friend and writer Clifford Odets felt about the situation as he said to her, "Well, I can tell you what I am going to do before those bastards on the Committee. I am going to show them the face of a radical man and tell them to go fuck themselves." Lillian Hellman, *Scoundrel Time* (New York: Bantam Books, 1976), 38–39, 62–63.

21. Addison Gayle, *Richard Wright: Ordeal of a Native Son* (Garden City, N.Y.: Anchor Press and Doubleday, 1980), 153.

22. Ibid., 155. Wright had quit the party, but in a letter to friend Joe Brown in

1938, he communicated his support of radical organizations: "Boy, you don't know how good it made me feel to know that you had joined the YCL [The Young Communist League]! Joe! that's great! You are now in the main stream of mankind's history. You have taken your place along side of those who are changing this world. That, in my opinion, is the best thing a Negro can do in this day." See *Richard Wright: Letters to Joe C. Brown*, ed. Thomas Knipp (Kent, Ohio: Kent State University Libraries, 1968), 7.

23. Alan Wald, *The New York Intellectuals: The Rise and Decline of the Anti-Stalinist Left from the 1930s to the 1980s* (Chapel Hill: University of North Carolina Press, 1987), 236. Walker calls *Native Son* "protest fiction with a Marxist philosophy or Communist ideology and socialism based on economic determinism" (121). See Margaret Walker, *Richard Wright: Daemonic Genius* (New York: Warner, 1988). The same words could apply to the early work of Grossman's own protest art, so it is no wonder he respected Wright's work.

Native Son was a literary sensation in 1940, presenting a powerful indictment of American racism as observed in the life of a fictional man brought up in poverty and illiteracy. Six weeks after the book's publication, over one-quarter of a million hardcover copies had been sold, the title was placed in the Book of the Month Club series, and it remained on bestseller lists for twelve to fifteen weeks. Its sensational, horrifying story appealed to popular readers (although it is unclear how many appreciated the book's exploration of racism). Reviews were strong in their praise or criticism. Irving Howe wrote in *Dissent* (1963): "The day *Native Son* appeared, American culture was changed forever. . . . It made impossible a repetition of the old lies. . . . A blow at the white man, the novel forced him to recognize himself as an oppressor. A blow at the black man, the novel forced him to recognize the cost of his submission" (quoted in Walker, *Richard Wright*, 153–54). Some white critics despised the book, implying that Wright's race denied him true talent. Wright himself wrote a friend asking, "What do the whites say of old Bigger? Did he scare them? I hope he did!" In Knipp, ed., *Richard Wright*, 11.

Wright depicted the Communist friends of Peggy as using Bigger to get a firsthand, though superficial, look at black life, just as the Russian-named lawyer, Mr. Boris Max—"that Godless Communist" as one reactionary character calls him—uses Bigger to advance Communist Party ideals (he argues for a life sentence, not acquittal, even though he blames the capitalist system for Bigger's actions). Peggy's liberal father, although a supporter of the NAACP, will not rent his properties in white neighborhoods to blacks–also pointing to the social hypocrisy of some white leftists. The murders, the first an "accidental" strangling of the white woman, Peggy, because Bigger fears he will be caught in the bedroom and accused of rape, and the second, of his girlfriend Bessie, whom he intentionally kills during his fearful flight, Wald contends, do not reinforce a simplistic notion of responsibility and oppression but instead allow for individual motives and self-determination. The critical reception among black writers varied, because Wright presented a complex and enriching mix of issues obscuring any simplistic polemical message (the plot presents no "either-or" or "good-evil" choices).

24. Robert Justin Goldstein, *Political Repression in Modern America from 1870 to the Present* (Boston: G. K. Hall, 1978), 295–96.

25. Richard Wright, *Native Son* (New York: Harper, 1940), 46, 137, 163, 270–72.

26. Ibid., 57.

27. Walker, *Richard Wright*, 172, 228–29, 198–200. As Walker shows, Wright's self-exile to Paris was a painful, deliberate decision. He went there in 1946, returned to the United States in 1947, and then left permanently in August of that year.

28. Frances K. Pohl, *Ben Shahn: New Deal Artist in a Cold War Climate, 1947–1954* (Austin: University of Texas Press, 1989), 30, 54, 55.

29. Joe Schwartz, telephone conversation with author, April 27, 1998.

30. Turner Browne and Elaine Partnow, *Macmillan Biographical Encyclopedia of Photographic Artists and Innovators* (New York: Macmillan, 1983), 370. Naomi Rosenblum, "Jerome Liebling," in *Contemporary Photographers* (New York: St. Martin's Press, 1982), 609. Liebling, born and raised in New York City, went to Brooklyn College (1942, 1946–48) and then the New School of Social Research (1948–49), where he studied film, and later he joined the Photo League. He studied with Rosenblum, Strand, and Lewis Jacobs (Browne and Partnow, *Macmillan Biographical Encyclopedia*, 369).

31. [League News], *Photo Notes* (March 1948): 13.

32. Thomas H. Johnson, *The Oxford Companion to American History* (New York: Oxford University Press, 1966), 368. May 4, 1886, was marked by the Haymarket riot in Chicago, which had grown out of labor strikes calling for an eight-hour working day. The day before this riot, the police had killed some strikers and wounded others, prompting an anonymous worker to throw a bomb at assembled police forces the next day. In the resultant confusion, seven policemen were killed and many more injured. Seven rioters were sentenced to death because of this action; four were hanged, one committed suicide, and two received commuted sentences of life imprisonment (in 1893 a new governor would pardon the survivors). After this event, the fourth day in May reminded many workers of such labor struggles. More recently, Eduardo Galeano, Uruguayan novelist and journalist, visited the Haymarket district of Chicago to salute the workers who died in the labor movement, but he was surprised to find no statues marking the event. As he writes, May Day, in the United States, "is a day like any other. . . . [A]lmost no one remembers that the rights of the working class did not spring whole from the ear of a goat, or from the hand of God or the boss." Eduardo Galeano, *The Book of Embraces* (New York: Norton, 1989), 117–18. Ironically, Richard Wright left the Communist Party during a May Day parade, when he was physically ejected from their ranks during the celebration (Gayle, *Richard Wright*, 167). Union Square, where many league images were shot, was a center of radicalism in New York City and the site of most May Day parades (Tucker, "A History of the Photo League," 176).

33. Angela Calomiris, *Red Masquerade: Undercover for the FBI* (New York: J. B. Lippincott, 1950). Excerpted in *Creative Camera*, no. 223/224 (July/August 1983): 1054. She added that all photographs "were blown up to a uniform eight by ten and carefully bound in a thick 'May Day Parade' book with appropriate captions. Every face was labeled with a number keyed to a name or names in the back."

34. Morris L. Ernst and David Loth, *Report on the American Communist* (New York: Capricorn, 1952), 41.

35. Chiarenza, *Aaron Siskind*, 19, 22.

36. Dan Weiner, *Dan Weiner*, ed. Sandra Weiner and Cornell Capa (New York: Viking Press and International Center of Photography Library of Photographers,

1974), 37. In the same book, Weiner reflects on the broader, humanistic aspects of documentary photography: "My restless lens keeps probing at the central issues of our day and . . . pushed the photographic horizons farther and deeper into the shape of the world and men's relation to one another." His photograph *May Day* (1948) expanded the league's usual take on police by including an element of humanism and humor, by portraying a laughing, portly policeman. Weiner maintained his documentary vision throughout his photojournalistic career (ended prematurely by a plane crash in 1959), at various assignments in South Africa, Montgomery, Alabama (during the bus boycotts), Russia, and Eastern Europe—pivotal places in the world of cold war politics. He is listed as a student of Grossman's in the *International Center of Photography Encyclopedia of Photography*.

Strand is documented, in Rae Russel's photographs, attending rallies with league members in 1948 (including one for Henry Wallace's campaign). Depoliticization of Strand's life and art is both false and irritating to those studying documentary work.

37. Dejardin, "The Photo League," 170; personal collection of Anne Tucker; Cohen, telephone conversation with author, 1998. Cohen adds that Grossman was anxious to fight fascism in Europe, but at his induction in Grand Central Station he registered dangerously high blood pressure. At his insistence, they took his blood pressure again after he had rested, reluctantly, Cohen says, letting him join the armed forces. Later he would learn that an FBI dossier had already been compiled on his "activities," which led to his being sent to Panama (which Cohen calls "Siberia") instead of the European theater. In Panama, while moving files one day for an officer, Grossman read his own file and saw the FBI's warnings to keep an eye on him in case he tried to overthrow the country.

38. Tucker, "Sid Grossman," 1040. Browne and Partnow, *Macmillan Biographical Encyclopedia*, 235; Vestal, "Sid(ney) Grossman," 392; Cohen, telephone conversation with author, 1998 (concerning the damaged negative). Photographers of the late 1940s and 1950s—especially Robert Frank, Garry Winogrand, William Klein, and Louis Faurer—would continue this aesthetic direction in their work as well. Livingston calls this work Grossman's culminating "epiphany," when "his best, or at least his most intense, images began to enter into . . . a new, and to this day, unique plane," earning Grossman a place in the pantheon of individualist modernists in the medium. Jane Livingston, *The New York School: Photographs 1936–1963* (New York: Stewart, Tabori, and Chang, 1992), 289.

39. Arthur Goldsmith, telephone conversation with author, July 8, 1989.

40. The aesthetic, theoretical implications of photographic meaning coupled with technique are too complicated for the scope of this chapter. The dichotomy between documentary realism and more self-conscious photography approaching "fine art" has existed since the medium's invention. Allan Sekula, in his "On the Invention of Photographic Meaning," in *Photography in Print*, ed. Vicki Goldberg (New York: Simon and Schuster, 1981) explores such discourse between two photographers, Hine and Stieglitz. He posits two socially invented poles in photographic meaning—"affective" meaning (the spiritualist's fetishized, precious object) and "informative" meaning (with a more empiricist function). Hine's work, then, like Grossman's, "displays a manifest politics and only an implicit esthetics, while the Stieglitz discourse displays a manifest esthetics and only an implicit politics." Estelle Jussim explores similar problems in the essay "Icons or Ideology: Stieglitz and Hine," in *The Eternal*

Moment (New York: Aperture, 1989), 141–51. She disdains the simple poles often constructed around these two photographers: beauty versus truth, "the elite versus the hoi polloi," inner need versus social need.

Serge Guilbaut has said that a similar conception of a "crude" polar division existed, more generally, in cold war rhetoric, which "tended to present two adversary empires striking at each other," whereas, in reality, politics of the time were far more complex and contradictory. Jean Baudrillard has also written that such "hot-cool" paradigms can create a sense of "symbolic world balance, a balance of terror." In short, such polarities, while not existing in the real, living worlds of art or society as pure states of being, serve to illustrate the culturally defined binary oppositions that citizens internalize, for example: Democratic-Republican, liberal-conservative, pro-choice—anti-abortion, and so on. Serge Guilbaut, "Postwar Painting Games: The Rough and the Slick," 31–32, and Jean Baudrillard, "Hot Painting: The Inevitable Fate of the Image," 17, both in *Reconstructing Modernism*, ed. Serge Guilbaut (Cambridge, Mass.: MIT Press, 1990).

41. Tucker, "Sid Grossman," 1040.

42. Vestal, "Sid(ney) Grossman," 392. *Documentary Photography*, 112.

43. *International Center of Photography Encyclopedia of Photography*, 235; Vestal, "Sid(ney) Grossman," 392; Tucker, "Sid Grossman," 104; Cohen et al., eds., *Journey to the Cape*, n.p. Miriam Cohen also remembers a Coney Island photograph of an older couple "making out" on the beach, which Sid loved for its naturalism and vitality. She does not recall Grossman using any of the terms Vestal applies to these photographs (e.g., "explosive shapes," "blasted"). Cohen, telephone conversation with author, 1998.

44. Paul Goodman, *Growing Up Absurd* (New York: Vintage, 1960), 42–43. Grossman himself said he was attracted to "these children who had these feelings, these limbs, these relationships, who had this peculiar kind of energy" (quoted in Tucker, "Sid Grossman," 1041).

45. *Contemporary Photographers*, 590–91.

46. Bonnie Yockelson, *Arthur Leipzig: A Retrospective* (New York: Long Island University and Hillwood Art Gallery, 1989), 3–4.

47. Sid Grossman, "Three Young Photographers Exhibit," *Photo Notes* (November 1947): 4–5.

48. Rosenblum, "A Personal Memoir," 139–40. Cohen, telephone conversation with author, 1998. Rosenblum also maintains that Grossman and Strand "were never very friendly. They were not on the same wavelength" (Rosenblum, interview by author, 1992). Both Rosenblum and Cohen credit Ed Schwartz as a leader of the radical cell in the league.

49. Rosenblum, "A Personal Memior," 141, 144–45, 147.

50. Anne Tucker, "Strand as Mentor," in Stange, ed., *Paul Strand*, 129.

51. Beaumont Newhall, "Two Schools: A Review," *Photo Notes* (fall 1948): 23–24.

52. Rosenblum, interview by author, 1992.

53. *International Center of Photography Encyclopedia of Photography*, 558.

54. The dichotomy between these poles of meaning, truth versus aesthetic beauty, is not inherent to the medium of photography but is often invented by artists, historians, and critics. Sekula points out: "The misleading but popular form of this opposition is 'art photography' versus 'documentary photography.' Every photo-

graph tends, at any given moment of reading in any given context, toward one of these two poles of meaning." However, many tended to accept these polarities within the context of the Photo League during this time. White firmly supported the modernist tradition of transcendent correspondence and synesthesia of the senses, and in his magazine, *Aperture*, as Sekula writes, he "proposes a community of mystics united in the exchange of fetishes." Sekula, "On the Invention of Photographic Meaning," 472, 467.

55. Tucker, "A History of the Photo League," 183.

56. Tucker, "Sid Grossman," 1041.

57. Russell Porter, "Girl Aide of FBI Testifies of Seven Years as 'Communist,'" *New York Times*, April 27, 1949, sec. 1, pp. 1, 11. Dejardin, "The Photo League," 171. After testifying that Sidney Grossman (described at the time as the league's director) had asked her to join the party (then Leona Saron, Communist branch organizer in the Tenth Assembly District, and Marion Hill [Hille]), Calomiris mentioned Grossman's name in another context: "'I was told by Grossman and Miss Saron to take an assumed name,' she said, 'and so used the name of Angela Cole.'"

58. Patricia Hills, *Alice Neel* (New York: Harry N. Abrams, 1983): 87.

59. Ibid., 189, 86, 87.

60. Russell Porter, "Witness Swears Communists Set Up Wallace Party in 1947," *New York Times*, May 3, 1949, sec. 1, p. 3.

61. Cohen, telephone converstaion with author, 1998. The source that expressed "glee" remains anonymous.

62. Porter, "Girl Aide of FBI Testifies," 11.

63. Ibid., 6.

64. Calomiris, *Red Masquerade*, 28–29.

65. Ibid., 33.

66. Harvey Breit, "Talk with Miss Calomiris," *New York Times Book Review*, November 26, 1950, sec. 7, p. 16.

67. "That Statement Still Stands" (accompanied by a reprint of letter to the Attorney General of the United States, Washington, D.C.), n.d., and "Dear Sirs," May 1949, both at Howard Greenberg Gallery, New York. The first statement was released by the executive committee of the league immediately after the listing. In the more current commentary, the committee admitted to their disgust, given the listing's detrimental effect on the organization, that with more than five hundred pages of testimony, "references to the Photo League take up just about one single page." After excerpting a portion of Calomiris's testimony, the statement also mentioned there was "nothing to show that in her activity as secretary did she do a single thing that in any way tied the Photo League to the Communist Party." Why then, they asked, would she testify against them? The league had become a "scapegoat," members maintained, "in the current attacks upon the civil liberties of the American people. . . . These are tense times." The statement defended Grossman as well as his wife, Marion Hille (whom he would soon divorce). The statement praised Hille, in fact, "for keeping the Photo League alive during the war years." Finally, Calomiris, it stated, "has no place among honest people, among people of trust, people that desire progress in our lifetime. . . . Her name should be forever removed from our books . . . as a warning to those debased elements who so misjudge the anger of American people, that they expect them to remain silent and apprehensive in the face of these

attacks on their freedom." The consequences for Grossman were profound; he had begun giving private classes in his own home and lost students as a direct result of this naming by Calomiris. Model and her husband, a painter, began attending such classes in 1949 or 1950 (during the time Grossman was under surveillance) as, she said, "a gesture of support." Thomas, *Lisette Model*, 1990), 95). For more information on enrollment and membership, see Tucker, "A History of the Photo League," 183.

68. Ernst and Loth, *Report on the American Communist*, 29, 143. Aaron Siskind, interview by author, tape recording, Providence, R.I., June 23, 1989. Calomiris, *Red Masquerade*, 37.

69. Goldstein, *Political Repression*, 296. Ernst and Loth, *Report on the American Communist*, 33. Ernst and Loth continue, "The peak membership of more than 100,000 was reached during the time of our war alliance with Russia" (33).

70. Anonymous telephone conversation with author.

71. Helen Gee, interview by author, tape recording, June 17, 1989, New York. See also Gee, *Limelight*.

72. Osman, "Walter Rosenblum," 1021; Rosenblum, interview by author, 1992. Rosenblum believes "Sid's involvement with the Photo League was such it really prevented him from becoming a really important photographer. Either he spent too much time or he lived too much through other people." Such words demonstrate the difficulties Grossman faced after 1949 because of his dedication to the league.

73. Osman, "Walter Rosenblum." Rosenblum, interview by author, 1992.

74. Calomiris, *Red Masquerade*, 48, 29. Rosenblum maintains that "They called us subversive to frighten us"; thinking league members would "destroy the system," however, "was stuff and nonsense." He points instead to the general climate, when officials wanted to make life difficult for "any progressive. They wanted to scare everyone to death" in order to fuel the government and spend money on military contracts. The cold war, to Rosenblum, "was a feeding trough for everybody"; "a lot of people . . . paid with their lives for what was going on" (Rosenblum, interview by author, 1992). As Garry Wills writes, "war was the best [economic] thing that had happened to this country in a long time" (Garry Wills, Introduction to Lillian Hellman's *Scoundrel Time*, 12).

75. Telephone conversation with author, February 22, 1990. This league member, who had joined in 1936, did not ask for anonymity but was speaking freely, not clearly understanding that his statements might be made public. He had very harsh words for Grossman and called him a political leftist who was not a humanitarian in his own dealings with people in the league.

76. Goldsmith, telephone conversation with author, 1989. At a more personal level, Goldsmith recalled the FBI calling him about a couple of his friends in college, one of whom was a Communist, forcing a very shaken Goldsmith to quickly "fudge" as much as he could. In light of the recent history of Hitler's Nazi Party, the event caused him to think, "it could happen here."

77. Siskind, interview by author, 1989.

78. Cohen, interview by author 1998.

79. Cohen, interview by Anne Tucker, personal collection of Anne Tucker. Cohen, interview by author, 1998. David Vestal, telephone conversation with author, July 1996.

80. Copies of rough transcriptions of these reels (labeled "Taped Sessions with

Grossman") are at the Howard Greenberg Gallery, New York, and the personal collection of Anne Tucker, Houston. Livingston notes that these reels consist of four sessions recorded by Harry Lapow in 1949 and 1950 during private evening classes (Livingston, *The New York School*, 281).

81. Livingston, *The New York School*, 260, 262, 280–81, 283. Miriam Cohen mentions a paperback of Grossman's she found—*The Life of Forms* by Henri Focillon (1934)—which discusses aesthetics and recurring forms in the history of art. As his widow points out, Grossman was "an artist," not just an "ideologue," as his reading of "bourgeois literature" to the Communist Party would indicate (Cohen, telephone conversation with author, 1998).

82. Vestal, "Sid(ney) Grossman," 391–92. Tucker, "Sid Grossman," 1041. Grossman married Emma Marion Hille in 1941 and divorced her around 1949; he lived with Miriam Echelman (Cohen) beginning in 1947 and they were married in 1949 (the year of Calomiris's testimony).

83. Livingston, *The New York School*, 285.

84. Vestal, "Sid(ney) Grossman," 392. A comparison between these two books illustrates key differences between the two photographers. Each book combines text with images, although Frank's is less narrative (having only a short introduction by his friend Jack Kerouac) and represents a more serious, sustained vision on a single topic (the United States). Frank's book flows gracefully from image to image (featuring photographs taken during a two-year period in the mid-1950s), whereas Grossman's covers decades and has no sense of overall unity. But Frank was, chiefly, the Guggenheim-sponsored auteur of *The Americans*, while *Journey to the Cape* was published after Grossman's death—therefore the organization of the latter work had no definable influence by the photographer.

85. Miriam Grossman Cohen, upon reading this analysis, says it is "a stretch," but imaginative; the fish in the picture was, she says, simply a one-hundred-pound tuna they had caught off the Cape.

86. Goldstein, *Political Repression*, 377 (on Lampell's blacklisting). Tucker, "Sid Grossman," 1041 (on Waldemar Hille). Mitgang, *Dangerous Dossiers*, 219–20. Seeger formed the Weavers in 1949, but blacklisting in the early 1950s ruined their success (Pohl, *Ben Shahn*, 95). Seeger resisted the HUAC court's efforts to make him name names; but he did offer, at trial, to sing songs. Victor S. Navasky, *Naming Names* (New York: Viking Press, 1980), 84.

87. Helen Gee, "Photography in Transition: 1950–1960," in *Decade by Decade*, ed. James Enyeart (Tucson: University of Arizona and Center for Creative Photography), 63.

88. Rosenblum, interview by author, 1992. Again, this dichotomy is not presented as a "natural" law of photography but rather as a polarity seen to exist by many within the league during the late 1940s. As noted in Chapter 1, Elizabeth Timberman, in her review of Siskind's art, derisively called his photographs "just abstractions," without "a single specimen of the human race." Elizabeth Timberman, "Aaron Siskind," *Photo Notes* (June 1948): 10. Siskind's perceptions of league criticism were justified.

89. Chiarenza, *Aaron Siskind*, 41, 48–49. Siskind certainly felt rebuffed by the league and found another creative road to travel. Rosenblum, however, argues that Siskind's version of history (that the league disliked his more formal images), is "an

absolute canard . . . a total lie. He needed an excuse to leave. . . . No, [*Tabernacle City*] was well received, there was no problem at all" (Rosenblum, interview by author, 1992). But Siskind maintains his version of events, saying "that was one of the reasons why I finally gave up on the Photo League. . . . I was condemned for taking pictures of middle-class and rich people" (Siskind, interview by author, 1989).

90. Chiarenza, *Aaron Siskind*, 44, 48–49.

91. *Documentary Photography*, 95.

92. "Taped Sessions with Grossman," 1949–50; also in *Documentary Photography*, 95. Cohen, phone conversation with author, 1998.

Chapter Three: Subtle Subterfuge

1. Edward Steichen, for the Museum of Modern Art, *The Family of Man*, prologue by Carl Sandburg (New York: Maco Magazine Corporation, for the Museum of Modern Art, 1955). This catalog is still in print; a thirtieth anniversary edition was published in 1986 with minor revisions (Steichen's introduction was moved to precede Sandburg's prologue). The most current edition was issued in 1996 by MoMA and distributed by H. N. Abrams.

The numbers of photographers and works are stated in the catalog and demonstrate the methodological nightmare such volume creates in terms of who to pick as representatives of the show and how to maintain its original thematic and visual intent. An added difficulty is that, after all these years in print, the catalog still does not include an index of photographers (another indication that the individual artists' identities were deemphasized in favor of the overall philosophy of the show). I encourage readers to get a copy of the catalog to refer to while reading this chapter, since few photographs can be reproduced here.

2. David Potter, *People of Plenty* (Chicago: University of Chicago Press, 1954); John Kenneth Galbraith, *The Affluent Society* (New York: Houghton Mifflin, 1958).

3. Richard Alan Schwartz, *The Cold War Reference Guide: A General History and Annotated Chronology, with Selected Bibliographies* (Jefferson, N.C.: McFarland, 1997), 88–89, 90.

4. Quoted in William Hauptman, "The Suppression of Art in the McCarthy Decade," *Artforum* (October 1973): 48–52.

5. Cockcroft's research isolates the ideological use of abstract expressionist art ("the symbol of political freedom") in international exhibitions organized by the Museum of Modern Art. "Links between cultural cold war politics and the success of Abstract Expressionism," she writes, "are by no means coincidental, or unnoticeable. They were consciously forged at the time by some of the most influential figures controlling museum policies and advocating enlightened cold war tactics designed to woo European intellectuals." The tangled web of relationships Cockcroft delineates includes MoMA, the CIA, the United States Information Agency, the Office of War Information, and Nelson Rockefeller's Office of the Coordinator of Inter-American Affairs (an organization in charge of touring art in Latin America, where Rockefeller had significant economic investments). Her research persuasively indicates the complex (and hardly neutral) relationships between art and politics during the cold war. Eva Cockcroft, "Abstract Expressionism, Weapon of the Cold War," in *Pollock and After: The Critical Debate*, ed. Francis Fascina (New York: Harper and Row, 1985), 125–32.

6. W. T. Lhamon, Jr., *Deliberate Speed: The Origins of a Cultural Style in the American 1950s* (Washington, D.C.: Smithsonian Institution Press, 1990), 147. Jonathan Green, *American Photography: A Critical History 1945 to the Present* (New York: Harry N. Abrams, 1984), 48. Gerry Badger, "From Humanism to Formalism: Thoughts on Post-War American Photography," in *American Images: Photography 1945–1980*, ed. Peter Turner (New York: Penguin Books and Barbican Art Gallery, 1985), 12–13.

7. Grace Mayer, interview by author, tape recording, New York, June 22, 1989. Grace Mayer worked closely with Steichen at the Museum. In the first two weeks alone more than 35,000 viewers came to see it at MoMA, "smashing all previous attendance records for any photographic exhibition ever held by the museum." Arthur Goldsmith, "The Family of Man," *Popular Photography* 36 (May 1955): 147.

At the time of this research at MoMA in 1989, the bulk of *The Family of Man* archive materials in the Department of Photography (including memos, press clippings, letters, etc.) were not cataloged with other museum resources but filed separately by Grace Mayer, Steichen's assistant for many years, who kindly allowed me, after our taped interview, full access to her personal files, boxes, and cabinets; such materials are noted here as part of the Edward Steichen Archive. Subsequent to this time and after Ms. Mayer's death, however, some of these materials may have become part of other collections, such as the Grace M. Mayer Collection.

8. Eric Sandeen, *Picturing an Exhibition: The Family of Man and 1950s America* (Albuquerque: University of New Mexico Press, 1995), 95.

9. Edward Steichen, "From Edward Steichen to Members of the Picture Division," *Picturescope: Newsletter of the Picture Division, Special Libraries Association* 3, no. 2 (July 1955): 6. This article was based on an informal talk Steichen gave to members of the New York Picture Group at the Museum of Modern Art, March 7, 1955. In *Steichen: A Life in Photography*, he more specifically recalls finding this phrase in Carl Sandburg's biography of Lincoln. Edward Steichen, *Steichen: A Life in Photography* (New York: Doubleday, 1963; New York: Harmony Books and Museum of Modern Art, 1985), n.p.

10. Steichen's place in the history of American photography could fill thousands of pages. Born in Luxembourg, he and his family immigrated to the United States when he was two; he became an American citizen in 1900 at age twenty-one. Steichen joined the Stieglitz circle of the Photo-Secession group, which urged a more progressive modernism in American art. He was already familiar with modernist directions, having studied art in Paris. He later focused on commercial photography, portraiture, and fashion photography (primarily for Conde Nast publications *Vogue* and *Vanity Fair*). During World War I, Steichen served as commander of the photographic division, and at age sixty-two he enlisted in the U.S. Navy to command combat photographers during World War II (Wayne Miller was among those in his special six-man photographic unit for Naval Aviation). Marianne Fulton, *Eyes of Time: Photojournalism in America* (Boston: Little, Brown, 1988; Rochester: George Eastman House, 1988), 155. Also see Penelope Niven, *Steichen: A Biography* (New York: Clarkson Potter, 1997).

11. Sandeen, *Picturing an Exhibition*, 17. As Sandeen notes, many combat photographers realized photography's emotional power: Robert Capa at D-Day, Margaret Bourke-White at Bergen Belsen, W. Eugene Smith in the South Pacific, and Wayne Miller in Hiroshima.

12. Quoted in Christopher Phillips, "The Judgment Seat of Photography," in *The Contest of Meaning*, ed. Richard Bolton (Cambridge, Mass.: MIT Press, 1989), 27.

13. Frank had accompanied Steichen on part of his European tour. Photographs in the Edward Steichen Archive include a very young Frank sitting alongside Steichen, pouring over piles of photographs.

14. Joseph Breitenbach, "The Abstractionists Go on Parade," *Infinity* (April/May, 1951): 6. This article quoted Steichen's own definition of *abstract*: "a convenient handle with which to tag a wide range of intelligent, artful experimentation, as well as the significant creative achievements." His loose definition allowed him the latitude to show more than 150 "more or less" abstract works by artists as divergent as Roman Vishniak, Harry Callahan, Henri Cartier-Bresson, Barbara Morgan, László Moholy-Nagy, Man Ray, Christien Shad, and Mathew Brady.

15. MoMA's press release (May 21, 1952) for "Diogenes with a Camera" also said Steichen chose the title "to indicate photography's contribution to the search for truth." The series, more generally, aimed "to demonstrate how the art of photography has added to our knowledge of the truth," not only observable facts but those "penetrating to significant meanings."

Many Photo Leaguers had similar beliefs. Dan Weiner, for instance, reviewed the second Diogenes show for *Infinity*. He clearly articulated his own position on the purpose of art when he wrote, in response to Ansel Adams's rhetoric, "photography has greater functions than to serve for the mere self-glorification of the ego of the 'artist.'" For Weiner, Lange's images were the highlight, as she dealt with social issues, while Siskind's abstractions were the low point. The Diogenes theme suited Weiner, documentarian and former Photo League member, perfectly. But Steichen's vision was not so narrow that it did not include various other types of image makers in this series. Dan Weiner, "Again Diogenes," review, Museum of Modern Art, *Infinity* (December 1952): 14–15, 22.

16. Edward Steichen, tape recording on his seventy-fifth birthday (March 25, 1954), transcript in Edward Steichen Archive, MoMA, New York. Most of these transcripts were reprinted in Tom Maloney, ed., *U.S. Camera Annual 1956* (New York: U.S. Camera, 1955), 18–51. The United Nations Educational, Scientific, and Cultural Organization (UNESCO) was founded in 1946 and, like the United Nations, was committed to the defense of global peace. In 1950 Steichen (with Shahn) also participated in a committee trying to review the masses' interest in art. Frances K. Pohl, *Ben Shahn: New Deal Artist in a Cold War Climate, 1947–1954* (Austin: University of Texas Press, 1989), 103.

17. Walter Benjamin, "The Author as Producer," in *Art After Modernism: Rethinking Representation*, ed. Brian Wallis (New York: New Museum of Contemporary Art; Boston: David R. Godine, 1984), 303. Originally this article was delivered as an address to the Institute for the Study of Fascism in Paris, 1934.

18. Bob Adelman, telephone conversation with author, February, 1990.

19. Steichen, "From Edward Steichen to Members of the Picture Division," 8. Edward Steichen, tape recording on his seventy-fifth birthday, 21.

20. Walter Rosenblum, "A Personal Memoir," in *Paul Strand: Essays on His Life and Work*, ed. Maren Stange (New York: Aperture, 1990), 146; Walter Rosenblum, interview by author, tape recording, Long Island City, N.Y., June 16, 1992. Rosenblum added during the 1992 interview:

Steichen called me one day, when the listing came out, and he said to me, "Walter, this is terrible. I know you, you used to bring [your] class up to the Museum." . . . He was so sweet, he couldn't be nicer. He called me up [and said], "I'm meeting with Stryker tomorrow and we're going to do something about it." I said, "terrific." Never heard from him again. Never saw him, he never called me, he disappeared completely. The pressure got too high. After all, you're dealing with boards of trustees that are difficult so you don't fool around, if you want your job and your position.

21. Steichen, "From Edward Steichen to Members of the Picture Division," 6.

22. Arthur A. Ekirch, Jr., *The Decline of American Liberalism* (New York: Antheneum, 1976), foreword, 315–17.

23. Jacob Deschin, "Steichen Reports," *New York Times*, December 14, 1952, sec. 2, Part 2, p. 17. Deschin also reported that the project seemed vague to some photographers: "Not everybody understood the project. Some disapproved; others tried to fathom the intent, but could make little headway." Perhaps photographers were confused by Steichen's take on documentary; the traditionally critical rhetoric of social documentary was obscured within his positive discourse and visionary purpose.

24. "Last Call," *Infinity* (February 1954): 8–9.

25. Arnold Gassan, interview by author, tape recording, Athens, Ohio, spring 1989. Orkin's images of her daughter playing cards were handpicked by Wayne Miller while going through her work (Sandeen, *Picturing an Exhibition*, 42).

26. Helen Gee, *Limelight: A Greenwich Village Gallery and Coffeehouse in the Fifties* (Albuquerque: University of New Mexico Press, 1997), 80. Gee adds that "pricing was a problem" since there "was no precedent; no one knew what to charge" (87). Gee decided on $25, on average, for new work by exhibiting artists. To put this point into further perspective, during the time *Aperture* was launched in 1952, a free print of Ansel Adams's *Moonrise over Hernandez* was offered to prospective subscribers as incentive to send money. Decades later, at auction, the same print would sell for thousands.

27. Rosenblum, interview by author, 1992. Rosenblum's irritation with the show was complicated by his loyalty to Beaumont Newhall, who, Rosenblum felt, had been "forced out" of MoMA's photography department in order to make room for Steichen in 1947 (who had "lots of contacts" and "a lot of money to bring in").

28. "'The Family of Man' Exhibition," *Image* 3, no. 3 (March 1954): 24.

29. Ibid.; "Last Call," *Infinity* (February 1954): 8.

30. Arthur Goldsmith, telephone conversation with author, July 8, 1989.

31. "The Family of Man, MoMA, Edward Steichen," *Aperture* 2, no. 1 (1953): 29–30. Eric Sandeen notes that White likened the show to a Cecil B. DeMille extravaganza (Sandeen, *Picturing an Exhibition*, 40).

32. Helen Gee, interview by author, tape recording, June 17, 1989, New York. Gee added that "today, of course, no one buys the idea of 'truth' in photography." But photographers in the 1950s, she recalls, "had a sense of belonging—you could make a statement and be heard."

33. "The Family of Man, MoMA, Edward Steichen," *Aperture* 2, no. 1 (1953): 29–30.

34. Ibid.

35. Gee, *Limelight*, 95, 100–101. The only restored permanent installation of the show is housed in Clervaux Castle, Luxembourg.

36. *The Family of Man* press release, MoMA, New York, January 26, 1955. Changes in the show were made; the "hokey" mirror that implicated each viewer was removed, criticized as a distraction from the bomb room (Sandeen, *Picturing an Exhibition*, 50).

37. Patricia Bosworth, *Diane Arbus: A Biography* (New York: Knopf, 1984), 114.

38. Cockcroft, "Abstract Expressionism, Weapon of the Cold War," 126, 128. Stange, ed., *Paul Strand*, 140–41. See also Francine Carraro, "Seeing Red: The Dallas Museum in the McCarthy Era," in *Suspended License: Censorship and the Visual Arts*, ed. Elizabeth C. Childs (Seattle: University of Washington Press, 1997). Carraro provides useful background on censored work and Senator Joseph McCarthy's and George Dondero's attacks on the arts; she discusses, for instance, Dondero's speech in the House, "Communist Conspiracy in Art Threatens American Museums" (March 17, 1952).

39. Maloney, ed., *U.S. Camera Annual 1956*, 18. The annual reprinted Rockefeller's address.

40. "Partial List of Guests at Preview of Family of Man," January 14, 1955, Edward Steichen Archive. Bourke-White had seven images in the show, Frank seven, Levitt two, Penn three, and Smith four. Ben Shahn had one FSA image in the show, and he and his wife were besieged at the time by FBI investigations because of Shahn's participation in leftist organizations. Even as early as 1951, at a Harvard talk, as if anticipating the myriad of later articles on the same topic, Shahn argued that there was a connection between the rise of abstraction after the war and right-wing attacks on liberal New Deal policies. Despite continued attacks from the government and media (he was blacklisted by CBS), Shahn openly continued pursuit of his liberal ideals. His 1952 poster design proclaimed Adlai Stevenson the best candidate for president, not Eisenhower (Pohl, *Ben Shahn*, 112, 120, 126). By July, 1959 Shahn was called before an HUAC court and monotonously intoned "I respectfully refuse to answer." His presence in the exhibition and at the opening of *The Family of Man* represented a branch of the family of American men who were increasingly unempowered during this decade.

41. Steichen, "From Edward Steichen to Members of the Picture Division," 7. Dorothy Norman, who was asked by Steichen to select "short evocative, poetic statements from the literatures of the world, of all time . . . [emphasizing] the important themes of the show," was shown an image of lovers embracing and suggested the end of James Joyce's *Ulysses*: "And then I asked him with my eyes to ask again yes and then he asked me would I yes . . . and first I put my arms around him yes and drew him down to me so he could feel my breasts all perfume yes and his heart was going like mad and yes I said yes I will Yes." Norman recalled, "Steichen looks at me aghast. 'You can't possibly use that.' I stiffen . . . I argue; Steichen gives in." This text appears in its entirety on page seven of the *Family of Man* catalog. Dorothy Norman, *Encounters: A Memoir* (New York: Harcourt, Brace, Jovanovich, 1987), 291–92.

42. Wynn Bullock's image, *Child in Forest*, was taken in 1951. Bullock came to photography from a decidedly broad philosophical background, having studied music, languages, art history, and law. In the early 1940s, his California studies in photography and semantics with Alfred Korzybski impressed him deeply; he learned that

sign systems are not fixed but fluctuating and often ambiguous—that "the word as symbol is not the thing symbolized." Given this background, he believed images should evoke "a stream of consciousness about something that is not directly related to that thing. . . . I think we have to evoke new symbols . . . that expand our minds so that we may be more at home in this scientific and terrifying age we live in." Turner Browne and Elaine Partnow, *Macmillan Biographical Encyclopedia of Photographic Artists and Innovators* (New York: Macmillan, 1983), 84–85. It is ironic, given Bullock's interest in non-narrative, associative meaning that his image should so evocatively illustrate *The Family of Man*'s introduction. The press release from MoMA stated that Bullock's image was placed at the head of the stairs and pictured a "young child lying in an ancient redwood forest linking the past and the future."

43. Herbert Mitgang, *Dangerous Dossiers: Exposing the Secret War against America's Greatest Authors* (New York: Donald I. Fine, 1988), 87. Mitgang's quoted phrase refers to the title of Carl Sandburg's epic poem of the 1930s, "The People, Yes".

44. Ibid., 89–90. Penelope Niven, *Carl Sandburg: A Biography* (New York: Charles Scribner's Sons, 1991), 637.

45. Mitgang, *Dangerous Dossiers*, 90–92.

46. Niven, *Carl Sandburg*, 511, 513, 632. "The People, Yes," was published as a book in 1936; this portion is from section 101. A dominant metaphor in the epic poem, Niven adds, is "the Family of Man" (510).

47. Westbrook Pegler, "America's Worst Foot Often Forward at Fair in Moscow," *Fort Wayne (Indiana) News-Sentinal*, August 14, 1959, sec. 1, p. 1. This King Features column by Pegler was also printed in other papers, including the *New Haven (Connecticut) Register* (August 14, 1959). Pegler's view that Sandburg "liked" the Russians provoked him to write: "That may make him a good Russian or at best an impudent boor but it certainly impugns his respect for our Constitution." He added at the end of this essay that Sandburg hardly encouraged any approval from Nixon, whom Pegler considered a brave statesman and politician in the thick of the cold war.

Another Associated Press wire story, published on July 20, 1959, appeared with numerous and telling headlines across America: "Red Exhibit Is Praised by Sandburg," *Asheville (N.C.) Times*; "Soviet Displays Win Praise of Writer, Artist [Steichen]," *Stamford (Conn.) Advocate*; "Sandburg Sees Great Worth in Red Exhibit," *Cincinnati Enquirer*; "Soviet Exhibit Called 'Great,'" *Charleston (W. Va.) Mail*. Steichen and Sandburg's trip to the Soviet Union was covered widely across the nation. *The Family of Man*'s critical reception there deserves more study; it afforded, alternately, an opportunity for some critics to damn its authors or, more typically, praise them for introducing Russian Communists to American ideals of freedom.

48. Edward Steichen, letter to "Marianna," October 5, 1959, Edward Steichen Archive. Grace Mayer believed that Marianna was Steichen's guide in the Soviet Union.

49. "The Family of Man," *Infinity* (December 1954/January 1955): 12, emphasis in original. This issue contains many additional articles relating to the show, including portions of the NBC broadcast with Steichen in 1954.

50. Wayne Miller quoted in ibid., 13.

51. Sandeen, *Picturing an Exhibition*, 122–23.

52. Ibid., 1, 150.

53. Quoted in "MoMA Memorandum" from Circulating to Edward Steichen re-

garding letter from the Director of the Des Moines, Iowa, Art Center, April 11, 1956, Edward Steichen Archive.

54. Edward Steichen, "Keynote Address at the Ab[s?]ilomar," handwritten notes, September, 1961, Edward Steichen Archive.

55. Steichen, "From Edward Steichen to Members of the Picture Division," 7.

56. Steichen probably had more in common with the photographers Luce employed than with the publisher himself. Henry Luce (1898–1967) was born in China, the son of missionaries; he attended Yale and studied at Oxford. He founded *Time* in 1923, *Fortune* in 1930, *Life* in 1936, and *Sports Illustrated* in 1954. *Fortune* and *Life* became "showcases for American photojournalism" (Bourke-White was the first photographer Luce hired for *Fortune*). Luce's biographer, John Kobler, wrote that Luce "rejected objectivity as a journalistic ideal from the beginning of his career. . . . 'Show me a man who claims he's completely objective,' he said, 'and I'll show you a man with self delusions.'" However, *Life* in particular was "word driven," as Marianne Fulton puts it; photographers were subordinate to writers who originated, narrated, and outlined picture essays. Similarly, photographers would, in *The Family of Man*, be subordinate to the overall vision of Steichen. Said one editor: "No matter how much Luce [and others] . . . raved about them and their vital importance to the magazine, the photographers, as a group, did not really enjoy the highest standing, even though their work made *Life*" (Fulton, *Eyes of Time*, 309, 131, 180–81).

57. Mission statement as stated in *Life*'s prospectus (1936), quoted in Colin Osman, "Photography Sure of Itself (1930–1950)," in *A History of Photography*, ed. Jean-Claude Lemagny and André Rouillé (Cambridge: Cambridge University Press, 1987), 168. Fulton, *Eyes of Time*, 135–37. Sandeen, *Picturing an Exhibition*, 8, 18. Sandeen expands on *Life's* popularity in the 1950s as well as the magazine's mission.

58. John Phillips, *It Happened in Our Lifetime: A Memoir in Words and Pictures* (Boston: Little, Brown, 1985), 120.

59. William Manchester, *In Our Time: The World as Seen by Magnum Photographers* (New York: W. W. Norton and the American Federation of Arts, 1989), 7.

60. Jim Hughes, *W. Eugene Smith: Shadow and Substance* (New York: McGraw-Hill, 1989), 50–52. Fulton, *Eyes of Time*, 136–38. Calculating the number of images from each country, photographer, or agency in the catalog is difficult because, first, some photographs are credited with two agencies as well as an individual photographer and, second, some country's names have changed over the decades. All calculations here are approximate; some deviation may occur with each scholar's indexing methodology.

61. Steichen, "From Edward Steichen to Members of the Picture Division," 6. Absolute identification of each photograph's content by location and each photographer's nationality has not been researched at this time. All numbers compiled here, then, are approximations based on the caption information in *The Family of Man* catalog.

62. Quoted in Osman, "Photography Sure of Itself," 185.

63. Steichen, "From Edward Steichen to Members of the Picture Division," 7.

64. Heyer's image is from from the Pix Agency files; Page's nine photographs were independently submitted (only two were associated with a magazine, *Argosy*). Ishimoto had two images in the show, both of the United States. Born in San Francisco, he studied with Harry Callahan and Siskind at the Chicago Insitute of Design.

After graduating in 1952, he too became a freelance photographer (Browne and Partnow, *Macmillan Biographical Encyclopedia*, 299).

65. W. Eugene Smith, "My Daughter Juanita," *Life*, September 21, 1953, 165.

66. Phoebe Lou Adams, "Through a Lens Darkly," *Atlantic Monthly* 195 (April 1955): 70. Eugenia Kaledin, *Mothers and More: American Women in the 1950s* (Boston: Twayne, 1984), 27. Kaledin analyzes 1950s gender roles through popular culture. Although Lucy's TV husband would not let her work, in real life obviously, Lucille Ball was a working mother. Furthermore, as Kaledin points out, even though Lucy was not permitted to say the word *pregnant*, over two million more people watched the episode in which little Ricky was born than had watched Eisenhower's inaugural address.

Kaledin also notes a parallel between *The Family of Man* and the burgeoning feminist movement of the early 1970s. The show stressed the importance of world peace, including "many examples of women's photographic skills, as well as many sympathetic illustrations of women involved in identical family rituals all over the world." By the 1970s, such "sentimental" values "would be considered part of a new feminist ideology" (Kaledin, *Mothers and More*, 23).

67. Sid Grossman, "Three Young Photographers Exhibit," *Photo Notes* (November 1947): 4. Reprinted in *Photo Notes, 1938–1950*, ed. Nathan Lyons (Rochester: Visual Studies Workshop, 1977).

68. Simone de Beauvoir, *The Second Sex* (New York: Vintage, 1974), xviii. This key literary source of midcentury gender roles and sexism is far too rich for a satisfying analysis here. *The Family of Man* is an interesting source of visual material concerning gender bias during this time, which can be studied in conjunction with such writings. Also see Rochelle Gatlin, *American Women Since 1945* (Jackson: University of Mississippi Press, 1987), 44.

69. Browne and Partnow, *Macmillan Biographical Encyclopedia*, 318. Maurice Berger, "Subjective Documentation," *Art in America* 82, no. 1 (January 1994): 51–55.

70. Wini Breines, "The 1950s: Gender and Some Social Science," *Sociological Inquiry* 56, no. 1 (winter 1986): 75. She also summarizes Barbara Ehrenreich's research of 1950s gender roles (*The Hearts of Men*, 1983), when male expectations increasingly converged "toward the feminine." Furthermore, she adds (quoting Ehrenreich), "many males writing in the 1950s believed that 'conformity destroys not only men's souls, but their very manhood'" (75). Not surprisingly, "anxiety about masculinity," Breines notes, was "closely linked with fears of female strength" (76). Of even more interest is her discussion of studies linking masculinity, fatherhood, homosexuality, and Communism in sociological studies of the 1950s. A family without a strong male role model (which risked "maternal overinvolvement"), it was feared, encouraged the formation of weak sons who might become homosexuals, Communists, or emasculated adults unable to battle against Communist forces.

71. It is interesting to trace where Frank's images are within the total narrative of *The Family of Man*. Two are in the pregnancy section (both of his wife at that time, Mary); one, of women in a New York City hamburger joint, is in the eating section; another, from Spain, pictures an older woman with a baby (surrounded by other grandmotherly types holding babies); a Peruvian peasant is pictured in the "Lonely" section; an image of an English street musician is surrounded by FSA images, mostly Shahn's and Lange's; and a photograph of a Welsh miner is found alongside the hope-

ful text, "Behold, this dreamer cometh" (in a section in which all subjects look upward toward the heavens). Most of Frank's images were posited, ironically, within the more upbeat, positive sections.

72. "And a Little Child Is Cast Out!" *Denver Post*, August 28, 1959, vol. 68, no. 26, p. 18. Sandeen, *Picturing an Exhibition*, 155. An Associated Press story from Moscow ran in many newspapers and reported on the incident, stating the image was removed "in response to Soviet objections" even though the director, Harold McClellan, felt the picture "had a rightful place in the collection." Such incidents continue; *National Geographic*'s more recent cover of a Tibetan boy was cancelled due to objections from the Chinese embassy (Kenneth Brower, "Photography in the Age of Falsification," *Atlantic Monthly* [May 1998]: 102).

73. Steichen, "From Edward Steichen to Members of the Picture Division," 7. The issue of delinquency was more topical by the mid-1950s than it had been in Grossman's time. Many Americans were becoming worried about youths' alienation, as evidenced by teen heroes such as Marlon Brando, James Dean, and even Holden Caufield. Increasing incidences of drug use were troubling as well, as seen in the 1953 *U.S. Camera Annual*'s inclusion of a photograph entitled "Marijuana Aftermath." In it a barely dressed young woman, who had been found only in her shoes in the yard of her Bronx home after a "marijuana binge," is carried away by arresting policemen (Maloney, ed., *U.S. Camera Annual 1953*, 298). The popularity of low-budget movies about juvenile delinquents skyrocketed in the 1950s, including, for instance, *The Violent Years* (1956). That movie's poster shows a leather-clad female gang with guns while the text reads, "See what actually happens behind the locked doors of a pajama party." Alan Betrock, *The I Was a Teenage Juvenile Delinquent Rock-n-Roll Horror Beach Party Movie Book!* (New York: St. Martin's Press, 1986).

74. James Enyeart, *Invisible in America: An Exhibition of Photographs by Marion Palfi*, foreword by Lee Witkin, catalogue essay by James Enyeart (Lawrence, Kans.: University of Kansas Museum of Art, 1973), n.p. Marion Palfi (1917–78) was born in Berlin to Hungarian parents but left Germany during Hitler's regime. She went on to become an activist photographer and was sponsored in 1945 by the Council against Intolerance in America, leading to her show *Great American Artists of Minority Groups and Democracy at Work*. As an artist, she was dedicated to creating a better world by picturing disenfranchised minorities. She said: "I want to make people aware . . . that the diversity of people in America is their strength. I believe enormously in the truth" (n.p.). Steichen appreciated Palfi's political photographs enough to put her on MoMA's walls. Within the photographic community she may be neglected and regarded as somewhat marginal in that she considered herself more of a documentary journalist or sociologist than an artist. Her emphasis on content marginalized her as an artist, just as she empowered the marginal in her own work.

75. An interesting side note is *The Family of Man*'s reception when it was shown in South Africa later in the decade. The Coca Cola Bottling Company of Johannesburg sponsored the show and reported record attendance in their newsletter. An Associated Press story ironically notes the show was "a hit here where the government's ideal is two separated families of man, black and white" ("Family of Man Show Hailed in South Africa," *Christian Science Monitor*, sec. 1, vol. 50, no. 253 [September 23, 1958]: 4). Although the show "gives almost equal emphasis to white and black hu-

mans . . . there was not a murmur of official protest." The story also notes that while there was no "color bar," few blacks attended.

76. Bob Schwalberg was a freelance photographer whose work appears in numerous photography annuals of the 1950s. He also wrote articles on 35mm technology, such as "The New Films," in *Photography Annual 1956*, on new high-speed films such as Tri-X, and "How Fast Can You Go?" *Infinity* (November) 1952.

77. Victor S. Navasky, *Naming Names* (New York: Viking Press, 1980), 9–10.

78. *The Family of Man*, press release, MoMA, 2. Wayne Miller, "The Family of Man," *Infinity* (December 1954/January 1955): 13; Arthur Goldsmith, "The Family of Man," *Popular Photography* (May 1955): 148; Ira Latour, "Family of Man," *Photo Vision* 2, no. 6 (May 1955): 35, 37; Judith Crist, "Modern Museum to Show 'Family of Man' Photos," *New York Herald Tribune*, January 23, 1955, 48.

79. William E. Leuchtenburg, *A Troubled Feast: American Society Since 1945* (Boston: Little, Brown, 1973), 104. Also see David Halberstam, *The Fifties* (New York: Fawcett Columbine, 1993); Niven, *Steichen*, 645.

80. Paul A. Carter, *Another Part of the Fifties* (New York: Columbia University Press, 1983), 264–65.

81. Tom Maloney, ed., *U.S. Camera Annual 1954* (New York: U.S. Camera, 1953), 368. Sandeen notes Steichen's need to make nuclear devastation visually shocking, given the number of numbing images American viewers had already been exposed to. Even the 1953 image of a house disintegrating could not convey the scope of an atomic bomb's destructive power (see also "A-Bomb vs. House," *Life*, March 30, 1954, 21). Shocking an American public more interested in TV, consumer goods, and social stature into the recognition of nuclear horror was one of Steichen's goals. It is this image that provokes Sandeen to call the show "one of the most significant cultural productions of 1950s America" (Sandeen, *Picturing an Exhibition*, 39, 65–66, 170).

82. I. F. Stone, *The Haunted Fifties, 1953–1963* (Boston: Little, Brown, 1963), 85. More subtle undertones of death exist throughout the show as well; Raphel Platnick's image of an inert soldier lying in sand with his shirt blasted open was taken in Eniwetok, an atoll in the Marshall Islands of the west central Pacific, which was the site not only of battle but also of numerous atomic tests by the United States. It must be noted that Steichen also included photographs of nuclear scientists and experiments in the show. The image following these, however, is of a desolate bombed German town.

83. "The Family of Man," *Infinity* (December 1954/January 1955): 15.

84. Norman, *Encounters*, 292–93. Mumford was a social critic and writer best known for his book on American art, *The Brown Decades* (1931).

85. Rosenblum, interview by author, 1992.

86. Richard H. Pells, *The Liberal Mind in a Conservative Age: American Intellectuals in the 1940s and 1950s* (New York: Harper and Row, 1985), 71. Stone, *The Haunted Fifties*, 90.

87. O. N. Solbert, "Edward Steichen and the Family of Man," *Image* 4, no. 2 (February 1955): 14.

88. Hughes, *W. Eugene Smith*, 330; 331–32. According to Hughes, assistant Wayne Miller had found a tattered photo of the same image in the *Life* files and asked Smith to send negatives for enlargement. Smith said he'd make his own prints, even

though *Paradise Garden* was to be 3 x 4 feet, a print far larger than he was used to making. In addition, the museum requested multiple prints in order to create traveling versions of the show. Miller, afraid that Smith might not come through with the print, had the photography department at the museum make copy negatives and prints, which they used for the shows. Smith eventually brought his own prints in one week after the show opened but declared the museum's prints superior.

89. Ibid., 189–91

90. Ibid., 191–92, 333.

91. Edward Steichen, "The Story of Man in One Picture," *This Week*, Sunday Magazine of the *New York Herald Tribune* (December 4, 1955): 2.

92. Crist, "Modern Museum to Show 'Family of Man' Photos," 48.

93. Steichen, "From Edward Steichen to Members of the Picture Division," 7. Grace Mayer said in 1989 that she knew nothing of the retraction of the lynching photograph. Sandeen, *Picturing an Exhibition*, 49–50, expands on the problematic "legibility" of the image and writes that Steichen "had the photograph removed" after it attracted great attention (49).

94. Cartier-Bresson's ten images in the show were all from Magnum and included photographs taken in France, Indonesia, Bali, the United States, Kashmir, Iran, Java, and China. Many of his images of China had already been published in "Report on Communist Shanghai" (text by Robert Doyle, photographs by Cartier-Bresson), *Life*, October 17, 1949. His influential book *The Decisive Moment* had just been published in 1952, and *The People of Moscow* followed in 1955.

95. Goldsmith, telephone conversation with author, 1989. Goldsmith still has "positive feelings" about the show; it was a form of public consciousness-raising, proving to the mass of viewers that photography was "an art form which should be taken seriously."

Rollie McKenna, "Photography," *New Republic* 132 (March 14, 1955): 30. McKenna said the show was "essentially journalistic" but had expressive and creative work as well. He felt the show deserved its enormous success but was troubled by its "cosmic One Man declaration." He also believed the design of the show detracted from the power of the photographs, though, in the end, "no amount of tricky exhibition technique can destroy really great photographs."

Professor Gary Kirksee (personal communication, Athens, Ohio, 1989) discussed his belief with me that this image is a "trophy shot," as he termed it. His sensitive explication clearly proved to me that the issue of race and racism in the context of the controversial show needs further and more profound analysis. One African American artist who saw the original show claimed positively that she had never seen so many representations of blacks in a white institution; others are more troubled by the show's imaging of "otherness." Some interesting questions to pose in future studies are: What is the ratio of black subjects to images of "undeveloped" countries; Which thematic areas are they found in; and, How many of the photographers themselves are African American?

96. From an unidentified article on "Rodin's Funeral" in unmarked box, p. 6, Edward Steichen Archive. Later, when the show was touring overseas, even without the lynching image, the issue of racism was often initiated. Theophilus Ucokonkwo, a Nigerian student, wrote "Why I Tore Down America's Pictures at Moscow Fair," for the *Afro-American* newspaper in Washington, D.C. He felt some pictures at the

American exhibit in Moscow "showed Africans in an unfavorable light," as "social inferiors–sick, raggerty, destitute, and physically maladjusted . . . half-clothed or naked. . . . It was insulting, undignified, and tendencious" (*Afro-American*, August 22, 1959, 1). Ucokonkwo urged more American understanding and cooperation with the Soviets. Other miscellaneous clippings in the Steichen Archive also allude to such issues. Bob Considine, reporting for the San Francisco *Examiner* (July 30, 1959) stated that the Russians frequently asked about American "treatment of minorities, notably Negroes," reflecting Soviet curiosity and skepticism of democracy in the United States. Wayne Hall, in the Columbus, Ohio, *Dispatch* (September 8, 1959) voiced a similar concern: "Racial discrimination was an issue in many a conversation, especially around the four Negro guides [at the Moscow exhibit]," who were "harassed" by individuals "mechanically mouthing loaded questions." Also see Niven, *Steichen*, 672.

97. bell hooks, *Black Looks: Race and Representation* (Boston: South End Press, 1992), 13. hooks examines the issues surrounding white liberal ideology toward African Americans that often obscure or negate the social and historical realities of racial discrimination; her analyses could greatly enhance understanding of the show. That the one image of murderous oppression by whites, the lynched figure, was removed (against, perhaps, Steichen's objections) negated a specific, visual instance of white racism. By the same token, however, no text was, presumably, included with the image to address the social realities of discrimination or clarify the reasons for its inclusion.

98. Goldsmith, "The Family of Man," 88, 147–49.

99. Ibid. Fred Ringel, "The Family of Man—A Minority Report" (Letters to the Editor), *Popular Photography* (May 1955): 6, 10. This writer decried Steichen's illustrative uses of photography "fit for a magazine." Furthermore, he felt the whole idea, given human diversity, was built on a lie—"Biologically, we are of course a family: genus. But in social, moral, ethical values we differ enormously." Irritated with the lack of artistic individuality, he wrote, "it's the message, not the artist, that counts." "The Semantics of Photography" (Candid Shots by the Editors), *Popular Photography* (February 1956): 32.

100. Latour, "Family of Man," 37.

101. Sandeen, *Picturing an Exhibition*, 4, 95. In one of many such instances, "La Famille Américaine," in *Informations et Documents* (Les Services D'Information des États-Unis), 36–42, the show was used to glorify American ideals. One article outlined the show, "La Grande Famille des Hommes," while the next focused specifically on American family life, complete with pictures (not in the show) of contented nuclear families by the hearth, eating, praying at the table, maintaining their lawns, and playing music in the living room (these images included a black family, too). In future analyses of *The Family of Man* as cultural persuader, it would be especially intriguing to study its inclusion in the 1959 exhibition of American technology and values in Moscow.

102. Typed letter from Dorothea Lange to Edward Steichen from Saigon," September 25, 1958, Edward Steichen Archive.

103. "UAW-CIO and The Family of Man," *UAW-CIO Ammunition* (March 1955): 3–25. See also Martin S. Dworkin, "'The Family of Man,'" *Progressive* (August 1955): 25. Dworkin's review in this leftist publication mentions the "cavils among

critics and photographers" regarding the universalist theme and manner of print presentation, but Dworkin admits "the show has been nothing if not popular." He saw themes of social struggle and conflict: "People are fundamentally good and kind; but they struggle. . . . The United Nations Assembly represents their hope organized; the atomic cataclysm the potentiality of obliteration, futility."

Some critics distrusted *The Family of Man*'s popular appeal, as masses swarmed to museums across the country in unprecedented numbers. This issue relates to more recent events in museum history; another controversial photo show on a single theme, *Harlem on My Mind* (1969), at the Metropolitan, made open the elite museum space to the African American community. Comparisons of *The Family of Man* with shows such as this (which also suppressed individual photographers' identities and used large-scale blow-ups of images) could illuminate the relationships between and presumed attractions of a popular audience and museum presentations (John Clarke, personal communication, March 1993).

104. Edwin Rosskam, "Family of Steichen," *Artnews* (March 1955): 34–36. Rosskam was kind to Steichen but said he "is simply too gentle." However, Rosskam harshly criticized the show's design; for instance, "the over-employment of devices . . . tend to make the visitor suspicious."

105. "The Controversial Family of Man," *Aperture* 3, no. 2 (1955): 8. Many other articles, reprinted reviews, and commentary are included in this issue.

106. "The Controversial Family of Man," *Aperture* 3, no. 2 (1955): 8, 11.

107. George Wright and Cora Wright, "One Family's Opinion," ibid., 20, 21. The Wrights were editors and writers; Cora Wright also wrote a column for *Popular Photography* under the name Kennedy (Gee, *Limelight*, 104).

108. Dorothy Norman, "The Controversial Family of Man," *Aperture* 3, no. 2 (1955): 14–16. In her biography, Norman would later qualify her approval of the show, admitting aesthetic "misgivings about certain of its aspects: blowups of fine photographs are often grainy and dilute the quality of the originals; some purely journalistic images offend" (Norman, *Encounters*, 292).

109. Adams, "Through a Lens Darkly," 69–71.

110. Ibid. Ernst Fischer, *The Necessity of Art: A Marxist Approach*, trans. Anna Bostock (Middlesex, England: Penguin Books, 1986), 96. Originally published as *Von der Notwendigkeit ker Kunst* (Dresden: Verlag der Kunst, 1959). Fischer was analyzing and quoting Colin Wilson's *The Outsider* (New York: Delta, 1956), a "seminal book on the alienation of modern man," as the book cover advertised. Similarly, Hilton Kramer denounced the show for obscuring real and specific problems in the world; see Hilton Kramer, "Exhibiting the Family of Man: 'The World's Most Talked about Photographs,'" *Commentary* 20 (October, 1955): 365–67.

111. An interesting parallel could be made here between Adams's review and Pells's history of American liberal intellectuals of the decade. Pells notes that after 1945 the leftists did not know who to blame or who to champion; there were "no archenemies to denounce and no movements to join. Thus two of the major post-war journals were christened *Commentary* and *Dissent*, as if intellectuals could only comment upon and dissent from but never hope to transform the prevailing social order" Richard Pells, *The Liberal Mind in a Conservative Age: American Intellectuals in the 1940s and 1950s* (New York: Harper and Row, 1985), 119. Adams herself could be likened to the disgruntled critic who has no constructive criticism or hopes for im-

provement but can only cynically dislike and disapprove of public tastes. But, in the context of the times, she could thus safely prove her critical "powers" without taking any clear, public (or controversial) stand. The magazine she wrote for, the *Atlantic Monthly*, might have been a better target for her disgust; David Cohn's review of *Native Son* in that magazine was openly racist, moving Richard Wright to send letters vehemently arguing against Cohn's review. Margaret Walker, *Richard Wright: Daemonic Genius* (New York: Warner, 1988), 151.

112. Sandeen argues against the notion that modernism was absent in the show, especially in regard to its Bauhaus-inspired installation design, which forced viewer interaction (Sandeen, *Picturing an Exhibition*, 60–61).

113. Osman, "Photography Sure of Itself," 184.

114. Susan Sontag, *On Photography* (New York: Farrar, Straus and Giroux, 1973), 31–32. Sontag's scholarship may be said to represent a complete rupture of photographic privileging of authoritative "truth." Steichen and Arbus provide her with a methodological polarity of "American partiality to myths of redemption and damnation. . . . What we have left of Whitman's discredited dream of cultural revolution are paper ghosts and a sharp-eyed witty program of despair" (Sontag, *On Photography*, 48).

115. John Szarkowski, *Mirrors and Windows: American Photography Since 1960* (New York: Museum of Modern Art and New York Graphic Society, 1978), 17.

116. Phillips, "The Judgment Seat," 31, 34. Later, Phillips reviewed another show in 1984 that had deliberately copied *The Family of Man*. This postmodern reexamination of the show allowed him to further pursue the issues of "truth" and objectivity in photography; he posited that photographs are commonly seen as "natural, unproblematic mode[s] of visual reproduction and communication." But, following Jean Baudrillard, Phillips concluded that, in reality, "all becomes undecidable." Today, the inability of signs to convey specific meaning is familiar to scholars acquainted with deconstruction and postmodern theory. See Christopher Phillips, "In a Family Way," *Afterimage* (May 1984): 10–11. Past photographers such as Hine, Grossman, or Steichen were not so completely unsophisticated that they believed in a single, iconic sense of truth or social mission in photography; however, in some recent criticism they have often been poorly reduced to rather naive artists with little understanding for the "artful" multivocality of photography.

117. Badger, "From Humanism to Formalism," 12–13.

118. Aaron Siskind, interview by author, tape recording, Providence, R.I., June 23, 1989; Burt Glinn, interview by author, tape recording, New York, June 18, 1989; Gee, interview by author, 1989.

119. Sandeen, *Picturing an Exhibition*, 71.

120. Roland Barthes, "The Great Family of Man," in *Mythologies* (New York: Hill and Wang, 1972), 101. Emmett Till, a black fourteen-year-old visiting Mississippi from his native Chicago, had been accused, by a white woman, of asking her out for a date in 1955 (various accounts of the story exist). The woman's husband and three other men confessed to kidnapping him at gunpoint. Till's body was dragged from the Tallahatchie River, dead from a gunshot wound to the head. An all-male, all-white jury acquitted all involved and no one ever served time for Till's murder. Just months later, in December 1955, Rosa Parks initiated the Montgomery bus boycott (Lhamon, *Deliberate Speed*, 33–34).

121. Barthes, "The Great Family of Man," 100–102; Sandeen, *Picturing an Exhibition*, 54–55; Wilson, *The Outsider*, 15.

122. Roland Barthes, *Camera Lucida*, trans. Richard Howard (New York: Hill and Wang, 1981), 34.

123. Crist, "Modern Museum to Show 'Family of Man' Photos," 48. Steichen, "From Edward Steichen to Members of the Picture Division," 7.

Chapter Four: Robert Frank

1. More academic attention has been given to Frank than, perhaps, to any other photographer of his generation. The number of dissertations, exhibitions, textbook chapters, articles, and general scholarly references indicate the centrality and importance accorded his visions of America in the 1950s. Concurrently, less attention has been paid so far to the years before he published *The Americans* (1959)—his years in Switzerland, the importance of his European heritage, his advertising and photojournalistic careers. The concentration on Frank has resulted, in some cases, in hyperbolic rhetoric concerning his impact on American photohistory, to the detriment of other contemporary workers in the field (notable examples of neglected photographers include William Klein and Louis Faurer). The concentration on Frank developed especially after 1969, the year a new edition of *The Americans* came out. As just a general indication of the accolades subsequently heaped on Frank: John Brumfield maintains that Frank's work "has been the most influential vision in American photography"; Judith Mara Gutman writes that Frank "broke all the rules and created a new photojournalistic style . . . photography became freer, more subjective, an art with no holds barred"; and Sandra Lipshultz says that time has proven him "one of the most revolutionary and influential artists of the twentieth-century". John Brumfield, "'The Americans' and The Americans," *Afterimage* (summer 1980): 9; Judith Mara Gutman, "One-Shot Hero," *Connoisseur* (November 1987): 138; Sandra Lawall Lipshultz, "Robert Frank: New York to Nova Scotia," *Arts* (April 1987): 14. One of the most adulatory texts is by David B. Cooper, who writes that Frank has "become one of the most famous and revered photographers of this century . . . he shaped a new power and even majesty of the photographic process." Cooper also lists others' accolades as "proof" while exploring Frank's images of political conventions over the years. David B. Cooper, *Robert Frank and American Politics* (Akron, Ohio: Akron Art Museum, 1985), 4.

2. Frank came armed with letters of recommendation from at least five jobs in Switzerland, indicating his background in photography while still in Europe. His references indicate apprenticeships or training in several companies: Segessner Photography, in Zurich, noted that Frank had worked in its studio for three years, beginning in January 1941. Gloriafilm, also in Zurich, recommended Frank in 1942 for his assistance in still photography during his tenure at this film company. Beginning in August 1942, Frank worked at the photography and cinema studio of M. Wolgensinger in Zurich. The photography studio of V. Bouverat (Geneva) employed Frank from December 1944 to June 1945. The Hermann Eidenbenz studio (Basel) employed Frank as their photography and laboratory head from May 1946 through August 1946. Copies of these letters and documents were found in the Museum of Fine Arts, Houston, Archives (Box 7, Folder 4). Such experiences suggest Frank's early exposure to European photography.

3. Some of these student photographs have been reproduced in *The Lines of My Hand* (1989), which contains an overview of his prints from his European studies, including images that seem to presage his style in America (such as the isolated horse's behind or the Lisette Model-like female figure on the street), as well as those that could be described as mainstream photographs appropriate for Swiss postcards (skiers on snow-covered mountains and the like). Other student prints are housed in the archives of the Museum of Fine Arts, Houston, and also aptly demonstrate Frank's technical abilities. The subject matter of these prints includes a closeup of a pile of cut wood (which indicates a clear facility for translating texture), an abstraction of ovoid shapes against a dark ground, a outdoor crowd scene of laughing children and adults, a caged howling monkey, and a scene of tempestuous clouds not unlike one of Stieglitz's "equivalents" of earlier years. Clearly Frank experimented with small-format cameras, social documentary, street photography, traditional landscape, still life, portraiture, and other photographic styles and subjects. It may be found, through further research, that his "vision" of an anti-aesthetic, as it has been called, was more in place before his arrival to the United States than has been previously appreciated.

4. "Robert Frank" (interview), in *Photography within the Humanities*, ed. Eugenia Parry Janis and Wendy MacNeil (Danbury, N.H.: Addison House, 1977), 65.

5. *40 Fotos*, ca. 1946–47 includes forty-two pages of photographs mounted back to back with images of Switzerland—an early experiment in the juxtaposition of sequential photographs. According to Alexander, this was probably the body of work Frank showed Brodovitch that helped him earn his position at *Harper's Bazaar*. Stuart Alexander, *Robert Frank: A Bibliography, Filmography, and Exhibition Chronology 1946–1985* (Tucson: Center for Creative Photography and University of Arizona, 1986), 1.

6. Anne Wilkes Tucker and Philip Brookman, eds., *Robert Frank: New York to Nova Scotia* (Houston: Museum of Fine Arts, 1986), 14. Gee remembers Frank's disgust during a discussion about a friend who had died in a taxi cab at an early age—"It's this god-damned country," he reportedly muttered. Helen Gee, *Limelight: A Greenwich Village Gallery and Coffeehouse in the Fifties* (Albuquerque: University of New Mexico Press, 1997), 115.

7. "International Photography," in Tom Maloney, ed., *U.S. Camera Annual 1951* (New York: U.S. Camera, 1950), 411, 142. Frank's work in Steichen's *51 American Photographers* at MoMA (August-September 1950) was mentioned in at least two articles: a preview by Steichen in *Art News* and a review by Samuel Grierson in *American Photography* (Alexander, *Robert Frank*, 6).

8. Alexander notes the publication of at least ten *Harper's Bazaar* assignments by Frank in 1951, all concerning fashion accessories like bathing suits, blouses, shoes, or hairstyles (Alexander, *Robert Frank*, 7–8). *Life* magazine printed a photo essay of Frank's work entitled "Speaking of Pictures: A Photographer in Paris Finds Chairs Everywhere," which included eleven images (*Life*, May 21, 1951, 26–28). The portrait of Wright Morris accompanied a *Time* magazine book review (*Time*, May 28, 1951, 110).

9. The November 26, 1951, issue of *Life* announced the winners of their "Young Photographers Contest." Frank's second prize was heralded by a title, "Poet's Camera Sees Everything." Among the judges was Steichen, as well as Edward K. Thompson, Julius H. Klyman (of the St. Louis *Post-Dispatch*), James Wong Howe, Frank

Scherschel, Peter Stackpole, and Roy Stryker. The winners (all under thirty, according to competition specifications) in the Individual Pictures category included (from first to fifth place): Carroll Seghers, Robert Frank, Ruth Orkin, Louis Stettner, and John P. Goeller. In the Picture-Story category, winners were (from first to fifth place): Dennis Stock, Elliott Erwitt, Esther Bubley, Alfred Gescheidt, and Regina Fisher. Also see "*Life*'s Contest Winners" in *Modern Photography* (January 1952), which alluded to the fact that many winners were already established workers in the field: "All ten were names known to picture editors and others who follow the doings of the magazine photographer world" (100–101).

10. "Robert Frank: Swiss Mister," *Photo Arts* (December 1951): 594–99. This article endeavors to articulate the differences between European and American photography of the time, suggesting that Frank was adopting a more American point of view in evoking mood over compositional formalism.

11. Martha Rosler, "Lookers, Buyers, Dealers, and Makers: Thoughts on Audience," in *Art after Modernism: Rethinking Representation*, ed. Brian Wallis (Boston: David R. Godine; New York: New Museum of Contemporary Art, 1984), 330. Rosler's article represents seminal scholarship in the research of twentieth-century photography and how penetrating cultural forces can "create" careers. Another, more recent scholar, Abigail Solomon-Godeau, similarly writes that Frank represents the "simultaneous apogee and rupture . . . [of] photographic modernism's heroic period." Abigail Solomon-Godeau, "Winning the Game When the Rules Have Been Changed: Art Photography and Postmodernism," *Exposure* (spring 1985): 5–15.

12. Alexander, *Robert Frank*, 8–9. This self-published book (ca. 1952), includes images from Spain, London, Paris, South America, and New York. The cover and layout were attributed to Frank's Swiss friend, photographer Werner Zryd. The copy inscribed to Steichen is in the MoMA archives.

Edward Steichen, "Photography at the Museum of Modern Art," *Museum of Modern Art Bulletin* 19, no. 4 (April 1952): n.p. Steichen's words in this MoMA bulletin indicate his aesthetic focus was perhaps not as narrow as has been often presumed: "There is a new kind of aliveness in the melting pot of American photography . . . [the medium] is young, elastic and has elbowroom to grow it—lots of elbowroom!"

13. "The Top Prize-Winners in Black and White: Why the Judges Picked Them," *Popular Photography* (December 1953): 143. In the Black and White category, Farrell Grehan came in first, Fran Nestler second, Richard Pousette-Dart third, Robert Frank fourth (with his image *Masque*, one of many he submitted), and Saul Leiter fifth. The text under "Meet the Prize Winners," page 166, includes the following information on Frank and indicates the periodical's respect for his accomplishments: "Frank has a comprehensive background in photography; he specializes in work for magazines, and has done a considerable amount of fashion photography as well as commercial and industrial shots . . . he now works entirely on a free-lance basis." The six judges were Arthur Rothstein, Irving Penn (*Vogue*), W. Eugene Smith (*Life*), Frank Zachary (*Holiday*), Edward Steichen, and Wilson Hicks (former executive director of photography at *Life*). For his shots, Frank used a Leica camera, low shutter speeds, and fast film, which often increased the grain, an aesthetic growing in popularity among younger photographers of the time.

14. Frank's trip to Europe in 1953 also aided Steichen in his organization of the exhibition *Post-War European Photographers* (as well as *The Family of Man*), as noted in Frank's interview in Janis and MacNeil, eds., *Photography within the Humanities* (52).

15. William S. Johnson, "History—His Story," in *The Pictures Are a Necessity: Robert Frank in Rochester, N.Y., November 1988*, ed. William S. Johnson, Rochester Film and Photo Consortium Occasional Papers, No. 2 (Rochester: George Eastman House, Occasional Papers No. 2, 1989), 37. In "Robert Frank," (interview), in Janis and MacNeil, eds., *Photography within the Humanities*, Frank called Steichen "the personification of sentimentality," adding, "I can't stand that" (65).

16. Robert Frank, "Letter from New York," *Creative Camera* 61 (July 1969): 234.

17. Jonathan Green, *American Photography: A Critical History 1945 to the Present* (New York: Harry N. Abrams, 1984), 76–77. Frank's *Portrait of Willem de Kooning* is dated 1957, and Green dates his *Portrait of Franz Kline* at 1956. Green's text also includes Frank's portraits of Beat writers Allen Ginsberg, Gregory Corso (ca. 1955), and Jack Kerouac (ca. 1959–60). In Tucker and Brookman, eds., *Robert Frank*, Frank's collage of portraits of artists he knew in the New York scene includes Franz Kline, John Grillo, Richard Bellamy, and Alfred Leslie (who designed the collage on the back cover of the dust jacket of the 1959 edition of *The Americans*), as well as artists more often associated with the 1960s (Red Grooms, Allen Kaprow, and Claes Oldenburg). Although his circle of friends and acquaintances was broad, Frank has repeatedly praised and embraced the influence of abstract expressionism, not pop art or conceptual art.

18. "Robert Frank," (interview), in Janis and MacNeil, eds., *Photography within the Humanities*, 61, 63.

19. Helen Gee, "Photography in Transition: 1950–1960," in *Decade by Decade*, ed. James Enyeart (Tucson: University of Arizona and Tucson Center for Creative Photography, 1989), 63. It is impossible within this context to do justice to the scholarship of researchers such as Serge Guilbaut, Max Kozloff, the Shapiros, and Eva Cockcroft in exploring the relationships between abstract expressionism, politics, and the cold war. These writers have noted the rise of abstraction and the development of avant-garde art markets in post–World War II American society. This form of abstraction, according to Guilbaut, laid "the groundwork for the art of peacetime" by virtue of its emphasis on individualism and its distance from previous styles of more overtly politicized realism. Serge Guilbaut, *How New York Stole the Idea of Modern Art: Abstract Expressionism, Freedom, and the Cold War*, trans. Arthur Goldhammer (Chicago: University of Chicago Press, 1983, 78.

20. "Robert Frank," (interview), in Janis and MacNeil, eds., *Photography within the Humanities*, 60.

21. Johnson, ed., *The Pictures Are a Necessity*, 31, 45, 123–24, 167, 172, 182, 130. See also Cooper, *Robert Frank and American Politics*, 4–8. Cooper writes that Frank said politics are "close to religion. To believe in a voice—that is what I think much of it is about. But I think it is better to believe in religion than to believe in politicians." *The Americans*, Frank maintained, "was very political. It really talked about the period of America – it showed that period in an unmistakable way, how I felt about it, where I stood. . . . How I live, that's my politics" (Cooper, *Robert Frank and American Politics*, 7).

22. Johnson, ed., *The Pictures Are a Necessity*, 130.

23. Lucy Lippard, "Trojan Horses: Activist Art and Power," in Wallis, ed., *Art after Modernism: Rethinking Representation*, 349, emphasis in original.

24. Johnson, ed., *The Pictures Are a Necessity*, 110, 135. In personal interviews, when asked generally whether Frank's work was "political," his colleagues and friends answered, typically, that he was absolutely political or not at all political, displaying the ambiguities and confusion over just what constitutes "political" art. Emile de Antonio maintains that *The Americans* was unintentionally but "absolutely" political (Emile de Antonio, interview by Anne Tucker, transcript, New York, New York, October 18, 1985. Curatorial Records, Anne W. Tucker Records, Robert Frank Files. Archives, the Museum of Fine Arts, Houston, Box 7, Folder 17).

25. Telephone conversation with author, New York, February 1990 (this source prefers not to be identified). Louis Faurer, telephone conversation with author, New York, March 6, 1990. Frank and Faurer experimented with similar aesthetics in their investigations of street photography and 35 mm cameras, although Faurer's contributions in this area have been ignored in comparison to Frank's. However, according to Patricia Bosworth, the two men shared a darkroom from 1947 to 1951, so artistic interchange between them was certainly unavoidable. Patricia Bosworth, *Diane Arbus: A Biography* (New York: Knopf, 1984), 142. Faurer also worked with Frank at *Harper's Bazaar*, and the two men felt a compatible disdain for the others working there: Frank said, "The others were different. Photographers like Mark Shaw and George Hoyningen-Huene were consumed with the commercial work. Lou was only one like me. I went to Peru to get away from that make-money crowd" (Tucker and Brookman, eds., *Robert Frank*, 90).

26. Bob Adelman, interview by author, New York, February 1990.

27. Johnson, ed., *The Pictures Are a Necessity*, 173. Edna Bennett, "Black and White are the Colors of Robert Frank," *Aperture* 9, no. 1 (1961): 22.

28. Frank certainly put the work of W. Eugene Smith on a higher conceptual plane than that of other contemporary photojournalists; "I do not call him a journalist, I think he is the Franz Kafka of photography . . . don't try to twist him into being a journalist . . . [he] photographed only for himself." Frank added that Smith rejected mainstream capitulation to magazine editors and overall narrative by saying he was "true to himself at the expense of the subject." See Paul Hill and Thomas Cooper, eds., *Dialogue with Photography* (New York: Farrar, Straus, Giroux, 1979), 270. Smith himself has been quoted as saying that *The Americans* was "one man's very opinionated statement about what he saw in America. I think this is fine. . . . Bob [Frank] just looks at the world in a rather grouchy fashion" (*Dialogue with Photography*, 272).

29. "Robert Frank," (interview), in Janis and MacNeil, *Photography within the Humanities*, 56.

30. Jacob Deschin, "European Pictures: Modern Museum Presents Collection by Steichen," *New York Times*, May 31, 1953, sec. 2, p. 13. "Post-War European Photography" (review of *Post-War European Photography* exhibition at MoMA), *U.S. Camera* (September 1953): 37–42. Byron Dobell, ed., "Feature Pictures: Robert Frank . . . The Photographer as Poet," *U.S. Camera* (September 1954): 77–84.

31. Minor White, "The Light Sensitive Mirage," *Aperture* 6, no. 2 (1958): 79.

32. Nancy Newhall, "Pirkle Jones Portfolio," *Aperture* 4, no. 2 (1956): 49. Myron Martin, "Of People and for People," *Aperture* 4, no. 4 (1956): 136.

33. Gee, *Limelight*, 115; Johnson, ed., *The Pictures Are a Necessity*, 160–61.

34. Dave Heath, *Dialogue with Solitude* (New York: Horizon Press, 1965), preface.

35. Johnson, ed., *The Pictures Are a Necessity*, 27.

36. Rosler, "Lookers, Buyers, Dealers, and Makers," 330–31.

37. Andy Grundberg, "Photography View: A Show That Puts a Social Critic in a Larger Context," *New York Times*, July 7, 1985, sec. 2, p. 23.

38. The entire Guggenheim application form Frank submitted is reproduced in Tucker and Brookman, eds., *Robert Frank*, 20–21. The editors also note that despite the printed warning that documents should reach the foundation no later than October 15, Frank's application was received October 21.

39. Ibid., 9. Photographer Todd Webb was also awarded a Guggenheim Fellowship in 1955, for his projected plan to walk across the United States taking photographs of pioneer trails. His project, too, was renewed in 1956. See *Todd Webb Photographs* (Fort Worth, Tex.: Amon Carter Museum, 1965).

40. "Pablo and Meyer Schapiro" is dated 1953 (in Alexander, *Robert Frank*, 103); Frank also met Walker Evans in 1953 (in Tucker and Brookman, eds., *Robert Frank*, 9).

41. "Robert Frank" (interview), in Janis and MacNeil, eds., *Photography within the Humanities*, 58, 65. "Beauties of the Common Tool," *Fortune*, July 1955, 103–7 (a photo essay Frank assisted Evans on). "The Congressional," *Fortune*, November 1955, 118–22 (photographs by Frank, essay by Evans). See Alexander, *Robert Frank*, 13.

Tod Papageorge has more fully explored this relationship and Frank's stylistic indebtedness to Evans by comparing Evans's work in *American Photographs* (1938) and Frank's *The Americans* (1959). Evans, according to Papageorge, was considered relatively obscure by most 1950s photographers. However, Frank found Evans's influence and support personally and professionally gratifying. See Tod Papageorge, *Walker Evans and Robert Frank: An Essay on Influence* (New Haven: Yale University Art Gallery, 1981).

42. Walker Evans to Ray Mackland, Office Memorandum, October 16, 1956 (Time-Life, Inc.), Museum of Fine Arts, Houston, Archives (Box 2, Folder 9).

43. Tucker and Brookman, eds., *Robert Frank*, 10. The chronology in the Houston exhibition catalog notes that Frank moved to 34 Third Avenue near Tenth Street in 1956; Alfred Leslie lived next door and de Kooning lived in the building across Frank's backyard (10).

44. *Photographie als Ausdruck* (Helmhaus, Zurich, Switzerland, 1955); Gotthard Schuh, "Exhibition 'Photography as a Means of Expression,'" *Camera* (March 1955): 102–28; John Barkley Hart, "Seven Types of Ambiguity in a Greenwich Village Coffee Shop," *Intro Bulletin: A Literary Newspaper of the Arts* (October 1955): 1–2.

Frank was represented briefly by the Gamma agency in the 1950s. While Frank could truthfully maintain that *Life* rejected his work on many occasions, they did not reject his two images from Gamma. Alexander, *Robert Frank*, 13.

45. Frank's South American photographs were published under a variety of titles, including *Indiens pas morts* (Paris: Delpire, 1956), *From Incas to Indios* (New York: Universe Books, 1956), *Incas to Indians* (London: Photography Magazine, 1956), *Indios* (Zurich: Manesse, 1956), and *Dagli Incas agli Indios* (Milan: Feltrinelli, 1957), as well as in periodicals.

46. "Robert Frank: Indians of Peru," in Tom Maloney, ed., *U.S. Camera Annual 1952* (New York: U.S. Camera, 1951), 64–65. The published versions of this book

garnered a number of favorable reviews in popular periodicals. Book reviews were published in: R. L. Duffus, "Lands to the South," *New York Times Book Review*, November 4, 1956, 14; "Book Reviews: Sons of the Incas Record in Pictures," *Springfield (Mass.) Sunday Republican*, December 2, 1956, 10; "Books: Good to Look At," *Time*, December 17, 1956, 107. More reviews followed in 1957 in *Camera 35*, *Image*, and the *Manchester Guardian* (see Alexander, *Robert Frank*, 14–16).

47. "Robert Frank," (interview), in Janis and MacNeil, eds., *Photography within the Humanities*, 61. The term *indecisive moment* was noted by writers such as Louise Abbott: "What Frank captured so well was not the decisive, but the seemingly indecisive moment, when people and situations were in a state of flux" (Louise Abbott, "Robert Frank's Photos Angered the Experts," *The (Montreal) Gazette*, November 20, 1980, 43.) Jean-Claude Lemagny writes that Frank's images were "no longer a matter of 'decisive moments.' What count are the moments 'in between,' in between the ones which appear to be full of significance and harmony. . . . After Frank, photographers knew that there were no significant moments. It is we who give them significance" (Jean-Claude Lemagny and Andre Rouillé, eds., *A History of Photography: Social and Cultural Perspectives* (Cambridge: Cambridge University Press, 1986), 193.

Frank, like Grossman before him, was rather contemptuous of the famous and influential photojournalist Henri Cartier-Bresson in later interviews: "He travelled all over the goddamned world, and you never felt that he was moved by something that was happening other than the beauty of it, or just the composition. That's certainly why *Life* gave him big assignments. They knew he couldn't come up with something that wasn't acceptable." Such overt concern for the aesthetics of beauty sickened Frank and compromised the artistic freedom and personal expression he felt. He also recounted a story of Cartier-Bresson (as well as Capa and Erwitt) rejecting his work for Magnum; "I really couldn't have done it. I felt that they didn't really want me, and it was more a personality thing" ("Robert Frank," [interview], Janis and MacNeil, eds., *Photography within the Humanities*, 56, 64). Johnson writes that Frank "was invited to join Magnum photo agency at one point, but declined." According to Johnson, Frank "simply could not or would not tailor his extremely personal vision to accommodate the needs of the editors of the mass circulation magazines," thus he heroically rejected mainstream journalism in favor of individual expression (Johnson, ed., *The Pictures Are a Necessity*, 34).

48. Tom Maloney, ed., *U.S. Camera Annual 1958* (New York: U.S. Camera, 1957), 89. That year's annual included a special insert of the images Frank had made during his Guggenheim travels, and includes many photographs that were not chosen for publication in *The Americans.*

49. Walker Evans, "Robert Frank," in Tom Maloney, ed., *U.S. Camera Annual 1958* (New York: U.S. Camera, 1957), 90.

50. Robert Frank, "A Statement," in Maloney, ed., *U.S. Camera Annual 1958*, 115. Also reprinted in *Photography in Print*, ed. Vicki Goldberg (New York: Simon and Schuster, 1981), 400–401, and Tucker and Brookman, eds., *Robert Frank*, 31.

51. Ibid.

52. Michael Schumacher, *Dharma Lion: A Biography of Allen Ginsberg* (New York: St. Martin's Press, 1992), 209. *Howl* is certainly political in its evocation of specific antihumanist social phenomena of the times, as evidenced in the presence of "Moloch," a "black cloud" not unlike the atom bomb, destroying human spirit. As Schumacher

points out, however, compared to Ginsberg's later works, *Howl* was far less specific in regard to historical events and consequences.

53. Tucker and Brookman, eds., *Robert Frank*, 9. Frank had placed an expired plate in his trunk after purchasing a 1950 Ford from Ben Schultz.

54. Robert Frank, letter to Mary Frank (July 1955), reprinted ibid., 22.

55. Lieutenant R. E. Brown, letter to Captain Alan R. Templeton, Little Rock, Arkansas (December 19, 1955) reprinted ibid., 24.

56. Robert Frank, letter to Walker Evans (November 9, 1955), reprinted ibid., 26. Nathaniel H. Janes, letter to Robert Frank (December 31, 1955), reprinted ibid., 27. In a later interview, Frank remembered the horror and fear of this event, saying the officers kept him "in jail for almost three days. I didn't know anybody; they could have killed me" ("Robert Frank," [interview], Janis and MacNeil, eds., *Photography within the Humanities*, 56). In 1947, *Photo Notes* published a letter from W. Eugene Smith, who also had been thrown in jail (this time in Fayetteville, North Carolina) for potentially illegal (but unspecified) activity. See "Letter to the Editor," *Photo Notes* (August–September 1947): 4. Reprinted in *Photo Notes, 1938–1950*, ed. Nathan Lyons (Rochester: Visual Studies Workshop, 1977). Also see Jim Hughes, *W. Eugene Smith: Shadow and Substance* (New York: McGraw-Hill, 1989), 207–8.

57. Robert Frank, *The Lines of My Hand* (New York: Pantheon Books, 1989), n.p.

58. Another difference between Frank and some earlier social documentarians is found in their use of titles. Frank's photographs, even when they picture specific figures he has encountered, rarely exhibit any hint of a developed relationship; the pictures' titles in *The Americans* carry the information of place only, never a person's name or position, a textual device Frank would probably find too descriptive. Some photographs in *The Americans* even show his subjects' distrust or anger upon seeing his lens pointed in their direction. Others never even knew he photographed them (for example, those figures populating bars or streets whom he secretly "shot from the hip.") While scholars today have, on occasion, tracked down the tenant farmers FSA workers photographed in order to chronicle these lives in later years, there is little hope the same could be done for Frank's subjects. Instead, they remain anonymous symbols of class, region, or race. While some might find this *de*humanizing, Frank's tack perfectly suits his intention to chronicle and unify a wide diversity of citizens, from the privileged elite to downtrodden outsiders and nonconformists, in Eisenhower's America.

59. Jack Kerouac, *On the Road* (New York: New American Library, 1985), 111. Originally published in 1955, *On The Road* has become a modern classic. Similar thematic views of cultures exist in other books of the 1950s, including: Andreas Feininger's *The Face of New York* (1954) and *Changing America* (1955); Cartier-Bresson's *Les Europeans* (1955) and *The People of Moscow* (1955); Cecil Beaton's *Japanese* (1959); Emil Schulthess' *Africa* (1960); and many others. Furthermore, Frank's critique of American culture in *The Americans* was communicated through his forceful sequencing of images. The methodological difficulty of discussing specific images, yanked from their context, parallels similar problems in analysis of *The Family of Man*. Our understanding of each photograph is enriched by its interaction with and impact upon other accompanying images.

60. Ulrich Keller, *The Highway as Habitat: A Roy Stryker Documentation, 1943–1955* (Santa Barbara, Calif.: University Art Museum, 1986), 23, 21. Ulrich Keller's

catalog essay for this 1986 show provides essential research into European preconceptions concerning American highway life.

Frank was also personally cognizant of the dangers of driving in America, as he did not want his wife to use an automobile, fearing for her safety; in a 1955 letter to his parents he wrote: "Mary has it rough—it is too bad, that Mary cannot drive" (Tucker and Brookman, eds., *Robert Frank*, 28). In a copy of this letter in the Museum of Fine Arts, Houston, Archives (Box 1), he expanded on the dangers of driving and his desire that Mary not learn to drive; but he admitted that without that freedom she became confined to the house and children.

61. Keller, *The Highway as Habitat*, 10–11. Keller also recounts the concerns of Soviet visitors Ilya Ilf and Eugene Petrov, written during their tour of the the United States in the mid-1930s. They commented on things such as the well-constructed roads, "built for eternity," and the ritual of gas service. The iconography of the American road is a potentially rich subject, as many more images in *The Americans* deal with this, including *Butte, Montana, U.S. 91, Leaving Blackfoot, Idaho, Covered Car–Long Beach, California, Car Accident–U.S. 66, between Winslow and Flagstaff, Arizona, Sante Fe, New Mexico* (which includes the sign "SAVE" above gas pumps), and *St. Francis, Gas Station*, and *City Hall–Los Angeles*, among others. Most of these images, featuring long stretches of desolate road, are from the West, bringing to mind the potential iconography of immigration and Western expansion. Jonathan Green links Frank's sublime images of the American automobile with the spiritual decrepitude of contemporary consumer society and Beat literature: "The world of spirit exists only in the world of things. . . . What remains of the old sacred rituals has become occult in this cold, highway world" (Green, *American Photography*, 87).

62. Keller, *The Highway as Habitat*, 14. Sidra Stitch, *Made in USA: An Americanization in Modern Art, the '50s and '60s* (Berkeley: University Art Museum and University of California Press, 1987), 64–65. Also see "Road Builders on the New Highway Network," *Time*, June 24, 1957, 92. In 1969, approximately 56,000 Americans died in car accidents, almost 20,000 more than had died in 1950 (Stitch, *Made in USA*, 172).

Bradley Smith, "Pictures on the Highway," *Popular Photography* 35, no. 3 (September 1954): 82, 118, 120; Joan Lewis, "More Pictures to the Gallon" (Section 1, "On the Road"), *Popular Photography* 44, no. 5 (May 1959): 66–67, 125–26. The cover picture for this 1959 article includes a long, turning stretch of road, misty ("impressionistic") with rain. The text added, "Your car is your magic carpet to summer picture places, but don't think of it only as a means of transportation. A car can actually be a photographic accessory."

63. Tom Clark, *Jack Kerouac: A Biography* (New York: Paragon House, 1990), 167, 134, 184. The history of Kerouac's efforts to publish *On the Road* could fill one chapter alone, as could his complex political affiliations during the cold war. Gerald Nicosia states that his *On the Road* journals date from 1948 to 1949. Clark maintains that the first version of *On the Road* was written in November 1948 and was based on his travel accounts from 1947 (79). Gerald Nicosia, *Memory Babe: A Critical Biography of Jack Kerouac* (New York: Grove Press, 1983), 71.

As Green notes, Kerouac and Frank teamed up again in 1958 when they traveled to Florida together (Green, *American Photography*, 85). "On the Road to Florida" (text by Kerouac, photographs by Frank) was finally published in *Evergreen Review* 74 (January 1970): 42–47, 64.

64. Kerouac, *On the Road*, 9.

65. Arthur Knight and Kit Knight, eds., *The Beat Vision* (New York: Paragon House, 1987), 23.

66. Quoted in Green, *American Photography*, 83–84. Frank felt more kinship with Kerouac than he did with Ginsberg; "[Kerouac] really loved America in a very simple and good way, and in a quiet way. He didn't scream about it, like Ginsberg screams about it," (Johnson, ed., *The Pictures Are a Necessity*, 173). In his *Pull My Daisy*, the ultimate Beat film of 1959, Frank is rather absent, even in later historical descriptions of it, as if he only neutrally wielded the camera or didn't even exist. The thorny issue of control versus "spontaneity" (and its potential mythological dimensions) in the making of *Pull My Daisy* still lives on as well, a theoretical discourse applicable to Frank's overall picture-taking; Frank states: "I assure you *Pull My Daisy* was totally spontaneous" (Johnson, ed., *The Pictures Are a Necessity*, 155).

67. "An Off-Beat View of the USA," *Popular Photography* 46, no. 5 (May 1960): 105.

68. Sandra Weiner and Cornell Capa, eds. *Dan Weiner* (New York: International Center of Photography, Grossman Publishers, and Viking Press, 1974), 45.

69. *Invisible in America: An Exhibition of Photographs by Marion Palfi*, foreword by Lee Witkin, catalogue essay by James Enyeart (Lawrence, Kans.: University of Kansas Museum of Art, 1973), n.p.

70. Jack Kerouac, "Introduction," in Robert Frank, *The Americans* (1959; New York: Pantheon Books, 1986), 8. Gilbert Millstein, "In Each a Self-Portrait" (Reviews of *The Americans* and *Journey to the Cape*), *New York Times Book Review*, January 17, 1960, 7.

71. Maren Stange, *Symbols of Ideal Life: Social Documentary Photography in America, 1890–1950* (Cambridge: Cambridge University Press, 1989), 147. Stange concludes her book with Frank's hovering image pointing to "the beginning of a new chapter in photographic expression, one with its own logic and direction" (148). Her implication is that Frank alters all expectation and perhaps, even, the history of photography.

72. Eugenia Kaledin, *Mothers and More: American Women in the 1950s* (Boston: Twayne, 1984), preface, n.p. See also: Wini Breines, "The 1950s: Gender and Some Social Science," *Sociological Inquiry* (winter 1986); Betty Friedan, *The Feminine Mystique* (New York: Dell, 1983); Rochelle Gatlin, *American Women Since 1945* (Jackson: University Press of Mississippi, 1987); Elaine Tyler May, *Homeward Bound: American Families in the Cold War Era* (New York: Basic Books, 1988); Margaret Mead, *Male and Female: A Study of the Sexes in a Changing World* (New York: William Morrow, 1949).

73. George Lefferts, *Special for Women* (New York: Avon, 1961), 135. This popular press book provided "eight dramatic investigations into problems of deep concern to both men and women in today's world" (from the cover) by discussing the following "types" of women (listed as chapters in the table of contents): The Cold Woman, The Trapped Housewife, The Single Woman, and The Working Mother, as well as a chapter on "The Glamour Trap." "'The Glamour Trap' was written as a comment on the worship of youth and beauty in our society. The extent of this worship, as our research found, is overwhelming . . . [Women] spent 24 million dollars for hairpins alone . . . The implications are clear . . . if you're *not* young and beautiful, these joys of life are not for you, sister, regardless of your other attributes" (135).

Such sources indicate the contemporary concerns over women's internalization of society's conception of beauty. Ironically, Frank's own wife at the time, Mary Frank, is often remembered in subsequent interviews for her beauty, not her own struggling, burgeoning artistic career. See Museum of Fine Arts, Houston, Archives for more interviews, Emile de Antonio's in particular, which mentions that everyone was "in love" with her (Emile de Antonio, interview by Anne W. Tucker); also Tucker and Brookman, *Robert Frank*, 91 ("Mary was beautiful, and men remember her with wonder").

For more on women in 1950s film, see Marjorie Rosen, *Popcorn Venus: Women, Movies and the American Dream* (New York: Coward, McCann, and Geohegan, 1973), 282–99; Brandon French, *On the Verge of Revolt: Women in American Films of the Fifties* (New York: Ungar, 1978); Molly Haskell, *From Reverence to Rape: The Treatment of Women in the Movies* (New York: Penguin, 1974).

74. Annette Kuhn, *The Power of the Image* (London: Routledge and Kegan Paul, 1985), 11, 13. Frank turned to glamour women as subjects elsewhere in *The Americans*, notably in another image of the same title, *Movie Premiere, Hollywood*, wherein a "star" resembling Carol Lynley looks off screen, posing for the male gaze (guarded, prepared, erect, and iconic). In another reproduction of this image, however, published in Ann Thomas's *Lisette Model* (Ottawa: National Gallery of Canada, 1990), 110, there appears a figure to the far left that was cropped out of the version in *The Americans*—a male figure looking at the woman. In the cropped version, then, we focus on the woman as the central object of our gaze, whereas in the full-frame image we are forced to confront more fully that gaze itself, as we see another figure participating in it as well. With Frank's archives now established at the National Gallery, scholars will be able to further research such issues of cropping.

75. Simone de Beauvoir, *The Second Sex* (1953; New York: Vintage Books, 1974), 630.

76. Anne Tucker, "The Photo League," *Creative Camera* no. 223/224 (July/August, 1983): 1016.

77. Johnson, ed., *The Pictures Are a Necessity*, 29.

78. Lou Stettner, "Speaking Out: Politics of Despair," *Camera 35* 17, no. 2 (March 1973): 9, 12. Stettner was a columnist for *Camera 35* beginning in 1971. Turner Browne and Elaine Partnow, *Macmillan Biographical Encyclopedia of Photographic Artists and Innovators* (New York: Macmillan, 1983), 587.

79. Lou Stettner, "Speaking Out: On the Windshield of My Mind," *Camera 35* 17, no. 1 (January/February 1973): 26, 74.

80. Ibid., 74.

81. David Vestal, "Review: *The Lines of My Hand*," *Camera 35* 17, no. 2 (March 1973): 27.

82. Robert Frank, letter to Kazuhiko Motomura (November 2, 1981), Museum of Fine Arts, Houston, Archives (Box 1).

83. The inclusion of this text (collected by Alain Bosquet), an editorial decision in the hands of Delpire, not Frank, substantially differentiates the French edition and demands further investigation, as the text certainly alters readers' perceptions of the images. There are only minor differences between the French edition and the later American version in terms of images, size, and cropping of photographs (both have one image per two-page spread, with place-name captions). The quotations culled

for *Les Américains* lend a more politically critical aura to the images, with text discussing, among other subjects, popular culture, statistics, racism, "Le Dieu Dollar," "L'Intellectuel Est Suspect," juvenile delinquency, and even William Faulkner on Americans' love of cars. It was published as part of a series by Delpire entitled "Encyclopédie Essentielle, No. 5, Série Histoire, No. 3." The maquette is housed in the collection of the Museum of Fine Arts, Houston, Archives.

84. Johnson, ed., *The Pictures Are a Necessity*, 42. Alexander, *Robert Frank*, 19. The interest in work by followers who "received and understood" his "language" was appreciated by Frank: "They listened to voices that had no part in the 'system.' Aware of hypocrisy around them, dissatisfied with slogans from preachers and patriots, they began to question everything. *The Americans* became for many an affirmation of what they felt about their country . . . that's what I cherish the most" (Frank, *Lines of My Hand*, n.p.).

85. Green, *American Photography*, 83.

86. Johnson, ed., *The Pictures Are a Necessity*, 173, 42, 161).

87. "New Photo Books," *Modern Photography* 24, no. 6 (June, 1960): 32–33, 52. *The Americans* was reviewed (by "P. C.") alongside *Observations* (photographs by Richard Avedon and "comments" by Truman Capote), which another reviewer ("J. B.") "loved," and *Africa* (photographs by Emil Schulthess), which "P. C." highly recommended.

88. "An Off-Beat View of the USA," 104–6. Published under the "Books" section of the magazine, this article includes on the front page the cover of Frank's book (with the *Trolley* image) and notes, "Seldom has a book of photographs aroused as much controversy in the *Popular Photography* office as Robert Frank's *The Americans*. . . . The reactions of the editors ranged from admiration to contempt. Some of these opinions are reported here in the form of individual reviews." The reviewers included Les Barry, Bruce Downes, John Durniak, Arthur Goldsmith, H. M. Kinzer, Charles Reynolds, and James M. Zanutto. In a later interview, Goldsmith says that Frank's work "violated" all acceptable notions of photography, although it did so "brilliantly." Goldsmith claims he would "modify" his negative review now, but he would not "recant"—"It is a one-sided America . . . it isn't all that grim" (Arthur Goldsmith, telephone conversation with author, July 8, 1989).

The written response of some *Popular Photography* readers who took issue with the collective denunciation of *The Americans* has also been neglected. Tad Stamm of Toledo, Ohio, wrote a long letter received by *Popular Photography* on April 14, 1960, that takes issue with the reviews. However, when the letter by Stamm was printed in *Popular Photography* (July 1960), it had been edited so heavily that his points were barely discernable. In the same issue, Grove Press editor Barney Rosset wrote that he was "mystified by the almost complete failure to consider Frank as an artist (for better or for worse) and to look at the pictures, not beyond them" (6). A copy of Stamm's original letter, before editing, was found in the Museum of Fine Arts, Houston, Archives (Box 2, Folder 9).

89. Ed Grazda, interview by Anne Tucker, transcript, October 11, 1985. Curatorial Records, Anne W. Tucker Records, Robert Frank Files. Archives, the Museum of Fine Arts, Houston, Box 8, Folder 3.

90. Dorothy Nyren, "*The Americans*," review, *Library Journal* 85, no. 6 (March 15, 1960): 1104. Millstein, "In Each a Self-Portrait," 7. "Books: General," *New*

Yorker, May 14, 1960, 203–4. The *New Yorker*'s brief review was positive overall, like Nyren's and Millstein's: "The special quality of American life is here exposed with brutal sensitivity."

91. Donald Gutierrez, "Books: The Unhappy Many," review of *The Americans*, *Dissent* (autumn 1961): 515–16. Gutierrez finds moments of capitalist injustice throughout *The Americans*: "Here, in a country capable of vastly enlarging and beautifying the material life of its people, is a culture that not only produces an avalanche of dime-store trivialities but has succeeded in conditioning the population to accept them." The "vast commercial squalor" Frank makes visible affirms the national capitalist hegemony for this reviewer but leaves him wondering how to change this course.

92. Bennett, "Black and White," 22.

93. Frank was further mentioned in terms of his growing reputation as a filmmaker (a crucial aspect of Franks' career, but one not in the scope of this chapter), as the seminal Beat film *Pull My Daisy* was released in 1959. By this time Frank was living in elegance compared to other bohemians of the time. Around 1960, playwright Jack Gelber remembers Frank's surprise at Gelber's cold-water flat, while he, Frank (according to Gutman's paraphrasing of Gelber), "needed $2,000 a month to live on—this at a time when most young professionals were delighted with one- third of that." As Gutman points out, "Frank found that just as he could not live with bourgeois values, he could not live without them, either" (Gutman, "One-Shot Hero," 141).

94. John Szarkowski, *Mirrors and Windows: American Photography Since 1960* (New York: Museum of Modern Art, 1978; Boston: New York Graphic Society, 1978), 18, 19. Frank and White offer two similar yet very divergent tangents in the artistic pursuit of personal expression; Frank's vision is more naturalistic, while White's is based on a more mystical understanding of non-European philosophy. While both are indebted to the modernist tradition in the arts, Frank's brand of "realism" forces viewers, more obviously, to contemplate his relationship to the social documentary tradition.

Szarkowski praises Kinzer's "basically sympathetic" review as well as that of Downes. However, he also notes that "among the more intellectually ambitious journals, it is difficult to find mention of the book's publication." It would be helpful to research just which "ambitious journals" took consistent note of small press releases of photography books at all; perhaps their ignoring *The Americans* was not so much a deliberate oversight as it was an indication of the more general, peripheral condition of photographic criticism at the time.

95. *Candy Mountain* (Xanadu Film, 1987), directed by Robert Frank and Rudy Wurlitzer, chronicles the adventures of Julius, who is in search of the great historical figure and guitar-maker Elmore Silk (on behalf of unscrupulous New York capitalists who want to exploit Silk). In the movie, the guitar-maker has taken refuge from the world in Mabou, Nova Scotia. However, whereas Silk destroys all his original guitars rather than have them marketed by exploitive forces, Frank is currently represented by a successful New York gallery.

Postscript: The Triumph of American Photographic Expressionism

1. "Promotional sheet for a workshop on 'reading' photographs, 1956," *Henry Holmes Smith: Collected Writings, 1935–1985*, ed. James Enyeart and Nancy Solomon (Tucson: University of Arizona and Center for Creative Photography, 1986), 26, 52–

53. This interest in "reading" photography, in developing a more critically attuned and visually literate audience, would also filter into the popular presses during the mid to late-1950s, in articles such as Ralph Hattersley, "How to 'Read' A Photograph," *Popular Photography* (March 1958): 61, which includes a section "Ask These 20 Key Questions Whenever You Study a Picture."

2. Jacob Deschin, "Picture Meanings: University Course in How to Read Photos," in Enyeart and Solomon, eds., *Henry Holmes Smith*, 26 (originally published in the *New York Times*, April 1, 1956).

3. Martha Rosler, "Lookers, Buyers, Dealers, and Makers: Thoughts on Audience," in *Art after Modernism: Rethinking Representation*, ed. Brian Wallis (Boston: David R. Godine; New York: New Museum of Contemporary Art, 1984), 338. Rosler adds that "social configurations enfold and constrain art production." While she is discussing art within the context of Reaganism, parallels certainly exist with the McCarthy-Eisenhower cold war years.

4. J. A. Vaughan, "Letter to the Editor," *Popular Photography* 43, no. 3 (March 1958): 6. Technical issues of clarity and detail were central to the new 35 mm aesthetic so many were pursuing. Yet even *Popular Photography* was publishing articles on new interests in the medium, demonstrating the new aesthetic's initiation and acceptance within mass popular culture. See, for instance, "Abstractions—They Emphasize Design," *Popular Photography* 38, no. 2 (February 1956): 62–63. However, many photographers, typically documentarians, still took issue with abstraction, as is evidenced by Weiner's comments on Siskind's "dehumanizing" photographs, depicting "a nether realm peopled by indefinite shapes and indiscriminate mishmash." Dan Weiner, "Again Diogenes," review, Museum of Modern Art, *Infinity* (December 1952): 22.

5. Clemens Kalischer, "Letters to the Editor," *Aperture* 5, no. 1 (1957): 42. Kalischer bemoaned photography in "conscious imitation of painting styles," with its "formalism and pictorialism." His criticism points to the displacement of, in Allan Sekula's terms, documentary's implicit politics by more manifest aesthetics. Kalischer, born in 1921 in Bavaria, studied in Paris, Cooper Union, and the New School. He freelanced and photographed for *Coronet* magazine (1948–49) and for the France Press News Agency (1947–48). Turner Browne and Elaine Partnow, *Macmillan Biographical Encyclopedia of Photographic Artists and Innovators* (New York: Macmillan, 1983), 317).

6. Roland Barthes, *Camera Lucida* (New York: Hill and Wang, 1981), 87, 115. John Tagg, "Introduction," in *The Burden of Representation: Essays on Photographies and Histories* (Amherst: University of Massachusetts Press, 1988), 1, 14–15. The growth of poststructuralist theory in Europe and its earliest manifestations in American art philosophy demand further research in relation to the criticism and historiography of photography in the late 1950s and early 1960s. In gross summary, Foucault, Barthes, and others questioned signification (including the arbitrary relationship between the signifier and signified). As evidenced in the investigations of contemporary semioticians and poststructuralists, such a theory readily applied to the visual world of photography. One photographer, Wynn Bullock, studied semiotics as early as 1940 to 1941, with Alfred Korzybski (Browne and Partnow, *Macmillan Biographical Encyclopedia*, 85.) White's aesthetic sophistication in *Aperture* articles of the 1950s certainly seems to point to the possibility of his having some understanding of the

shifting nature of signs and complex issues of connotation and denotation in representations. This could, in turn, be seen as a coping device within the context of the cold war, during which time artists might have desired to reconcile their (covert) capitulation to censoring forces with their (overt) desire for personal expression.

Frank's images are often exciting to critics engaged in postmodernist theory, such as John Brumfield, who, in a 1980 *Afterimage* article, attempts a more deconstructivist response to the images in *The Americans* and claims "Frank's has been the most influential vision in American photography." He further praises Frank's works' "connotative potential," noting "the literal structure of the image operates as a metaphor." See John Brumfield, "'The Americans' and The Americans," *Afterimage* (summer 1980): 9–15.

7. "The Experience of Photographs: Five Photographs by Aaron Siskind," *Aperture* 5, no. 3 (1957): 118–19. Five reviews by five readers were published: Henry Holmes Smith, Kurt Safranski, Myron Martin, Walter Chappell, and Sam Tung Wu.

8. Margery Mann, "The Controversial Aaron Siskind," *Infinity* (March 1968): 16. Mann discusses the "canonization" of Siskind in this article, also mentioning Rosenberg's introduction to the book *Aaron Siskind: Photographs* (New York: Horizon Press, 1954) and his lack of understanding of the photographic process. However, the adjectives she uses to describe Siskind's work could apply to Frank as well in the current popular understanding of his work in *The Americans.* Despite their differences, Siskind must have appreciated Frank's photographs; he published a portfolio by Frank (and Callahan) in the magazine *Choice* (1962), for which he was photography editor.

9. Jonathan Green, *American Photography: A Critical History 1945 to the Present* (New York: Harry N. Abrams, 1984), 71.

10. Harold Rosenberg, "Evidences," introduction to *Aaron Siskind: Photographs*, n.p. Rosenberg's own personal and critical evolution from the 1930s through the 1950s could offer another interesting glimpse into the changes in America's art scene. Rosenberg was more radical in his politics than was Clement Greenberg, and he was greatly informed by existential philosophy in his understanding of the solitary modern artist. Action, or gestural, painting, he felt, signified personal liberation and preserved individuality. Serge Guilbaut observes that the artists surrounding Rosenberg and Robert Motherwell "took account of both art and politics but did not particularly concentrate on either. Instead, man was the central focus: the artist himself embodied both art and politics and through his work resolved the contradictions between them" Serge Guilbaut, *How New York Stole the Idea of Modern Art: Abstract Expressionism, Freedom, and the Cold War*, trans. Arthur Goldhammer (Chicago: University of Chicago Press, 1983), 156. Rosenberg also honored risk as crucial to creativity; his idea that "there is no point to an act if you already know what it contains" and his respect for "the discipline of the Open Road of risk" would be more compatible with Frank and Siskind's creative efforts than with those of earlier documentarians (such as Grossman), although he took risks both in his art *and* his life. See Max Kozloff, "The Critical Reception of Abstract-Expressionism," *Arts Magazine* (December, 1965), reprinted in *Abstract Expressionism: A Critical Record*, ed. David Shapiro and Cecile Shapiro (Cambridge: Cambridge University Press, 1990), 143.

11. Minor White, "*Aaron Siskind: Photographs*," review, *Aperture* 7, no. 3 (1959): 124.

12. Rosenburg, "Evidences," n.p. Minor White, "Book Reviews," *Aperture* 3, no. 3 (1955): 32. Siskind had little patience with simplistic polarities and categories in photography; rather than ignore or disparage documentary work, he practiced it and taught it to his students on a number of occasions.

13. Rosenberg, "Evidences," n.p. In a personal interview, Siskind said that he had originally asked Clement Greenberg to write the introduction, since Greenberg "liked . . . and admired" him, but, Siskind continued: "His point of view about me was 'you can't do that.' . . . And I would say, 'Well, I'm doing it.' . . . Photography is something to make representations with and I was doing what painters were trying to do." Greenberg, according to Siskind, also said he couldn't write the introduction for free. However, Rosenberg agreed to write the piece even though he "had never shown any interest in photography. . . . Of course photographers didn't like it but I thought it was quite intriguing. . . . All I wanted was somebody that would write something that was intelligent, interesting, intriguing." (Aaron Siskind, interview by author, tape recording, Providence, R.I., June 23, 1989).

14. Tagg, "Introduction," 13–15. He adds: "The historicist reduction of complex practices to stylistic streams, defined, opposed or reconciled by a privileged criticism and gathered in the transcendent space of the Museum, typified the strategic attempt to impose a corporatist hegemony in a reasserted cultural hierarchy" (14–15).

15. Minor White, "Editorial: The Pursuit of Personal Vision," *Aperture* 4, no. 1 (1956): 3.

16. Green, *American Photography*, 79. Green excludes the Photo League from this historical text of photography "1945 to present" (only mentioning it briefly in the context of Paul Strand's career). This exclusion of the league could be partly due to the fact that its historical documents are not conveniently housed in easily accessible archives: many have been stored away, planned for use in Anne Tucker's book on the league (planned since the 1970s). But many of the artists of the league are still alive and working as photographers, although most seemed surprised by any attention to their histories at this point in time.

17. Meyerowitz quoted in Judith Mara Gutman, "One-Shot Hero," *Connoisseur* (November 1987): 139. Such sentiments concerning Frank's overall contribution to American photography are plentiful. William Johnson credits Frank with freeing photography from the rhetoric of documentary: "Frank was able to evoke a newer visual syntax, one which could lead to a richer dialogue about the nature of the country." *The Pictures Are a Necessity*, ed. William S. Johnson (Rochester: George Eastman House, Occasional Papers No. 2, 1989), 39. Ralph Gibson's oft-quoted remark was that *The Americans* "hit the photographic community with the impact of a pole axe" (Brumfield, "'The Americans' and The Americans," 11). Green adds that "it was Frank's genius and good fortune . . . to revitalize American photography by way of the European tradition," (Green, *American Photography*, 90).

18. "*U.S. Camera Annual 1958*," review, *Aperture* 5, no. 4 (1957): 173. Ironically, these words were describing the section in the *U.S. Camera Annual* on Robert Frank's Guggenheim-sponsored photographs; his "Frank approach" and use of "irony in photography" is applauded.

Selected Bibliography

Archives at the following institutions have been utilized in the research of this book: Howard Greenberg Gallery, New York; Humanities Research Center, University of Texas, Austin; Museum of Fine Arts, Houston, Texas; Museum of Modern Art, New York.

Abbott, Louise. "Robert Frank's Photos Angered the Experts." *Gazette (Montreal)*, November 20, 1980, 43.

Adams, Ansel. "The Profession of Photography." *Aperture* 1, no. 3 (1952): 3, 32.

Adams, Phoebe Lou. "Through a Lens Darkly." *Atlantic Monthly* 195 (April 1955): 69–72.

Alexander, Stuart. *Robert Frank: A Bibiliography, Filmography, and Exhibition Chronology, 1946–1985*. Tucson: Center for Creative Photography and University of Arizona, 1986.

Alinder, Mary Street. *Ansel Adams: An Autobiography*. New York: Henry Holt, 1996.

Badger, Gerry. "From Humanism to Formalism: Thoughts on Post-War American Photography." In *American Images: Photography, 1945–1980*, ed. Peter Turner. New York: Penguin Books and Barbican Art Gallery, 1985: 11–22.

Baigell, Matthew, and Julia Williams, eds. *Artists against War and Fascism: Papers of the First American Artists' Congress*. New Brunswick: Rutgers University Press, 1986.

Barry, Les. "The Legend of Sid Grossman." *Popular Photography* 47, no. 5 (November 1961): 51, 94.

Barthes, Roland. "The Great Family of Man." In *Mythologies*. New York: Hill and Wang, 1957.

———. *Camera Lucida*. New York: Hill and Wang, 1981.

Bennett, Edna. "Black and White are the Colors of Robert Frank." *Aperture* 9, no. 1 (1961): 20–22.

Berger, Maurice. "Subjective Documentation." *Art in America* 82, no. 1 (January 1994): 51–55.

Betrock, Alan. *The I Was a Teenage Juvenile Delinquent Rock-n-Roll Horror Beach Party Movie Book!* New York: St. Martin's Press, 1986.

Bezner, Lili Corbus. "Interview: Aaron Siskind." *History of Photography* 16, no. 1 (1992): 28–33.

"Books: General." Review of *The Americans*. *New Yorker*, May 14, 1960, 203–4.

Bosworth, Patricia. *Diane Arbus: A Biography*. New York: Knopf, 1984.

Breines, Wini. "The 1950s: Gender and Some Social Science." *Sociological Theory* 56, no. 1 (winter 1986): 69–92.

Breit, Harvey. "Talk with Miss Calomiris." *New York Times Book Review*, November 26, 1950, Sec. 9, p. 16.

Breitenbach, Joseph. "The Abstractionists Go on Parade." *Infinity* (April/May 1951): 6.
Brower, Kenneth. "Photography in the Age of Falsification." *Atlantic Monthly* 281 (May 1998): 92–111.
Browne, Turner, and Elaine Partow. *MacMillan Biographical Encyclopedia of Photographic Artists and Innovators*. New York: Macmillan, 1983.
Brumfield, John. "'The Americans' and The Americans." *Afterimage* (summer 1980): 9–15.
Butterick, George F., ed. *Charles Olson and Robert Creeley: The Complete Correspondance*. Vol. 1 (Santa Barbara: Black Sparrow Press, 1980.
Calomiris, Angela. *Red Masquerade: Undercover for the FBI*. New York: J. B. Lippincott, 1950. Also excerpted in *Creative Camera* no. 223/224 (July/August 1983): 1054–55.
"Candid Shots by the Editors." *Popular Photography* 38, no. 2 (February 1956): 32.
Carraro, Francine. "Seeing Red: The Dallas Museum in the McCarthy Era." In *Suspended License: Censorship and the Visual Arts*, ed. Elizabeth C. Childs, 235–58. Seattle: University of Washington Press, 1997.
Carter, Paul A. *Another Part of the Fifties*. New York: Columbia University Press, 1983.
Chancellor, John. Introduction to *The Fifties: Photographs of America*. New York: Pantheon Books, 1985.
Chiarenza, Carl. *Aaron Siskind: Pleasure and Terrors*. Boston: Little, Brown, 1982.
Clark, Tom. *Jack Kerouac: A Biography*. New York: Paragon House, 1990.
"Common Bonds of Man." *Life*, February 14, 1955, 132–43.
Contemporary Photographers. New York: St. Martin's Press, 1982.
"The Controversial Family of Man." *Aperture* 3, no. 2 (1955): 8–27.
Cooper, David B. "Robert Frank and American Politics." In *Robert Frank and American Politics*. Akron, Ohio: Akron Art Museum, 1985: 4–8.
Creeley, Robert, ed. *Selected Writings of Charles Olson*. New York: New Directions, 1966.
de Beauvoir, Simone. 1953. *The Second Sex*. New York: Vintage Books, 1974.
Dejardin, Fiona M. "The Photo League: Left-wing Politics and the Popular Press." *History of Photography* 18, no. 2 (1994): 159–73.
Dobell, Byron. "Feature Pictures: Robert Frank . . . The Photographer as Poet." *U.S. Camera* (September 1954): 77–84.
Documentary Photography. New York: Time-Life Books, 1972.
Duberman, Martin Bauml. *Paul Robseson*. New York: Knopf, 1988.
Dworkin, Martin S. "The Family of Man." *Progressive* (August 1955): 25–26.
Ekirch, Arthur A., Jr. *The Decline of American Liberalism*. New York: Antheneum, 1976.
Enyeart, James, *Invisible in America: An Exhibition of Photographs by Marion Palfi*. Foreword by Lee Witkin. Lawrence: University of Kansas Museum of Art, 1973.
Ernst, Morris L., and David Loth. *Report on the American Communist*. New York: Capricorn Books, 1952.
Evans, Walker. *American Photographs*. New York: Museum of Modern Art, 1988. Originally published by Museum of Modern Art, 1938.

The Family of Man. Curated by Edward Steichen; prologue by Carl Sandburg. New York: Museum of Modern Art, 1955.
"The Family of Man." *Infinity* (December 1954/January 1955): 12–15.
"'The Family of Man' Exhibition." *Image* 3, no. 3 (March 1954): 24.
"The Family of Man, MoMA, Edward Steichen." *Aperture* 2, no. 1 (1953): 29–31.
Fascina, Francis, ed. *Pollock and After: The Critical Debate*. New York: Harper and Row, 1985.
Featherstone, David, ed. *Observations: Essays on Documentary Photography*. Carmel, Calif.: Friends of Photography, 1984.
Feininger, Andreas. *Successful Photography*. Englewood Cliffs, N.J.: Prentice-Hall, 1954.
Fischer, Ernst. *The Necessity of Art: A Marxist Approach*, trans. Anna Bostock. New York: Penguin Books, 1986. Originally published as *Von der Notwendigkeit ker Kunst* (Dresden: Verlag der Kunst, 1959).
Frank, Robert. *Les Américains*. Text edited by Alain Bosquet. Paris: Robert Delpire, 1958. Maquette in Museum of Fine Arts, Houston Archive.
———. *The Americans*. Introduction by Jack Kerouac. New York: Pantheon Books, 1986. Originally published by Grove Press, 1959.
———. "Highway 61 Revisited." Interview by Marlaine Glicksman. *Film Comment* (August 1987): 32–39.
———. "Letter from New York." *Creative Camera* 60 (June 1969): 202–3.
———. "Letter from New York." *Creative Camera* 61 (July 1969): 234–35.
———. *The Lines of My Hand*. New York: Pantheon Books, 1989.
[Frank, Robert.] "Speaking of Pictures: A Photographer in Paris Finds Chairs Everywhere." *Life*, May 21, 1951, 26–28.
French, Brandon. *On the Verge of Revolt: Women in American Films of the Fifties*. New York: Ungar, 1978.
Friedan, Betty. 1963. *The Feminine Mystique*. New York: Dell Publishing, 1983.
Fulton, Marianne. *Eyes of Time: Photojournalism in America*. Boston: Little, Brown, 1988; Rochester: George Eastman House, 1988.
Gablik, Suzi. *Has Modernism Failed?* New York: Thames and Hudson, 1984.
Galeano, Eduardo. *The Book of Embraces*. New York: W. W. Norton, 1989.
Gatlin, Rochelle. *American Women Since 1945*. Jackson: University of Mississippi Press, 1987.
Gayle, Addison. *Richard Wright: Ordeal of a Native Son*. Garden City, N.Y.: Doubleday, Anchor Press, 1980.
Gee, Helen. *Limelight: A Greenwich Village Photography Gallery and Coffeehouse in the Fifties*. Albuquerque: University of New Mexico Press, 1997.
———. "Photography in Transition: 1950–1960." In *Decade by Decade*, ed. James Enyeart, 62–71. Tucson: University of Arizona and Tucson Center for Creative Photography, 1989.
Goldberg, Vicki. *Photography in Print*. New York: Simon and Schuster, 1981.
Goldsmith, Arthur. "The Family of Man." *Popular Photography* 36 (May 1955): 80–88, 147–49.
Goldstein, Robert Justin. *Political Repression in Modern America from 1870 to the Present*. Boston: G. K. Hall, 1978.
Goodman, Paul. *Growing Up Absurd*. New York: Vintage Books, 1960.

Green, Jonathan. *American Photography: A Critical History 1945 to the Present.* New York: Harry N. Abrams, 1984.

Grossman, Sid. Text by Millard Lampell. *Journey to the Cape*, ed. Miriam Cohen, Sy Kattelson, Charles Pratt, and David Vestal. New York: Grove Press, 1959.

Guilbaut, Serge. *How New York Stole the Idea of Modern Art: Abstract Expressionism, Freedom, and the Cold War.* Trans. Arthur Goldhammer. Chicago: University of Chicago Press, 1983.

———, ed. *Reconstructing Modernism*, Cambridge, MA: MIT Press, 1992.

Gutman, Judith Mara. *Lewis Hine and the American Social Conscious.* New York: Walker, 1967.

———. "One-Shot Hero." *Connoisseur* (November 1987): 138–43.

Gutierrez, Donald. "Books: The Unhappy Many." Review of *The Americans. Dissent* (autumn 1961): 515–16.

Gwathmey, Rosalie. *Photographs from the Forties.* East Hampton, N.Y.: Glenn Horowitz Bookseller, 1994.

Hall, James Baker. *Minor White: Rites and Passages.* Millerton, N.Y.: Aperture Monograph, 1978.

Hart, John Barkley. "Seven Types of Ambiguity in a Greenwich Village Coffee Shop." *Intro Bulletin: A Literary Newspaper of the Arts* (October 1955): 1–2.

Hattersley, Ralph. "Ask These 20 Key Questions Whenever You Study a Picture." *Popular Photography* 42, no. 3 (March 1958): 61.

Hauptman, William. "The Suppression of Art in the McCarthy Decade." *Artforum* (October 1973): 48–52.

Heath, David. *Diaglogue with Solitude.* A Community Press Publication. New York: Horizon Press, 1965.

Hellman, Lillian. *Scoundrel Time.* New York: Bantam Books, 1976.

Hill, Paul, and Thomas Cooper, eds. *Diaglogue with Photography.* New York: Farrar, Straus, Giroux, 1979.

Hills, Patricia. *Alice Neel.* New York: Harry N. Abrams, 1983.

hooks, bell. *Black Looks: Race and Representation.* Boston: South End Press, 1992.

Hughes, Jim. *W. Eugene Smith: Shadow and Substance.* New York: McGraw-Hill, 1989.

International Center of Photography Encyclopedia of Photography. New York: Pound Press and Crown Publishers, 1984.

International Center of Photography. "Program Guide and Directory: Fall, 1992." New York: 1992.

Janis, Eugenia Parry, and Wendy MacNeil, eds. *Photography within the Humanities.* Danbury, N.H.: Addison House; Wellseley, Mass.: Wellseley College, 1977.

Johnson, Thomas. *The Oxford Companion to American History.* New York: Oxford University Press, 1966.

Johnson, William S. "Photo Notes 1938–1950: Annotated Author and Photographer Index." *History of Photography* 18, no. 2 (1994): 185–95.

Johnson, William S., ed. *The Pictures Are a Necessity: Robert Frank in Rochester, N.Y., November, 1988.* Rochester Film and Photo Consortium Occasional Papers, No. 2. Rochester: George Eastman House, 1989.

Jussim, Estelle. "Icons or Ideology: Stieglitz and Hine." In *The Eternal Moment*, 141–51. New York: Aperture, 1989.

Kaledin, Eugenia. *Mothers and More: American Women in the 1950s.* Boston: Twayne, 1984.

Kalischer, Clemens. "Letters to the Editor." *Aperture* 5, no. 1 (1957): 42.

Keller, Ulrich. *The Highway as Habitat: A Roy Stryker Documentation, 1943–1955.* Santa Barbara: University Art Museum, 1986.

Kerouac, Jack. 1955. *On the Road.* New York: Signet; New American Library, 1985.

Knight, Arthur, and Kit Knight, eds. *The Beat Vision.* New York: Paragon House, 1987.

Kramer, Hilton. "Exhibiting the Family of Man: 'The World's Most Talked about Photographs.'" *Commentary* 20 (October 1955): 365–67.

Kuhn, Annette. *The Power of the Image*, London: Routledge and Kegan Paul, 1985.

Larkin, Oliver. 1949. *Art and Life in America.* New York: Holt, Rinehart and Winston, 1960.

"Last Call." Advertisement for *The Family of Man* entries. *Infinity* (February 1954): 8–9.

Latour, Ira. "The Family of Man." *Photo Vision* 2, no. 6 (May 1955): 32–37.

Lefferts, Georg. *Special for Women.* New York: Avon, 1961.

Leipzig, Arthur. *Arthur Leipzig: A Retrospective.* New York: Long Island University and Hillwood Art Gallery, 1989.

Lemagny, Jean-Claude, and André Rouillé, eds. *A History of Photography: Social and Cultural Perspectives.* Cambridge: Cambridge University Press, 1986.

Leuchtenburg, William E. *A Troubled Feast: American Society Since 1945.* Boston: Little, Brown, 1973.

Lewis, Joan. "More Pictures to the Gallon." *Popular Photography* (May 1959): 66–67, 125–26.

Lhamon, W. T., Jr. *Deliberate Speed: The Origins of a Cultural Style in the American 1950s.* Washington, D.C.: Smithsonian Institution Press, 1990.

"*Life* Announces the Winners of the Young Photographers Contest." *Life*, November 26, 1951.

"*Life*'s Contest Winners." *Modern Photography* 16, no. 1 (January 1952): 100–101.

Lipshultz, Sandra Lawall. "Robert Frank: New York to Nova Scotia." *Arts* (Minneapolis Society of Fine Arts) (April 1987): 14–17.

Livingston, Jane. *The New York School: Photographs, 1936–1963.* New York: Stewart, Tabori, and Chang, 1992.

Maloney, Tom, ed. *U.S. Camera Annual 1951.* New York: U.S. Camera, 1950.

———. *U.S. Camera Annual 1956.* New York: U.S. Camera, 1955.

———. *U.S. Camera Annual 1958.* New York: U.S. Camera, 1957.

Manchester, William. *In Our Time: The World As Seen by Magnum Photographers.* New York: W. W. Norton and the American Federation of Arts, 1989.

Mann, Margery. "The Controversial Aaron Siskind." *Infinity* (March 1968): 16.

———. "West: The Americans Revisted." *Camera 35* (January 1975): 14, 74–75.

Martin, Myron. "Of People and for People." *Aperture* 4, no. 4 (1956): 134–41.

May, Elaine Tyler. *Homeward Bound: American Families in the Cold War Era.* New York: Basic Books, 1988.

McKenna, Rollie. "Photography." *New Republic* 132 (March 14, 1955): 30.

Mead, Margaret. *Male and Female: A Study of the Sexes in a Changing World.* New York: William Morrow, 1949.

Millstein, Gilbert. "In Each a Self-Portrait." Reviews of *The Americans* by Robert Frank and *Journey to the Cape* by Sid Grossman. *New York Times Book Review*, January 17, 1960, 7.

Mitgang, Herbert. *Dangerous Dossiers: Exposing the Secret War against America's Greatest Authors.* New York: Donald I. Fine, 1988.

Monroe, Gerald M. "Art Front." *Studio International* (September 1974): 66–70.

———. "The Artists' Union of New York." *Art Journal* (fall 1972): 17–20.

Natanson, Nicholas. *The Black Image in the New Deal: The Politics of FSA Photography.* Knoxville: University of Tennessee Press, 1992.

Navasky, Victor S. *Naming Names.* New York: Viking Press, 1980.

Newhall, Beaumont. *The History of Photography.* Boston: Little, Brown; New York: Museum of Modern Art, 1982.

———. "Photographing the Reality of the Abstract." *Aperture* 4, no. 1 (1956): 32.

———. *Photography at Mid-Century.* Rochester: George Eastman House, 1959.

Newhall, Nancy. *From Adams to Stieglitz: Pioneers of Modern Photography.* New York: Aperture, 1989.

———. *This Is the Photo League.* N.p. Photo League exhibition catalog, 1948–49.

———. "Pirkle Jones Portfolio." *Aperture* 4, no. 2 (1956): 49–57.

"New Photo Books." Reviews of *The Americans* by Robert Frank, *Observations* by Richard Avedon and Truman Capote, and *Africa* by Emil Schulthess. *Modern Photography* 24, no. 6 (June 1960): 32–33, 52.

Nicosia, Gerald. *Memory Babe: A Critical Biography of Jack Kerouac.* New York: Grove Press, 1983.

Niven, Penelope. *Carl Sandburg: A Biography.* New York: Charles Scribner's Sons, 1991.

———. *Edward Steichen: A Biography.* New York: Clarkson Potter Publishers, 1997.

Norman, Dorothy. "The Controversial Family of Man." *Aperture* 2 (1955): 12–16.

———. *Encounters: A Memoir.* New York: Harcourt, Brace, Jovanovich, 1987.

Nyren, Dorothy. Review of *The Americans, Library Journal* 85, no. 6 (March 15, 1960): 1104.

"An Off-Beat View of the USA." Reviews of *The Americans. Popular Photography* 46, no. 5 (May 1960): 104–6.

Ollman, Leah. "The Photo League's Forgotten Past." *History of Photography* 18, no. 2 (1994): 154–58.

Oren, Michel. "On the 'Impurity' of Group f/64 Photography." *History of Photography* 15, no. 2 (summer 1991): 119–27.

Osman, Colin. "Biographical Notes." *Creative Camera* no. 223/224 (July/August 1983): 1027.

Papageorge, Tod. *Walker Evans and Robert Frank: An Essay on Influence.* New Haven: Yale University Art Gallery, 1981.

Pells, Richard H. *The Liberal Mind in a Conservative Age: American Intellectuals in the 1940s and 1950s.* New York: Harper and Row, 1985.

Phillips, Christopher. "In A Family Way." *Afterimage* (May 1984): 10–11.

———. "The Judgment Seat of Photography." In *The Contest of Meaning*, ed. Richard Bolton. Cambridge, Mass.: MIT Press, 1989.

Phillips, John. *It Happened in Our Lifetime: A Memoir in Words and Pictures.* Boston: Little, Brown, 1985.
The Photo League, 1936–1951. New Paltz: College Art Gallery, College at New Paltz and State University of New York; New York: Gallery Association of New York State and Photofind Gallery, n.d.
"Photography at the Museum of Modern Art." *Museum of Modern Art Bulletin* 19, no. 4 (April 1952): n.p.
Plattner, Steven W. *Roy Stryker: USA, 1943–1950.* Austin: University of Texas Press, 1983.
Pohl, Frances K. *Ben Shahn: New Deal Artist in a Cold War Climate, 1947–1954.* Austin: University of Texas Press, 1989.
Pollitt, J. J. *Art and Experience in Classical Greece.* Cambridge: Cambridge University Press, 1972.
"Post-War European Photography." Review of Edward Steichen's *Post-War European Photography* exhibition, Museum of Modern Art, New York. *U.S. Camera* (September 1953): 37–42.
Ringel, Fred. "The Family of Man—A Minority Report." Letters to the Editor, *Popular Photography* 36, no. 5 (May 1955): 6, 10.
Rosen, Marjorie. *Popcorn Venus: Women, Movies and the American Dream.* New York: Coward, McCann, and Geohegan, 1973.
Rosenblum, Naomi. "Jerome Liebling." In *Contemorary Photographers.* New York: St. Martin's Press, 1982.
Rosenblum, Walter. Interview by Colin Osman. *Creative Camera* no. 223/224 (July/August 1983): 1019–21.
———. *Walter Rosenblum.* Dresden: Verlag der Kunst, 1990.
Rosskam, Edwin. "Family of Steichen." *Artnews* (March 1955): 34–37.
Sandeen, Eric J. *Picturing an Exhibition: The Family of Man and 1950s America.* Albuquerque: University of New Mexico Press, 1995.
Schuh, Gottard. "Exhibition 'Photography as a Means of Expression.'" *Camera* (March 1955): 102–28.
Schumacher, Michael. *Dharma Lion: A Biography of Allen Ginsberg.* New York: St. Martin's Press, 1992.
Schwartz, Joe. *Poems I've Never Written.* San Luis Obispo: California Polytechnic State University, 1994.
Schwartz, Richard Alan. *The Cold War Reference Guide: A General History and Annotated Chronology with Selected Biographies.* Jefferson, N.C.: McFarland, 1997.
Shahn, Ben. *The Shape of Content.* Cambridge: Harvard University Press, 1957.
Shapiro, David, and Cecile Shapiro, eds. *Abstract Expressionism: A Critical Record.* Cambridge: Cambridge University Press, 1990.
Siskind, Aaron. *Aaron Siskind: Photographs.* Introduction by Harold Rosenberg. New York: Horizon Press, 1959.
———. *Harlem Photographs, 1932–1940.* Washington, D.C.: National Museum of American Art, 1981.
———. "Interview: Aaron Siskind." Interview by Lili Corbus Bezner. *History of Photography* 16, no. 1 (spring 1992): 28–33.
Smith, Bradley. "Pictures on the Highway." *Popular Photography* 35, no. 3 (September 1954): 82, 118, 120.

Smith, Henry Holmes. *Henry Holmes Smith: Collected Writings, 1935–1985*, ed. James Enyeart and Nancy Solomon. Tucson: Center for Creative Photography, University of Arizona, 1986.
Smith, Henry Holmes, et al. "The Experience of Photographs: Five Photographs by Aaron Siskind." *Aperture* 5, no. 3 (1957): 118–19.
Smith, W. Eugene. "Gene Smith." Interview by Beverly Bethune. 1976. *Creative Camera* no. 223/224 (July/August 1983): 1017, 1055.
Solbert, O. N. "Edward Steichen and the Family of Man." *Image* 4, no. 2 (February 1955): 9–16.
Solomon-Godeau, Abigail. "Winning the Game When the Rules Have Been Changed: Art Photography and Postmodernism." *Exposure* (spring 1985): 5–15.
Sontag, Susan. *On Photography*. New York: Farrar, Straus, and Giroux, 1973.
Stamm, Tad. "Letters to the Editor." *Popular Photography* 47, no. 1 (April 13, 1960): 6.
Stange, Maren. *Symbols of Ideal Life: Social Documentary Photography in America, 1890–1950*. Cambridge: Cambridge University Press, 1989.
———, ed. *Paul Strand: Essays on his Life and Work*. New York: Aperture, 1990.
Steichen, Edward. "From Edward Steichen to Members of the Picture Division." *Picturescope* 3, no. 2 (July 1955): 6–8.
———. *A Life in Photography*. Garden City, N.Y.: Doubleday and Museum of Modern Art, 1963. New York: Harmony Books and Museum of Modern Art, 1985.
———. Foreword to *Memorable Life Photographs*. New York: Time-Life, 1951.
———. "The Story of Man in One Picture." *This Week* (Sunday Magazine of the *New York Herald Tribune*) December 4, 1955, 2.
———, for the Museum of Modern Art, *The Family of Man*, prologue by Carl Sandburg. New York: Maco Magazine Corporation, for the Museum of Modern Art, 1955.
Stettner, Louis. "Cezanne's Apples and the Photo League." *Aperture* 112 (1988): 14–35.
———. Interview by Colin Osman. *Creative Camera* no. 223–24 (July/August 1983): 1021.
———. "Speaking Out: On the Windshield of My Mind." *Camera 35* 17, no. 1 (January/February 1973): 26, 74, 76.
———. "Speaking Out: Politics of Despair." *Camera 35* 17, no. 2 (March 1973): 9, 12, 71.
Stitch, Sidra. *Made in USA: An Americanization in Modern Art, the '50s and '60s*. Berkeley: University of California Press and University Art Museum, 1987.
Stone, I. F. *The Haunted Fifties, 1953–1963*. Boston: Little, Brown, 1963.
Stott, William. *Documentary Expression and Thirties America*. Chicago: University of Chicago Press, 1973.
Szarkowski, John. *Mirrors and Windows: American Photography Since 1960*. New York: New York Graphic Society and Museum of Modern Art; Boston: Little, Brown, 1978.
Tagg, John. "The Currency of the Photograph." In *Thinking Photography*, ed. Victor Burgin, 110–41. London: MacMillan, 1982.
———, ed. *The Burden of Representation: Essays on Photographies and Histories*. Amherst: University of Massachusetts Press, 1988.

Thomas, Ann. *Lisette Model*. Ottawa: National Gallery of Canada, 1990.
"The Top Prize-Winners in Black and White: Why the Judges Picked Them." *Popular Photography* 33, no. 4 (October 1953): 90–98, 143, 148.
Trachtenberg, Alan, and Isabelle Storey, eds. *In the Presence of Walker Evans*. Boston: Institute of Contemporary Art, 1978.
Tucker, Anne. "A History of the Photo League: The Members Speak." *History of Photography* 18, no. 2 (1994): 74–184.
———. "The Photo League." *Creative Camera* 223/224 (July/August 1983): 1012–18.
———. "The Photo League." *Ovo Magazine* 10 no. 40/41 (1981): 3–7.
———. "Sid Grossman: Major Projects." *Creative Camera* 223/224 (July/August 1983): 1040–41.
Tucker, Anne Wilkes, and Philip Brookman, eds., *Robert Frank: New York to Nova Scotia*. Houston: Museum of Fine Arts, Houston, 1986.
"UAW-CIO and The Family of Man." International Union of United Automobile, Aircraft and Agricultural Implement Workers of America. *UAW-CIO Ammunition* (March 1955): 3–25.
U.S. Congress. House. Committee on Un-American Activities. *The American National Exhibition, Moscow, July 1959*. 86th Congress, January 7, 1959. Washington, D.C.: U.S. Government Printing Office, 1957.
———. *Report on the Communist Party of the United States as an Advocate of Overthrow of Government by Force and Violence*. 80th Congress, 2nd sess., May 11, 1948. House Report No. 1920. Washington, D.C.: U.S. Government Printing Office, 1948.
Vaughn, J. A. "Letter to the Editor." *Popular Photography* 42, no. 3 (March 1958): 6.
Vestal, David. "Review: *The Lines of My Hand*." *Camera 35* 17, no. 2 (March 1973): 27.
———. "Sid Grossman." *Contemporary Photographers*. New York: St. Martin's Press, 1982: 391–92.
Wald, Alan. *The New York Intellectuals: The Rise and Decline of the Anti-Stalinist Left from the 1930s to the 1980s*. Chapel Hill: University of North Carolina Press, 1987.
Walker, Margaret. *Richard Wright: Daemonic Genius*. New York: Warner Books, 1988.
Wallis, Brian, ed. *Art after Modernism: Rethinking Representation*. Boston: David R. Godine; New York: The New Museum of Contemporary Art, 1984.
Webb, Todd. *Todd Webb Photographs*. Fort Worth, Tex.: Amon Carter Museum, 1965.
Weiner, Dan. "Again Diogenes." Review, Museum of Modern Art. *Infinity* (December 1952): 14–15, 22.
Weiner, Sandra, and Cornell Capa, eds. *Dan Weiner*, New York: International Center of Photography, Grossman Publishers, and Viking Press, 1974.
Whelan, Richard. *Robert Capa*. New York: Ballantine Books, 1985.
White, Minor. "Book Reviews." *Aperture* 3, no. 3 (1955): 32.
———. "Editorial." *Aperture* 2, no. 3 (1953): 3.
———. "Editorial." *Aperture* 4, no. 2 (1956): 47–48.
———. "Editorial: The Pursuit of Personal Vision." *Aperture* 4, no. 1 (1956): 3.
———. "The Light Sensitive Mirage." *Aperture* 6, no. 2 (1958): 74–80.
———. "*Aaron Siskind: Photographs.*" Review. *Aperture* 7, no. 3 (1959): 123–24.
Wilson, Colin. *The Outsider*. New York: Delta, 1956.

Wright, George, and Cora Wright. "One Family's Opinion." *Aperture* 3, no. 2 (1955): 19–23.

Wright, Richard. *Letters to Joe C. Brown*, ed. Thomas Knipp. Kent, Ohio: Kent State University Libraries, 1968.

———. *Native Son.* New York: Harper and Brothers, 1940.

Yavno, Max. "Max Yavno." Interview for Oral History project, George Eastman House, 1977. Excerpted in *Creative Camera* 223/224 (July/August 1983): 1018.

Yockelson, Bonnie. "Arthur Leipzig." In *Arthur Leipzig: A Retrospective.* New York: Long Island University and Hillwood Art Gallery, 1989.

Index

LILI CORBUS BEZNER, an associate professor of art history at the University of North Carolina at Charlotte, was born in Tallahassee, Florida, in 1957, and was raised in Sarasota. She received a B.A. in anthropology from Kenyon College, an M.A. in American studies from the University of Maryland, College Park, and completed a Ph.D. in art history at the University of Texas, Austin. She has written articles for *History of Photography* and the *Southern Quarterly*, and *Studies in Popular Culture* on wedding photography, contemporary documentary, the Limelight Gallery, and other subjects. She has also curated art exhibitions and written numerous catalog essays on, most recently, women in the Photo League.

Other Center-Sponsored Books in Photography Published by Johns Hopkins

Alligators, Prehistoric Presence in the American Landscape
Martha A. Strawn, with essays by LeRoy Overstreet, Jane Gibson, and J. Whitfield Gibbons

Belonging to the West
Eric Paddock

Between the Landscape and Its Other
Paul Vanderbilt

Bravo 20: The Bombing of the American West
Richard Misrach, with Myriam Weisang Misrach

Disarming the Prairie
Terry Evans, with an introductory essay by Tony Hiss

Invisible New York: The Hidden Infrastructure of the City
Stanley Greenberg, with an introductory essay by Thomas H. Garver

Measure of Emptiness: Grain Elevators in the American Landscape
Frank Gohlke, with a concluding essay by John C. Hudson

The Nature of Photographs
Steven Shore, with a foreword by James L. Enyeart

The New American Village
Bob Thall

Nuclear Landscapes
Peter Goin

Old Order Amish: Their Enduring Way of Life
Lucian Niemeyer and Donald B. Kraybill

The Perfect City
Bob Thall, with an essay by Peter Bacon Hales

Library of Congress Cataloging-in-Publication Data

Bezner, Lili Corbus.
Photography and politics in America : from the New Deal into the Cold War / Lili Corbus Bezner.
p. cm.
"Published in cooperation with the Center for American Places Santa Fe, New Mexico, and Harrisonburg, Virginia."
Includes bibliographical references and index.
ISBN 0-8018-6187-X (alk. paper)
1. Photography—United States—History—20th century. 2. Documentary photography—United States—History—20th century. 3. Photography—Political aspects—United States. I. Title.
TR23.B48 1999
070.4'9'0973—dc21 99-23281 CIP